WEAVING AT BLACK MOUNTAIN COLLEGE

WEAVING AT BLACK MOUNTAIN COLLEGE

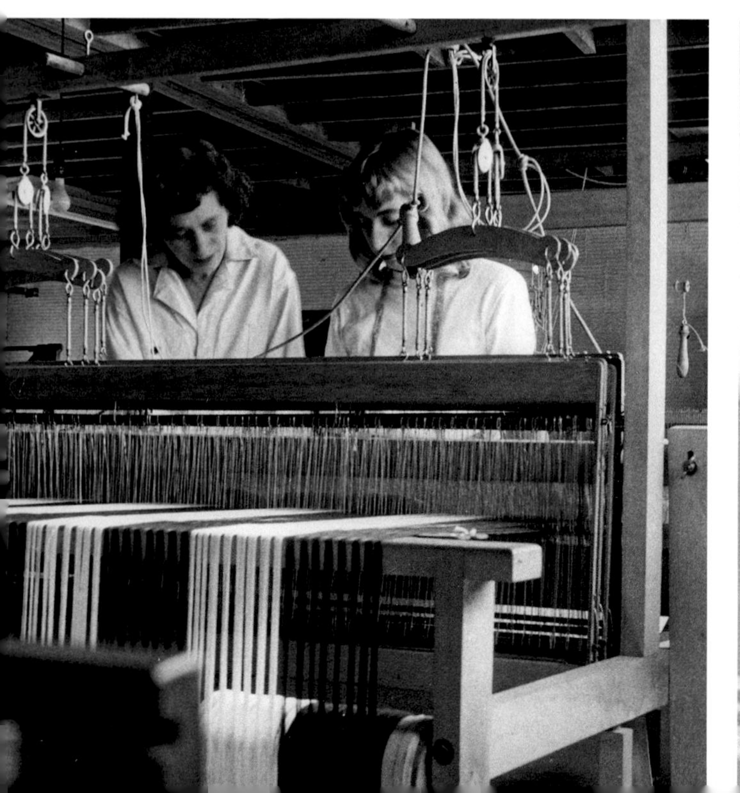

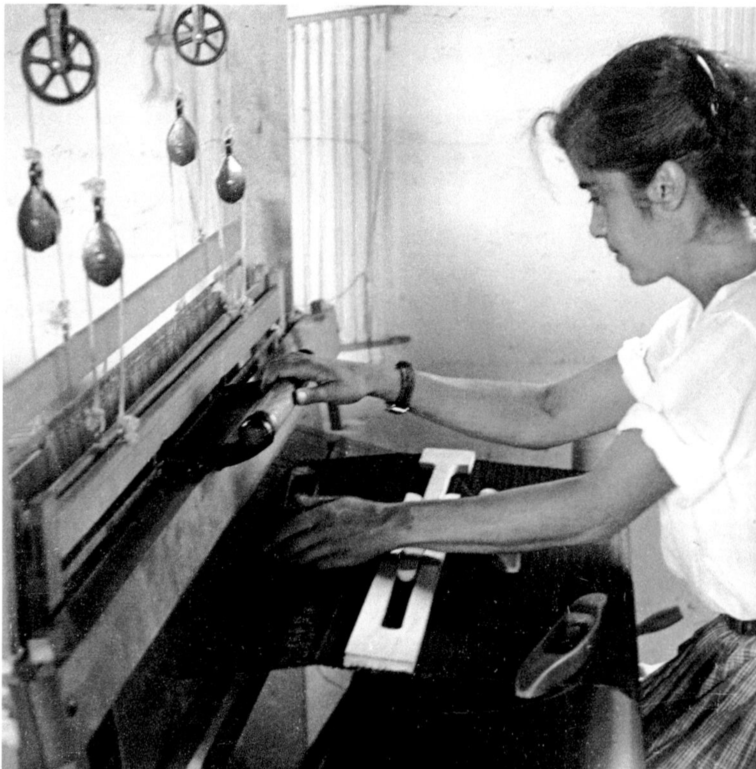

ANNI ALBERS, TRUDE GUERMONPREZ, AND THEIR STUDENTS

MICHAEL BEGGS
JULIE J. THOMSON

WITH ADDITIONAL TEXTS BY
Brenda Danilowitz
Jennifer Nieling
Erica Warren

Black Mountain College
MUSEUM ✛
ARTS CENTER

DISTRIBUTED BY
Yale University Press,
New Haven and London

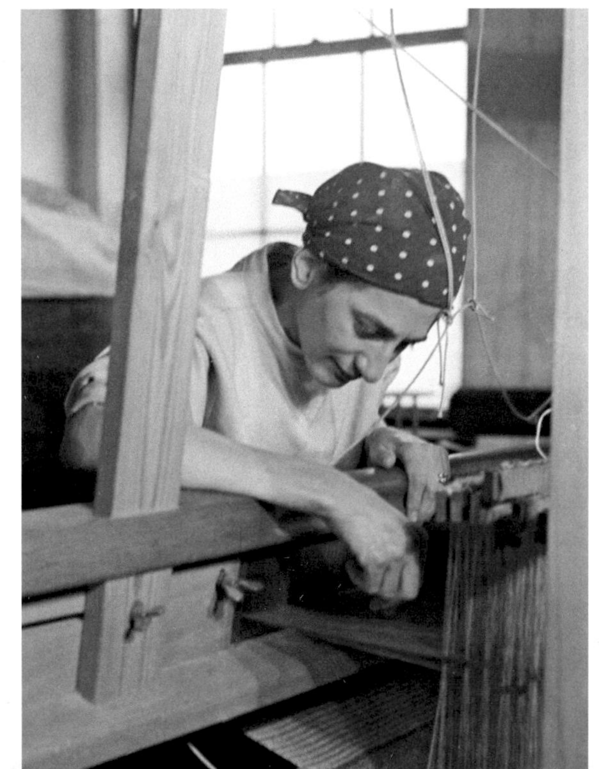

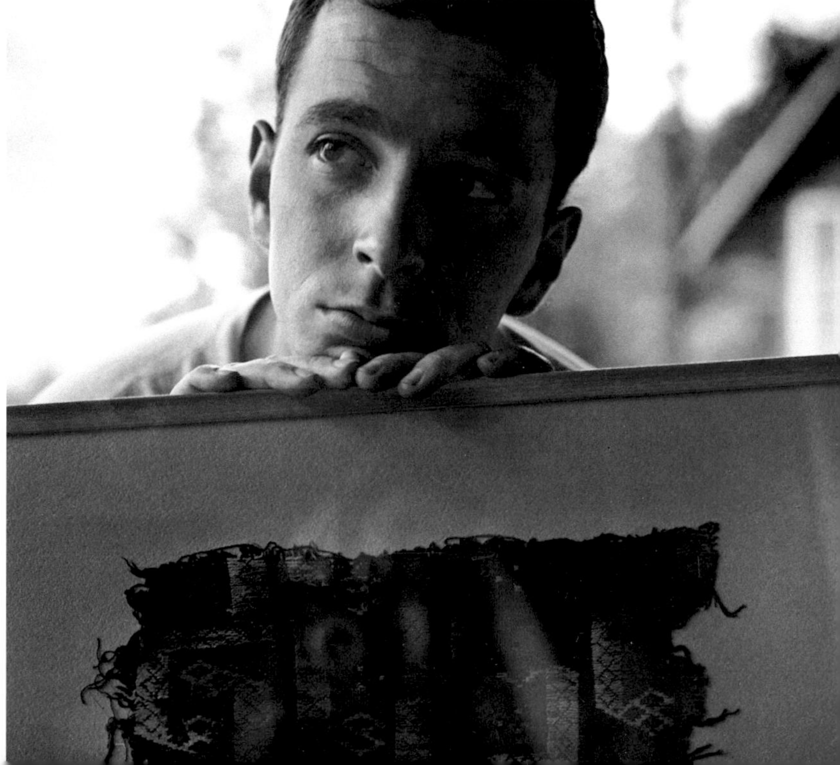

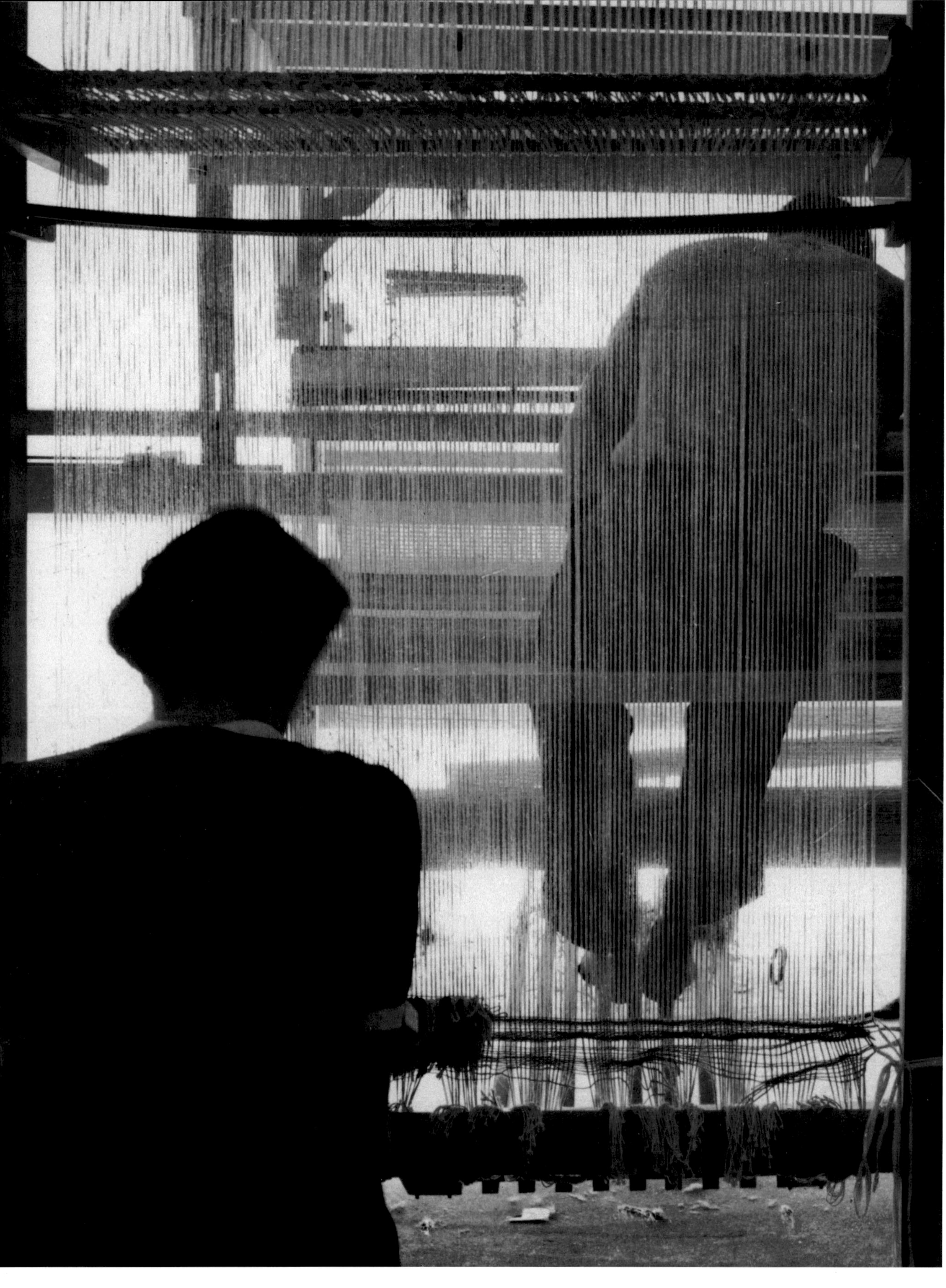

1. Nevalie Ropp and Alex Reed at looms, 1938.
Photograph by John Stix.

CONTENTS

FOREWORD

Black Mountain College (BMC) has long been acknowledged as an international crossroads for some of the most innovative artists of the twentieth century. A close study of BMC's weaving program offers new and dynamic ground to reexamine and expand what we already know about the history and the work produced at the college.

It is impossible to consider any part of the history of BMC without first acknowledging the school's relationship to the environment and the natural world. BMC was set in the rural South in the mountains of western North Carolina. Within this remote and beautiful landscape there was a profound aspiration to create an experiment in education through communal living, experiential learning, and a commitment to discovery. Faculty, students, and staff placed an emphasis on purpose and hoped to function as a whole. BMC teacher Buckminster Fuller's synergy comes to mind—the interaction of parts that, when combined, produce a total effect that is greater than the sum of the individual contributions.

Anni Albers started teaching weaving at BMC in 1934, drawing on her experiences at the Bauhaus. Her approach embraced experimentation and imagination, with special focus on structure and material, the role of the designer, and professional weaving techniques. Albers's teaching explored the importance of design and how design connects to craft, art, and multidisciplinary education.

Weaving at Black Mountain College: Anni Albers, Trude Guermonprez, and Their Students traces the many chapters of the Weaving Workshop from its beginnings in 1934 to the last weaving class in 1956 and the many communities that this work touched after the closure of BMC in 1957. Following the threads of the weaving program through the work of teachers and the many weaving students adds nuance and context to the larger history of BMC.

Michael Beggs's and Julie J. Thomson's careful and passionate scholarship provides an inspired call to refocus the history of weaving and design at Black Mountain College. The inclusion of the Harriett Engelhardt Memorial Collection of Textiles is one of many important and lesser known highlights that sheds light on the scale and seriousness of weaving pedagogy at BMC.

Profound thanks to Michael and Julie for their commitment to the history and scholarship of BMC and for their curatorial vision for this book and the exhibition: *Weaving at Black Mountain College: Anni Albers, Trude Guermonprez, and Their*

Students, at Black Mountain College Museum + Arts Center from September 29, 2023 through January 6, 2024.

My thanks and appreciation to Brenda Danilowitz, Jennifer Nieling, and Erica Warren for contributing thoughtful and insightful essays to this publication. Special thanks to Kay Sekimachi, Jen Bervin, Bana Haffar, Porfirio Gutiérrez, and Susie Taylor for exquisite and inspiring work both in the publication and exhibition. Additional thanks to Tom Eykemans and Taylor Miles Hopkins for the incredible design work on this book.

We are grateful for support from the National Endowment for the Arts, Robert Lehman Foundation, Andy Warhol Foundation for the Visual Arts, and Furthermore grants in publishing, a program of the J. M. Kaplan Fund.

Many thanks to our small team at BMCM+AC, including Alice Sebrell for her continued passion and expertise on all of our work but especially with this project.

On behalf of the board and staff we would like to acknowledge and thank the many other individuals and organizations that have contributed to this work including Brenda Danilowitz, chief curator at the Josef and Anni Albers Foundation, and Heather South, lead archivist at the Western Regional Archives.

Our museum exists to educate the public on the history and legacy of Black Mountain College. We accomplish that goal through our work as both a dedicated history museum and a contemporary arts center. We deeply admire all the scholars whose work lends new insights to the ongoing story of BMC, and we take great pride in supporting their work. Our museum has been fortunate to work with Michael and Julie on previous projects, and we are very grateful for their dedication, enthusiasm, and endless energy. Through rewarding partnerships with Yale University Press, the Josef and Anni Albers Foundation, and the Western Regional Archives, this project is an exceptionally collaborative effort.

Final thanks to the incredible BMC community that keeps all of the history and work alive.

Jeff Arnal
Black Mountain College Museum + Arts Center, Executive Director

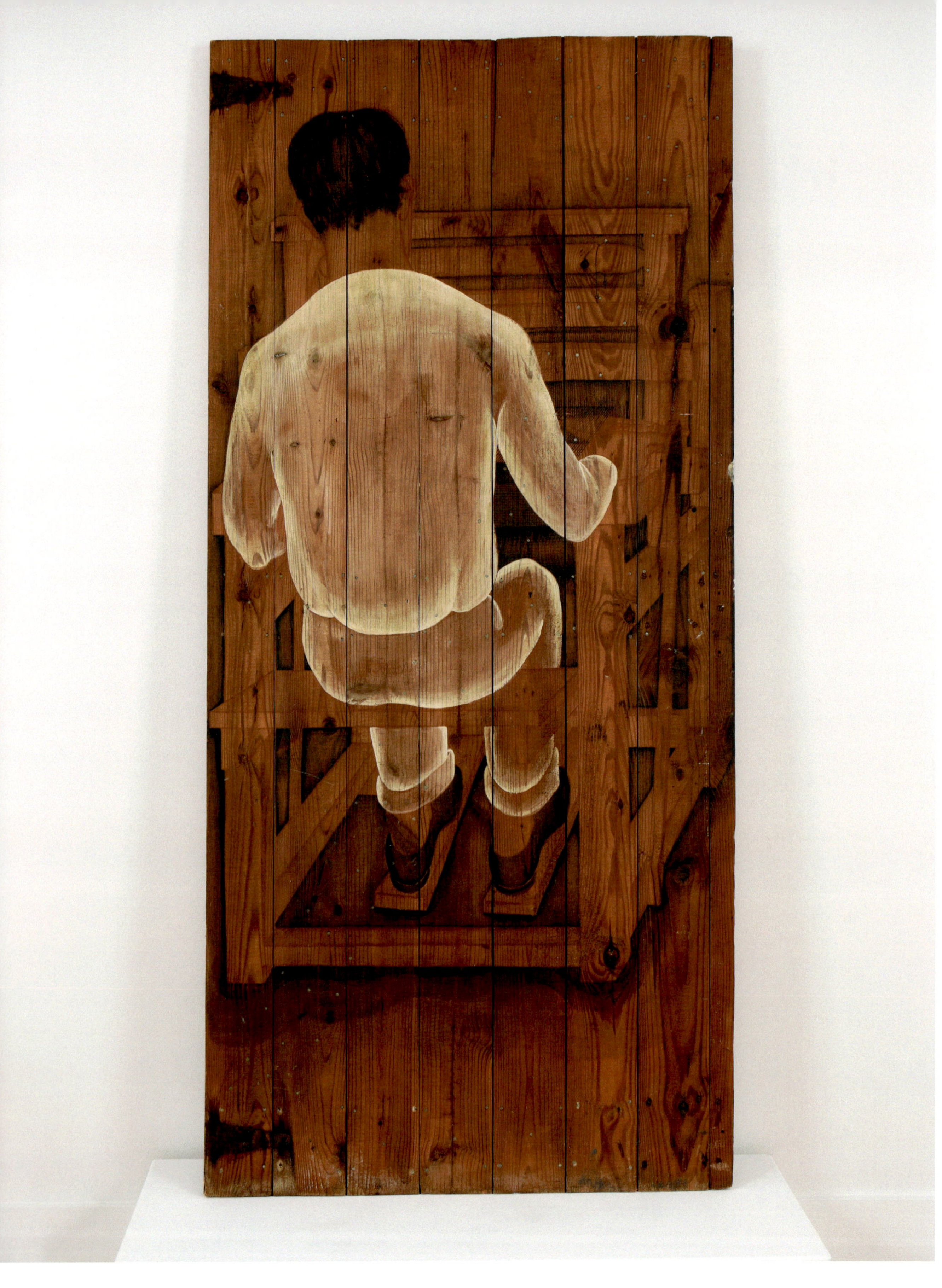

2. Faith Murray Britton, *Door to the weaving room
from the Lake Eden campus,* ca. 1941–1942. Oil on
wood. 81 × 38 × 1⅓ in.

INTRODUCTION

We must come down to the earth from the clouds where we live in vagueness and experience the most real thing there is: material. —Anni Albers, *Work With Material,* 1937

MICHAEL BEGGS + JULIE J. THOMSON

In late November 1933 when Anni Albers arrived at Black Mountain College (1933–1957), no one could have predicted that this tiny liberal arts college, located in the mountains of western North Carolina far from traditional centers of the art world, would one day be regarded as one of the most important art schools of the twentieth century. The College, founded by a group of disaffected professors just a few months before, was radically experimental. Deeply influenced by the educational philosophies of John Dewey and Alfred North Whitehead, Black Mountain College sought "to educate a student as a person and as a citizen."[1] Owned and governed democratically by its faculty, without a large administrative body or even a board of trustees, Black Mountain stressed complete academic and pedagogic freedom for its faculty and self-determined, experiential education for its students. In the words of founding faculty member John Andrew Rice: "Our central and consistent effort is to teach method, not content; to emphasize process, not results; to invite the student to the realization that the way of handling facts and himself amid the facts is more important than facts themselves."[2]

Black Mountain College was always small, never exceeding a total population of around a hundred students and twenty faculty members, all of whom worked, ate, and lived on the campus together. Daily operations were managed through a work program in which both faculty and students contributed, including helping with the College's farm and participating in an extensive building program to build, renovate, and maintain college buildings. Although each student had their own private study in which to work, the intimacy and constant activity of community life could be overwhelming for some.

What a student gained from Black Mountain College was largely left up to the individual, though their development and progress was reviewed and discussed by the faculty. Although course offerings could be highly contingent on BMC's faculty at any given time, the curriculum was interdisciplinary, with the arts given a crucial central position, something unique within American higher education at the time.

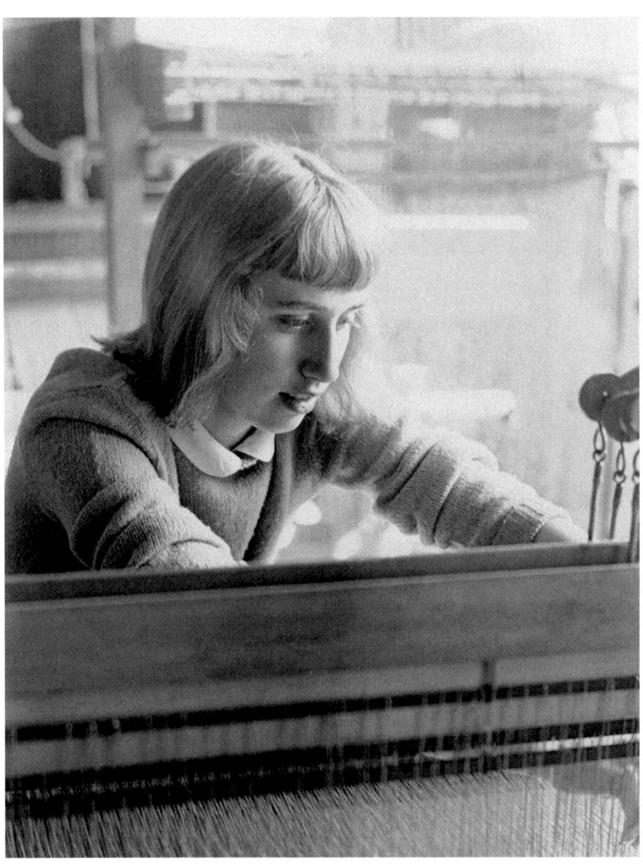

Josef and Anni Albers, who were recruited to Black Mountain after the demise of the Bauhaus in Germany, were central to the College's success as an art school. While the Bauhaus had trained students for specialization as artists or designers, at Black Mountain the Alberses recalibrated their teaching to serve a broader audience, most of whom would not become artists. They brought a rigorous, experiential process to teaching that emphasized self-discipline, the fallibility of human perception, a deep regard for materials and process, and a sense of wonder for the ordinary.

Despite constantly struggling to keep itself afloat financially, Black Mountain College attracted a dazzling roster of students, faculty, and guests who would collectively shape the social and artistic attitudes of the United States in the second half of the twentieth century. In addition to the Alberses, notable long-term faculty included M. C. Richards, Charles Olson, Heinrich Jalowetz, and Max Dehn; students included Ruth Asawa, Arthur Penn, Kenneth Noland, Ray Johnson, Robert Rauschenberg, Dorothea Rockburne, and Michael Rumaker; and visiting faculty included John Cage, Merce Cunningham, R. Buckminster Fuller, Jacob Lawrence, Beaumont and Nancy Newhall, and Willem de Kooning. From its founding in 1933 to its legal closure in 1957, BMC maintained its experimental mission and its commitment to interdisciplinary education with the arts at the center.

While Josef Albers's art classes have long been recognized as an essential part of Black Mountain College's curriculum, the weaving program created by Anni and the classes she, Trude Guermonprez, and the six other weaving faculty members taught, have been largely treated as craft lessons with a subservient role in the curriculum.[3] This was far from the case. The weaving program was Black Mountain's most sophisticated and successful design program, and had a widespread influence both on the College itself and in the fields of design and weaving in midcentury America.

Working from student enrollment records from the Black Mountain College Papers housed in the North Carolina Western Regional Archives, we have compiled the first comprehensive list of all the students formally enrolled in weaving at Black Mountain College.[4] With this list and close readings of surviving weavings, student notes, and other primary sources, a radically new and exciting picture of Black Mountain College's weaving program emerges.

In total more than 120 students—about 10 percent of all students to ever attend Black Mountain College—took at least one class in weaving and textile design. Unlike the Bauhaus, where the subject was gendered as feminine, at Black Mountain both men and women studied weaving. This book examines the many ways in which weaving played a much larger role in Black Mountain's legendary art and design curriculum than previously assumed.

This book is divided into six major sections, which roughly follow the College's chronology from its first weaving classes in early 1934, to its last in 1956. Within most sections there are longer thematic essays, which identify key figures and trends within the narrative of weaving at Black Mountain, and briefer subject essays, which explore specific topics in greater detail. These sections are further enlivened by historic primary texts and guest essays by textile experts Erica Warren, Brenda Danilowitz, and Jennifer Nieling.

BEGINNINGS, 1933–1940

Within her first few months at Black Mountain College, Anni Albers (BMC faculty, 1934–49) was teaching weaving and beginning to shape a weaving program that reflected her philosophies on the role of handweaving and the relationship between art, craft, and design. This section lays out Albers's general approach to teaching, and the ways in which her weaving classes served as Black Mountain's primary design program. We also explore how Albers's writing, weaving, and teaching related to broader national discourses that were shaping the nascent field of design in the United States in the 1930s and 1940s.

This section contains two of Albers's essays, "Work with Material" and "Handweaving Today: Textile Work at Black Mountain College"; each show how she positioned herself within Black Mountain's curriculum and situated her approach to weaving within larger design and craft discourses in the United States. This section also includes a subject essay, "Making Clothes at Black Mountain College," which examines the formal and informal ways in which Black Mountain students learned about using textiles to design and make clothes, and how the ideas of Irene Schawinsky and Berta and Bernard Rudofsky, who taught design classes in clothing, paralleled those of Anni Albers.

SPECIALIZATION AND GENERALIZATION, 1940–1947

Unlike Cranbrook Academy, the Institute of Design in Chicago, or the Rhode Island School of Design, Black Mountain College was a liberal arts college, and the weaving program was interdisciplinary; students who would never weave again learned how to design textiles at the same level of depth and seriousness as those who majored in the subject. This section considers the many levels at which students studied and worked with weaving at BMC. We examine the connections between the weaving program and the textile industry, including the industry experiences of students who found later work as woven and print textile designers. We also discuss the many ways in which Anni Albers worked to promote the weaving program at Black Mountain through nationally distributed publications and touring exhibitions.

weaving

Practical and theoretical work in hand-weaving; to develop a feeling for material and an understanding of the elements of form in textiles; to prepare for individual or industrial production of fabrics. Beginning with a free play of the given means, the work includes the set-up of the loom, draft-writing (for hand and for power loom), the development of new drafts, the analysis of fabric samples, the different weaving techniques (weaving on looms up to eight harnesses, gobelin, smyrna, etc.), the experimentation with unusual materials. On the one hand, studies in the free composition of texture, color, and the surface qualities of materials (that is, the work of art); and on the other hand, studies emphasizing the functional qualities of materials (that is, the useful textile).

Two semesters; one hour of theory, four hours of practice a week.   Mrs Albers

Two subject essays explore other facets of mid-1940s specialization: Erica Warren follows the legacy of Black Mountain College in the lives and work of specialist students Lili Blumenau and Else Regensteiner, who attended BMC to specifically study with Anni Albers. The essay "Weaving as Art" discusses the ways in which Black Mountain College's weavers, who treated weaving as a design medium for practical fabrics, also explored weaving as a medium for making art.

By contrast, in "Weaving Literacy," we attempt to understand ways in which weaving was connected to the general education at Black Mountain College. We offer the phrase *weaving literacy* to discuss how textile practices and ideas spread beyond the weaving program into other areas of study through informal interactions, lectures, texts, and exhibitions. Thanks to this interdisciplinary knowledge transfer, any student at Black Mountain College had many opportunities to interact with textiles and their making, and these interactions then informed work in other disciplines, including visual art, music, architecture, and dance as well as social sciences, literature, and mathematics.

4. Course description for Anni Albers's weaving class, in the *Black Mountain College Bulletin*, 1936.

A key part of the interdisciplinary diffusion of textile ideas at Black Mountain College was the Harriett Engelhardt Memorial Collection, a collection of nearly one hundred ancient and vernacular textiles, mostly from Mexico and South America, which Anni assembled from 1947 to 1949 and was housed and exhibited at Black Mountain College. The acquisition was funded by a gift from the estate of Harriett Engelhardt, a former weaving student, who, after serving in the Red Cross during World War II, tragically died in a car accident in Germany in 1945. After Black Mountain College closed in 1956, Anni was instrumental in moving the Engelhardt Collection to the Yale University Art Gallery, where it resides today. We examine Harriett Engelhardt's own engagement with weaving, Albers's intentions in developing the Collection, and how it taught weavers and nonweavers alike. The story of the Engelhardt Collection is a compelling example of the sophistication with which students at Black Mountain College examined, understood, and designed textiles.

GROWTH AND CHANGE, 1947–1956

While Anni Albers was the primary creator of the weaving program at Black Mountain College, she was not the only faculty member to teach weaving. Nevertheless Albers's fame tends to overshadow the work of her teaching colleagues at Black Mountain, whose contributions have never been fully credited, discussed, or realized. This is particularly true for Trude Guermonprez (BMC faculty, 1947–49), who was hired along with Franziska Mayer (BMC faculty, 1946–47) to teach weaving while Albers was on sabbatical. When Anni returned, Trude carried the primary course load while Albers was occupied with creating work for her 1949 solo exhibition at the Museum of Modern Art.

The first essay in this section examines how Trude Guermonprez taught weaving during Anni's absence, and the ways she shaped and added to BMC's weaving program. Guermonprez arrived at the College as an experienced textile designer who had worked in industry, but at Black Mountain she embraced a more personal textile expression, encouraging her students to explore freer and more pictorial approaches. Significantly, during her time at Black Mountain Trude discovered how much she enjoyed teaching, a realization that would ultimately lead her to teach hundreds of students in California at Pond Farm (Guerneville, California; faculty, 1949–51) and at the California College of Arts and Crafts (Oakland, California; faculty, 1953–76), where she trained a generation of weavers and teachers, including Kay Sekimachi.

Guermonprez returned to Black Mountain as a guest lecturer in 1952, and we reproduce her talk, "Design," to allow her voice and views to exist in conversation with Anni Albers's writing. In a subject essay Brenda Danilowitz expands upon the experiences of Albers, Mayer, Guermonprez, and Albers's former Bauhaus colleague, Marli Ehrman (BMC faculty, summer 1949) as German-born Jewish exiles and examines their personal and professional ties before and during their time at Black Mountain College.

This section's other subject essay, "Departures, Short Stays, and Closure" covers the last six years of the weaving program. After Ehrman, Ellen Siegel (BMC faculty, 1949–50), a graduate of Cranbrook Institute with a deep interest in unusual and synthetic materials, taught weaving. After Siegel's departure, Andy Oates taught as a student instructor for several terms, but after his classes ended Black Mountain had no official weaving teacher until San Francisco–based weaver Marie Murelius taught during the 1953 Summer Session. The weaving program's last faculty member, Anthony "Tony" Landreau (BMC faculty, 1954–56), had his first encounters with ancient textiles at Black Mountain College and would later become director of the Textile Museum in Washington, D.C., and an expert in Turkish weaving and rugs.

CONTINUANCES, 1957–PRESENT

Although Black Mountain College closed in 1957, many of the College's weavers continued to make work, building a collective legacy for the weaving program. Indeed, some former students, like Joan Potter Loveless, only blossomed as weavers long after leaving BMC behind. "Continuances" examines some of the later work of Black Mountain's weavers and considers the many ways in which weaving students continued to show an interest in textile practices. A subject essay by Jennifer Nieling explores the life and work of Black Mountain College alumnus Andy Oates, who had a long career as a teacher, designer, and master weaver at the small production studio Nantucket Looms.

Black Mountain College has a long and continuing afterlife. Our book closes with the work of four contemporary artists—Jen Bervin, Porfirio Gutiérrez, Susie Taylor, and Bana Haffar—who connect with and respond to the legacy of weaving at Black Mountain College in a myriad of structural, conceptual, and intuitive ways. Their work continues to explore the central concerns that motivated Anni Albers, Trude Guermonprez, their peers, and their students and shows how even after ninety years, the College and its weavers continue to educate and inspire us.

In 1971 Trude Guermonprez remarked, "the youngest generation seems to face the super technological world and turns to crafts, not so much as a rejuvenation for the existing technological world, but as a protest."[5] Today with screens and many sleek surfaces filling our digital lives, our tactile sensibility is weak and often fading. Weaving and texture have been part of human life for millennia, and we may need them both more than we realize. We invite you to look closely at the weavings and textiles made by these artists and to discover for yourself the possibilities that weaving still holds.

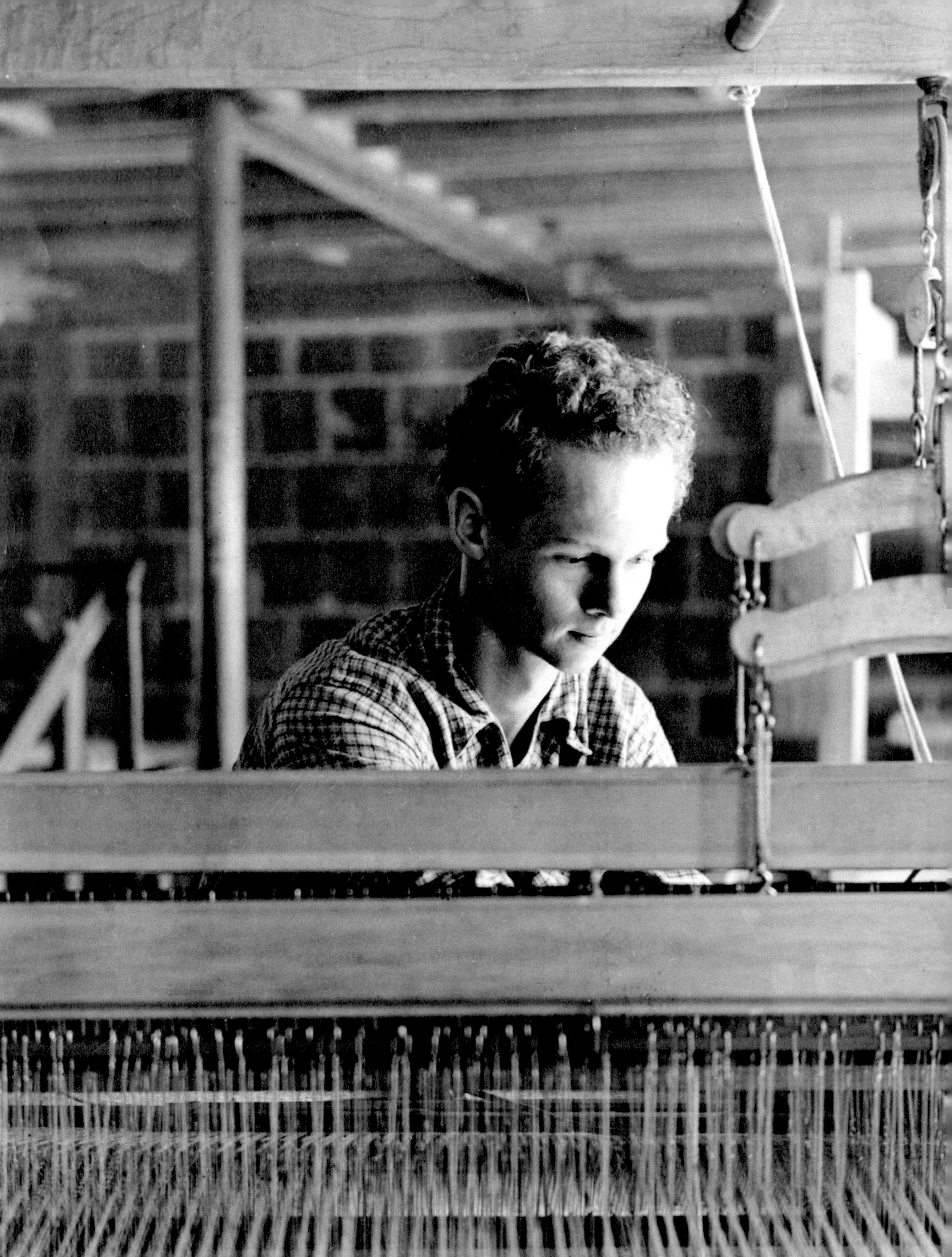

BEGINNINGS

1933–1940

6. Don Page at a Tapestry Loom, n.d.
Photographer unknown.

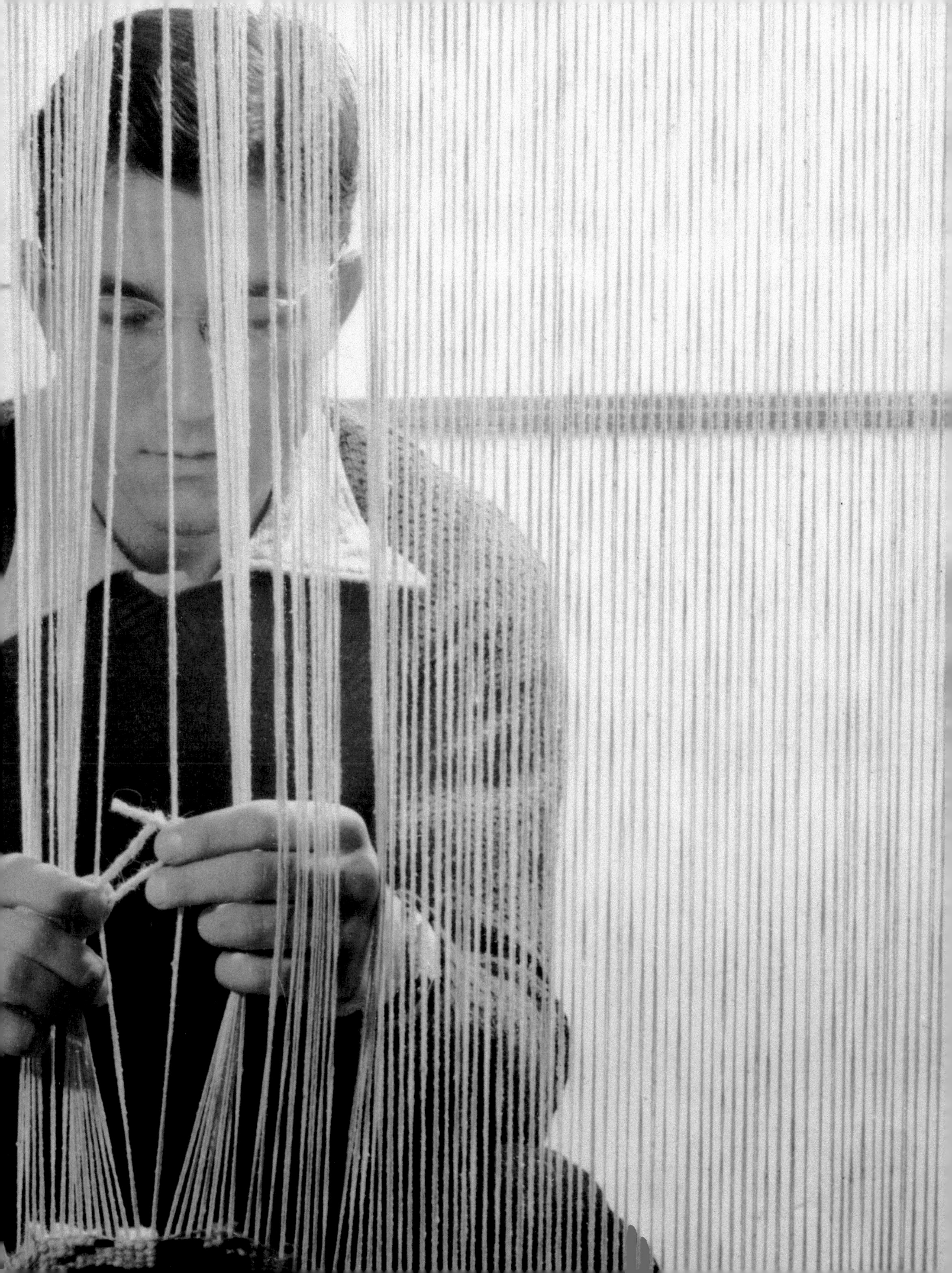

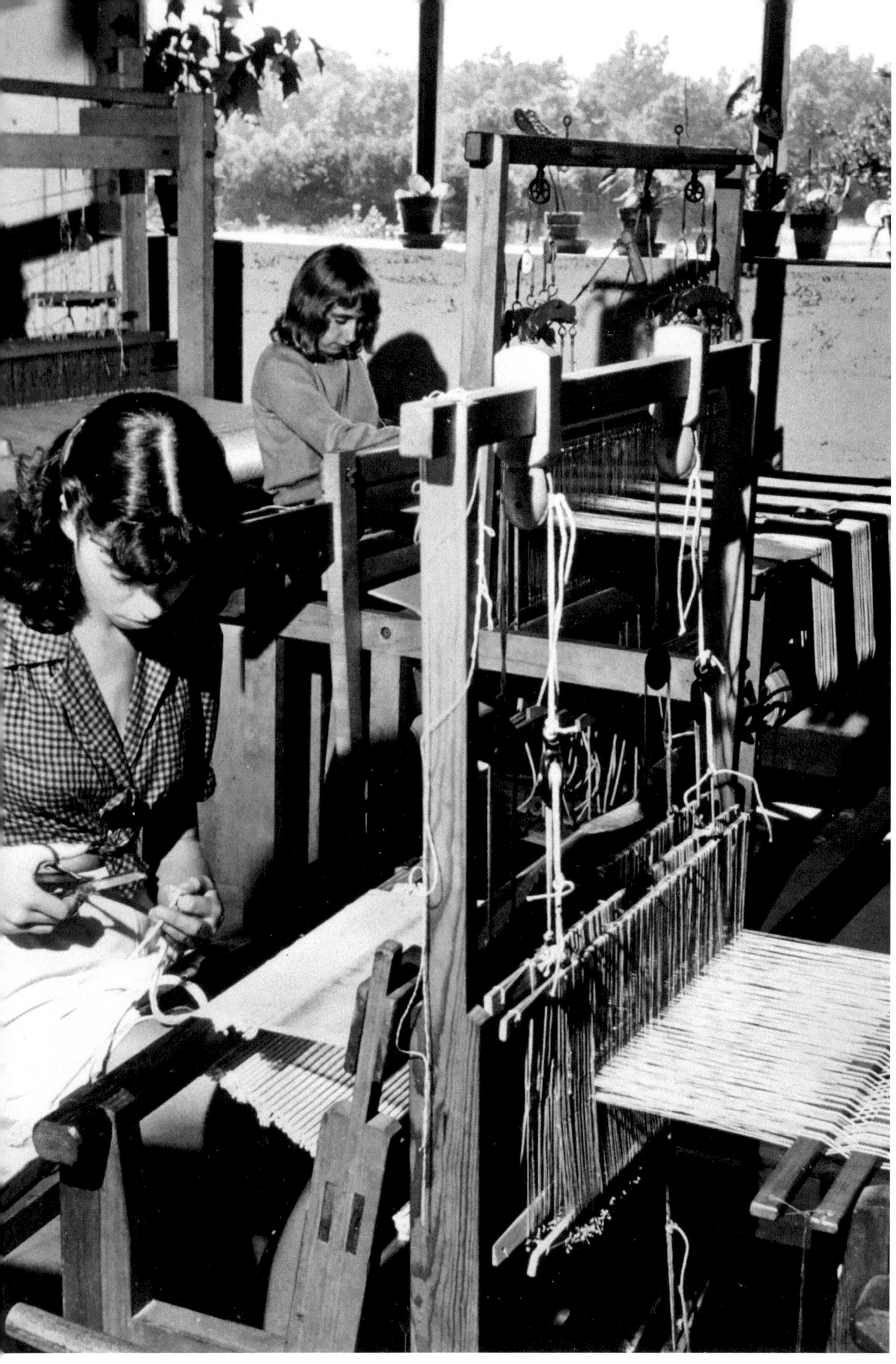

7. Ati Gropius and Mimi French weaving, summer
1944. Photograph by Josef Breitenbach.

ART, CRAFT, DESIGN

ANNI ALBERS'S VISION FOR THE WEAVING PROGRAM AT BLACK MOUNTAIN COLLEGE

MICHAEL BEGGS

When Anni Albers arrived at Black Mountain College in November 1933, nothing was certain. The College consisted of fewer than two dozen students and half as many faculty, and had been open less than three months. Anni's husband, Josef Albers, had been hired to teach art, which was to be at the center of Black Mountain College's liberal arts curriculum, but while the College's founders believed in the importance of the arts, none of them really knew how art should be taught or what kind of artist should be doing the teaching. They just had, as Anni put it, "a vague hunch that this might be a way of establishing a college."[1] In their early letters to Josef Albers, it was clear that what the College's founders meant by "art" was painting, drawing, and maybe sculpture. Neither craft nor design were mentioned.

While other faculty spouses filled administrative roles at the College, or taught kindergarten to a few children of faculty and local families, it was clear from the outset that Anni wanted to teach weaving.[2] In a letter to Ted Dreier written from Berlin on the October 31, 1933, Josef explained:

> my wife will bring her loom and hopes to be able to continue her weaving work there. since it is not your intention to train artists, she thinks she can give students an understanding of weaving materials and practices and perhaps some lessons.[3]

It took a few months after the Alberses' arrival for weaving lessons to begin. At first, Anni, who was not fluent in English but was far more proficient than her husband, was busy translating for Josef in his classes (and at all other times as well). Anni's loom was held up in customs for eight weeks, along with most of the couple's other belong-

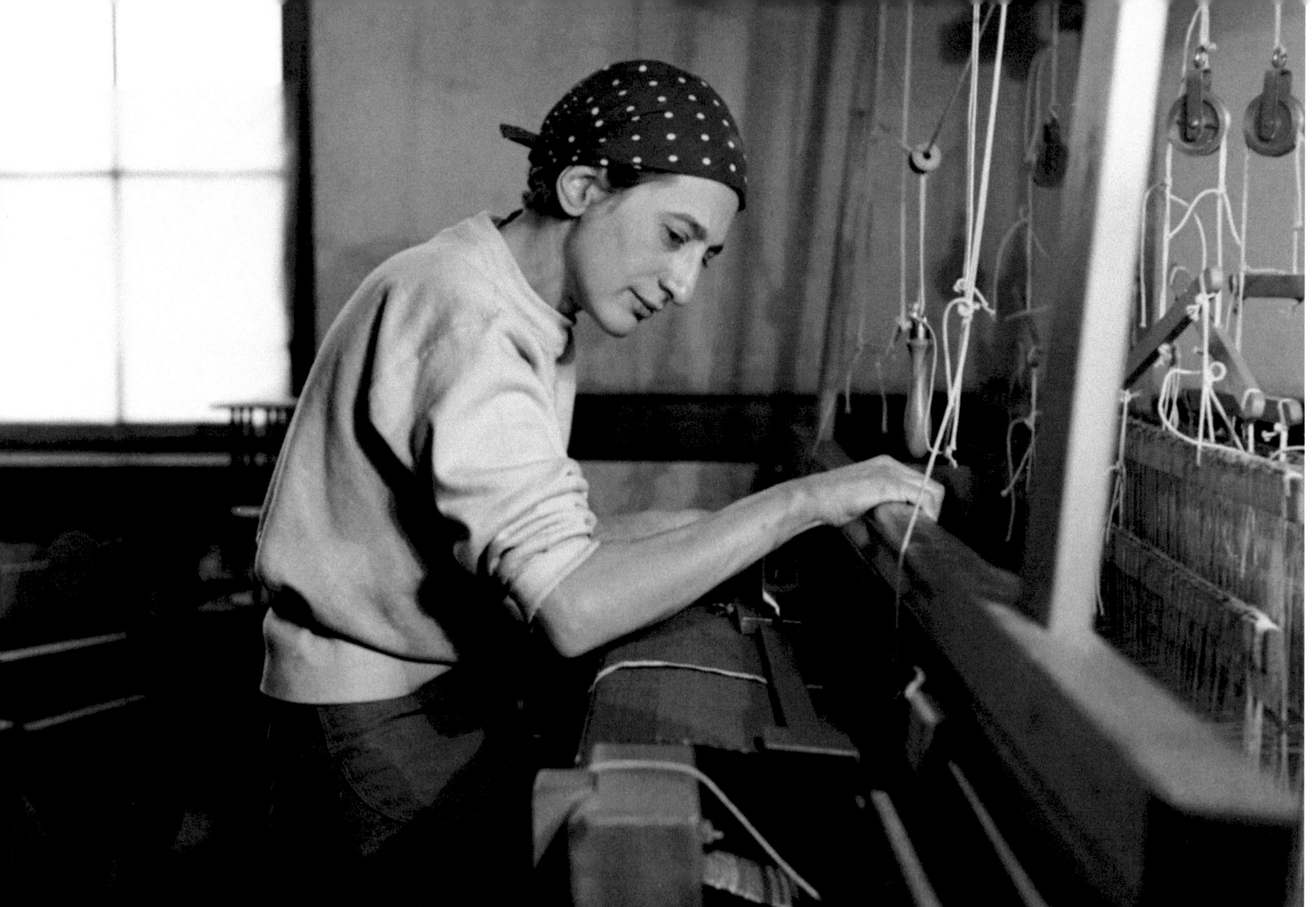

ings. When these items at last arrived at Black Mountain, the Alberses were devastated by what they found. Ten of Josef's artworks in sandblasted glass were shattered, some of their possessions were missing altogether, and Anni's weaving yarns were "in confusion and tangle," the result of poor handling by customs agents.[4] However, by the end of April 1934, Josef was able to report to Wassily and Nina Kandinsky, "weaving has started and my wife gives weaving lessons."[5]

The College's first weaving student was Alice Lee Swan in the winter term, followed by Laura Belle Fisher and Robert Orr in the spring term. But with only one loom, Anni's ability to teach weaving was limited. Adding to Albers's difficulties, weaving materials could be hard to come by, and Anni had no familiarity with the technical vocabulary of weaving in English, which inhibited communication with manufacturers and suppliers.[6] The situation was somewhat improved when additional looms, including a 42" countermarche loom made from maple, were built by chemistry professor and then-College Rector Frederick Georgia, who was a hobbyist cabinetmaker.[7]

Despite these hurdles, by the fall of 1934, three students were taking weaving classes: Robert Orr, Alan Brown, and Sara "Sally" Sylvester. The looms were located in a small white room in the basement of Lee Hall (since renamed Eureka Hall), directly to the west of the porch, where tall north-facing windows filled the space with ample daylight. Hampered by a lack of equipment, weaving classes remained capped at three or four students a semester until the late 1930s, but by 1935, weaving

8. Anni Albers weaving at Black Mountain College, 1937. Photograph by Helen M. Post Modley.

was established enough in the Black Mountain curriculum that Anni Albers was officially made a member of the College faculty. By the end of 1939, she and Josef were U.S. citizens.

DEFINING WEAVING: CRAFT, DESIGN, AND ART

What Josef Albers tentatively described in his letter to Ted Dreier as an informal program in weaving instruction quickly grew into something much more. At Black Mountain College the faculty were given complete control of how and what they taught in their classes, and both Alberses relished this academic freedom. The weaving program at Black Mountain was entirely Anni Albers's brainchild—developed with complete autonomy as an extension of and reaction to her experiences as a student and teacher at the Bauhaus.

Albers's weaving classes were fundamentally design classes, and weaving was the longest running and most successful design subject offered at Black Mountain College.[8] Her students learned about materials and weaving structures though direct experimentation on the loom and were expected to carefully develop the results of their experiments into finished objects. The results varied across the entire spectrum of woven fabrics: from simple utilitarian items like placemats and runners, to structurally ambitious functional fabrics suitable for industrial production, to original artworks at a variety of scales.

Albers's conception of weaving combined the three related strands of art, craft, and design within a single complex approach to the medium. Weaving was a craft and handweavers were craftspeople, but Albers recognized that traditional craft forms and methods were not suited to twentieth century needs or production. Craft had been superseded by industrial production, retired by the simple fact that "we need too much too quickly for any handwork to keep up with."[9] The creation of new industrial objects would be in the hands of a new discipline: "the craftsman is today outside of the great process of industrial production; the designer belongs to it."[10]

In July 1938, Albers visited Mary Hambidge and the Weavers of Rabun in Rabun Gap, Georgia, a visit that did not change her opinions on the role of craft production in the twentieth century. Describing the visit in a letter to Ted Dreier, Anni declared:

> i like machines and believe in them and always more after having seen and heard so much talk about the beauty of handwork. if you do a lot of it, it is just boring, and just as boring as working with machines. only handwork as artwork has sense, so i still and always more believe.[11]

Although Albers felt that there was little need for the crafts in the realm of production, the crafts had tremendous merit for teaching and design. Because a craftsperson is both producer and designer, craft centralizes a process that is otherwise divided by mechanization.[12] Albers emphasized that the crafts were useful for "their contact with material and their slow process of forming,"[13] In the case of weaving, the handloom imposed deliberation during production, which created the conditions for experimentation, learning and design. Writing in the magazine *Design*, Albers explained: "We learn patience and endurance in following through a piece of work. We learn to respect material in working it. Formed things and thoughts live a life of their own; they radiate a meaning." The resulting products could be highly practical, or could extend into

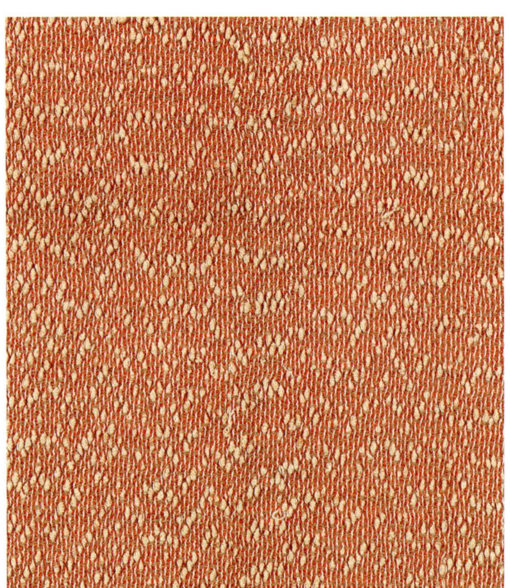

the spiritual realm of art: "handweaving can go both ways; to become art it needs nothing but its own high development and adjustment in all its properties, —to become utilitarian it needs today the help of machines if it is to be more than a mere luxury."[14]

When Josef and Anni Albers arrived at Black Mountain College, Josef's role was clear—to teach art classes—but Anni's was not. Anni Albers was often listed as one of Black Mountain College's art faculty (her byline in "One Aspect of Art Work" is "Assistant Professor of Art, Black Mountain College") but Anni's role at the College, even early in her tenure, was much more closely allied to design and utilitarian production than it was to art. While one of Josef's classes, *Werklehre*, which emphasized material, perceptual, and form studies, would be renamed "Basic Design" to make it less German sounding during World War II, his classes were always more concerned with the creation of visual art than with objects for use.[15] Weaving, and its inherent concern with utility, naturally suited Anni for the role as the College's design teacher, a role that was related to her husband's but distinct enough to merit a full program of her own.

The idea of teaching design at all was cutting edge. In 1933 when Black Mountain College was founded, this definition of the word design—as a verb describing a synthetic creative process that develops functional and aesthetic responses to a set of practical or creative constraints—did not really exist in American English.[16] But with the rise of industrial design as a high-profile discipline in 1930s America, associated with figures like Henry Dreyfuss and Raymond Loewy, who gave form to everything from telephones to locomotives, and with the arrival of émigré designers from Europe, including former *Bauhäusler* Anni and Josef Albers, Mies van der Rohe, and Walter Gropius, the meaning of design within architectural, craft, and artistic discourses began to change. In December 1939, the Museum of Modern Art made its first use of the newer sense of the word in an exhibition title for a holiday-season exposition, *Useful Objects of American Design under $10.00*.[17] By 1945, they had staged *Design for Use, Organic Design in Home Furnishings*, and *T.V.A. Architecture and Design*, among others.[18] By the time the Museum started the *Good Design* exhibition series in Chicago in 1950, the new definition of design had crystallized and was in common usage.

With articles like "Designing," published in *Craft Horizons* in 1943, and "Design: Anonymous and Timeless," published in *The Magazine of Art* in 1947, Anni Albers was an active participant in the discourses that defined the new discipline of design in the 1940s. She, and by extension Black Mountain College, showed how a designer learned, thought, and worked, laying the groundwork for the field of practice that would be occupied after World War II by such figures as Charles and Ray Eames, Paul Rand, George Nelson, and Alexander Girard.

LEARNING ON THE LOOM

To teach her students how to design, and more specifically how to design and weave textiles, Albers gave them the freedom to explore and experiment with materials, colors, textures and structures, both on and off the loom. In her 1965 book, *On Weaving*, she would praise the freshness of these first encounters: "beginning means exploration, selection, development, a potent vitality not yet limited, not circumscribed by the tried and traditional."[19]

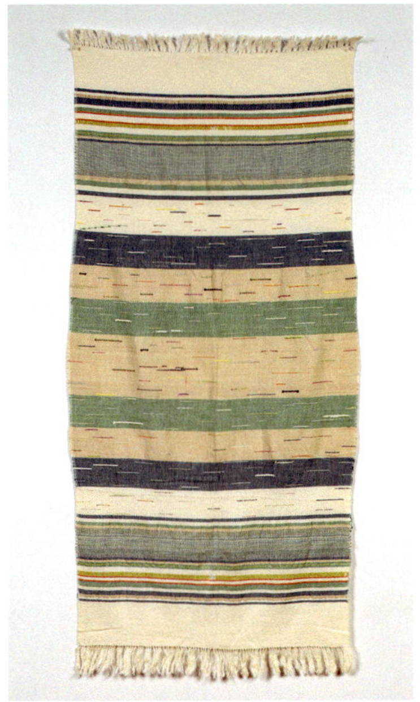

To Albers, the tried and traditional was the enemy of the potent vitality that made great works of art and design sing. Her goal with beginners was to give them time to develop their own sensibilities freely without the requirement to make something recognizable. When she first encountered the kinds of weaving that were being taught in the craft schools near Black Mountain College, she immediately diagnosed "a backlog of colonial weaving."[20] Anni felt teaching her students at Black Mountain to weave in such a traditional, pattern-based way would actively hinder their development as thinkers and designers: "It wouldn't have made any sense to have a student just doing this kind of reproductive work . . . I wanted a free experimentation and a much more professional approach than these mountain weavers had."[21] Like Black Mountain College itself, Anni's weaving classes married great freedom with great rigor. As student Claude Stoller recalled: "Anni Albers gave a wonderful weaving course. She was a most sensitive artist and quite a taskmaster. I admired her greatly."[22]

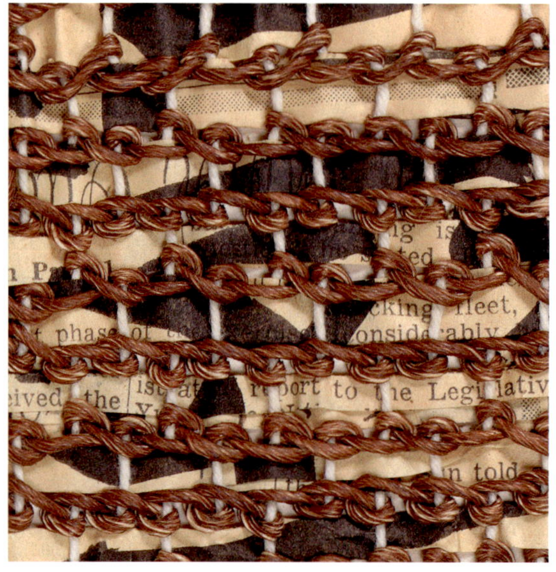

13. Anni Albers, *Studies made on the typewriter* (detail), n.d. Typewriter printing in blue ink on papers mounted on board.

14. Anni Albers, *Study of effect of construction weave* (detail), n.d. Newspaper, string, and fiber mounted on board.

students looked more closely at the characteristics of fibers: rayon and mercerized cotton are glossy and lustrous, but also slippery; wool is relatively weak in tension but because it is fibrous it can be warm and dust-repelling.[31] In addition, threads come in many different constructions: there are threads that vary in texture like bouclé, slub, flake, nub, and chenille, and threads made of specialty materials like cellophane and Lurex. As with the basic weave structures, students learned about these materials both by rote, with Albers lecturing them on their characteristics, and experientially, both through direct work with the materials in weaving and by handling samples among the many threads the college provided for student use. To keep track of what they learned, students took notes and made sample cards for reference.

Albers also created design exercises that encouraged students to explore textile characteristics on a larger scale than a single thread. Made away from the loom and frequently using materials that could not be woven at all, these studies often presented juxtapositions or combinations of found materials that were intriguing to touch, such as Lore Kadden Lindenfeld's study combining burlap with long corkscrews of metal shavings. These freer exercises developed the student's "tactile sensibility," asking them to give attention to their sense of touch, a sense that Albers felt was becoming less familiar with the march of progress.[32]

Often, these non-loom design exercises involved repetition and order, and were therefore more closely allied to textile characteristics. Students gathered the tasseled heads of grasses and laid them next to each other until they took on the character of twills or knitting, or they grouped and mirrored corn kernels into alternating wide and narrow bands, almost like a mock-leno weave. Other studies might use facture on a material with an existing structure, such as abrading and coloring corrugated cardboard to give it a textile-like appearance, or perforating paper with a multitude of pinpricks to create alternating smooth and rough bands. Another permutation used typewritten characters, in which case the exercise was no longer tactile or haptic but instead about creating a textile

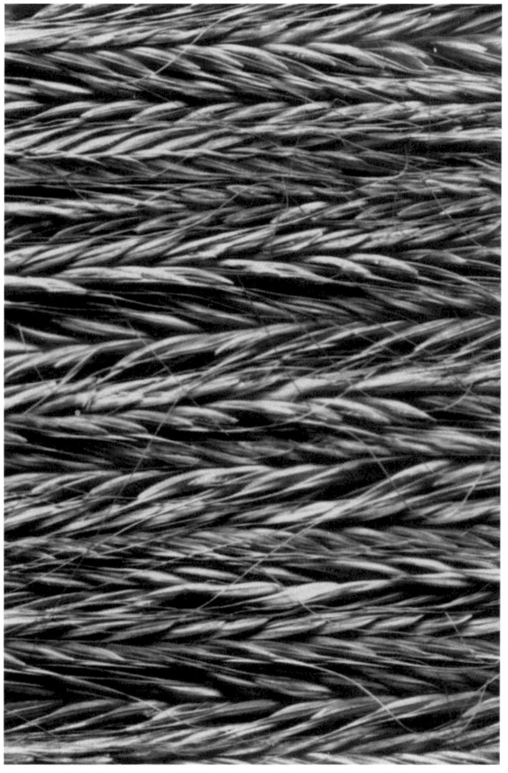

appearance through compounded letterforms and playing with the design elements of fabrics: lines and bands, openness and tightness, and directionality.[33] In all cases, these exercises freed the students, particularly beginners, from the rigors of determining how to achieve a textural or structural effect on the loom, in effect allowing

15. Material study made with grass seeds, Black Mountain College, 1940–41. Photograph by Claude Stoller.

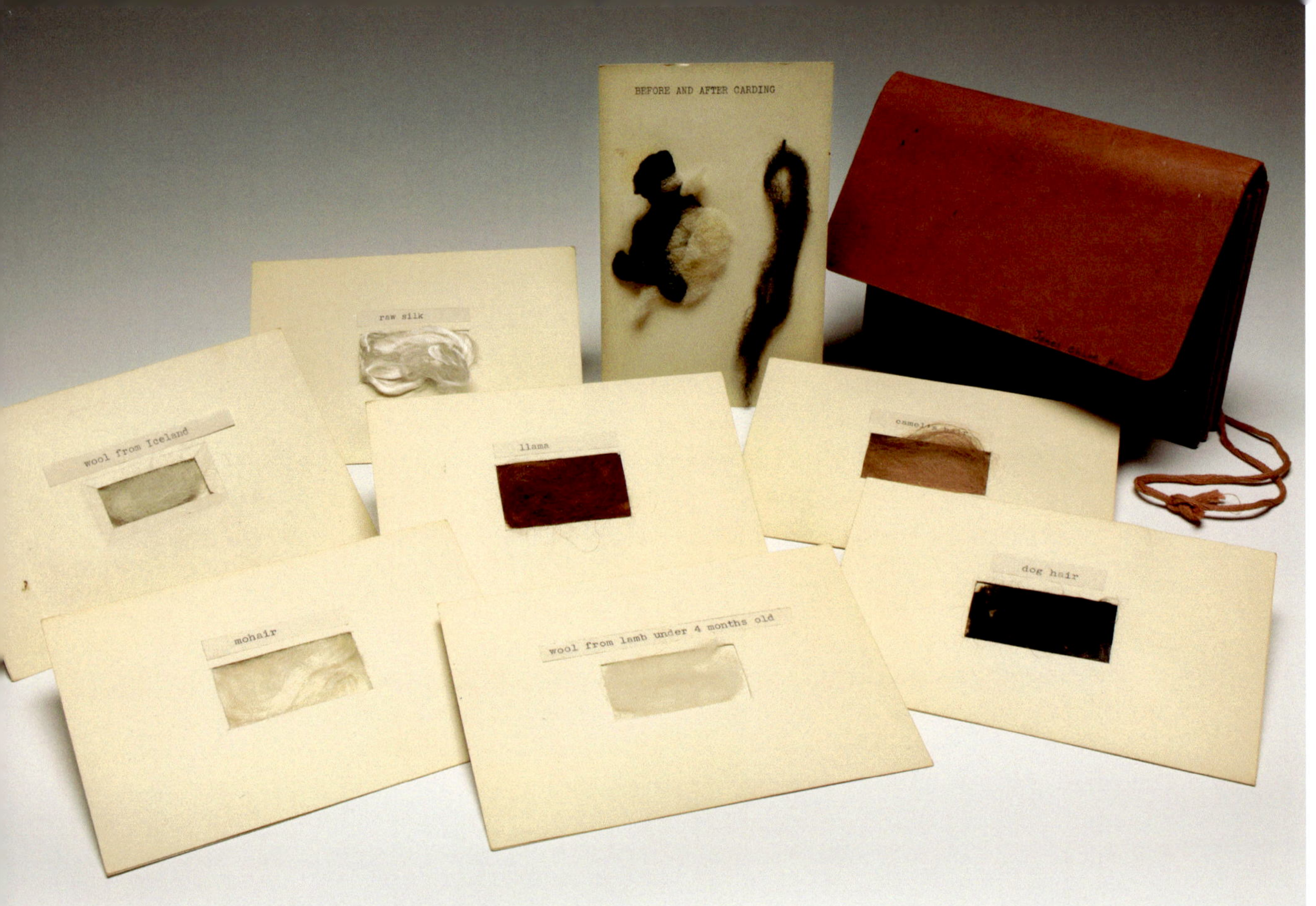

students to bring sophistication to their design thinking about what a textile's texture and appearance might be even when they did not yet have the sophisticated technique required to weave such a textile.[34]

AN EVOLVING PEDAGOGY

Albers's teaching methods developed and evolved over her time at Black Mountain College. According to Anni, she developed some of the non-loom design exercises when the College moved from Blue Ridge to the Lake Eden campus: "I had to teach a class without any roof over my head, or looms . . . we had to do something that could be done by just sitting down together, and we started by selecting grasses and seeds and so on and putting them in specific orders, which are textile orders."[35] By the mid-1940s, these exercises were a significant part of Albers's teaching. Both Janet Heling Roberts, who took weaving classes from 1944 to 1947, and Joan Potter Loveless, who took weaving in 1946 and 1947, remembered lots of material studies using "seeds and grains, sand, bits of bark—anything that could be glued down to create variations of texture and tune us in to this quality that was important in weaving."[36]

16. Janet Heling Roberts, *Fiber samples for Anni Albers's weaving class*, ca. 1944–47.
Index cards, typewriter ink, assorted fibers
8 cards, 4 × 6 in. each.

17. Anni Albers card weaving at Black Mountain College, n.d. Photograph by Claude Stoller.

Albers also introduced her students to weaving with backstrap looms beginning in the fall of 1939, after encountering them in Mexico during a trip there in the summer, where the Albers were joined by weaving and art student Alex Reed. In a letter to Ted Dreier, Anni explained:

> I found a very old primitive loom and bought it. It is a method of weaving with a few wood sticks, the warp tied to a tree and the other end to yourself. An Indian woman showed us how to set up the loom and how to weave. It is terribly tricky and Bill and I don't quite understand it yet although we went back to her village and had another lesson. It is strange that the primitive, so called, methods are so very complicated! I thought it would be interesting to show students this way of weaving.[37]

The extent to which backstrap weaving was quickly integrated into the weaving curriculum is clearly shown in a photograph made by John Harvey Campbell of Mimi French, Jane Slater, Marilyn Bauer, and a fourth student (possibly Virginia Osbourne) using backstrap looms on the porch of the studies building, probably in the spring of 1944 (fig 32.).[38] It is possible that Albers also added card weaving to the curriculum around the same time as the backstrap loom, as all existing card weavings from Black Mountain College (all known examples of which are belts) seemingly date to after 1940.[39]

Albers introduced these other looms and techniques not just as curiosities, but rather, to add context to her students's understanding of more modern looms: "Once they understand these basic elements, that the Peruvian backstrap loom has embedded in it everything that a high power machine loom today has . . .they understand it in a completely different sense than walking into a factory and seeing these things operate."[40] If handweaving imposed the slow and patient thought necessary for design when compared to machine looms, backstrap looms imposed an even slower and more manual process, which actually allowed the weaver more freedom and possibilities than a standard floor loom.

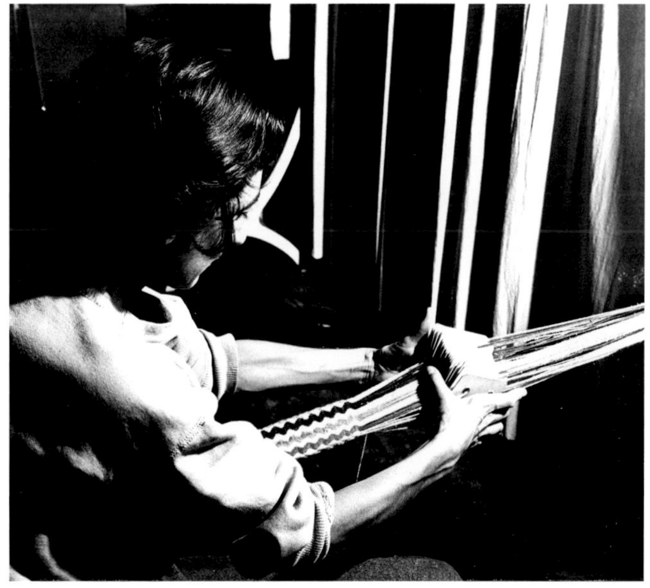

After leaving Black Mountain College, Albers taught privately in New Haven in the 1950s and 1960s, during which time her students included Sheila Hicks, Dolores Dembus Bittleman, and Dorothy Cavalier Yanik. Building off of her non-loom studies developed at BMC, Albers aimed to put her "students at the point of zero" by having them imagine themselves as pre-textile humans.[41] They would then slowly go through "pre-weaving structures: looping, twining, knotting" before "gradually we invented looms out of sticks and so on."[42]

LEARNING TO DESIGN FABRIC FOR A PURPOSE

Having experimented with the range of possibilities afforded by materials and structures, Anni's students would be asked to apply their experience to specific textile design problems. Lore Kadden Lindenfeld's notes from Anni's class in 1948 record several of these problems, including a tablecloth (must be washable, "pattern is desirable to not show spots"), stage curtains (fire proof, light weight, elegant look, "dark color for practical reasons, shine for festiveness"), and a partition between dining room and kitchen (must handle "smoke, smell, noise, dust, and fat").[43]

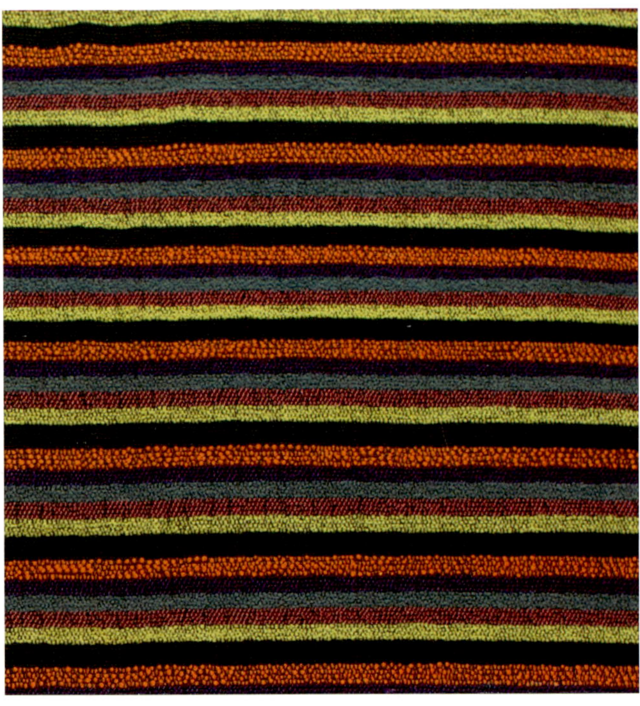

Albers liked to assign her students design prompts that she had previously solved. Lindenfeld's notes record Albers's own solution for a stage curtain, designed in 1928 for a theater in Oppeln: "Mrs. Albers wove such a stage curtain. Long stripes of material about 1 yard in width were pieced together in the vertical direction to give the appearance of width. Horizontal stripes were woven into each stripe in alternating fashion and were the design which made this curtain unique."[44] A note indicates that Albers's curtains were black with gold and blue stripes.[45] Lindenfeld's notes also describe the fabric for which Albers received her Bauhaus diploma, a wall covering in cotton, chenille and cellophane that was sound absorbing but light reflecting, made for the Allgemeinen Deutschen Gewerkschaftsbundeschule building in Bernau.

Albers relished the activating effect of a design prompt on her student's work. By considering fitness to purpose, her students moved from the realm of experimentation—more closely allied with art making—to the realm of production, and in the process became designers. In her 1938 essay "Bauhaus Weaving" written to accompany the landmark exhibition *Bauhaus 1919–1928* at the Museum of Modern Art, Albers evoked the same moment in her description of the evolution of the weaving workshop at the Bauhaus:

> This consideration of usefulness brought about a profoundly different conception. A shift took place from the free play with forms to a logical building of structures. . . . Concentrating on purpose now had a disciplining effect, now that the range of possibilities had been freely explored. The realization of appropriateness of purpose also introduced another factor: the importance of recognizing new problems arising with changing times, of foreseeing a development. . . . The creative impetus, previously coming from the world of appearance, now received its stimulus from the intellectual sphere of a recognized need. Only the imaginative mind can bring about the transformation of such rational recognition into a material form.[46]

Albers's design prompts to her students emphasized function because she saw usefulness as an activating impulse in the design process, but she was quick to note that the design process must also consider aesthetic fitness for purpose:

> The good designer is the anonymous designer, so I believe, the one who does not stand in the way of the material; who sends his products on their way to a useful life without an ambitious appearance. A useful object should perform its duty without much ado. The tablecloth that calls "Here I am, look at me," is invading the privacy of the consumer. The curtains that cry "We are beautiful, your attention please," but whisper "though not very practical, we will need much of your time to keep us in shape," are badly designed. The unknown designer or designers of our sheets or of our light bulbs performed their task well. Their products are complete in their unpretentious form.[47]

Alongside requirements that the fabric be an "expensive looking material which is cheap" that gives the "illusion of lots of material without using much," Anni's prompt for a display curtain for an expensive gift shop also stipulated that it should be a "neutral color to go with everything" and of "little textile interest."[48] The draperies Albers designed for Rena Rosenthal's exclusive Madison Avenue store in 1935 fit the bill exactly. These draperies were woven using a combination of rayon and cellophane so that the sparkle of the cellophane could give the draperies a luxurious appearance; had vertical stripes of contrasting textures which gave the appearance of being gathered; were also beige "to go with everything;" and fundamentally receded behind the housewares and pieces of decorative arts that Rosenthal hoped to sell.

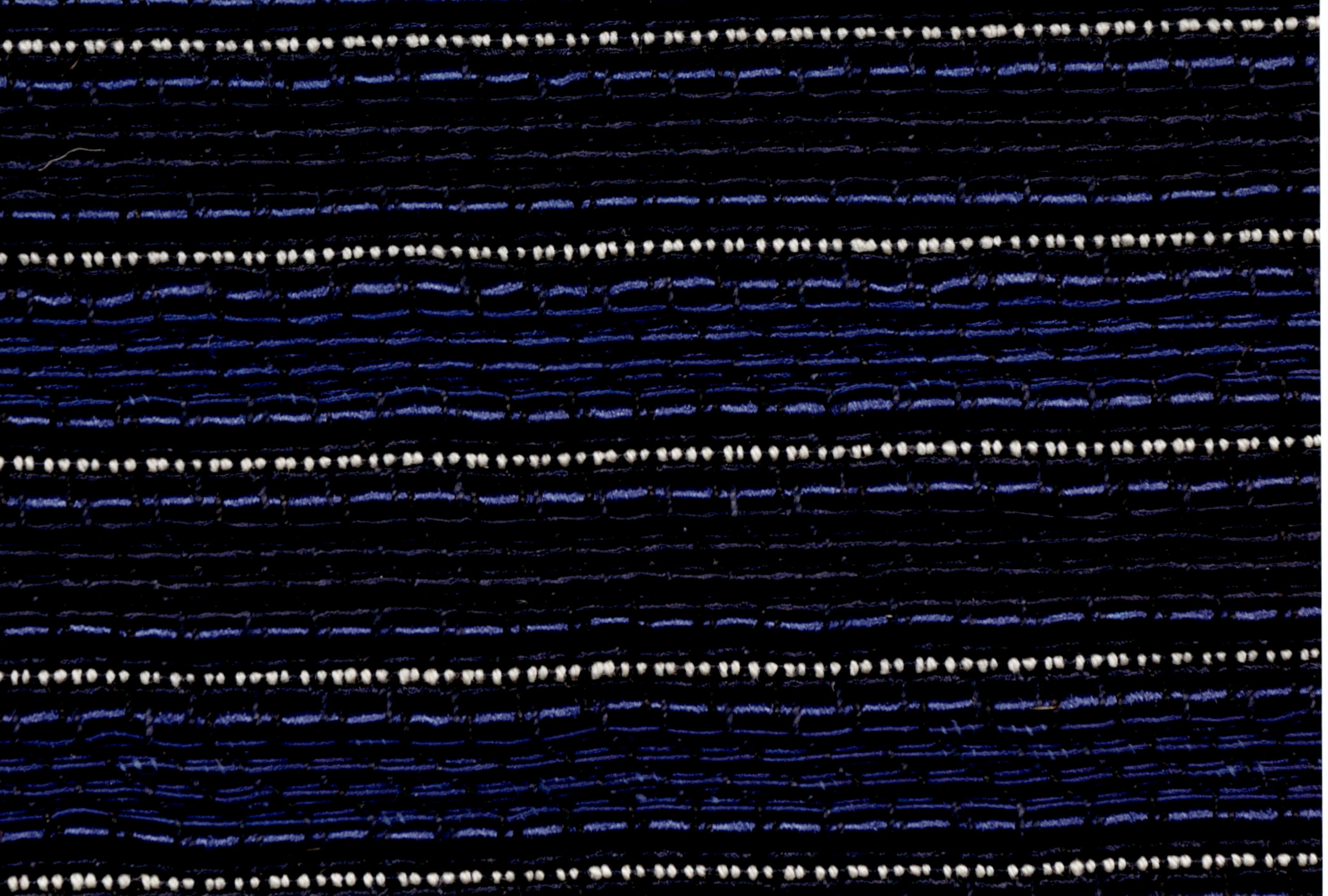

A STUDENT-DESIGNED FABRIC

Albers's experimental and pedagogical approach can be seen by looking at a practical textile designed and woven by Black Mountain College student Don Page around 1940 (fig. 19, above).

The fabric is not traditional or patterned: it doesn't depict a scene and is neither floral, nor herringbone, nor paisley. It is deceptively simple, just alternating stripes of blue and black highlighted by thin bright lines of gold. It seems modern and fresh, and is attractive but anonymous. At first glance, the fabric seems to be strongly weft-facing and woven in a single layer—the stripes within the fabric appear to be entirely made up of blue, black, or gold threads within a black or dark blue warp.

Looking closer, we see much more complexity. What we thought was a continuous weft thread in gold is discontinuous and is actually made up of many white warp threads that normally are hidden behind the mass of the blue or black stripes. And when we look closely at those stripes themselves, we see what appear to be multiple sizes and layers of weft threads. The more we look, the more we realize how highly-structured this fabric is.

As a designed object, the components of this textile work together to create a cohesive and functional whole. The thin row of white warp threads not only offers a pleasing highlight within the pattern of the face of the cloth, but also binds all those layers of threads together tightly to make the fabric thick and resistant to wear, while the dominance of the weft threads gives it a grain, which makes it easier to clean. The thicker blue threads are cords—threads bound in an outer sheath of blue wrapped threads—adding an extra layer of durability and smoothness to them. We might guess that this is a tough upholstery fabric—something meant for use in a car or on a surface that gets rougher treatment than a sofa or armchair. Zooming out, the overall appearance of the fabric is attractive but not gaudy or overpowering, again appropriate for utilitarian upholstery.

Weaving students at Black Mountain College were taught to understand practical textiles as designed functional objects made up of integrated complementary parts held together in a specific structure to fulfill a defined function. When Don Page wove this fabric he was designing a fabric to meet a function, and bringing a form for the fabric out of that function. The result does not mimic traditional fabrics in its appearance or construction or materials, but is instead thoroughly modern, meeting a twentieth century need (automobile upholstery) using twentieth century materials (mass-produced threads) in a way suitable for twentieth century means (industrial production).

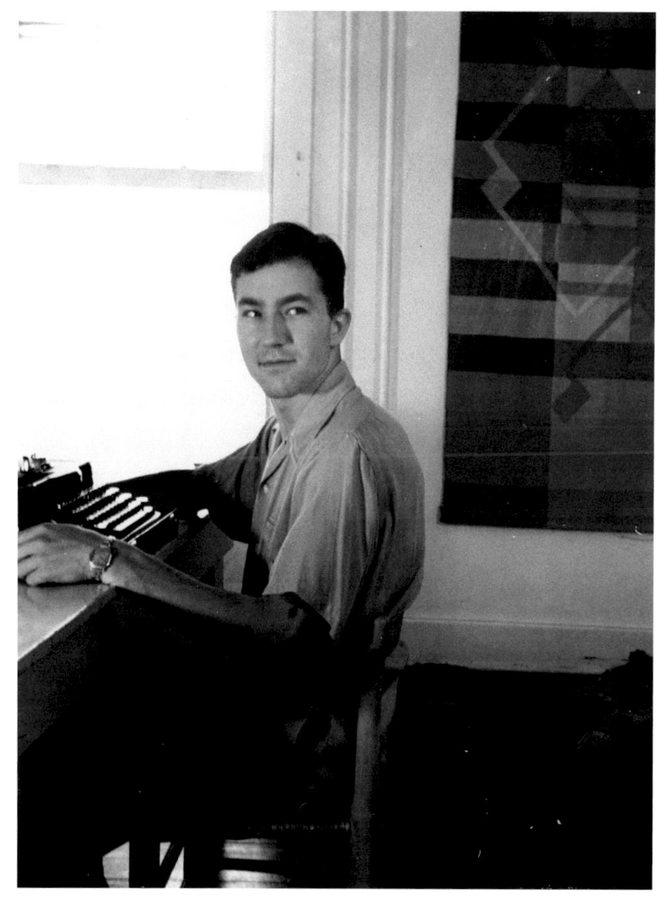

Apart from all its formal characteristics discussed above, this textile is a startling example of the success of Anni Albers's vision for the weaving program as a textile design program. Page's textile shows his sophisticated grasp of how design imperatives are turned into a finished object, a skill he developed and honed in Albers's classes through a rigorous and experiential course of applied experimentation. The resulting fabric is complex, professional, and thoroughly modern. It is designed and executed at a level on par with many of Albers's own fabrics. Black Mountain College may be best known as an art school, but many of the greatest design objects produced at the school are hiding in plain sight; products of the weaving program.

WORK WITH MATERIAL

1938

ANNI ALBERS

Life today is very bewildering. We have no picture of it which is all-inclusive, such as former times may have had. We have to make a choice between concepts of great diversity. And as a common ground is wanting, we are baffled by them. We must find our way back to simplicity of conception in order to find ourselves. For only by simplicity can we experience meaning, and only by experiencing meaning can we become qualified for independent comprehension.

In all learning today dependence on authority plays a large part, because of the tremendous field of knowledge to be covered in a short time. This often leaves the student oscillating between admiration and uncertainty, with the well-known result that a feeling of inferiority is today common both in individuals and in whole nations.

Independence presumes a spirit of adventurousness—a faith in one's own strength. It is this which should be promoted. Work in a field where authority has not made itself felt may help toward this goal. For we are overgrown with information, decorative maybe, but useless in any constructive sense. We have developed our receptivity and have neglected our own formative impulse. It is no accident that nervous breakdowns occur more often in our civilization than in those where creative power had a natural outlet in daily activities. And this fact leads to a suggestion: we must come down to earth from the clouds where we live in vagueness, and experience the most real thing there is: material.

Civilization seems in general to estrange men from materials, that is, from materials in their original form. For the process of shaping these is so divided into separate steps that one person is rarely involved in the whole course of manufacture, often knowing only the finished product. But if we want to get from materials the sense

21. Eva Zhitlowsky at a loom, n.d.
Photograph by Fred Stone.

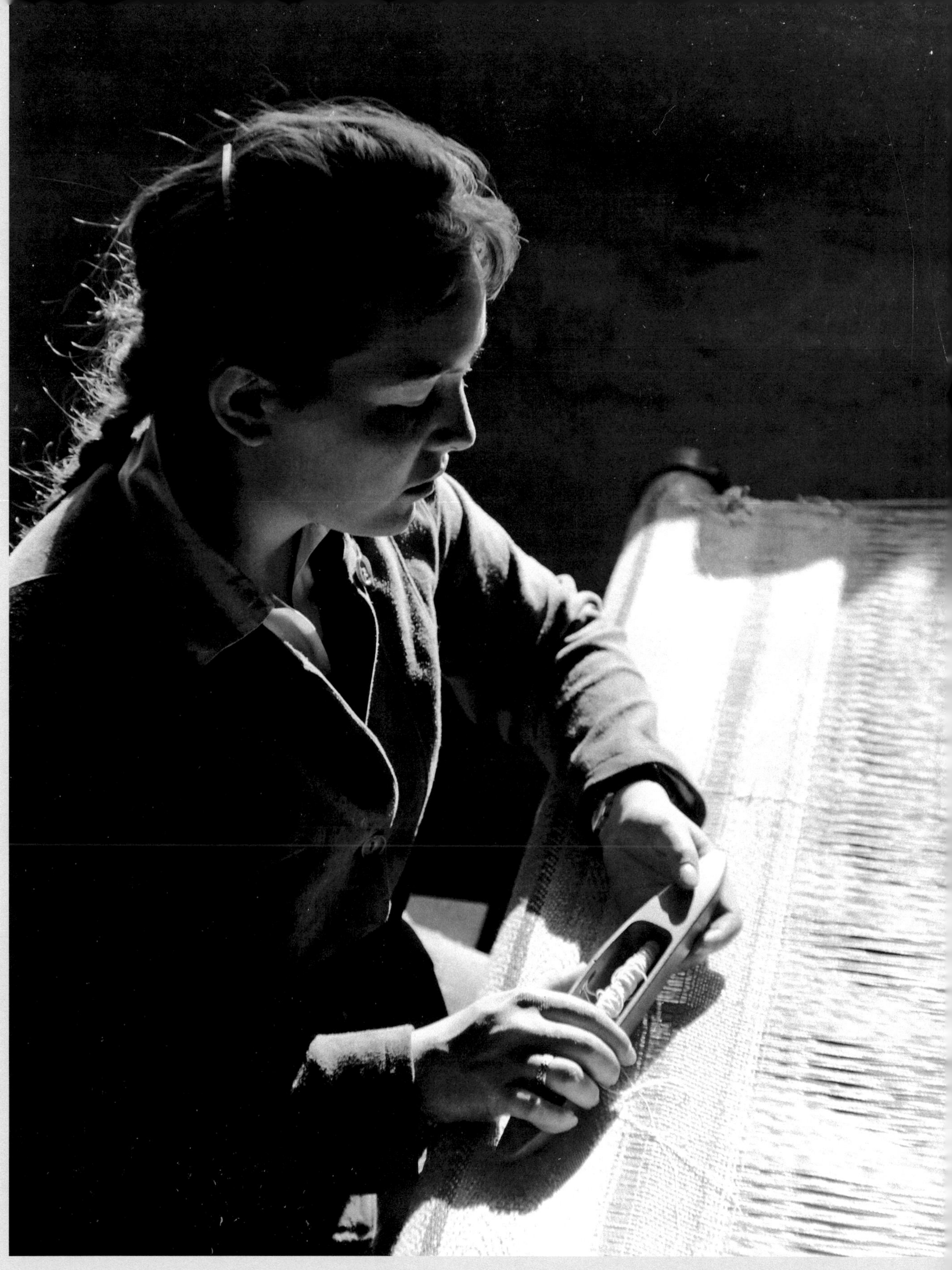

of directness, the adventure of being close to the stuff the world is made of, we have to go back to the material itself, to its original state, and from there on partake in its stages of change.

We use materials to satisfy our practical needs and our spiritual ones as well. We have useful things and beautiful things—equipment and works of art. In earlier civilizations there was no clear separation of this sort. The useful thing, could be made beautiful in the hands of the artisan, who was also the manufacturer. His creative impulse was not thwarted by drudgery in one section of a long and complicated mechanical process. He was also a creator. Machines reduce the boredom of repetition. On the other hand they permit a play of the imagination only in the preliminary planning of the product.

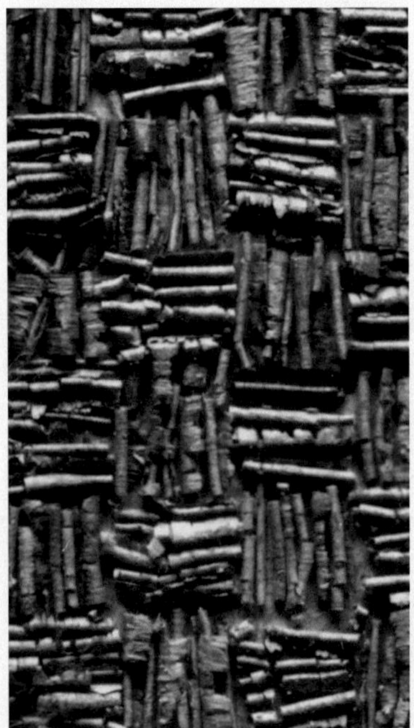

Material, that is to say unformed or unshaped matter, is the field where authority blocks independent experimentation less than in many other fields, and for this reason it seems well fitted to become the training ground for invention and free speculation. It is here that even the shyest beginner can catch a glimpse of the exhilaration of creating, by being a creator while at the same time he is checked by irrevocable laws set by the nature of the material, not by man. Free experimentation here can result in the fulfillment of an inner urge to give form and to give permanence to ideas, that is to say, it can result in art, or it can result in the satisfaction of invention in some more technical way.

But most important to one's own growth is to see oneself leave the safe ground of accepted conventions and to find oneself alone and self-dependent. It is an adventure which can permeate one's whole being. Self-confidence can grow. And a longing for excitement can be satisfied without external means, within oneself; for creating is the most intense excitement one can come to know.

All art work, such as music, architecture, and even religion and the laws of science, can be understood as the transformed wish for stability and order. But art work understood as work with a substance which can be grasped and formed is more suited for the development of the taste for exploration than work in other fields, for the fact of the inherent laws of material is of importance. They introduce boundaries for a task of free imagination. This very freedom can be so bewildering to the searching person that it may lead to resignation if he is faced with the immense welter of possibilities; but within set limits the imagination can find something to hold to. There still remains a fullness of choice but one not as overwhelming as that offered by unlimited opportunities. These boundaries may be conceived as the skeleton of a structure. To the beginners a material with very definite limitations can for this reason be most helpful in the process of building up independent work.

22. Material study made with wood shavings
and twigs, Black Mountain College, 1940–41.
Photograph by Claude Stoller.

23. Draft notation in Lolita Georgia's notebook
from Anni Albers's weaving class, ca. 1935.

The crafts, understood as conventions of treating material, introduce another factor: traditions of operation which embody set laws. This may be helpful in one direction, as a frame for work. But these rules may also evoke a challenge. They are revokable, for they are set by man. They may provoke us to test ourselves against them. But always they provide a discipline which balances the hubris of creative ecstasy.

All crafts are suited to this end, but some better than others. The more possibilities for attack the material offers in its appearance and in its structural elements, the more it can call forth imagination and productiveness. Weaving is an example of a craft which is many-sided. Besides surface qualities, such as rough and smooth, dull and shiny, hard and soft, it also includes color, and, as the dominating element, texture, which is the result of the construction of weaves. Like any craft it may end in producing useful objects, or it may rise to the level of art.

When teaching the crafts, in addition to the work of free exploring, both the useful and the artistic have to be considered. As we have said before, today only the first step in the process of producing things of need is left to free planning. No variation is possible when production is once taken up, assuming that today mass production must necessarily include machine work. This means that the teaching has to lead toward planning for industrial repetition, with emphasis on making models for industry. It also must attempt to evoke a consciousness of developments, and further perhaps a foreseeing of them. Hence, the result of craft work, work done in direct contact with the material, can come here to have a meaning to a far wider range of people than would be the case if they remained restricted to handwork only. And from the industrial standpoint, machine production will get a fresh impetus from taking up the results of intimate work with material.

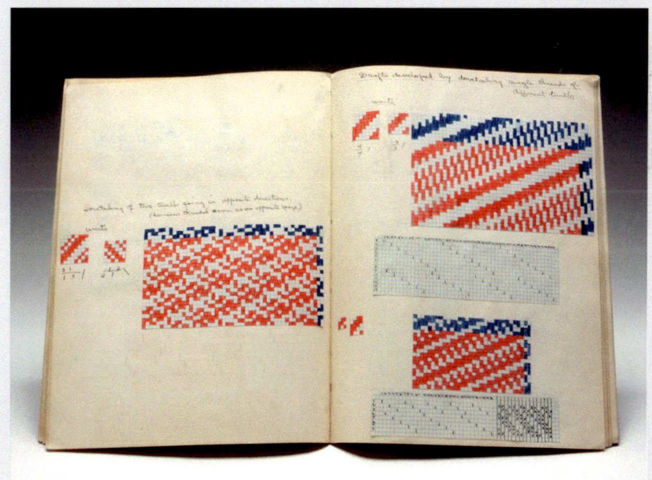

The other aspect of craft work is concerned with art work, the realization of a hope for a lawful and enduring nature. Other elements, such as proportion, space relations, rhythm, predominate in these experiments, as they do in the other arts. No limitations other than the veto of the material itself are set. More than an active process, it is a listening for the dictation of the material and a taking in of the laws of harmony. It is for this reason that we can find certitude in the belief that we are taking part in an eternal order.

Published in the Black Mountain College Bulletin, *5, 1938.*

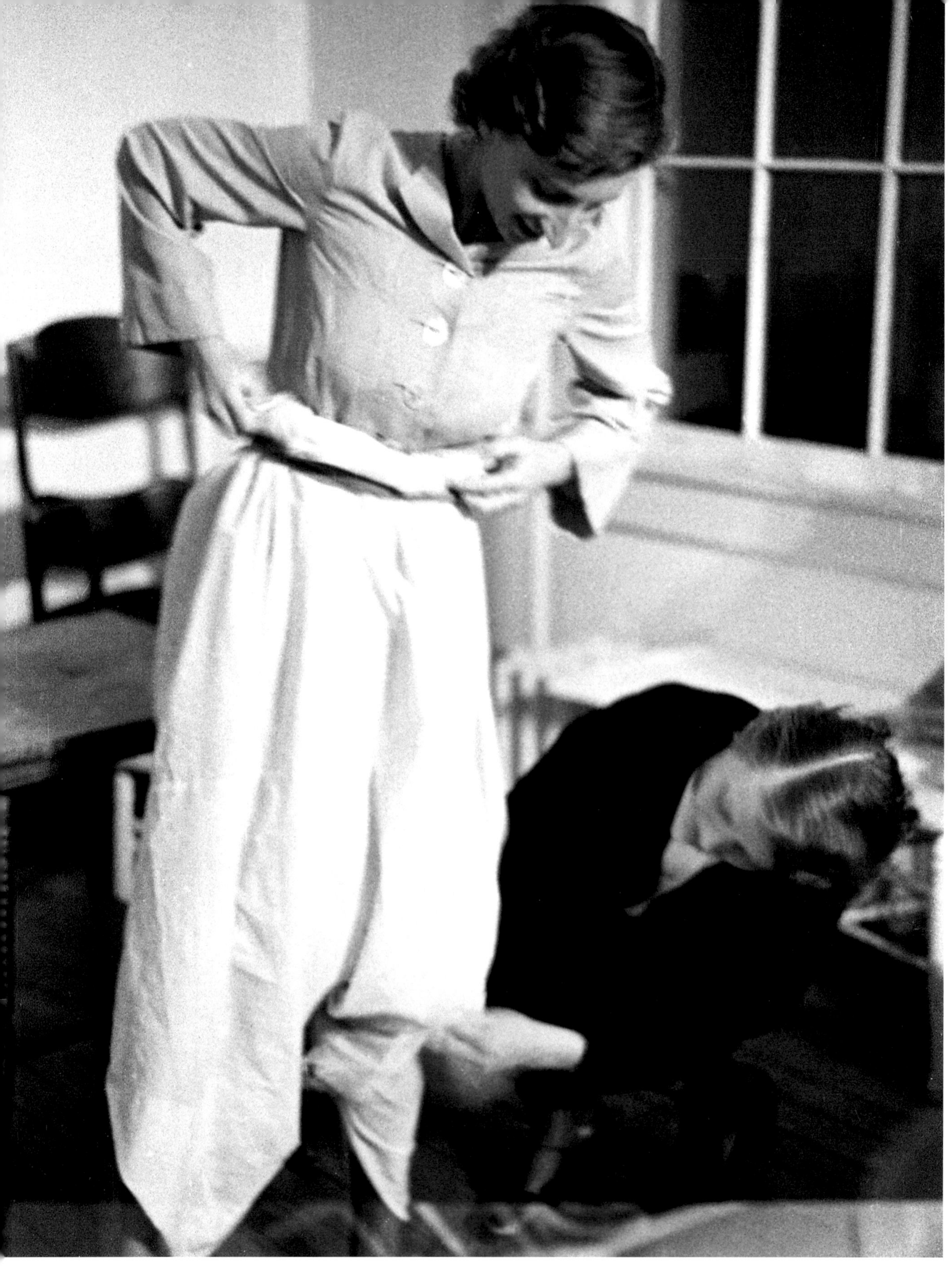

24. Bobby Dreier (left) and Irene Schawinsky
in Schawinsky's dressmaking class, spring 1937.
Photograph by Helen M. Post Modley.

MAKING CLOTHES AT BLACK MOUNTAIN COLLEGE

MICHAEL BEGGS

Throughout Black Mountain College's history, students and faculty made and mended their own clothing and accessories, sometimes making garments out of handwoven fabrics produced by the College's weaving program. Although this sewing was largely done on an extracurricular basis, organized classes were taught by Irene Schawinsky from 1937 to 1938, and by Bernard and Berta Rudofsky during the 1944 and 1945 summer sessions. Though generally speaking, attire was very casual at Black Mountain—many female students wore their first pair of jeans at BMC—clothing made at the College ran the gamut from casual clothes for sunbathing to practical box coats to formal evening dresses.[1] These clothes reflected the atmosphere of the College itself: a highly opinionated aesthetic environment with a strong self-sufficient, do-it-yourself ethos. Like any other college, at BMC looking the part went hand in hand with belonging.

When Irene Schawinsky arrived at Black Mountain College she was married to architect and stage designer Xanti Schawinsky, a former Bauhaus colleague of Josef and Anni Albers. She had been trained as a fashion designer in Paris and Berlin and taught dressmaking at the College from January 1937 until her departure in the summer of 1938.[2] Like Anni in her weaving classes, Schawinsky did not teach her students to merely replicate existing designs by cutting and sewing from patterns. Instead she taught them how to design clothes by combining experiential practice with theoretical instruction. The dressmaking class was attended by both men and women and included members of the faculty, such as Anni Albers and John Andrew Rice, and faculty spouses like Barbara "Bobby" Dreier.[3] For some students, the class was their introduction to working with textiles. After studying dressmaking with Schawinsky, Alex Reed would go on to study weaving with Anni in each subsequent semester up until his graduation.

Although Irene gave some instruction in the "English" method of panel dressmaking, her preferred method of design was what she called the "French" method, which relied on draping and was a more exploratory method of arriving at a final design.[4] In the photographs Helen M. Post took of Schawinsky's class in the spring of 1937, Irene and her students can be seen draping and pinning a variety of bodices onto a mannequin. "She had a marvelous way of making you feel how important draping the fabrics around the figure was," Don Page recalled, "she was very concerned about how a different shaped body required a different dress and what you should do for instance to accent some lines and soften others."[5]

Students in Schawinsky's classes were also encouraged to think about the interaction between material and structure in the construction of garments. In Anni's class the materials in question were single threads, in the dressmaking class the materials were finished textiles, which themselves had unique properties, including stretch, weight, transparency, and other qualities. Schawinsky explained how the direction in which segments of fabric were cut and joined mattered to the finished garment, explaining, for instance, that "a circular skirt that hangs evenly must be made of gores cut square to the weave, otherwise it stretches unevenly according to the weight of the material. The seams will be slightly bias and therefore they tend to stand out."[6]

Schawinsky was also conscious of the interaction between clothing and the moving body. Dreier's notes from the dressmaking class record how certain cuts of skirt,

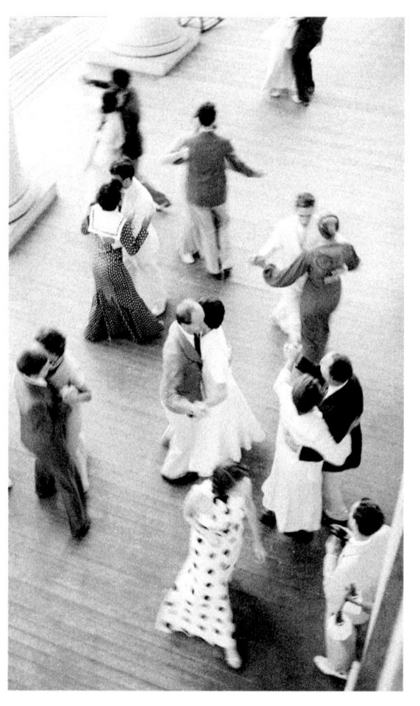

particularly when combined with the wrong kind of fabric, would get shorter if the wearer took too long a step.[7] Don Page remembered Irene going "down in the great hall at night [to try] out one of her new skirts . . . running around, jumping and dancing all by herself . . . seeing how it fell, how it moved."[8] In the 1930s, informal social dances, led by music teacher John Evarts at the piano, took place several nights a week in the evenings at Black Mountain College. These dances, as well as more formal occasions, were a great venue for trying out the products of the dressmaking class. "We had a marvelous time with it," Page recalled, "we had great fun making dance dresses for the girls for Saturday night."[9]

Irene and Xanti Schawinsky's marriage was tumultuous, and the College faculty privately worried that they set a poor model for their students.[10] When Xanti accepted a job at the ill-fated New Bauhaus run by László Moholy-Nagy in Chicago, BMC's faculty happily let the Schawinskys leave.[11] The Schawinskys ultimately moved to New York City, where they left teaching for their respective design professions.[12]

Unlike Anni, Irene Schawinsky never attained faculty status during her time at Black Mountain College, and it is not clear if her dressmaking classes were ever formally designated as classes taken for credit.

26. Anni Albers, Irene Schawinsky, and John Andrew Rice in Schawinsky's dressmaking class, spring 1937. Photograph by Helen M. Post Modley.

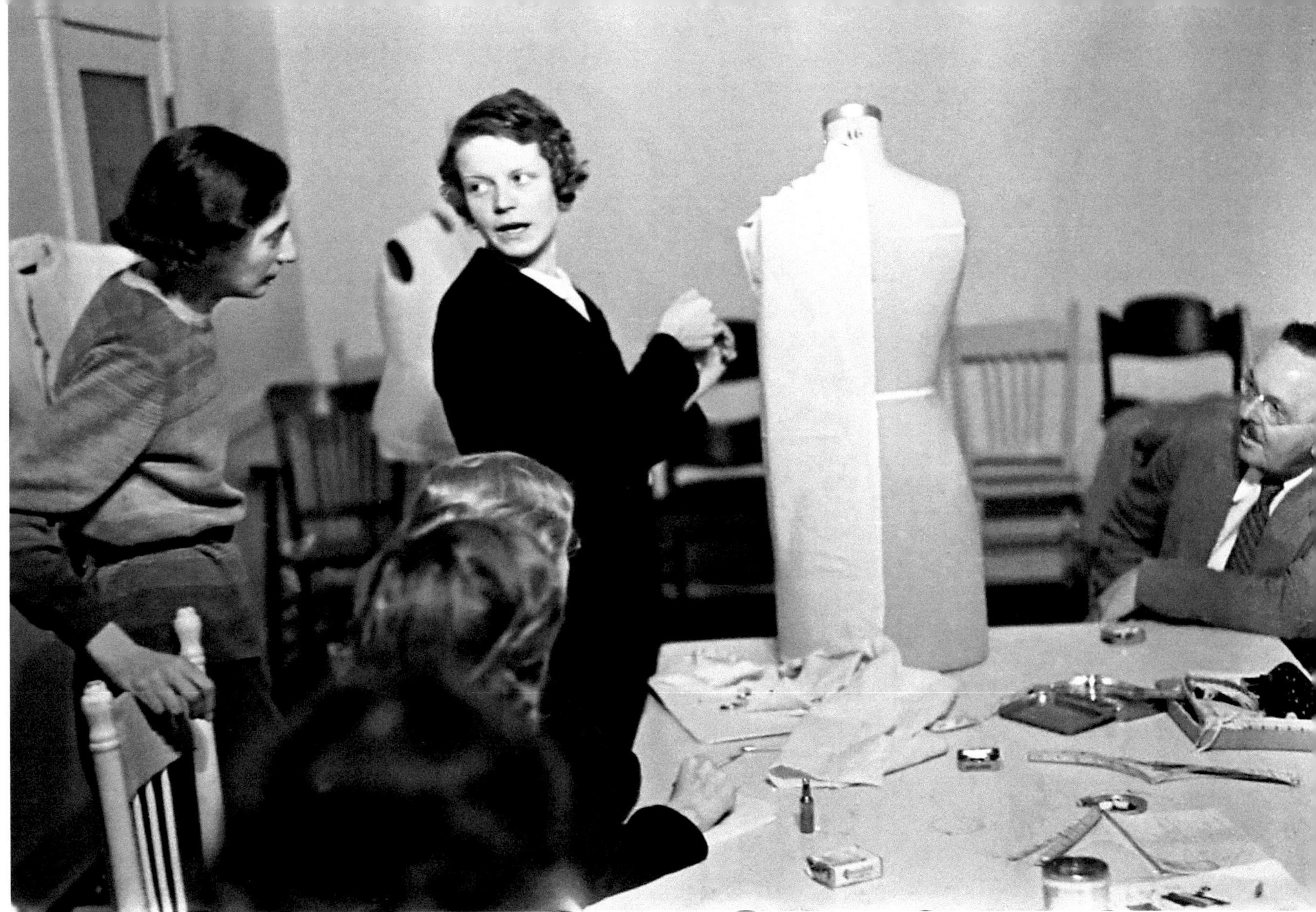

Clothesmaking at Black Mountain College did not cease with Schawinsky's departure, however. Anni Albers continued to make her own clothes—mostly very simple garments with store-bought cloth, such as halter tops and simple jackets. Albers seemingly seldom made clothing with handwoven fabrics, though one jacket, thought to be made in the early 1950s, is an exception. Faculty spouses with sewing skills also made their own clothes and accessories, including Bobby Dreier, whose reversible black-and-white jacket survives, and Johanna Jalowetz, who made a small purse as a gift for Ruth Asawa out of fabric woven by her daughter, Trude Guermonprez.[13]

Most of the clothes made at Black Mountain were made and worn by the College's students, and it was natural for some weaving students to want to make clothes out of the fabrics they wove. It took a certain commitment of time to weave enough fabric to make a garment, but being able to make something wearable once weaving was completed could be a tempting reward. Both beginners, like Lorrie Goulet, and more seasoned weavers, like Barbara Stone Rice, made clothes out of fabric they wove. In other cases, weaving students who had no interest or experience in making clothes, wove fabric for professionals or friends to turn into clothes, and it seems likely that as with other products of the weaving program, clothes (and the fabrics for making them) were also bought, traded, and given as gifts between students.[14] Their work was even published. In a feature on Black Mountain College in *Junior Bazaar* in 1946, Ati Gropius appears in a photograph by noted fashion

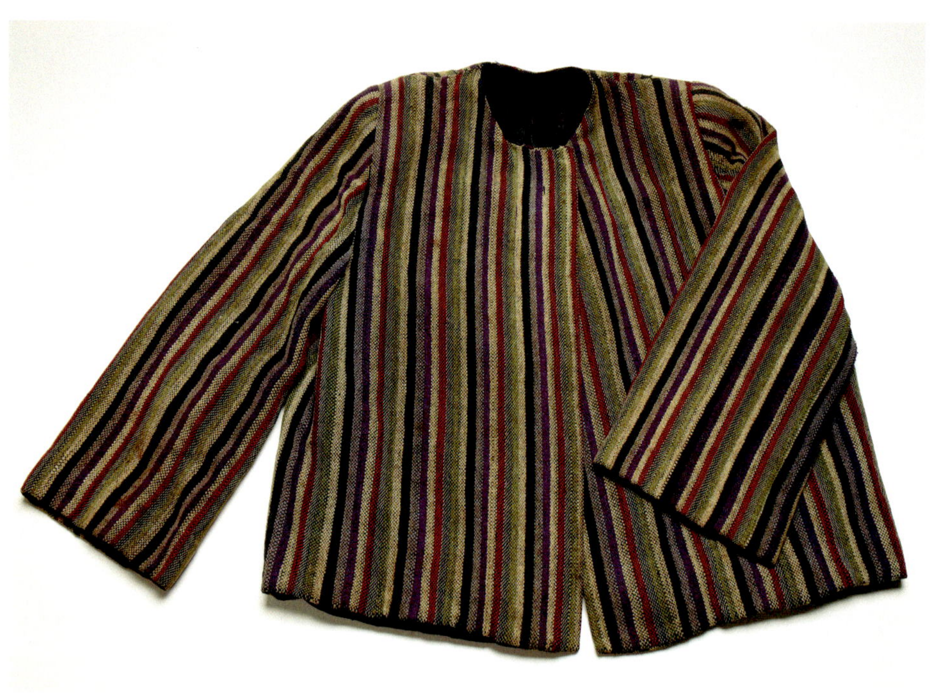

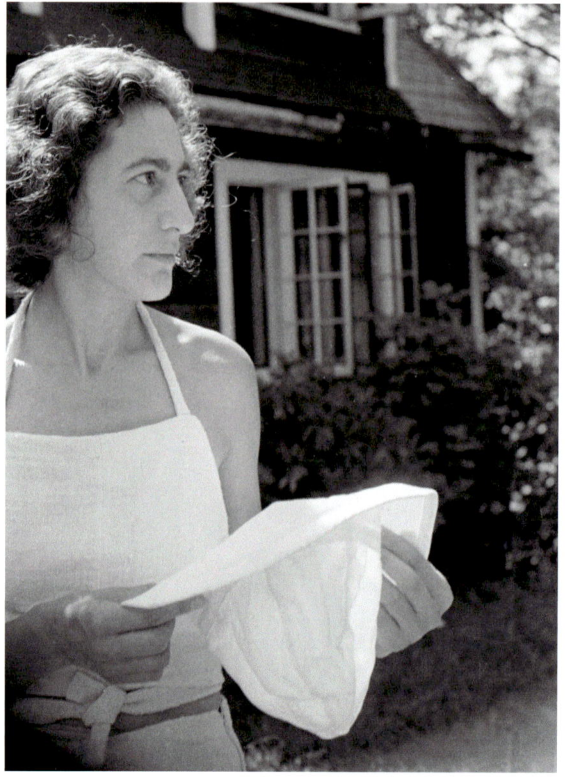

27. Lorrie Goulet, *Jacket*, ca. 1943
Cotton.

28. Anni Albers at Lake Eden, Summer 1938.
Photograph by Josef Albers.

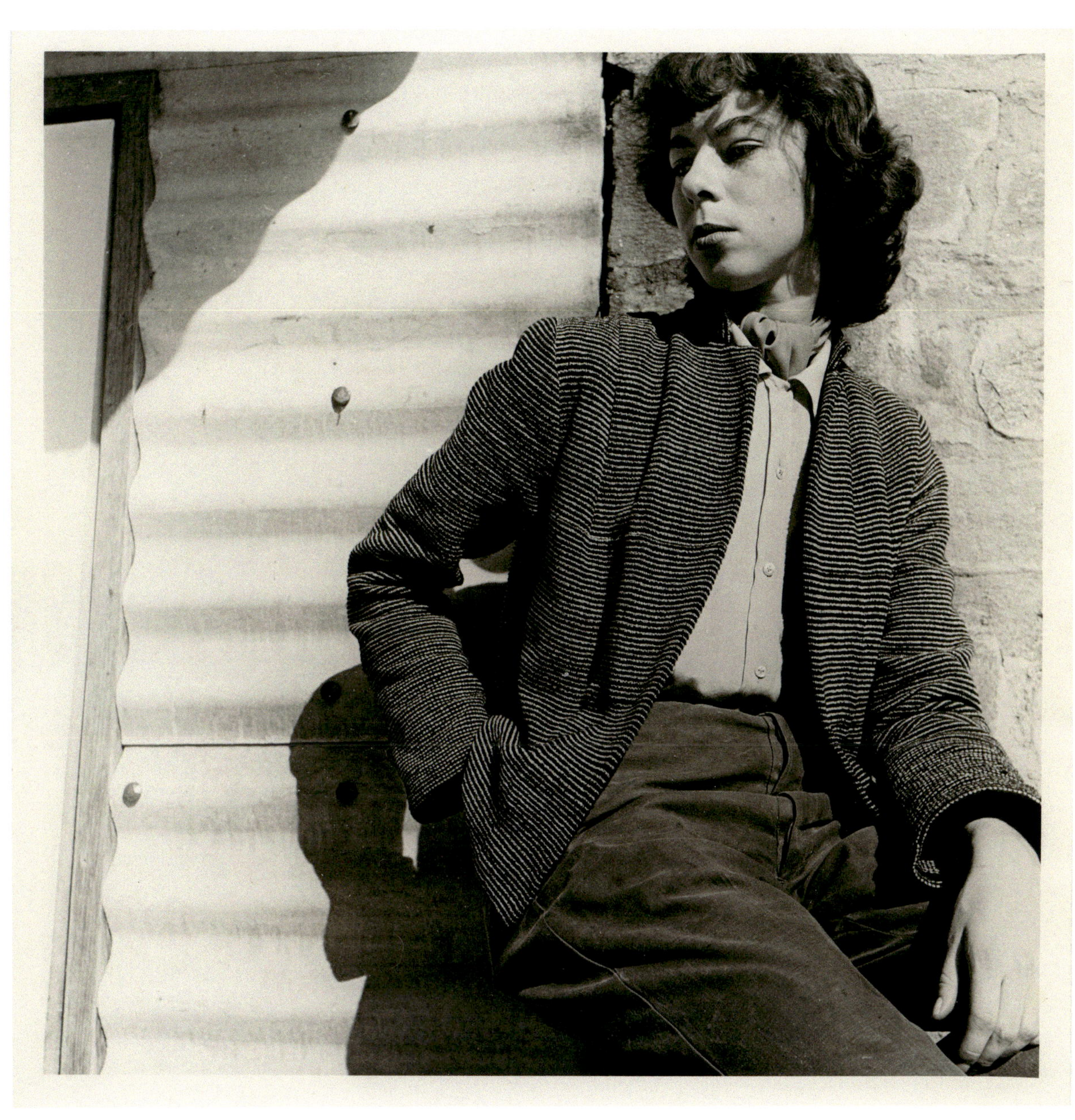

29. Ati Gropius in a jacket woven and designed in the textile workshop, 1946. Photograph by Genevieve Naylor.

photographer Genevieve Naylor wearing a box jacket "designed and woven in the textile workshop."[15]

For the 1944 Summer Session, the first to feature art as well as music faculty, Black Mountain College invited Viennese-born architect and aesthetic theorist

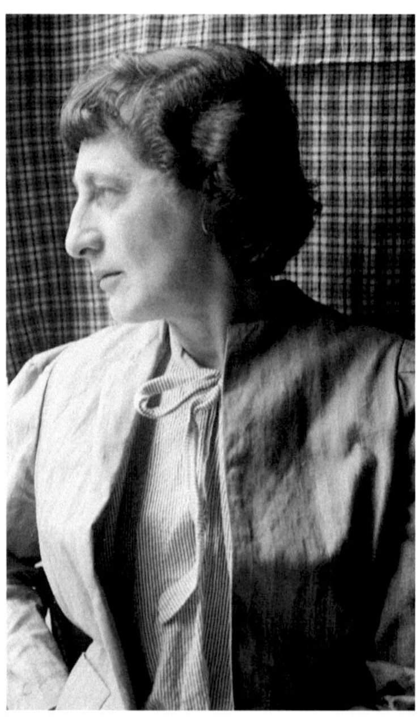

Bernard Rudofsky to teach a two-week class on clothing and deliver a series of lectures. Rudofsky was at the time putting together his first major exhibition, *Are Clothes Modern?*, which was shown at the Museum of Modern Art from November 1944 to March 1945 and was subsequently turned into a book of the same name in 1947. At Black Mountain, Rudofsky gave lectures based on his research, including "How Can People Expect to Have Good Architecture When They Wear Such Clothes?" and "The Unfashionable Human Body," the latter of which was likely similar in content to the chapter of the same name in his book.[16]

While Rudofsky was at Black Mountain, his wife, Berta, taught a popular impromptu practical class in leatherwork and sandal making.[17] Student-made sandals had been a fixture of Black Mountain College life since at least the late 1930s, and were worn by both men and women.[18] They were simple to make, and since they could be made in many different styles, they offered an opportunity for personalization within the otherwise utilitarian-casual BMC style.[19] The popularity of Bernard Rudofsky's lectures, and Berta's class in particular, was enough to convince Josef Albers to invite them to teach again the next year during the 1945 Summer Session.

Bernard Rudofsky's more theoretical exploration of clothing's modernity had parallels to ideas that Irene Schawinsky discussed with her students, including how fashions of the past emphasized or obscured different parts of the body, and the complex relationship between clothing and the ease or restriction of movement the piece caused the wearer. Indeed, some of Schawinsky's post-BMC design work was included in Rudofsky's exhibition and was promoted in the Museum of Modern Art's accompanying press release:

> Enlarged photographs of four contemporary garments (two dresses, two coats) designed and executed by Irene Schawinsky are shown as examples of clothing which can be made without mutilating the material by cutting a complicated pattern which almost requires an engineering degree to decipher. Each of these contemporary garments is composed of *one* or two pieces of material ingeniously joined. All four of the garments demonstrate that beauty and simplicity of line and fabric transcend the dictates of any period, style or fashion.[20]

In the book version of *Are Clothes Modern?*, published three years after the exhibition, one of Schawinsky's short coats is reproduced alongside three garments designed by pioneer sportswear designer Claire McCardell, which were "all made simply by seaming two rectangles of fabric up the sides."[21] Rudofsky's text explains that at the time of the exhibition, this approach "was derided by fashion writers as absurd and impractical," before he tacitly claims some credit by explaining that McCardell's versions, which he implies were designed after the exhibition, "are highly significant because they are not experimental, but are mass-manufactured and successfully sold."[22] By contrast, Schawinsky, whose designs were more experimental, and who did not have McCardell's fame or industry backing, didn't see long-term success as a result of her inclusion in Rudofsky's exhibition.

During his preparations for the 1945 Summer Session, Josef Albers also wrote to Irene asking if she would be interested in returning to the College (without Xanti), to give a four-week practical course in dress design to supplement Berta Rudofsky's class.[23] Irene responded enthusiastically, and she and Albers began to plan for her return. She anticipated that her class would be based on her recent work with minimal cutting that had been featured in *Are Clothes Modern?*. "If I really were to teach at Black Mountain for 4 weeks," Irene wrote Albers, "I would not want to cover conventional dressmaking at all, just three-dimensional tailoring, as Rudofsky calls it. I wouldn't give lectures, but instead give students the task of finding a Black Mountain style, which they would then execute in as many different materials as possible."[24] With its emphasis on material exploration and a design prompt that discarded traditional methods, Irene's proposed class would have been a perfect fit with the rest of the Alberses' art and design curriculum at BMC. Unfortunately, after almost two months of planning, Irene contacted Albers to tell him she would not be able to come after all.[25]

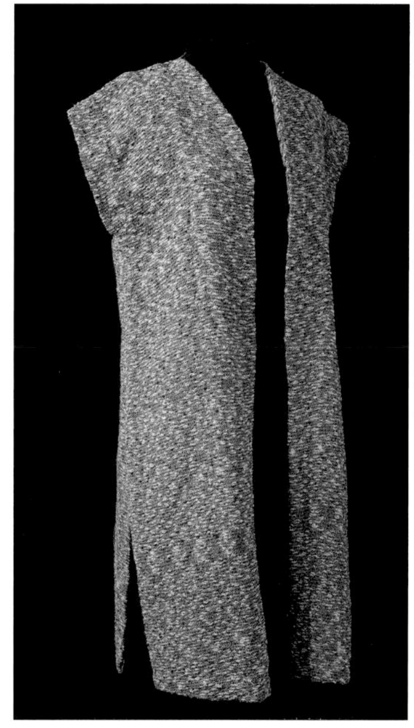

While Schawinsky did not return to Black Mountain to teach, in the winter of 1947 Anni Albers and Trude Guermonprez proposed further collaborations with Schawinsky as a part of their plans for a production weaving program at Black Mountain College. Anni met with Irene several times in New York City in December 1947, seemingly to discuss fashion and garment uses for cloth produced in the planned production weaving workshop.[26] Since, as Rudofsky stated, Schawinsky's designs made with a minimum of cutting enabled wearers to "again become aware of the inherent beauty of uncut materials," her proposed collaboration in the production weaving program is interesting to consider, since the fabric her clothes were made from—fabric designed and woven by Black Mountain College's weavers—would have been intrinsic to the beauty, utility, and success of the finished garments.[27]

HANDWEAVING TODAY
TEXTILE WORK AT BLACK MOUNTAIN COLLEGE 1941

ANNI ALBERS

Almost all textiles today are products of machine looms. They are turned out in great quantities, at high speed. Quantity and speed reflect on the design. In general we think today of more and more, of faster and faster, and only then of better and better.

In this situation the attempt to deal with textiles on a small scale, in a slow manner, with quality mainly in mind, may seem rather futile. This may appear to be retreat and seclusion, but actually have quite a different result. It is true that such work is often no more than a romantic attempt to recall a *temps perdu*, a result rather of an attitude than of procedure. But, if conceived as a preparatory step to machine production the work will be more than the revival of a lost skill and will take responsible part in a new development.

Handweaving the slow, and machine-weaving the fast method of the same process contrast only in velocity. Sameness of procedure is one of the justifications for hand-work preliminary to work for mass production. Weaving in any form is a constructive process; it is also a combinative process demanding aesthetic judgment as to surface, form and color qualities of the materials. Other problems enter, such as functional and social demands. All of these factors engage intellect and imagination if the craft is looked upon as still in formation.

Unfortunately today handweaving has degenerated in face of technically superior methods of production. Instead of freely developing new forms, recipes are often used, traditional formulas, which once proved successful. Freshness of invention, of intelligent and imaginative forming has been lost. If handweaving is to regain actual influence on contemporary life, approved repetition has to be replaced with the adventure of new exploring.

32. Students weaving on backstrap looms at BMC, 1945. Photograph by John Harvey Campbell.

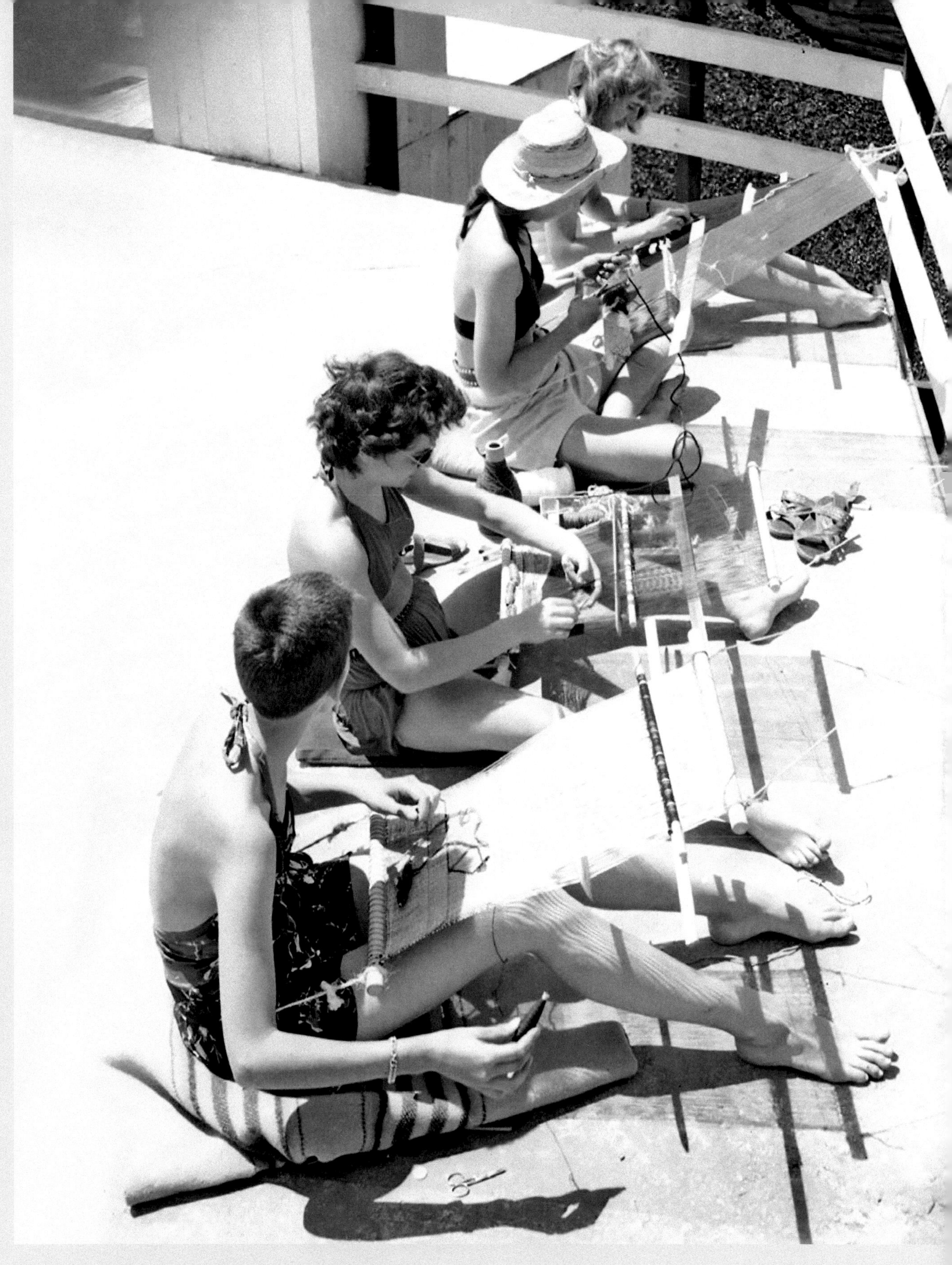

Such an attempt needs a careful foundation. It is only possible if we go back to the elements. Materials have accumulated to themselves set rules of working them. In going back to the fundamental principles we can open the field again for invention, imaginative use of intellectually recognized facts.

We have stated before that hand and machine weaving are fundamentally the same. The theory of the constructive process, the draftwriting, can therefore be taught so as to include both hand and machine possibilities. Handlooms today are often limited technically. Why fit the theoretical knowledge to the present limitations of handweaving? Rather the theoretical work should be developed, expanding beyond the boundaries set to it now, in order to stimulate new experimentation. The teaching should be the development of structures, from the elementary weaves to more complicated derivations rather than the passing on of patterns for weaving. Thus the work can be directed toward independent initiative.

The same return to the fundamentals needed for the structural work is also necessary for the combinative or aesthetic side of it, to clear the way for new forming. For the lack of invention often found in the handweaving of today is a general symptom of this time of standardization. If teaching attempts to direct the development of individuals as well as of peoples, it should try to avert a growing onesidedness which may prove fatal. For ability to form materials presupposes responsiveness towards the material, a flexibility of reaction, and this flexibility is one of the factors we will need

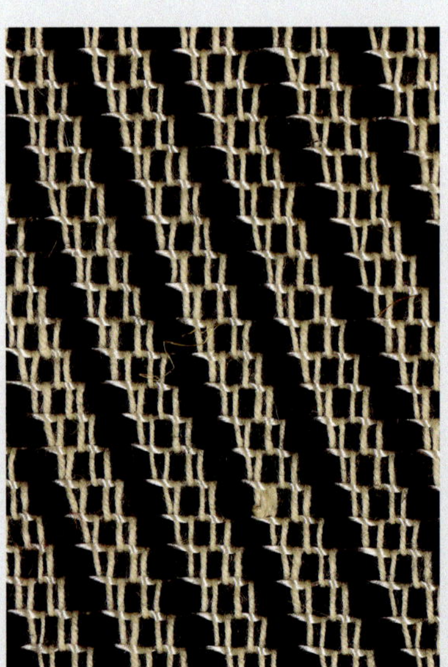

for times to come. Through working with material we can perhaps develop this ability to respond. More than intangible material, than tones or words, tangible material can teach that it has demands of its own and suggestions of its own for its forming, that it asks for a reaction. Creating means this reacting to material rather than the execution of a dream, as the layman conceives it. The first vision of something to be done gives more the mood of the work than its final form. The form emerges as the work progresses.

An elementary approach will be a playful beginning, unresponsive to any demand of usefulness, an enjoyment of colors, forms, surface contrasts and harmonies, —a tactile sensuousness. This first and always most important pleasure in the physical qualities of materials needs but the simplest technique and must be sustained through the most complicated one. For just this satisfaction coming from material qualities is part of the satisfaction we get from art.

For more advanced work considerations of utilitarian purpose arise. Although for the beginner the thought of practical usefulness has more a constraining than animating effect, conscious deliberations on function and useful objective are in a later stage stimulating, as is the material itself. Demands set by the practical use give the work a certain direction, unthought of before the problem came up, as to construction, choice of material, color and form. An example: The task of weaving a material to be used as wallcovering sets up certain requirements, strongly influenced by the specific tendencies of a period. It brings up the question of a light or dark material, light-reflective maybe, of resistance to dust, the question how it is to be attached to the wall. The answer will probably eliminate fuzzy fibers, loose, stretchable, plastic textures, and suggest straw-like qualities and a stiff, smooth, close construction of weave. The search for the fiber best uniting the requisite qualities may lead to one not used for weaving before. The experiments can result in a fabric equipped with new characteristics, a new fabric.

Awareness of the need for adaptation to purpose introduces one other factor: the importance of recognizing new problems as they appear, of foreseeing a development. "An unspecialized aptitude for eliciting generalizations from particulars and for seeing the divergent illustrations of generalities in diverse circumstances is required. Such a reflective power is essentially a philosophic habit," says Whitehead. The creative impetus, at first coming sensuously from the world of appearance, now receives its stimulus from the intellectual sphere of a recognized need. Only the imaginative mind can transform the intellectual recognition into a material form.

The special inclinations of certain times play a dominant part in the rise of new forms. Today's interest in hygiene, in light, in movable things, in short-lived things even, as far as the serviceable objects of our surroundings are concerned, become manifest in the objects we make. For textiles this means washable materials, transparent or light-reflective ones, materials repelling dust or water, reversible ones and materials which can easily be replaced. For durability need not necessarily be a value in itself, although this seemed a valuation set forever. Accumulation of material values rapidly loses its charm in face of the mutation of a world; thus durableness is no longer equivalent to value. There is a close correlation between demands arising in the course of time, being fulfilled by new materials, and new materials bringing about new demands. In the one case the demand acts as motive power, in the other the pleasure of free forming. Fulfillment of a demand confines a product to usefulness—the result of free forming can be art.

Handweaving can go both ways; to become art it needs nothing but its own high development and adjustment in all its properties, —to become utilitarian it needs today the help of machines if it is to be more than a mere luxury.

There is one other aspect of the work, one not intrinsically connected with the idea of future development; it is that of handweaving as a leisure-time occupation and as a source of income in rural communities. The importance of such work should not be overlooked. But it is necessary to keep in mind that handweaving here takes on the character of a means to an end and is not in itself the center of interest. It has to be admitted that at one point we discussed handweaving also as a means, when taking its educational value into account, shifting the emphasis from the result to the process. But the objective was to encourage experimenting which leads back to the core of these considerations.

Published in The Weaver *6 no. 1 (January–February 1941)*

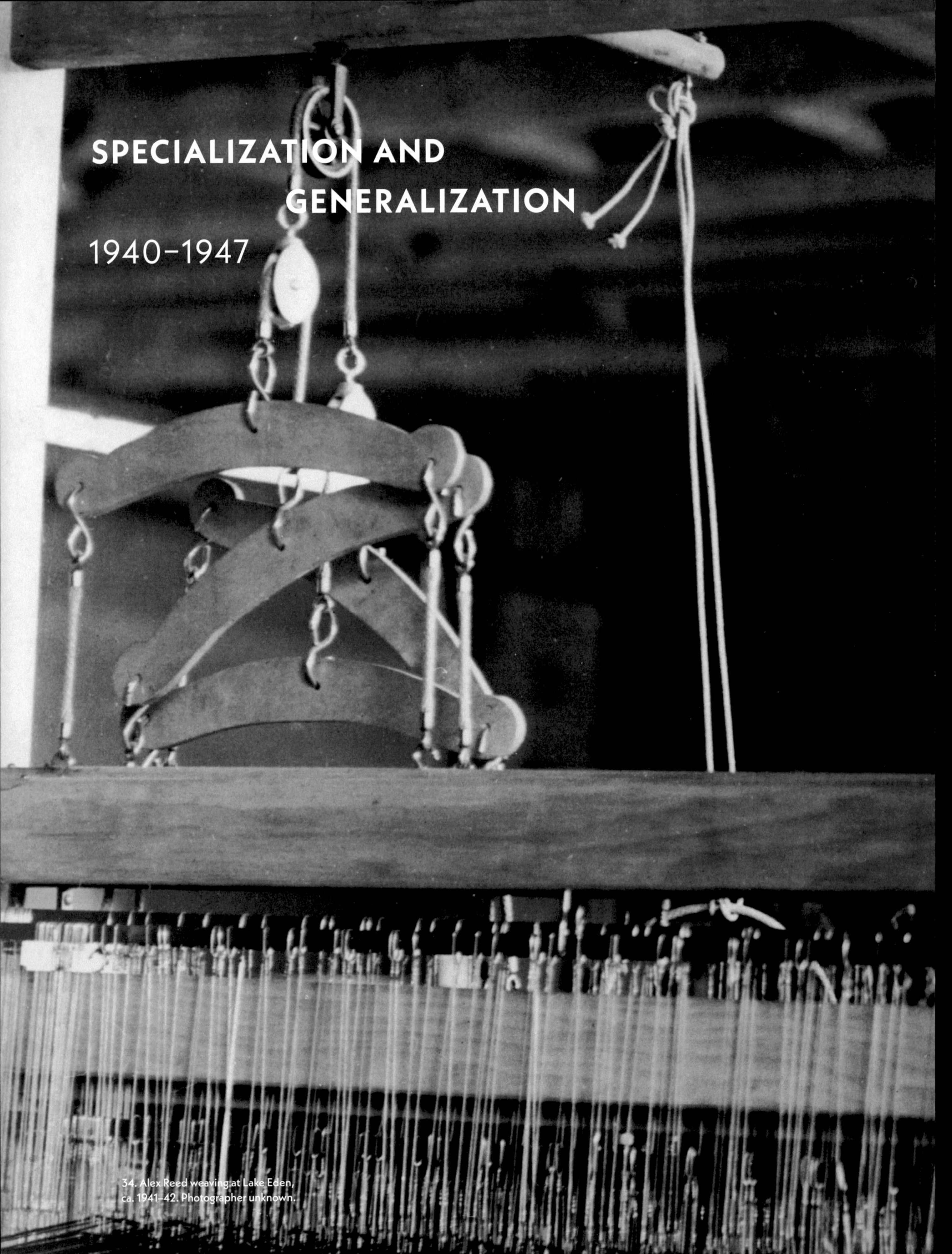

34. Alex Reed weaving at Lake Eden,
ca. 1941–42. Photographer unknown.

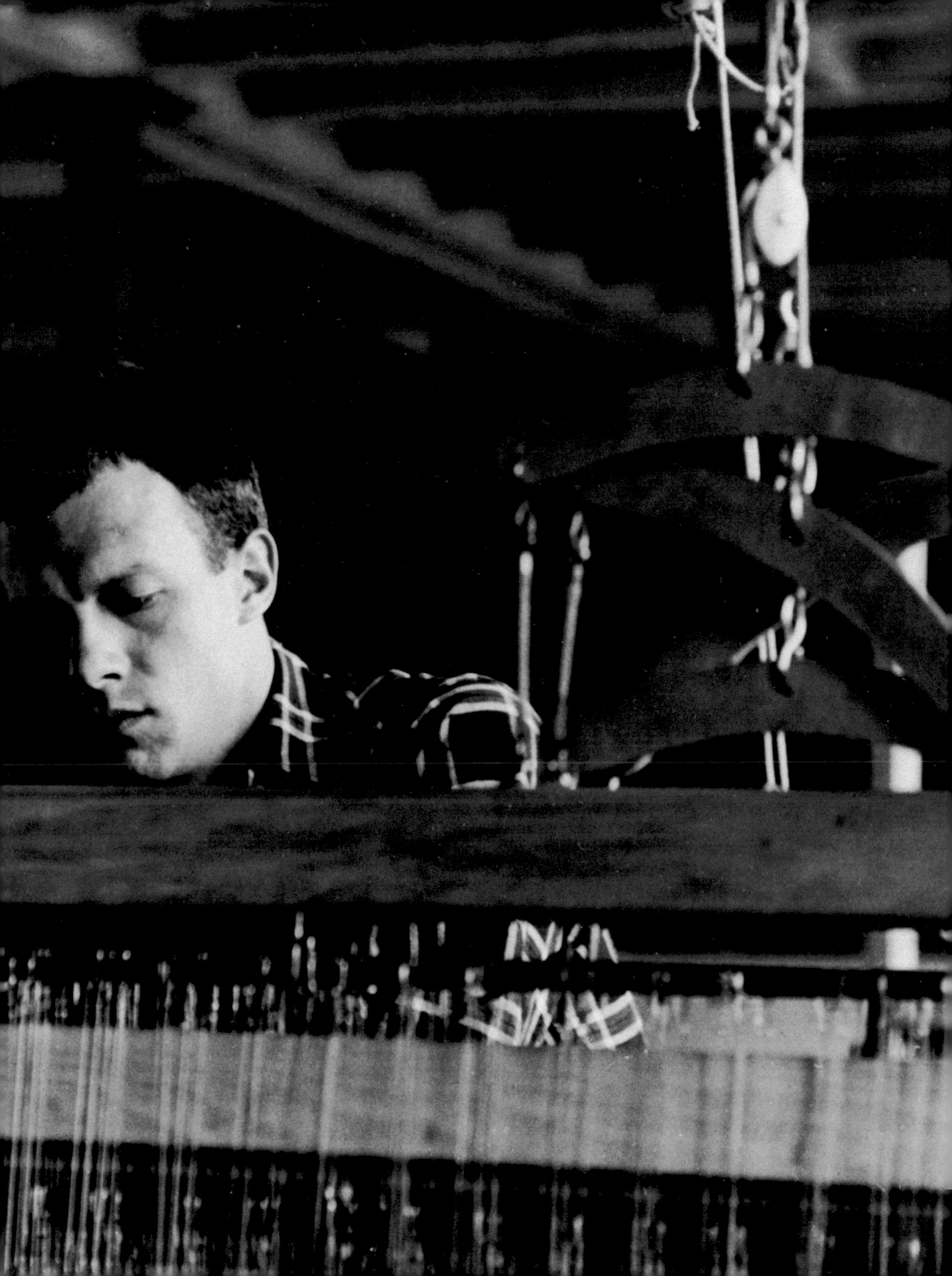

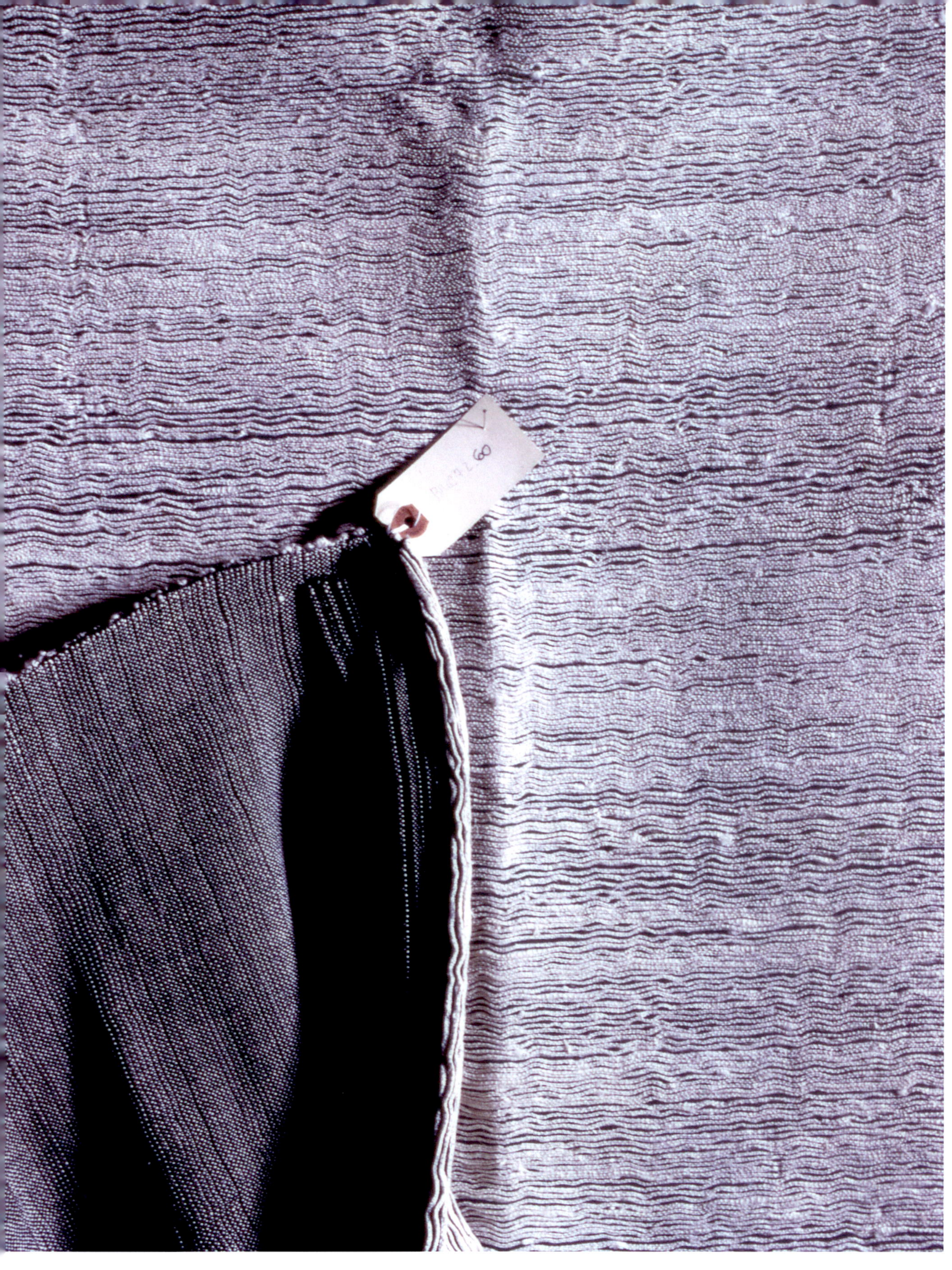

35. Textile sample made by Willie Joseph at
Black Mountain College ca. 1945–48.

SPECIALIZATION, PRODUCTION, AND PUBLICATION

MICHAEL BEGGS

From 1940 to 1947 the weaving program at Black Mountain College underwent significant changes. The College acquired more looms and, with the move to the Lake Eden campus in 1941, a larger dedicated space for weaving was set aside in the basement of the Studies Building, one end of which was often used for critiques and lectures in Josef Albers's classes. Black Mountain began hosting summer sessions for the work program, music, and art, turning the College into a year-round enterprise and establishing summer workshops as a new format for weaving classes. These workshops were sometimes attended by more experienced weavers, artists, and designers, who treated the summer session as a chance to have an intensive apprenticeship with Anni Albers.

The weaving program at Black Mountain College developed a more public face as it grew. Albers worked hard to promote the College and her vision for the evolving role of the designer and continued to write influential articles for publications like *Craft Horizons*, the *Magazine of Art*, and *Design Magazine*. She sought connections with industry and tried to expand the College's ability to produce textiles for sale or to fulfill commissions. Textiles designed and made by Albers and her students were also featured in numerous exhibitions around the country, including traveling exhibitions organized by the Museum of Modern Art. Albers's efforts to develop outlets and connections for the program paid off for some of her most talented students, who were able to make meaningful contributions as designers of mass-produced woven and print fabrics.

PRODUCTION WEAVING AND CONTACT WITH INDUSTRY

Almost as soon as the weaving program was established at Black Mountain, Anni Albers began trying to make industry contacts, both to further her own work as a textile designer and to try to build the kind of industry partnerships that had helped to publicize and financially support the Weaving Workshop at the Bauhaus.[1] Her initial American contacts seemed promising, and she saw particular interest from retailers who were interested in carrying modern or European-influenced products. As early as 1935, not much more than a year after starting to weave in the United States, Anni received a desirable commission: the design of curtains for Rena Rosenthal's exclusive decorative arts gallery on Madison Avenue in New York City. Throughout the 1930s Albers met whenever she could with representatives from both retail and industry and worked both her and the College's networks of contacts to develop new connections. These meetings sometimes occurred at Black Mountain College, as in the summer of 1938 when Albers reported to her brother that "we had here for days the head of the Sears Roebuck & Co. 'merchandise development department,'" or in December 1940 when Edgar Kaufmann Jr. visited to see Anni's work.[2]

But while Albers's work was appealing to those who wanted to market modernist luxury goods, she struggled to work with industrial textile mills, who were put off by the structural complexity of Anni's designs at a time when the American textile market was dominated by less expensive print fabrics.[3] While at Black Mountain, Anni received several major commissions for practical textiles—such as the curtains for the Philip Johnson–designed Rockefeller Guest House in Manhattan—but these commissions were invariably executed by production handweaving studios, often in or around New York City.[4] None of Albers's textile designs were put into mass production during her

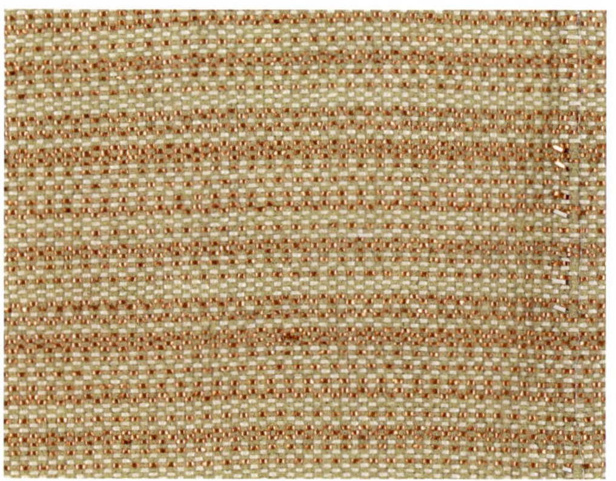

time at Black Mountain College. Instead, it was Black Mountain's most serious student weavers, especially those who graduated in weaving, who gained the most experience working directly with industry; their experiences are covered later in this essay.

Alongside Anni's mostly unsuccessful push for industry collaboration, Black Mountain College weavers produced fabrics on a craft basis for sale at the College. At both of BMC's campuses, the weaving room had display boards where student work was shown and items offered for sale. In the 1930s and 1940s, Anni and her students produced a steady stream of functional objects that were purchased by members of the College community for their own use or to give as gifts. Among these objects were wearables, like scarves and shirting and suiting cloth, and household textiles, like placemats, napkins, and doilies, which were the College's most

37. Anni Albers, *Handwoven placemat*, ca. 1940. Wool and cotton. 13½ × 16⅝ in.

popular items for sale. A May 1940 inventory of weaving supplies lists twelve woven materials suitable for exhibition or sale, consisting of seven pieces of drapery material, each 3 1/2 yards long; one wool blanket; three assorted fabrics, including one made of cotton and cellophane; and a tapestry by Don Page. Linens available for sale included sixty-four doilies, seventy-eight napkins, and three linen covers.[5]

Selling the products of the weaving program gave an outlet to the tremendous number of textiles made by students and also offset much of the costs of supplies and materials. Once the weaving program became established, the weaving room had a large supply of yarns for students to use, with a wide variety of fibers and characteristics. Students could use these materials for free provided they allowed their finished pieces to be sold. "When we wove something that we wanted to keep," student Marilyn Bauer Greenwald remembered, "we paid for the cost of the yarn. . . . If we didn't want to keep it, we didn't have to pay for it."[6]

Inevitably, selling textiles also led to some problems, the foremost of which was supplying the objects that people wanted to buy. Making students reproduce a single product dozens of times was in direct opposition to Albers's aims to make the weaving program experimental and open-ended enough to allow students to learn to design and work in a self-guided manner. As a result, Albers sometimes wound up filling orders herself. In response to an order from Bobby Dreier's sister, Margot Loines Morrow, the College's bookkeeper, Robert S. Kumabe, wrote: "Mrs. Albers has just informed me that your 20 doilies have been sent to you this morning. She expresses her regret that she could not send them earlier to you, but she has had many pending orders and had to finish them first." The doilies cost $1.50 each.[7] Student Don Page recalled that at other times, Anni "hired a woman [who] used to come up and work several hours a day just weaving these doilies and napkins that were sold at the College. . . . [T]hey were really very good material. They were Irish linen and just nice simple things."[8]

Page and Albers also designed simple textiles for cottage industry production under the auspices of the Works Progress Administration. One summer, probably in 1938, Page taught weaving to local and regional weavers in Wilmington and Charlotte, North Carolina. He recalled, "while [the students] did no designing—they wove the fabrics that we had designed for them—they learned the whole technique and [the WPA] hoped these women would eventually branch out and earn a living by weaving." According to Page, this program was set up by Albers in collaboration with an unnamed regional official for the WPA in North Carolina.[9]

Page was seemingly the first of Albers's students to have direct contact working in the textile industry. In the summer of 1939, Albers arranged for Page to have an apprenticeship in the Designing Division of the Sample Production Department at Callaway Mills in LaGrange, Georgia.[10] The experience was informative for Page, who "learned a lot about mill production, and how a big mill really works" but also found the textile industry "cut-throat and kind of unpleasant."[11] He was further discouraged by the lack of interest mills showed in the kinds of highly structured fabrics Black Mountain weavers were designing. "They were interested in materials that they could run through another mill and flatten out and print designs on," he recalled. His early negative experiences in the textile industry stayed with him and after graduating and then serving in the U.S. Army Air Corps, Page became an architect.[12]

Once Black Mountain College moved to its Lake Eden campus, where it owned its buildings outright, it was able to find another revenue source by renting the campus to visiting groups and conferences. In the mid-1940s, this practice led to an unexpected alliance between BMC and a different facet of the textile industry when, in September 1942, the Textile Workers Union of America rented the campus to hold the southern meeting of their Labor Institute at Lake Eden.[13] In this one-week training seminar, a group of about forty union members were trained in topics that included parliamentary law, collective bargaining, and textile unionism.[14] The union held the Labor Institute at Lake Eden again in 1943 and, later, in 1950.[15]

Beginning in the mid-1940s, Anni Albers began to more seriously consider developing a production weaving workshop at Black Mountain College. The first move toward a production-oriented workshop was made in the summer of 1943, when Anni Albers suggested that student Mimi French, who could no longer afford her tuition, return "not as a regular student, but in her capacity as a weaver and make pieces for sale in the textile department."[16] The idea was that Mimi's family and the College would jointly share in covering Mimi's living expenses while at the same time sharing in the profits from Mimi's production. It seems that French did indeed return to BMC for the 1943–44 school year and followed a modified version of this plan, as her enrollment in other classes was very limited.

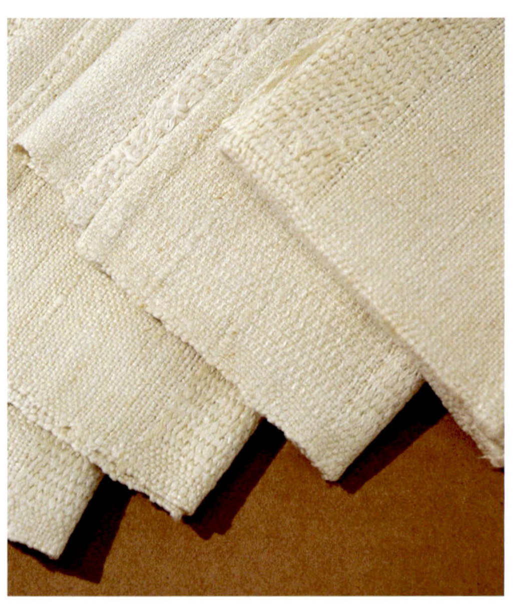

By 1946, Albers was considering purchasing a power loom for Black Mountain College. In April of that year, she wrote to Robert D. Sailors, assistant director and an instructor at Cranbrook Institute, asking him about his experiences working with the power loom Cranbrook had purchased in 1945. "We have been thinking about a powerloom [*sic*] for some time," Albers wrote, "but have not yet been able to set one up, nor do I myself feel able to handle it."[17] It is possible that working with a power loom would not only have advanced the College's production capabilities, but it would also have given Anni the chance to experiment directly with mechanical production, perhaps enabling her to design textiles that were more agreeable to industry partners.

With Josef and Anni Albers planning to go on sabbatical starting in the fall of 1946, these plans for production weaving were deferred, but the topic continued to be discussed in Albers's absence. In a lengthy state-ment to the College's Board of Fellows written in January 1947, interim weaving instructor Franziska Mayer, who had previous experi-ence with cottage industry weaving, outlined her concerns and questions with establishing a production weaving program. She worried that "it is quite a job in itself to build up a busi-ness" and suggested that the College do some research by consulting successful production weavers about "market, labor, equipment, source of raw materials, and type of product to be sold."[18] Mayer also raised ethical and economic concerns about using students as the labor in a production weaving workshop and worried about who would own and make

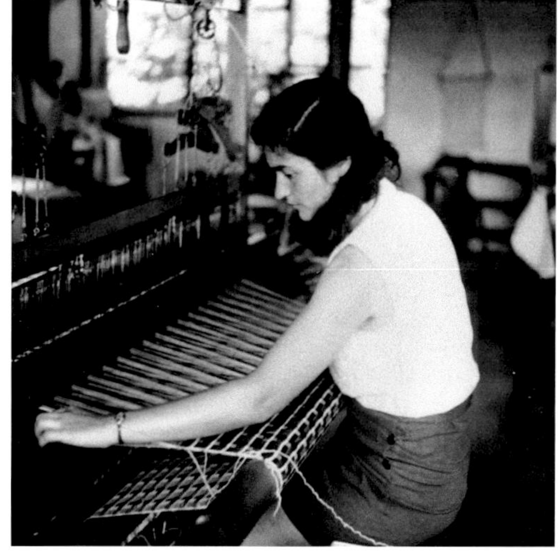

money on the intellectual property generated by the weaving program. Would it be "the [corporation] of B.M.C., or the members of the weaving department, teachers, students," who would receive credit? And who in that case should be paid for the success of the design? Mayer further wrote that she did not "believe that students would be interested in taking weaving if it meant making 100 scarves, 1 doz. bridgecloths, 60 luncheonsets [*sic*]. Could they give the steady time? What should they earn?"[19]

With Trude Guermonprez's arrival in early 1947, the College added another skilled textile designer with industry experience to its faculty. In the summer of 1947, after Mayer's departure and with Anni Albers expected to return in early 1948, the idea of a production arm of the weaving program continued to be discussed, in part as a way of justifying Guermonprez's continued employment by the College.[20] A production program could also take advantage of the promising and creative textile designers among the weaving students at this time, including Willie Joseph and Lore Kadden Lindenfeld. Like Mimi French before her, Anni and Trude proposed keeping Lindenfeld on at the College as a production weaver, even after her graduation, con-sidering her the only weaving student mature enough (Lindenfeld was twenty-six in 1947) to handle the demands and discipline required to weave what had to be woven, as opposed to what she wanted to weave, in the production model. This plan was approved by the Board of Fellows and Lindenfeld worked as a production weaver at BMC in 1947 and 1948, during which time she also occasionally assisted with teaching beginning weaving students.[21]

Unlike Don Page or Anni Albers herself, Lindenfeld was later able to satisfactorily meld the Black Mountain College structural approach to weaving with the demands of industrial production. After graduating Black Mountain College in 1948, Lore Kadden Lindenfeld had a successful ten-year career as a professional textile designer, working for companies in the greater New York City area, including Kanmak Textiles, John Walther Fabrics, Herbert Meyer, Inc., and Forstmann Woolens.[22] Prior to emigrating to the United States, Lindenfeld had trained as a fashion designer in Düsseldorf, and her shirting and suiting fabrics were in high demand from fashion designers like Pauline Trigère, Adele Simpson, and Molly Parnis, as well as retailers like Lord & Taylor.[23] A 1950 profile of Lindenfeld in *Mademoiselle* highlighted her drive and singled her out for being a woman in a male-dominated industry. At Forstmann, Lindenfeld "received permission to take the training program for young male employees—which teaches trainees what happens to wool between sheep's back and customer's."[24] Lindenfeld left the textile industry in the mid-1950s after her marriage and the birth of her second child.[25]

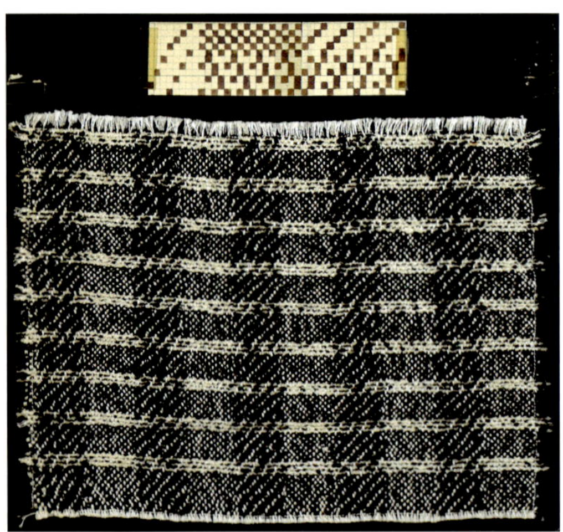

Anni Albers returned to the College for two weeks in November 1947, during which time she and Guermonprez wrote a proposal for production weaving at Black Mountain College, which was submitted to the Board of Fellows on November 11. In this proposal, Albers and Guermonprez suggested that weaving production could focus on developing textiles for mass production, which would be "machine produced outside the College" and sold "at the College, in stores throughout the country, and through agents" as well as developing designs for commissions from "architects and other individual customers (upholstery, drapery, wallcovering, dress material)" all of which were "to be produced within the College."[26] Guermonprez traveled to New York City in December 1947, where Albers was staying as she and Josef continued their sabbatical, to discuss the idea further and attempt to find industry and retail partners to support a production weaving program.

During her time in New York City, Anni agreed to a solo exhibition at the Museum of Modern Art. The exhibition, *Anni Albers Textiles*, held in 1949, was the first solo exhibition by a weaver at the Museum and immediately increased her personal and professional workload. When she returned to Black Mountain College in February 1948, she and Guermonprez shared teaching responsibilities, but plans for production weaving at the Black Mountain seemingly became less important as more pressing concerns about the College's future came to the fore. When Albers and Guermonprez both resigned in 1949, the possibility of production weaving at BMC left with them.

While weaving classes at Black Mountain College focused on the medium of weaving as the means of production and design for fabrics, students Don Wight, Donald Alter, and Ruth Asawa (who unlike Alter and Wight never took a weaving class) designed successful print textiles after leaving BMC. In all cases, these designers' fabrics built on work done at Black Mountain College not only in Anni Albers's classes but in Josef Albers's classes as well.

While a student at Black Mountain Ruth Asawa began covering whole sheets of paper with impressions of rubber stamps she borrowed from the College's laundry. These works, made of borderless, endless repetitions of "DOUBLE SHEET" or "BMC" both invert and reference the logic of the non-loom studies made by Albers and her students using typewriter characters (which themselves may have referenced print textiles designed by *Bauhäusler* Hajo and Katja Rose around 1930). Unlike Albers's typewriter exercises, where characters are combined to create "textile orders" without reference to their syntactic or semiotic function, in Asawa's stamp works the characters retain a verbal order and thus a meaning, either as words (DOUBLE SHEET) or as the College's monogram.[27]

The reordering or rearrangement exercises in Josef Albers's Basic Design classes were likely a greater influence on Asawa's stamp works.[28] In rearrangement studies, students took materials with an inherent order (printed matter, corrugated cardboard), cut them up, and collaged or pasted them into a whole with a new order—interrupting their internal pattern to create a new pattern. Asawa's stamp works bring the rearrangement into the realm of textile order by creating surfaces in which the pattern repeats endlessly, beyond the edge of the paper.

Asawa's BMC design was popular at the College and her classmates used BMC papers to cover their notebooks and other objects. It also reached a (limited) public audience in reproduction when it was printed as the cover of the 1947–1948 *Black Mountain College Photographic Viewbook* produced by Hazel Larsen Archer.[29] After leaving Black Mountain, Asawa sold the design to Everett Brown, who

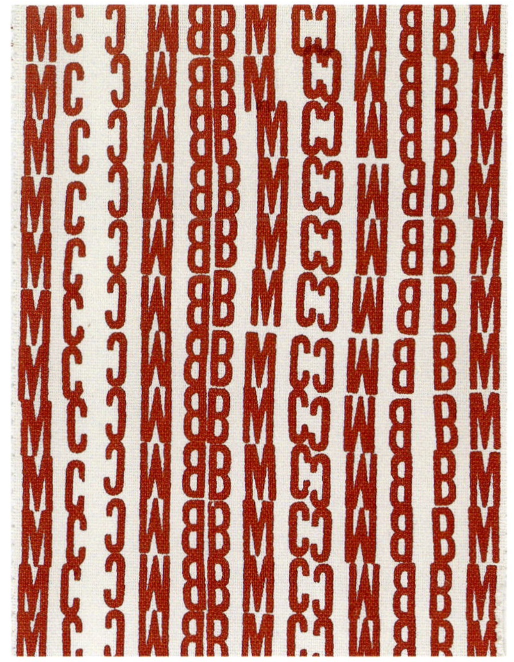

was given credit for the design when it was produced by Englander & Co. in 1952.[30] Despite the specific meaning of the BMC monogram, Asawa's design was sold as a fabric for all sorts of applications under the name *Alphabet*. While no other fabrics

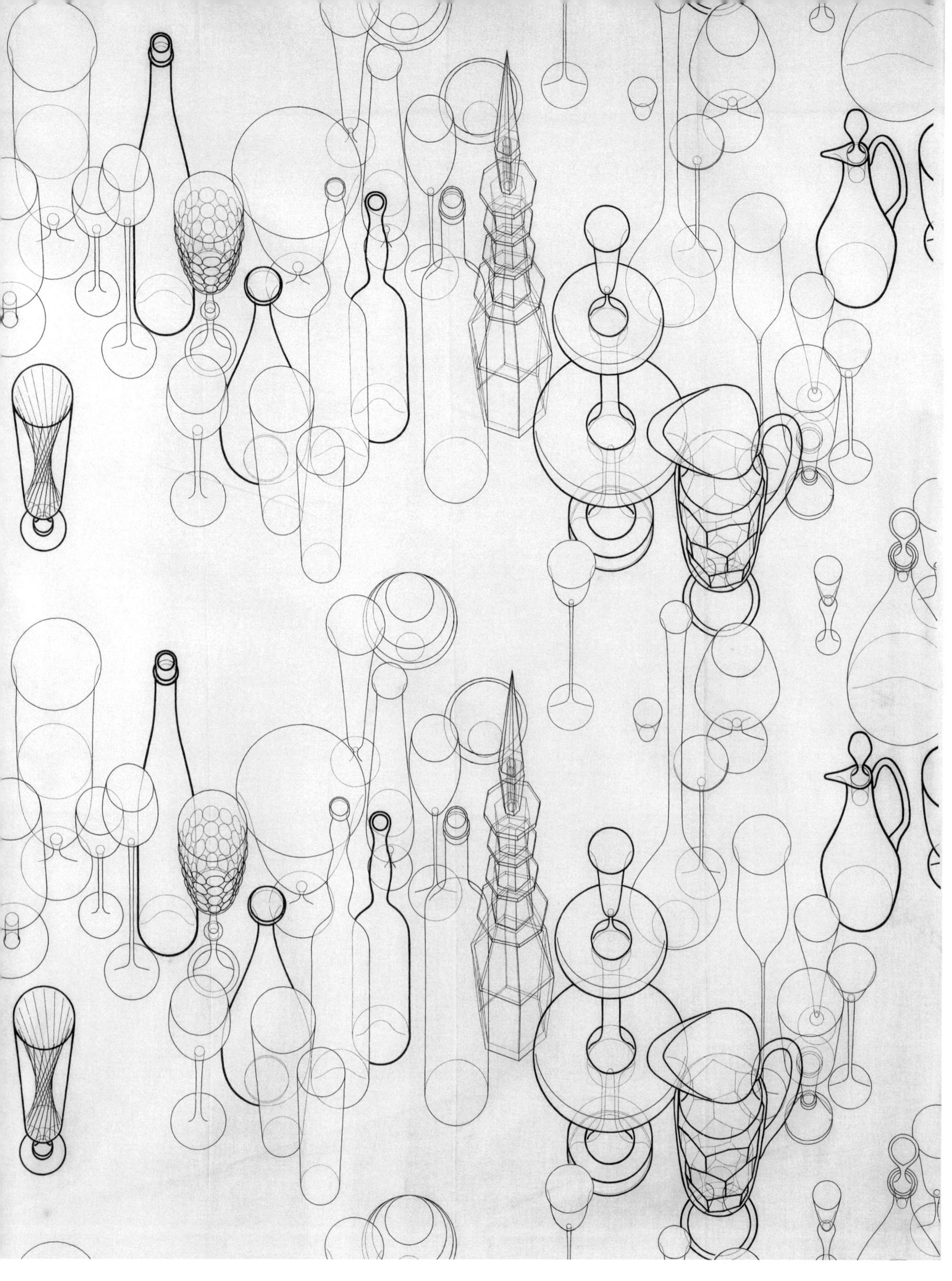

42. Don Wight, *Garden of Glass* (detail), ca. 1950.
Printed Cotton, manufactured by Quaintance
Fabrics.

43. A drawing of overlapping flowerpots by M.E.
Parker from Josef Albers's Basic Drawing class at
Yale University, ca. 1950–60.

designed by Asawa entered production, she continued to correspond with manufacturers throughout the 1950s, including L. Anton Maix and Jack Lenor Larsen.[31]

Donald Alter entered Black Mountain College in 1948 and took one weaving class in the spring of 1949 with Trude Guermonprez and Anni Albers, as well as Drawing and Color with Josef Albers. After Guermonprez and the Alberses resigned, Alter studied drawing and painting with Joseph Fiore and Pete Jennerjahn, leaving Black Mountain in 1951 when he was drafted.[32] After his tour of service, Alter attended Pratt Institute to study textile design and later formed two successful textile design studios,

New Line Designers, Inc., and Design Logic, Inc., both based in New York City. His print fabrics were primarily used in home furnishings and wallpaper, and he sold his own designs to industry and also received commissions. Alter's work as a textile designer was driven by his skilled draughtsmanship and strong pictorial sense, coupled with a lifelong love of painting. In 2014 he recalled that "during all those textile years, I painted every single day— never put a brush down all that time."[33] After thirty-five years in the textile industry, Alter retired in 1990 and began painting full time, a practice that continued, broadening into digital art, until his death in 2019.

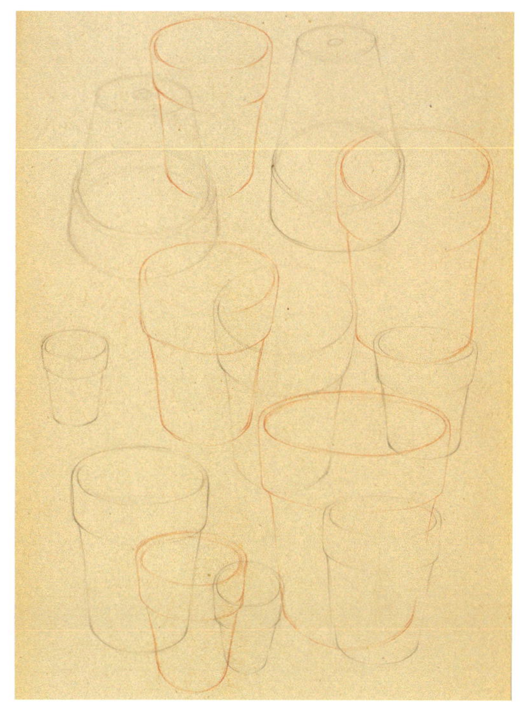

Don Wight attended Black Mountain College from 1945 to 1946 on the GI bill, having been told about Black Mountain College by Walter Gropius. Having previously studied for a year at Alfred University, Wight's studies at Black Mountain focused on the arts, including Drawing and Basic Design with Josef Albers, Woodworking with Molly Gregory, and music classes with Mark Fax and Charlotte Schlesinger.[34] In the 1946 Summer Session and into that fall, Wight took two weaving classes with Anni Albers and Franziska Meyer, and toward the end of his second class Wight designed an "experimental weaving using Christmas tinsel and cellophane thread."[35]

In a freelance career lasting several decades, Wight designed textiles for numerous clients, including Quaintance and, most notably, Jack Lenor Larsen, where he designed some of Larsen Design Studio's most successful fabrics. Wight was, in Larsen's words, "a great draftsman," and the textiles he designed with delicately drawn figures, such as *Bouquet Garni* and *Garden of Glass* recall his training in drawing classes at Black Mountain College, where Josef Albers emphasized contour drawing and eschewed shading.[36] The overlapping forms of bottles and glasses in *Garden of Glass* also echo Albers's class, where students drew the same figure over and over again, filling a single page with overlapping figures to save paper (and, pedagogically, to reduce the preciousness of a single drawing).

Some of Wight's fabrics for Larsen required a fair amount of technical experimentation to achieve. *Leaves of Grass* (1971) is dyed, rather than printed, using a multistep mechanized batik process that the Larsen Design Studio developed in the

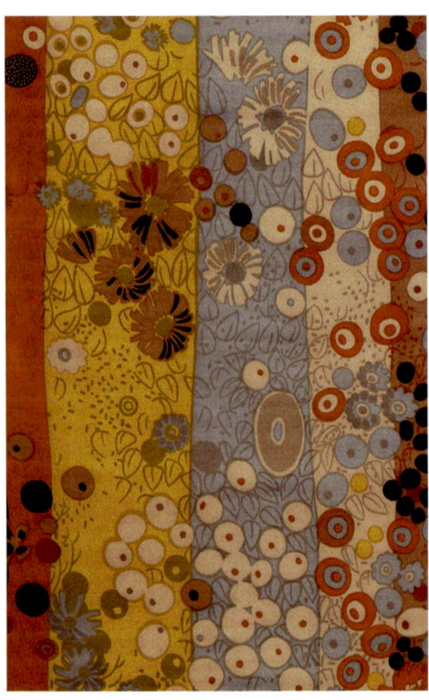

1960s.[37] Wight's most famous fabric, *Primavera*, designed in 1959 and produced until the 1980s, was the first screen-printed velvet fabric made in the United States. To achieve this, Larsen Design Studio experimented until they could produce a "cotton velvet, luxurious to the touch, with a pile low enough to take the hand screen print dye with no loss of color intensity." As Maleyene Syracuse explains, *Primavera* was wildly successful, "perfect for the freewheeling, exuberant residential market of the sixties. As a reviewer in the magazine *Industrial Design* noted: 'It is not easy to be rampantly luxuriant and succeed; [Primavera] does.' In fact, in its day, Primavera was the most successful printed velvet in the industry. Today it remains an icon of the period."[38]

Wight designed numerous other textiles for Larsen, including *Spindrift*, *Pastorale*, and *Paradise*. His design for *Midsummer*, first produced around 1958 and since printed on linen, velvet, and as a casement cloth, is still available today from Cowtan & Tout, who purchased Larsen Design Studio in 1997. The vast majority of Wight's textile designs were print textiles, but he also designed some woven textiles, including *Benin Brocade* in 1962 for Larsen, which was woven from wool, rayon, nylon, and silk.[39]

INTERLUDE + APPRENTICESHIP: WEAVING IN THE SUMMER ARTS INSTITUTES

In the 1940s, Black Mountain College began offering summer sessions. First organized as work camps to speed construction at the Lake Eden campus, in 1944 they grew to include the Music and Arts Institutes. Open to people who would not otherwise enroll in full-time education at Black Mountain, summer sessions allowed the College to boost enrollment, bring visitors to the College, and keep their own faculty occupied at a time when interstate travel was restricted due to wartime rationing. The institutes were popular and continued after the end of World War II, drawing notable visiting faculty and students and creating an environment rich with interdisciplinary collaboration. While these summer classes were publicly advertised as an opportunity for travel, the Black Mountain atmosphere of serious experimentation prevailed. Speaking at the opening of the 1945 Summer Session, Josef Albers explained, "We are here

45. Announcement for weaving classes in the
1944 Black Mountain College Summer Art
Institute.

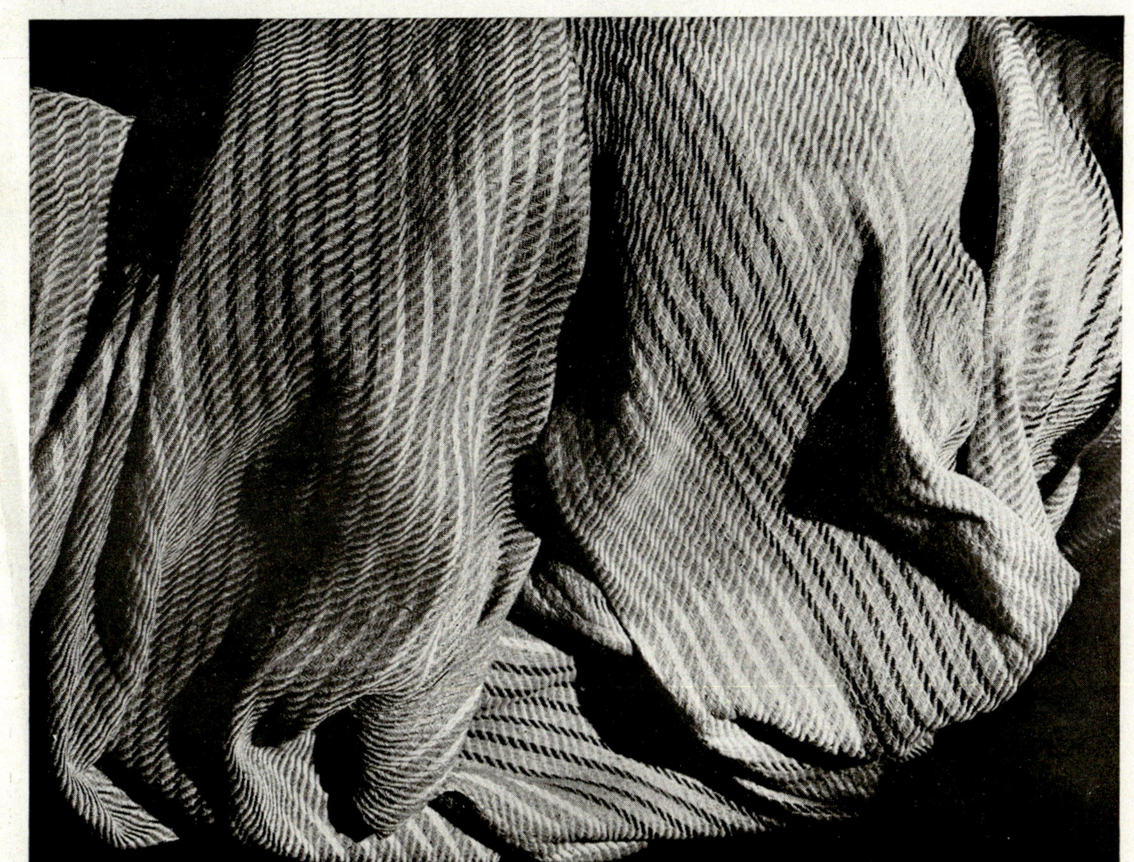

only for ten weeks . . . and art is a job for lifetime. . . . If anyone has come here for a vacation; sorry, we don't sell any."[40]

In 1944 Anni Albers's weaving classes were specifically advertised in a flyer directed at those interested in attending "a course in Textile Design" that included "construction of fabrics; . . . analysis of fabrics; designing on the loom for industrial production; . . . and work with primitive looms for the teaching of weaving in schools with limited equipment and for those interested in the study of some ancient techniques."[41] In addition, interdisciplinary connections were emphasized: "The Art Institute gives the student of textiles opportunity to complement his special studies with studies in other fields of art, [including] Drawing–Painting, General Design, Color, Sculpture, Wood Plastic, Photography, Clothing, Architecture, Planning, Art Theory, Art Appreciation, Art Education."[42]

As this flyer suggests, the summer sessions were aimed at a somewhat different audience than the College's regular students. Summer attendees were often older and some were more established in their careers. Some artists, designers, and art teachers attended the summer sessions to get an apprenticeship of sorts with Josef or Anni Albers. Among the art teachers to take Albers's weaving classes were people like Moreen Maser and Jane Cooper Bland (both at the Museum of Modern Art, New York), and Nuvart Bedrossian (Art Department, Asheville Teachers' College) in 1944.[43] Experienced weavers who came to Black Mountain to study with Anni Albers

included Wanda Nelles and Else Regensteiner in 1945 and Lili Blumenau in 1948. As
Erica Warren details in her essay in this book (pages 80–89), even these short contacts
with Albers and her methods had lasting impacts on summer session attendees, who
would further disperse Albers's methods through their own work and teaching.

PROMOTING WEAVING THROUGH PUBLICATION

The weaving program at Black Mountain was the second program Albers helped to
shape through her writing. T'ai Smith, in her book *Bauhaus Weaving Theory: From
Feminine Craft to Mode of Design*, masterfully demonstrates how Albers's writing at
the Bauhaus helped to distill and promote the ways in which the Weaving Workshop
at the Bauhaus situated their discipline as a specifically modernist project. As early as
1924, when her article "Bauhausweberei" was published in the magazine *Junge Menschen*, "through her carefully crafted text—the first of its kind on weaving—Albers proposed
a future of mass textile production even as she advocated for experimentation and a renewed
approach to design through handloom weav-ing."[44] This vision for the role of handweaving
in the age of mass production was one that she would continue to promote throughout her
career and especially through her writing proj-ects while a faculty member at Black Mountain
College.

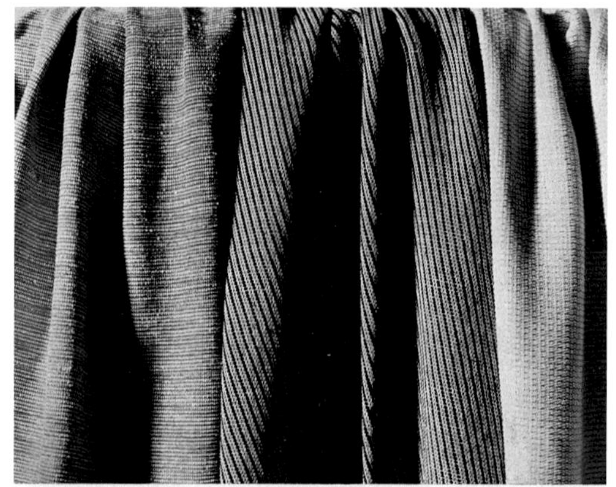

HANDWEAVING TODAY
Textile Work at Black Mountain College • by ANNI ALBERS

Where at the Bauhaus she had been part
of a movement—one member of a workshop
embedded in one of the leading institutions of
European modernism—in the United States,
Albers was a lone voice speaking to an audi-ence much less familiar with the tenets of modernism. As a result Albers's writing
became more generalized and dealt not only with concerns of industry, craft, art and
design but also implicitly taught the reader new (and modernist) ways of thinking about
the relationship between these different aspects of practice. Indeed, her first essay in
English, "Work with Material," published in the *Black Mountain College Bulletin* in 1938,
mentions weaving only once, as an example of a versatile craft that can teach many
different valuable skills. Other more general articles included "Designing" (published in
Craft Horizons 2, no. 2, May 1943), "Black Mountain College" (*Black Mountain College
Bulletin* 2, no. 3, December 1943), and "Art—A Constant" (lecture, 1939).

At Black Mountain College, Albers found both her voice as writer (in her second
language, no less) and pleasure in writing. While working on her second article in

46. Anni Albers's article "Handweaving Today:
Textile Work at Black Mountain College" featured
student-designed and produced drapery fabrics by
Ruth Bailey, Don Page (fig. 33) and Agatha Schurman.

English, "Weaving at the Bauhaus," Anni explained to Ted Dreier, "I am at a difficult point and have a hard time to say something clearly and always get it unclear again. A real tangle in the whole. But I like so much doing it and if in the end some sense comes out it would be wonderful."[45] As she became more confident as a writer and began to write more speculatively, her approach to writing became an act of construction itself. Weaving student Eva Zhitlowsky recalled:

> I learned about construction in writing by being Anni Albers's typist . . . She would think a paragraph in German, then slowly dictate in very precise, elegant English sentences. There was no outline. We then set the typesheets on the floor. She would walk around. I would walk around. Then she would paste and cut up and reconstruct the sentences. It always made perfect sense.[46]

Albers's care and precision is evident in everything she wrote and was likely a result of this iterative, combinative process described above. She pared and pruned and ordered and reordered her words into essays of great potency and economy. As originally published, Albers's essays are sparsely illustrated and rarely feature her own work. While today Anni is probably best known for her work as an artist, it is likely that when she left Black Mountain College in May 1949, she was more influential as a writer than as an artist.

Anni's articles were read by academics and art teachers, handweavers, artists, designers, and industry professionals, and the reach of her articles can be gauged by a survey of some of the responses she received. Joseph Hudnut, dean of the Graduate School of Design at Harvard University, and Jacques Barzun, professor of History at Columbia University, both sent Albers letters responding to her article "One Aspect of Art Work."[47] Arthur A. Brill of Cohn-Hall-Marx Textiles replied favorably to Albers's article "Constructing Textiles" in the special issue of *Design* devoted to Black Mountain College, writing, "it is a very accurate analysis of some of our design problems in the textile field today."[48] She was also read by emerging designers, like Alexander Girard, who wrote Albers to tell her, "I very much enjoyed your article ["Design: Anonymous and Timeless"] in *Magazine of Art*," the only known correspondence between the two legendary designers.[49]

Albers's ideas were not universally accepted, especially by the small (and generally traditional) handweaving community in the United States. Her article "Handweaving Today: Textile Work at Black Mountain College," published in the *Weaver* in 1941, is almost manifesto-like in its urgency and economy, a deft call to arms for weavers to use their handlooms as tools of design, rather than of (re)production. Sigrid Wortmann Weltge describes the controversy that surrounded the publication of "Handweaving Today," writing that "the sheer quantity and emotional outpouring of readers' letters prompted the editors [of the *Weaver*] to allot Mary M. Atwater space for a rebuttal entitled 'It's Pretty—But Is It Art?'"[50] Atwater, a staunch traditionalist (though one with a broad appetite for weaving from other cultures and traditions), was a highly respected handweaver and among the most-read authors on the subject in the United States. Atwater's response derisively summed up "Mrs. Albers' opinion [on handweaving] as expressed in her article: (1) the making of 'models' for industry—I fancy industry would consider this a big joke!—(2) for some rather vague 'educational' value, and (3) for profit or money. None of these things appear to me to be the 'why' of handweaving—today or any day."[51]

Reading Albers's articles, one can perhaps understand Atwater's viewpoint. In her vision for modernist handweaving, Albers leaves very little room for handweavers like Atwater who wove "because we like to do it, and . . . because we like to have our own beautiful textiles, made with our own hands."[52] Albers was always wary of people who vested value into craft objects merely because they were handmade, and it is notable that unlike her BMC colleague Trude Guermonprez, Albers did not embrace the craft revival of the 1960s and 1970s. This ambivalent and sometimes hostile attitude toward her medium's craftier side is ubiquitous in Albers's magnum opus, *On Weaving*, a text that avoids giving much in the way of direct instruction on how to weave and instead explores weaving as an ancient and modern design practice.[53]

On Weaving was not published until 1965, but a similar book to *On Weaving* might have been published almost two decades earlier. Albers had a contract with a publisher in 1946 to write a book on weaving and had begun the manuscript, which she intended to work on during her 1946–47 sabbatical year, but due to illness and other complicating factors, Albers was not able to fulfill her contract and was not able to find another interested publisher.[54] Given *On Weaving*'s lasting influence as a major text on twentieth-century weaving and design theory, one can only imagine that such a book, coupled with Albers's solo exhibition at the Museum of Modern Art in the fall of 1949, would have even further secured Albers's—and by extension Black Mountain College's—already notable position within midcentury design thought.

PROMOTING WEAVING THROUGH EXHIBITION

Alongside Albers's articles, the other primary venue for the promotion of textiles made by Black Mountain's weavers was public exhibitions. Between 1940 and 1950, textiles designed and woven by Albers and her students were featured in at least ten exhibitions. Because documentation of these exhibitions is scarce, it may never be possible to decisively fix the total number of times Black Mountain College textiles were shown publicly.

Some exhibitions, like *Exhibition of Hand-Weaving from Black Mountain College* held at Sophie Newcombe College in New Orleans in 1942, were solely devoted to works from Black Mountain. By contrast, in *Modern Textile Design*, which opened at the Museum of Modern Art in the fall of 1945 and traveled for about two years, the College was represented by only a handful of textiles—most designed by Albers, and

47. Installation view of "Exhibition of Hand-Weaving from Black Mountain College" at Sophie Newcomb College, New Orleans, 1942. Photographer unknown.

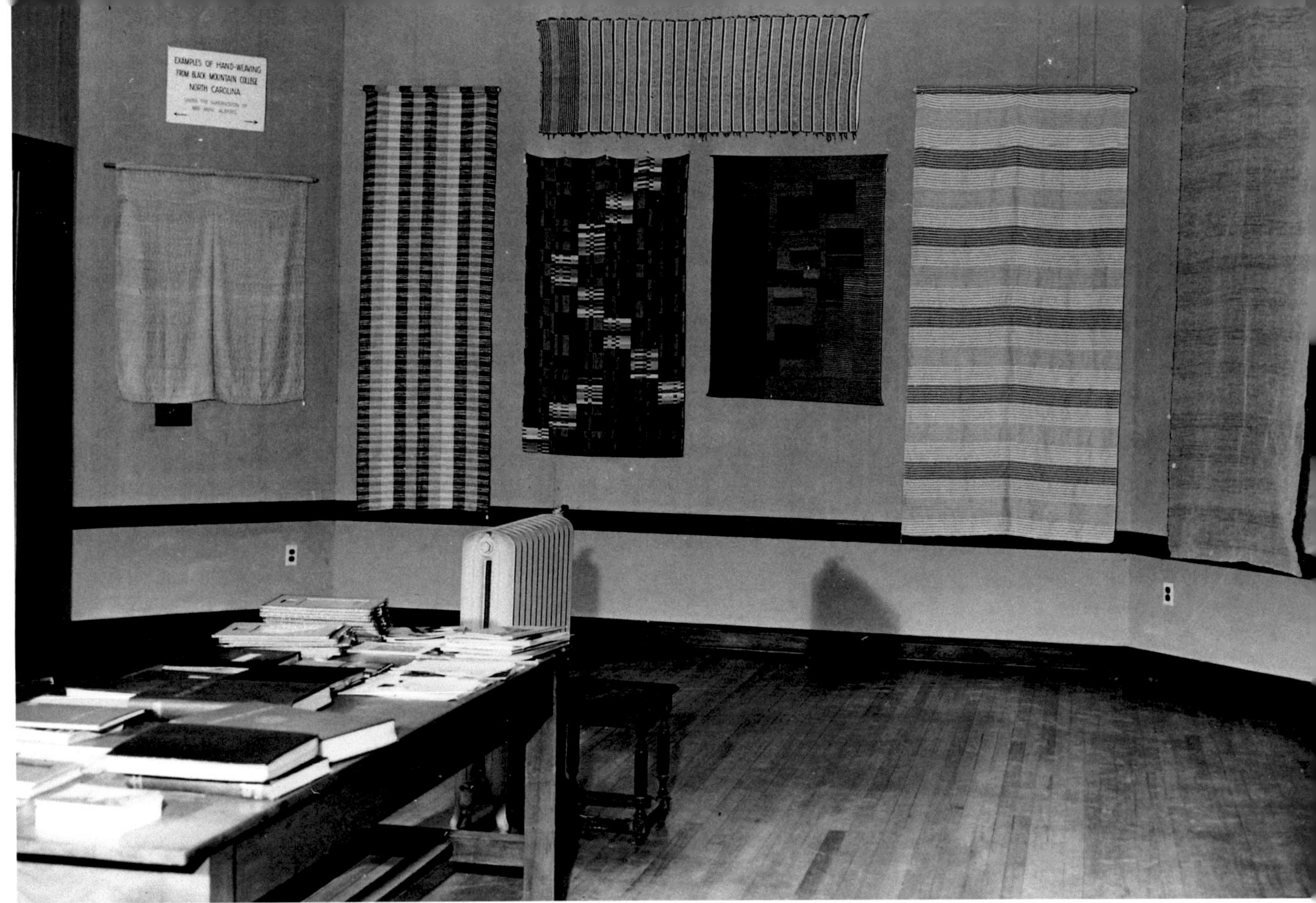

one other designed and woven by student John "Danny" Deaver.[55] Some exhibitions were local or regional, such as an exhibition of BMC textiles at the Mint Museum in Charlotte, North Carolina, in January 1943, which then traveled to Louisville, Kentucky.[56] Many of these small exhibitions were staged at college or university museums. In addition to the aforementioned exhibition at Sophie Newcombe, textiles from Black Mountain College were shown at the Skidmore College Gallery, Cranbrook Academy, Massachusetts Institute of Technology (MIT), and the Busch Reisinger Museum at Harvard University.[57]

The checklists of group exhibitions featuring textiles from Black Mountain paint a picture of the individuals and institutions in the College's peer group. In the *Exhibition of Modern Textiles* at MoMA, fabrics from Black Mountain were shown alongside textiles designed by Louise Bourgeois, Marianne Strengell, Dorothy Liebes, Marli Ehrman, Angelo Testa, and Robert D. Sailors.[58] The 1946 exhibition at MIT, which Anni Albers curated, "consisted of handwoven materials by outstanding textile designers from all parts of the country, and work from the Institute of Design in Chicago, Art Institute of Chicago, Cranbrook Academy, and Black Mountain. Mrs. Albers also gave a talk, sponsored by the museums committee of M.I.T. on 'Some Problems of Textile Designing.'"[59] Black Mountain College's inclusion in such exhibitions is a testament to the high esteem in which its weaving program was held nationally.

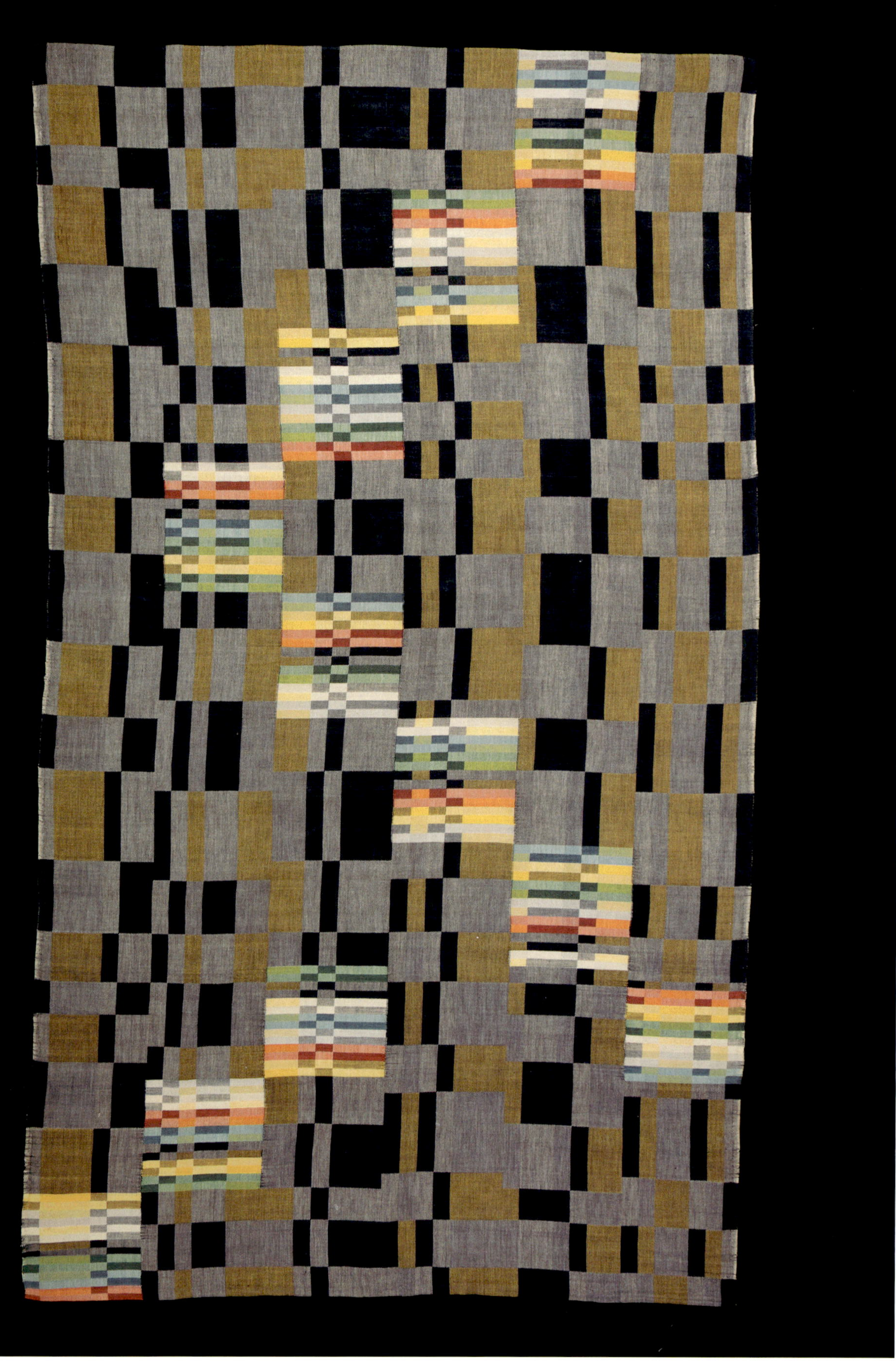

48. Don Page, *Untitled wallhanging*,
ca. 1939–41. Cotton. 62 × 37 in.

WEAVING AS ART

MICHAEL BEGGS

Although the primary purpose for the weaving practiced at Black Mountain College was to create fabrics for practical uses, students and faculty also made weavings intended to be viewed as artworks. This essay briefly considers the ways in which five of the College's most active weavers, Anni Albers, Don Page, Eva Zhitlowsky (Milton), Marilyn "Widget" Bauer (Greenwald), and Lore Kadden (Lindenfeld), found their own artistic expression within the medium of weaving.

ANNI ALBERS

In her own work, Albers had been making woven artworks since her time at the Bauhaus, where creating standalone artworks left her free to let her work be guided purely by composition rather than having to suit a design brief. In her wall hangings Albers also explored complex processes, such as triple cloth or Jacquard weaving, which were less readily adaptable to her practical textiles.

At Black Mountain College, Albers's woven art practice underwent significant changes. With less complex looms than those available at the Bauhaus (it seems the College never had a loom with more than eight harnesses), Albers's art became more manual, a change also attributable to her deepening interest in pre-Columbian weaving and vernacular methods like backstrap and card weaving. Anticipating her most mature and prolific phase as an artist-weaver in the 1950s and 1960s, her Black Mountain weavings became smaller in scale and increasingly used woven structure as

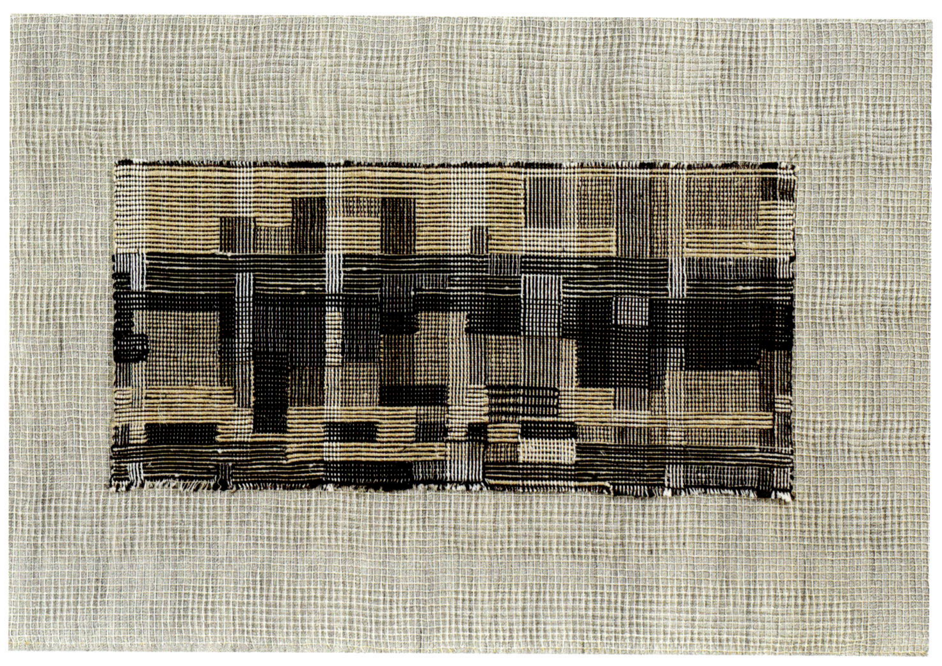

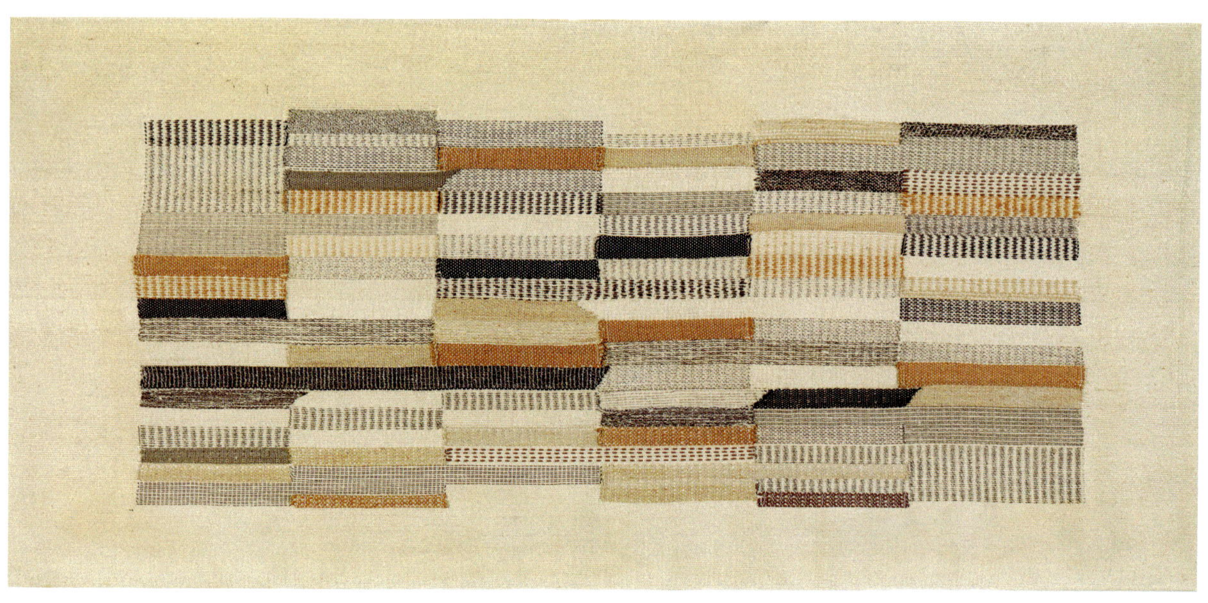

49. Anni Albers, *City*, 1949. Linen and cotton. 17½ × 26½ in.

50. Anni Albers, *Untitled*, 1941. Rayon, linen, cotton, wool, and jute. 21 × 46 in.

their primary pictorial language. This evolution can be clearly seen by comparing a work from 1936, *Monte Alban* (fig. 61), to *City*, 1949, woven either at Black Mountain College or shortly after Albers's resignation from the College. Where *Monte Alban* is figural, with pyramid- and hill-like forms made from supplementary wefts emerging from a single-cloth background, *City* is vague and impressionist. If *City*'s many stacked blocks of texture depict anything at all, the image of the city is very much implied; this is a weaving primarily made of and depicting woven structure applied as field, rather than figure. This change in Albers's approach to making art on the loom is captured in progress in Albers's *Untitled* weaving of 1941. Within a flat, even background of white wool, rectangular and oblong forms emerge made of different weave structures, with the ends of each weft pick often interlaced. This work, which was owned by Margot Loines Wilkie, the sister of Black Mountain College founder Bobby Dreier, was arguably Albers's first mature work to take weaving as its primary subject.

At Black Mountain College, Albers set no explicit expectation for her students to make woven artworks. If students made art, they did so on their own time or during free weaving periods, a pedagogical approach that paralleled her husband's, where classwork was treated as practice or rehearsal and artwork was a personal, self-driven pursuit. That said, Anni provided an outstanding role model as a weaver who alternately embodied craftsperson, designer, and artist, and this trinity of practice was clearly emulated by both her students and her peers (Franziska Mayer and Trude Guermonprez chief among them).

DON PAGE

Don Page, the College's first graduate in weaving, was a prolific and highly technical weaver of wall hangings. Whereas Albers's move toward woven structure as a medium led her to embrace more open and pick-up–based structures, Page's fascination with structure led to a prolonged experimentation with double weave in his wall hangings. His *Untitled* double weave (fig. 48) features an asymmetrical arrangement of multicolored blocks within a shifting, offsetting field of inverting blocks. In its fineness and flatness it recalls some of Albers's Bauhaus-era weavings, most notably her mid-1920s forays into double and triple weave wall hangings.

Page was a versatile weaver and another surviving weaving takes an entirely different approach. A smaller wall hanging (fig. 51, above) features a central figure

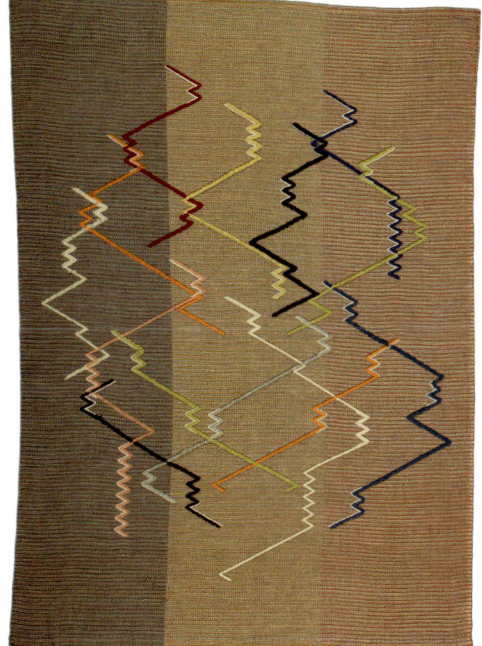

51. Don Page, *Untitled wallhanging,* ca. 1939–41. Cotton. 48 × 34 in.

of zigzagging embroidery floating against three fields of densely colored background. The vertical bands of color in the ground are controlled in the warp, which is moderated and modulated by the multiple colors and threads used in the weft, where the same colors are repeated along with other, related colors.

As an advanced weaver who worked toward his graduation in one-on-one study with Albers, Page also created pictorial designs for knotted and woven fabrics in a way that Albers's other students seldom did. Page's colored pencil sketches for textiles made using double weave show his sophisticated understanding and grasp of both the possibilities and technical requirements of the technique, with the warp designed to allow for great flexibility and variety when mixed with weft picks of the same set of colors.

ALEX REED

Alex Reed was a skilled visual artist who had already distinguished himself in Josef Albers's classes before taking up weaving. Today he is probably best known for his collaboration with Anni Albers on a series of necklaces made from pieces

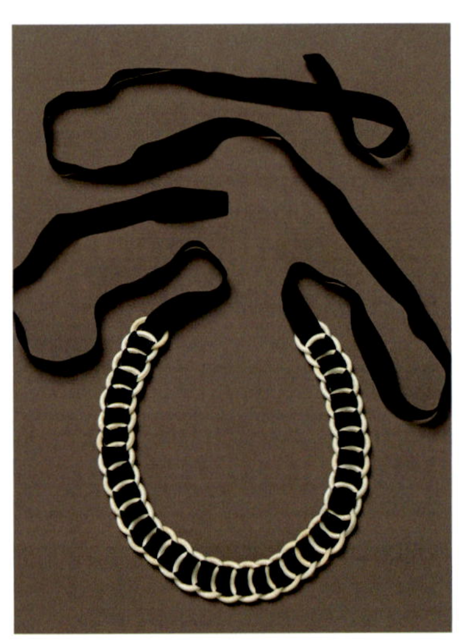

of hardware such as washers, electrical insulators, and springs. Inspired in part by pre-Columbian precedents, these necklaces were shown in the early 1940s at several modern-leaning galleries, and in 1946 in an exhibition called *Modern Jewelry* organized by the Museum of Modern Art, and which traveled to eight additional venues.[1] While Albers has sometimes received sole credit for these necklaces, in the original exhibitions both Reed and Albers were always credited, and a letter by Bobby Dreier identifies Reed as the originator of the necklace design featuring washers, apron rings, or other discs interlaced on a ribbon.[2]

Reed's work as a weaver is preserved in photographs. There are several photographs of Reed at work at the loom, both in his study at the Blue Ridge campus as well as in the weaving room at Lake Eden. This latter group includes a particularly evocative photograph by Claude Stoller of Reed's hands and a shuttle (the back cover of this book). Two of Reed's art-oriented weavings appear in photographs as well. One is a small but carefully woven tapestry with a design of tessellated parallelograms, a strong example of Reed's pictorial sensibility as applied to a rather conventional weft-facing tapestry.

The second weaving, which was featured in Albers's 1941 article "Handweaving Today: Textile Work at Black Mountain College" is structurally more nuanced (fig. 54). Woven in a balanced twill on a warp that is half white and half black, the

52. Anni Albers and Alex Reed, *Necklace*, ca. 1940. Plastic rings on black grosgrain ribbon.

53. Untitled tapestry by Alex Reed, ca. 1938–40. Photographer unknown.

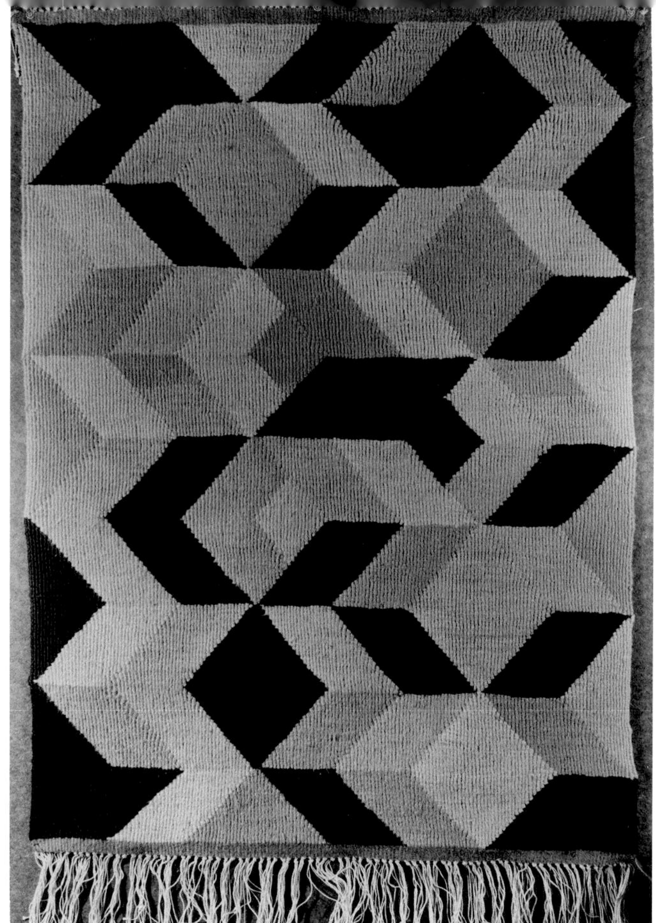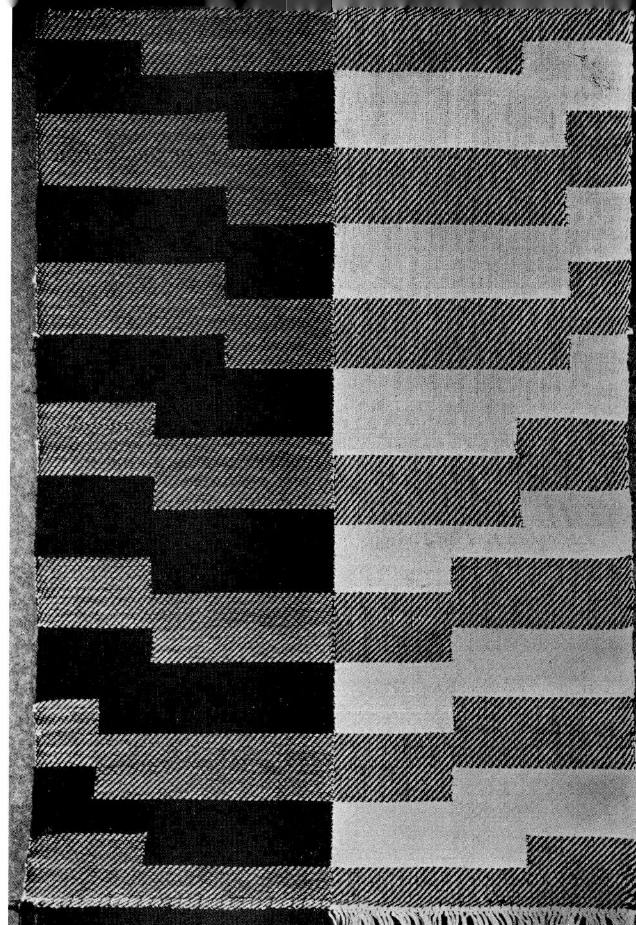

weaving features an undulating central figure the edges of which are implied, rather than fully delineated.[3] The third color of the composition, which bridges the black and white warp sections, is created by the even mixing of warp and weft, which requires that the color of the weft inverts on each half of the weaving (i.e., white weft with black warp and black weft with white warp).[4] While this work clearly owes much to Anni Albers's teaching and Reed's own grasp of the mechanics of structural weaving, its composition also recalls certain early 1930s works by Josef Albers, in particular his 1931 piece in sandblasted flashed glass, *Im Wasser*, which features implied undulating figures executed in three shades of gray.

EVA ZHITLOWSKY

Although she was manually skilled from prior experience in shop classes, Eva Zhitlowsky was not initially drawn to weaving, describing herself instead as "essentially a political animal."[5] But, as Zhitlowsky would explain, "I was fascinated by Anni Albers, who was a remarkable woman . . . I loved the people who were weaving and, in spite of myself, I found myself becoming a weaver."[6] She became one of the more structurally and materially experimental weavers at Black Mountain, and one of her designs

54. Untitled weaving by Alex Reed, ca. 1938–40
Photographer unknown. Reproduced in Anni
Albers's article "Handweaving Today: Textile
Work at Black Mountain College."

SPECIALIZATION AND GENERALIZATION, 1940–1947

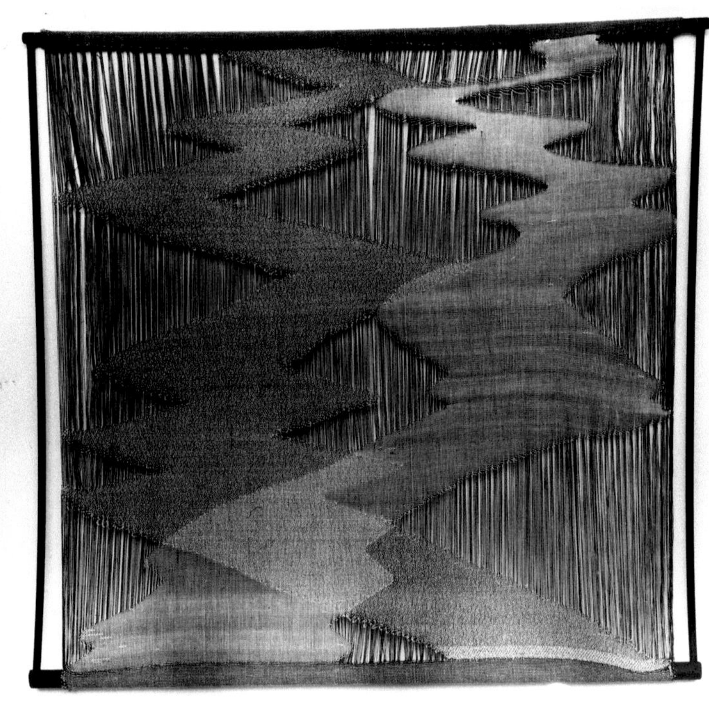

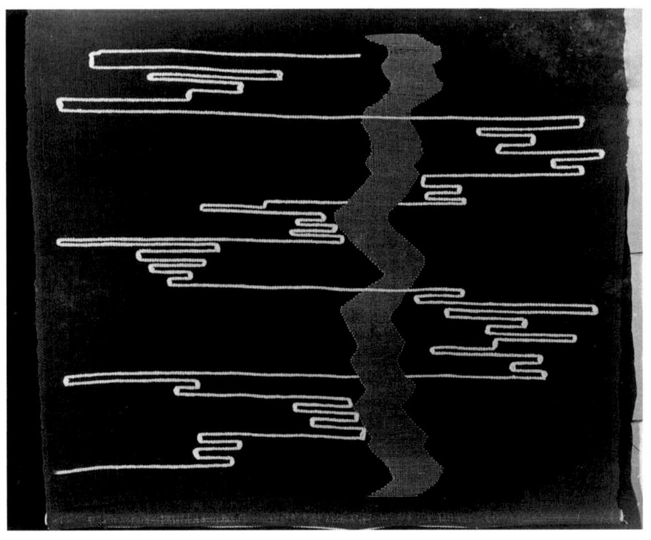

55. Untitled weaving by Eva Zhitlowsky,
ca. 1942. Photograph by Claude Stoller.

56. Untitled weaving by Eva Zhitlowsky,
ca. 1942. Photograph by Claude Stoller.

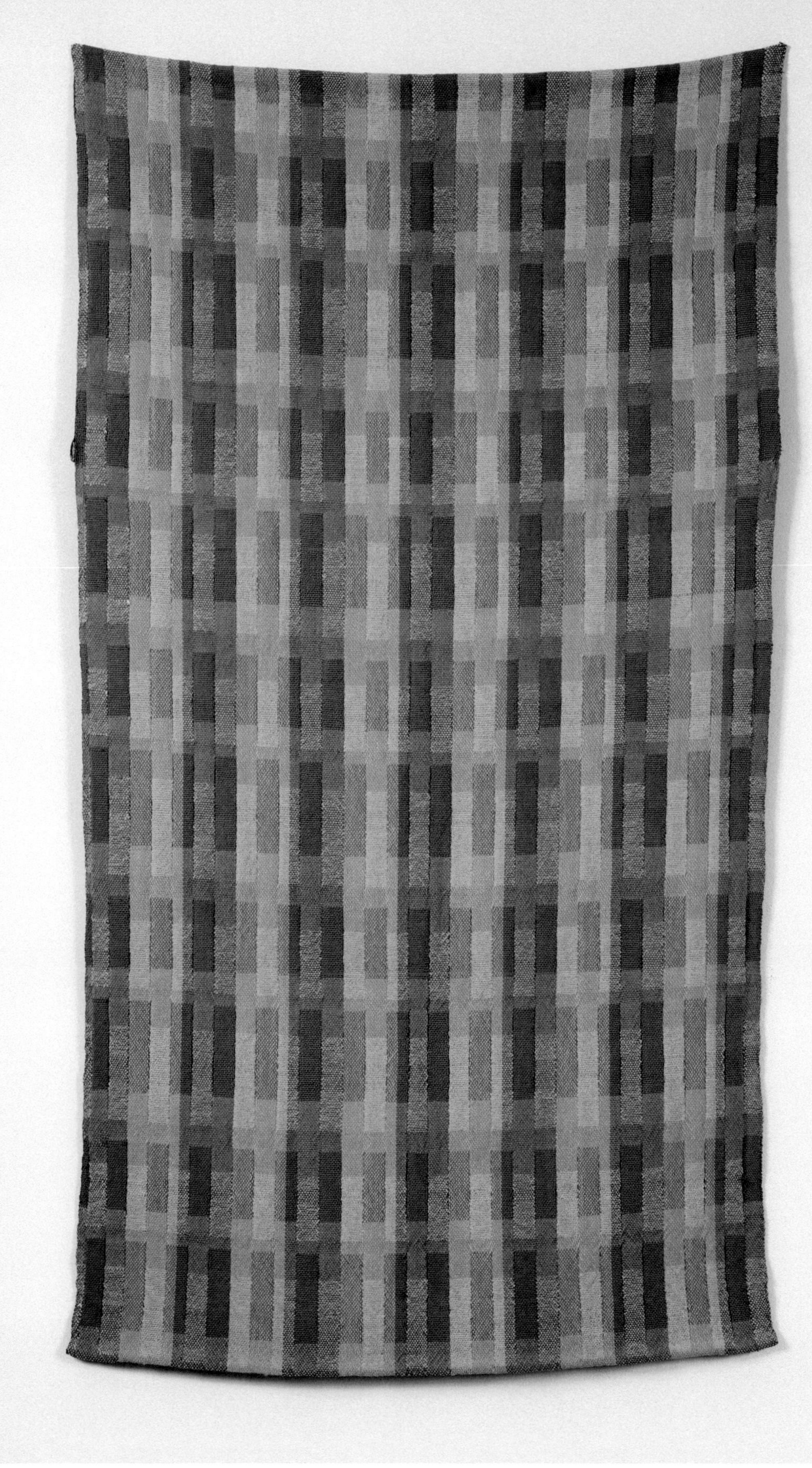

57. Marilyn Bauer Greenwald, *Untitled wallhanging*, n.d. Cotton.

SPECIALIZATION AND GENERALIZATION, 1940–1947

for a practical fabric, a heavily ribbed and possibly reflective fabric, was featured in Albers's article "Handweaving Today," where it was described as an "experiment for drapery material."[7]

But her freest expression as a weaver came in the numerous pictorial weavings with floating warp threads that she wove around 1942. In these pieces, she emulated (and anticipated) the work of her mentor Anni Albers by creating woven artworks that were structurally based but embraced manual, rather than industrial, techniques. Eva later recalled that she was so nervous to have anybody ask what she was making that she "waited until everybody, Don Page, Anni Albers, Mimi French, Danny Deaver, who were all the producing weavers . . . went to a conference at Chapel Hill. And they were gone for something like ten days which gave me night and day in which I produced, I think, four wall hangings."[8]

Zhitlowsky said her inspiration for the works was a period studying counterpoint in a music class at the BMC, which she tried to express in weaving instead. "Anni was so impressed," she recalled, "nobody asked me to explain why I left threads hanging and why I did not weave any of the other spaces." She later explained her decision further by saying, "I feel that weaving as a medium is very much related to sculpture in that you are forever butting yourself against the medium. It is demanding of you a certain conformity, and if you have any ideas at all, you want to change that, and so you push in another direction."[9]

MARILYN "WIDGET" BAUER

Marilyn Bauer, who was generally known as "Widget" during her time at Black Mountain College, was BMC's second graduate in weaving. She entered Black Mountain when she was seventeen in the fall of 1941, intending to study art. She graduated in 1945, and during her final year she assisted Albers by teaching weaving classes. Years later, Widget would recall that during this time "Anni Albers, for unstated reasons, completely withdrew from the community during my senior year so that I found myself teaching her classes for her, working toward graduation on my own, seldom ever seeing her."[10] Like Don Page before her, Bauer's graduation examiner in weaving was Marli Ehrman, who visited Black Mountain to evaluate Widget's work, which was put on display for several days in Molly Gregory's study.[11]

Bauer's own work shows her to have been a highly technically skilled weaver with a mature restraint in her use of color and compositions. Like Albers's later pictorial weavings, many of Bauer's fabrics, including both those woven for practical use and those intended as artworks, are best described as being a consistent field, rather than having figures. This field-like compositional strategy also extended to the textures of Widget's weaving, which were generally unified and less prominent than in a weaving like Albers's *City*. Although her material and color palettes in surviving pieces

58. Lore Kadden Lindenfeld, *Black and White Double Weave from Black Mountain College*, 1948. Cotton. 21½ × 24 in.

tend to be fairly limited, they are nevertheless different from Albers's own restrained palettes. Based on surviving weavings and photographs, Bauer balanced the neutrals and grays she favored with accents of bold, highly saturated colors like black and red. Bauer continued to weave after leaving Black Mountain and, in April 1947, showed her weavings at the Ten-Thirty Gallery in Cleveland, Ohio.[12]

LORE KADDEN LINDENFELD

The College's last graduate in weaving, Lore Kadden Lindenfeld, had a successful ten-year career as a textile designer (for more on her industry career see pages 59–60 in this book). Lindenfeld, who benefitted from Albers's guidance and her close relation-ship with Trude Guermonprez (see fig. 111), also created several artworks while at Black Mountain that combined double weave with the highly manual technique of pick-up leno. Two of these works survive, *Black / White Hanging*, in the collection of the Smithsonian American Art Museum, and the smaller *Black and White Double Weave* (1948, at right).

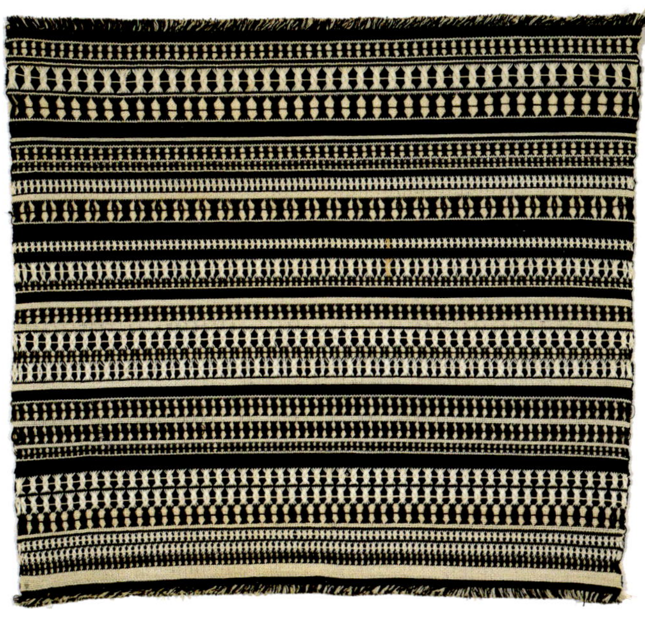

These works nod to the artworks Albers was making at this time, particularly in the way in which they feature woven structure itself as a primary element of the composition (they are works that could not possibly exist in another medium). Lindenfeld's prominent use of pick-up leno is also notable, as Albers herself would use the technique extensively in her mature artworks from the 1950s, in pieces like *Development in Rose I* (1952), *Blue and Red Layers* (1954), *Open Letter* (1958), *Pasture* (1958), *Variations on a Theme* (1958), and *Tikal* (1958). Since Albers seemingly did not use pick-up leno until 1950, it is possible that when she began using the technique, she was thinking of Lindenfeld's experiments with the technique during her time at Black Mountain College.[13]

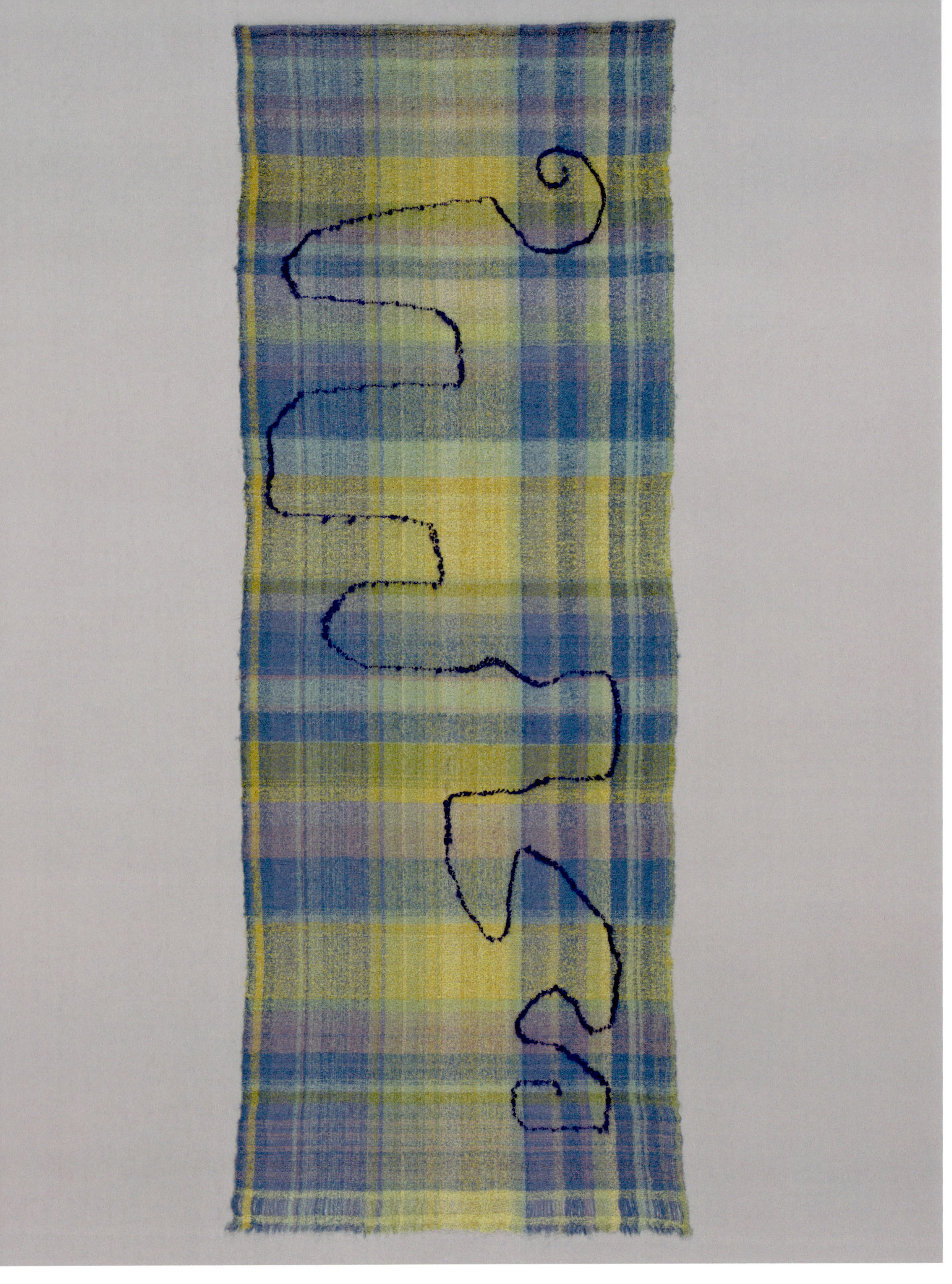

59. Else Regensteiner, *Blue River*, 1964. Rayon
and wool bouclé, 111⅞ × 43½ in.

FOLLOWING THE THREAD

BLACK MOUNTAIN COLLEGE AND WEAVING EDUCATION IN THE UNITED STATES, 1934–1956

ERICA WARREN

Within the history of modern art, Black Mountain College has achieved recognition as a progressive, albeit short-lived, art school with ties to artists often celebrated in canonical narratives, such as Josef Albers, John Cage, Merce Cunningham, Buckminster Fuller, and Robert Rauschenberg. Anni Albers and Ruth Asawa are arguably the most recognizable and frequently mentioned artists tied to narratives about weaving and textiles at Black Mountain, however, and more than one hundred of the students who enrolled at the remotely situated school took a weaving class. Perhaps unsurprisingly, the school, rooted in ideals of communal living and hands-on learning, also served as a site of connection and network building and can be understood as part of an expansive web of art programs, publications, schools, and teachers that specifically advanced weaving education and practice in the United States during, roughly, the second quarter of the twentieth century. This closely knit network shared the textile teachings of Black Mountain College across America.

In the summer of 1945, one of the students who took a weaving class at Black Mountain College was Else Regensteiner. Previously she had studied at the Institute of Design in Chicago (established as the New Bauhaus in 1937 by László Moholy-Nagy) under the tutelage of *Bauhausler* Marli Ehrman.[1] In recalling the impact of this experience, which included taking courses with both Alberses, Regensteiner reflected, "Josef was an enthusiastic teacher. He cured me of my timidity which I had from childhood. . . . I started to be more free in my work. This one class helped me a tremendous amount in my own teaching, in my approach, and in my whole life actually."[2] In 1942, Regensteiner, following Ehrman's path, was appointed as a weaving instructor at the Institute of Design as well as at Hull House. Founded in 1889 by Jane Addams and

Ellen Gates Starr, Hull House was the first settlement house in Chicago and served immigrants regardless of race or class.[3] Ehrman and Regensteiner both fled Germany during the Nazi regime and likely valued Hull House's founding proposition that "the social relation is essentially a reciprocal relation, it gives a form of expression that has peculiar value," a belief that would also guide their artistic endeavors.[4] These three formative educational experiences and environments (Black Mountain College, the Institute of Design, and Hull House) provided a pedagogical and practical framework for Regensteiner, who through her teaching and design work would inform and shape generations of designers, weavers, and artists with a textile-based practice. Moreover, the breadth of Regensteiner's career highlights the multivalent opportunities available to those interested in weaving practice at this time.

Regensteiner's *Blue River* (1964) (fig. 59), made twenty-eight years after her arrival in Chicago, visualizes her experience as a transplant, burgeoning weaver, and eventually prolific artist and professor making her way in a new land. The work debuted the year it was made in an exhibition at Illinois State University. The subtle yet luminous plaid pattern of the hanging's plain-weave ground has a softness of hue as well as line, an effect achieved in part through Regensteiner's use of bouclé yarns in cornflower blues and daisy yellows.[5] The delicate and irregular loops of the bouclé as well as the variations in shade moderate the strict rectilinearity of the structured plaid and provide a backdrop for the defining deep-blue supplementary brocading weft that winds and twists across and along the work, suggesting the titular stream of water. I see this thick dark brocading weft echoing the meander of Regensteiner's career and her definitive impact on the field, while the interlaced threads that ground it exemplify the finely wrought and interconnected network that constituted weaving education and practice across the United States during the second quarter of the twentieth century and well into the postwar period.

In 1945, after teaching at the Institute of Design and Hull House for three years, a time marked by material deprivation due to the products of industry being directed to the war effort, Regensteiner was recruited by Caroline Howlett, then head of the Art Education Department, to teach at the School of the Art Institute of Chicago.[6] The initial offer letter from SAIC, for the 1946–1947 school year, noted that she was being contracted to teach three periods for thirty-six weeks. A few months later, this offer was revised up to five periods, likely due to higher than expected enrollments.[7] Her courses remained popular throughout the late 1940s and 1950s, and during each school year, she taught five, and later six periods of weaving classes.[8] After twelve years of teaching and proving her indispensable value, in 1957 the Weaving Department was officially established as a degree-granting program and Regensteiner became its head.[9] The School Committee promoted her to professor that same year.[10]

As Regensteiner noted, her Black Mountain experiences informed her teaching at SAIC. Among the assignments she designed for her "third term" weaving students was a project titled "fabric textures taken from nature," which had the following directions: "Collect all kinds of natural materials: wood, stone, bark, leaves, shells, seeds, sponge, coal, etc. . . . . Make samples of fabric resembling closely these materials. Mat at least six samples opposite the natural object."[11] Exercises with natural materials were common at Black Mountain. In 1941, the weaving workshop was relocated to a newly built space, however before it was finished and set up with looms, Anni Albers reportedly "made her students go out and find any material they could and organize it in a rectangular format. . . . The weaving exercises were distinctive because they heightened an awareness of a haptic or tactile experience through the strict repetition of the same or similar elements, which in turn creates visible uneven irregularities that make these surfaces anything but formulaic or predictable."[12] Regensteiner's assignment suggests the impact of Albers's methods, a notion reinforced though the inclusion of Anni Albers's *On Designing* in Regensteiner's course syllabus reading list, under the heading "Books on Weaving."[13]

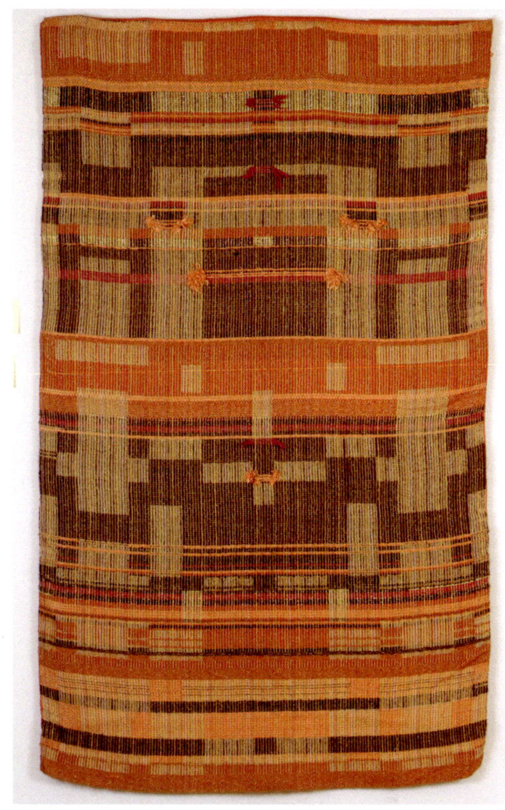

Regensteiner's work also reflects the impact of these exercises and practices, and two aesthetically distinct weavings demonstrate the breadth of possibilities she achieved through her experimental engagements with nature. Woven in 1948, just a few short years after her summer at Black Mountain and her start at SAIC, *Woodland* (fig. 60) has a modular rectilinear geometry similar to Anni Albers's *Monte Alban* (1936) (fig. 61), which references the recently excavated ancient city located in the Valley of Oaxaca in Mexico.[14] Albers employed a discontinuous supplementary weft technique for the first time in *Monte Alban*, using these wefts to envision the horizontal strata and stepped architecture of the ancient site. Regensteiner's abstract composition seems distant from the dense natural environment invoked in the title, yet the color palette of ochre, orange, and umber, with a hint of crimson and lime creates a late autumnal impression. The vertical striations and horizontal stripes in varied widths recall the bark of trees as well as the rings that chronicle their growth. Regensteiner used the ends of discontinuous wefts in the orange and crimson hues to produce small fluffy bursts of texture evocative of the crinkled character of fallen leaves. The contrast between lighter and darker shades throughout the work recalls a sun-dappled forest floor covered in leaf litter.

A few years later, when making *Wall Hanging with Sea Stars* (1951) (fig. 62), Regensteiner incorporated small desiccated sea creatures into a diaphanous open-warp

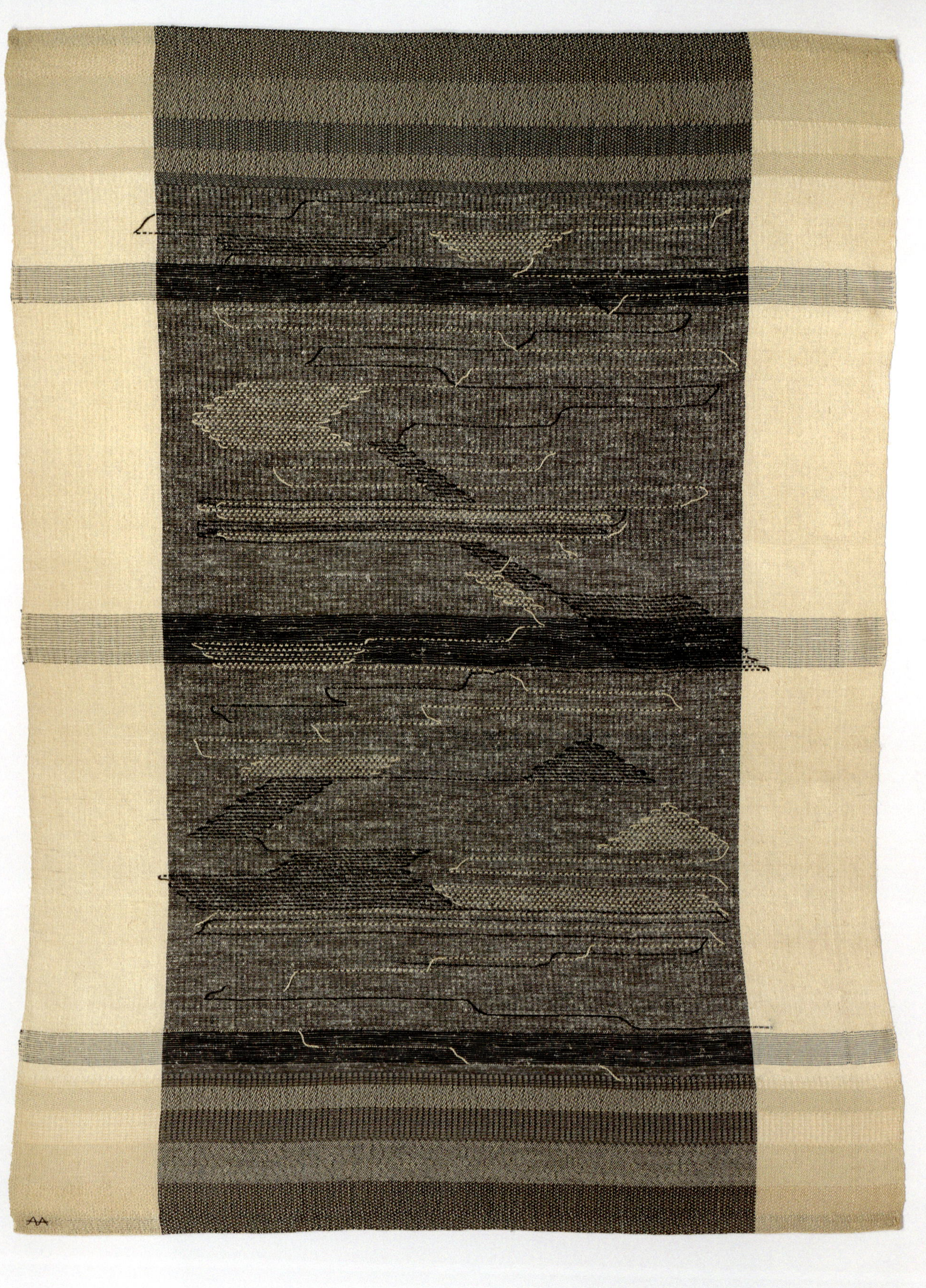

61. Anni Albers, *Monte Alban*, 1936.
Silk, linen, and wool. 57½ × 44⅛ in.

62. Else Regensteiner, *Wall Hanging with Sea Stars*, ca. 1959. Lace weave of unspun wool, Lurex, linen and rayon with dried starfish, sea urchin, and seahorse, 24 × 42 in.

weaving that echoes the shifting topography of sandy beaches with daily tides. In 1961, she affirmed that nature provided the primary inspiration for her practice and good design more broadly, stating in a lecture for the Ontario Handweavers and Spinner Conference, "When we want to weave a fabric, we should never copy, but always apply the principles of good design and our own judgement and imagination to the project. . . . Where do we find ideas and inspiration for our fabrics? . . . We find it in every tree, every branch, every leaf. We find unending variations."[15]

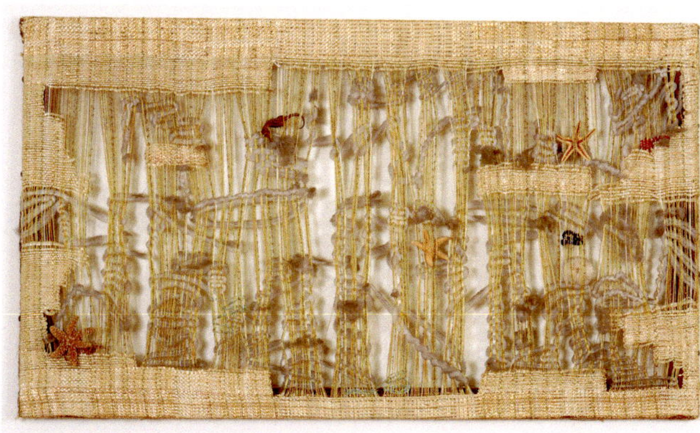

Regensteiner was not the only weaver who adapted ideas and lessons learned at Black Mountain College in her pedagogy and practice. Lili Blumenau, another artist who immigrated to the United States, where she established herself in New York City and went to study at Black Mountain in 1948, also encouraged experimentation and intermedial pursuits and emphasized the basics or fundamentals of weaving. After a summer in North Carolina, Blumenau returned to New York City, where she taught at Columbia University Teacher's College, the New York School of Textile Technology, and, in 1951, established her own weaving workshop, where she offering morning and evening classes during the fall and winter.[16] Her teaching, which received mention in the pages of *Women's Wear Daily*, was described thusly: "Classes follow no formal program; students are taught by 'trial and error' experimentation following several lectures which provide basic background information."[17]

In 1950 Blumenau's article "On Textures—Notes of a Contemporary Weaver" published in *Handweaver and Craftman* included material studies with macaroni and split peas, staples, leaves and stones, and matches, each organized "in a rectangular format" (fig. 63). These material arrangements have a clear kinship with Albers's studies that feature grass, metal shavings, twisted paper, and corn kernels, which she included in her foundational volume *On Weaving* in 1965.[18] Further echoing Albers, in the same article, Blumenau goes on to argue for intermedial engagements, asserting: "The nature and the handling of yarns and weaves may also be learned through working with other basic materials. Modern education has begun to encourage a wide and close acquaintance with materials."[19] This experimentation would prove invaluable as weavers grappled with incorporating new types of fibers, such as Lurex, polyester, wood, and even glass into their work. Blumenau's translucent and reflective wall hanging made of glass rods and Mylar yarns (fig. 64) foregrounds her experimental approach. The rigid clear glass rods that function as wefts are held in place by the fine and more densely woven Mylar warps and wefts. Like Albers and Regensteiner, Blumenau used

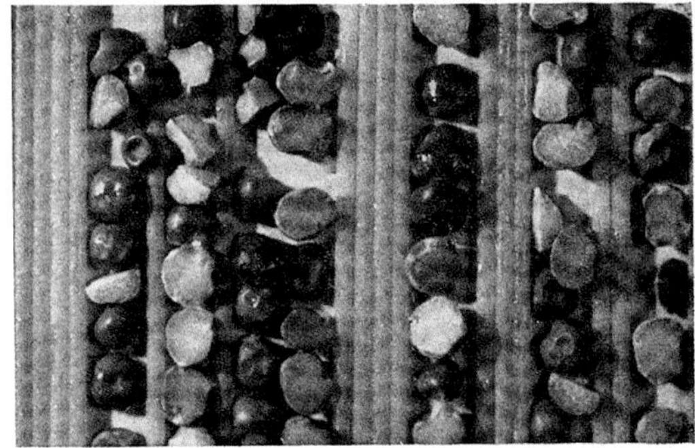

Corded design—macaroni and split peas.

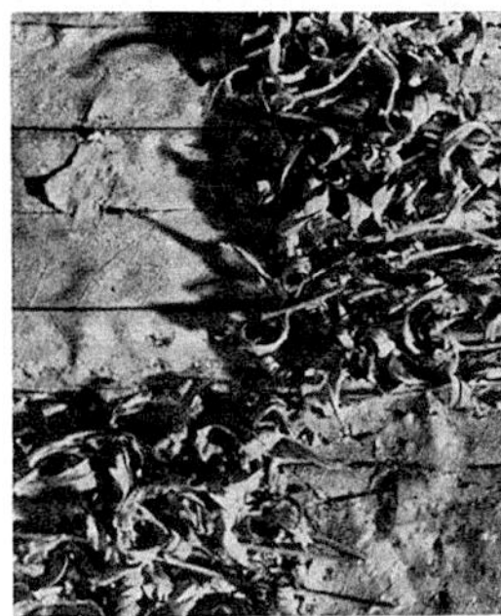

Pile effect—leaves and stones.

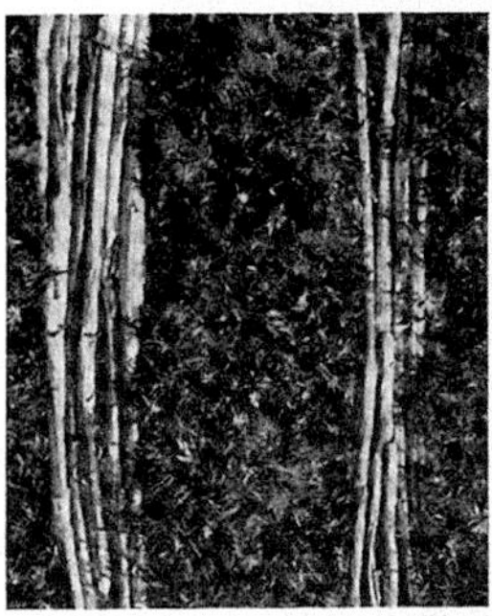

Weed seeds—soft as silk.

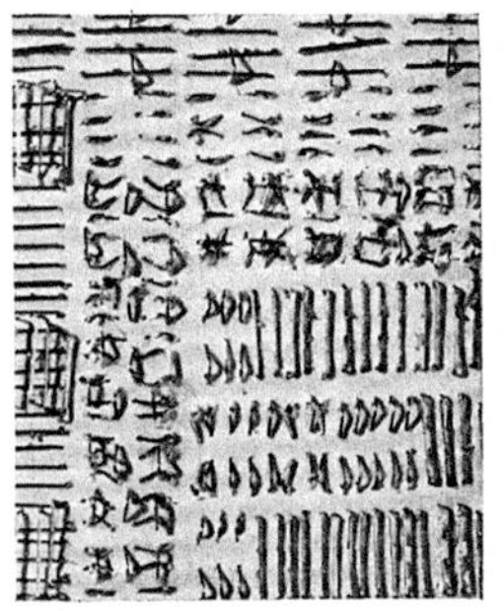

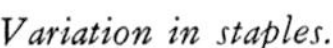

Variation in staples.

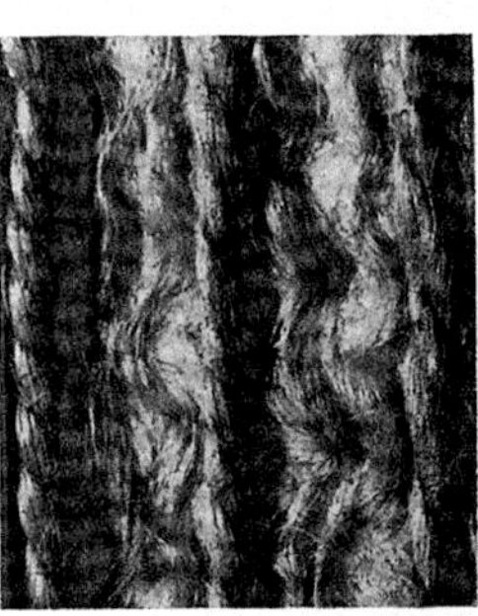

Luxury from raveled rope.

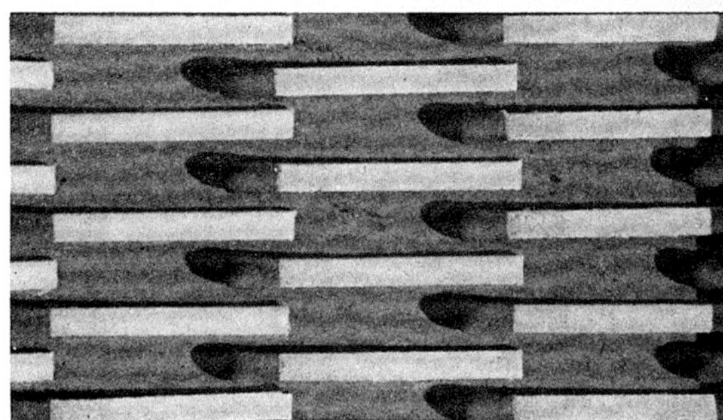

Matches assume a textile-like quality.

a supplementary weft to create a pattern, which fellow artist and weaver Alice Adams keenly described as a "whimsical play of graphic line over basic structure."[20]

Individualized study, weaving workshops, and summer residencies, in addition to degree-granting programs, proved integral to the growth of weaving education across the United States during this period. Regensteiner, acutely aware of the popular interest in weaving, followed Ehrman's example and embraced the vast community of handweavers across the United States regardless of their experience (the estimated number of handweavers in the United States and Canada in 1950 was, by one account, 300,000).[21] Gail Redfield, a design professor who took a summer handweaving workshop with Ehrman at Purdue University in 1954, described the workshop: "The weavers attending the workshop came with varying backgrounds . . . but all went away with a feeling of having added to their weaving knowledge and with a realization that no matter how much anyone knows there is always more to learn."[22] Ehrman's respect for handweaving and those practicing it at various skill levels was reiterated in a 1960 profile for *Handweaver and Craftsman*, "[Ehrman] believes that the foundation for industrial textile design should be handweaving, but also that there are important values in the handcraft for itself. Hence her continuing interest in weavers whose craft is only a rewarding leisure time activity and in weavers' guilds."[23] Ehrman centered handweaving in her teaching at the Institute of Design, through her involvement with Black Mountain College (where she taught weaving during the summer of 1949 and

63. Material studies featured in Lili Blumenau's "On Textures—Notes of a Contemporary Weaver," 1950.

64. Lili Blumenau, *Translucent Wall Hanging*, ca. 1955–1962. Glass rods and Mylar yarns, 60 × 30 in.

served as an outside examiner for a few BMC students), and during her summer at Haystack Mountain School of Crafts in Deer Isle, Maine, in 1956 (fig. 66).[24] Regensteiner likewise practiced this open-minded artistic and pedagogical ethos and led dozens of workshops for weaving guilds and textile societies across the United States and in Canada.[25]

Ehrman's stint at Haystack followed a particularly remarkable summer, which Jack Lenor Larsen, who began teaching at Haystack in 1953, chronicled in the article "The Weaver as Artist."[26] Haystack, established in 1950 and shaped in part by many of its collegiate predecessors, including the Penland School of Craft, Cranbrook Academy of Art, Black Mountain College, Arrowmont School of Arts and Crafts, and Pond Farm, provided summer courses for artists and students at all levels.[27] As Larsen noted, for the summer of 1955, he invited Anni Albers, Lili Blumenau, and Mariska Karasz to teach the twelve-week summer course with him. In recapping the experience, he described their approach, "Limitations form the very essence of weaving, and often the weaver's highest potential may be reached by the intuitive exploitation of these limitations. . . . We become, then, not instruments of our ambition, not the pupils of a master, but students of the interlacing of the warp and the weft."[28] Through his invocation of the fundamentals of weaving, Larsen sounds remarkably like Albers (and Blumenau), who in her essay "Handweaving Today: Textile Work at Black Mountain College" published in 1941 wrote, "Materials have accumulated to themselves set rules of working them. In going back to the fundamental principles we can open the field again for invention, imaginative use of intellectually recognized facts."[29] She reiterated this approach later in her essay "Design: Anonymous and Timeless," asserting, "Design is often regarded as the form imposed on the material by the designer. But if we, as designers, cooperate with the material, treat it democratically, you might say, we will reach a less subjective solution of this problem of form and therefore a more inclusive and permanent one."[30]

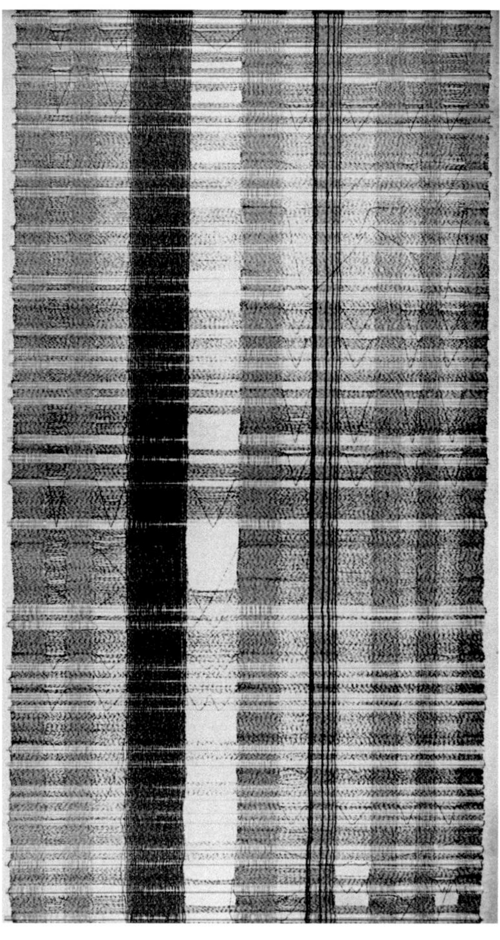

Albers wrote both of these essays during her time at Black Mountain and they surely reflect the teachings and ideas that she would have imparted not only to Regensteiner and Blumenau but to her many other students as well. These practical and

theoretical fundamentals come through in Regensteiner's teaching and practice, which rely on nature and the limits of the interlacing warps and wefts. *Blue River*, *Woodland*, and *Sea Stars* all derive their colors, and some, if not all, their materials, from the natural world. Moreover, Regensteiner's design approach across these works is rooted in the fundamental interlacing structure of two threads meeting at a ninety-degree angle and visually expressed in a grid. Years after making these works, when recounting her approach to her biographer, Regensteiner affirmed the impact of her time at Black Mountain, "When I came back [to Chicago], I did many of the assignments at home . . . and carried it over to my own teaching."[31] Like the supplementary weft in *Blue River*, Regensteiner carried those lessons with her, and when she intersected with other weavers, those teachings became further anchored in the fabric of American weaving practice.

Weaving pedagogy and practice found a significant platform in popular craft publications of the period, including *Craft Horizons*, *Handweaver and Craftsman*, and *The Weaver*. Larsen's article on the fruitful Haystack summer of 1955, which was published in *Craft Horizons* (now *American Craft*), draws attention to the role these magazines had in advancing and promoting weaving education. *Craft Horizons* launched in 1941 without a title but with a solicitation to readers to send in their suggestions, asking them to keep in mind the editorial focus on cultivating and elevating handicraft in America.[32] Similarly, Mary Alice Smith, the editor of the more specific *Handweaver*

65. Else Regensteiner, Sample, 1946. Rayon, wool, cotton, and Lurex. 16½ × 16½ in.

66. Haystack Mountain School of Crafts advertisement for "1956 Summer Session."

and Craftsmen (published from 1950 to 1975), acknowledged in the inaugural issue that she felt "a terrific responsibility" to their partners across the weaving community "interested in the development of sound craftsmanship."[33] At the time, these magazines provided an invaluable resource for weavers across the United States who were interested in finding educational opportunities to fit their needs, and retrospectively, the issues chart the growth in weaving education resources. These magazines published articles on weaving programs at art schools, including Cranbrook and Black Mountain; highlighted opportunities for summer studies at places such as Berea College, Penland, and Haystack; and featured advertisements for individualized study with weavers, including Mary Meigs Atwater, Lili Blumenau, and Berta Frey—the latter two were frequent contributors to *Handweaver and Craftsman*.[34] Blumenau also served as the textiles editor at *Craft Horizons* for twenty years and wrote two books *The Art and Craft of Handweaving* (1955) and *Creative Design in Wall Hangings: Weaving Patterns Based on Primitive and Medieval Art* (1967).[35] Together, these publications fostered and sustained a network of weavers with varied skill levels and practical expertise and kept them informed of happenings in the field.

Albers, Blumenau, Ehrman, and Regensteiner were émigrés and their significant involvement with the weaving community in the United States as well as their major impact on weaving discourse and education during and after their experiences at Black Mountain confirm craft scholar Jenni Sorkin's insightful argument that "the weaving workshop at Black Mountain strongly determined the emergent discourse on textiles in the United States, situating the medium as a vigorous champion of modernism and its skilled immersion in formalist issues of color, structure, and form."[36] Each of these artists took weaving seriously and advanced its practice through their numerous pedagogical pursuits. Their myriad connections are just a microcosm of the expansive network of weavers and elucidate the resounding impact that Black Mountain had on weaving education in America during this vibrant time for handcrafting.

ONE ASPECT OF ART WORK

1944

ANNI ALBERS

Our world goes to pieces; we have to rebuild our world. We investigate and worry and analyze and forget that the new comes about through exuberance and not through a defined deficiency. We have to find our strength rather than our weakness. Out of the chaos of collapse we can save the lasting: we still have our "right" or "wrong," the absolute of our inner voice—we still know beauty, freedom, happiness . . . unexplained and unquestioned.

Intuition saves us examination. We have to gather our constructive energies and concentrate on the little we know, the few remaining constants. But do we know how to build? Education meant to prepare us. But how much of education is concerned with doing and how much with recording? How much of it with productive speculation and how much with repeating? Research work and engineering work, when they are creative, are too specialized to give any general basis of constructive attitude. We neglect a training in experimenting and doing; we feel safer as spectators. We collect rather than construct. We have to learn to respond to conditions productively. We cannot master them but we can be guided by them. Limitation from the outside can stimulate our inventiveness rather than confine it. We need such flexibility of reaction in times of crisis. Too much of our education provides instead of prepares and thus loses its serving role and tends to become an end in itself. We are proud of knowledge and forget that facts only give reflected light.

Education in general means to us academic education, which becomes synonymous with an unproductive one. If we want to learn to do, to form, we have to turn to art work, and more specifically to craft work as part of it. Here learning and teaching are directed toward the development of our general capacity to form. They are

67. Anni Albers winding a bobbin, n.d.
Photograph by Claude Stoller.

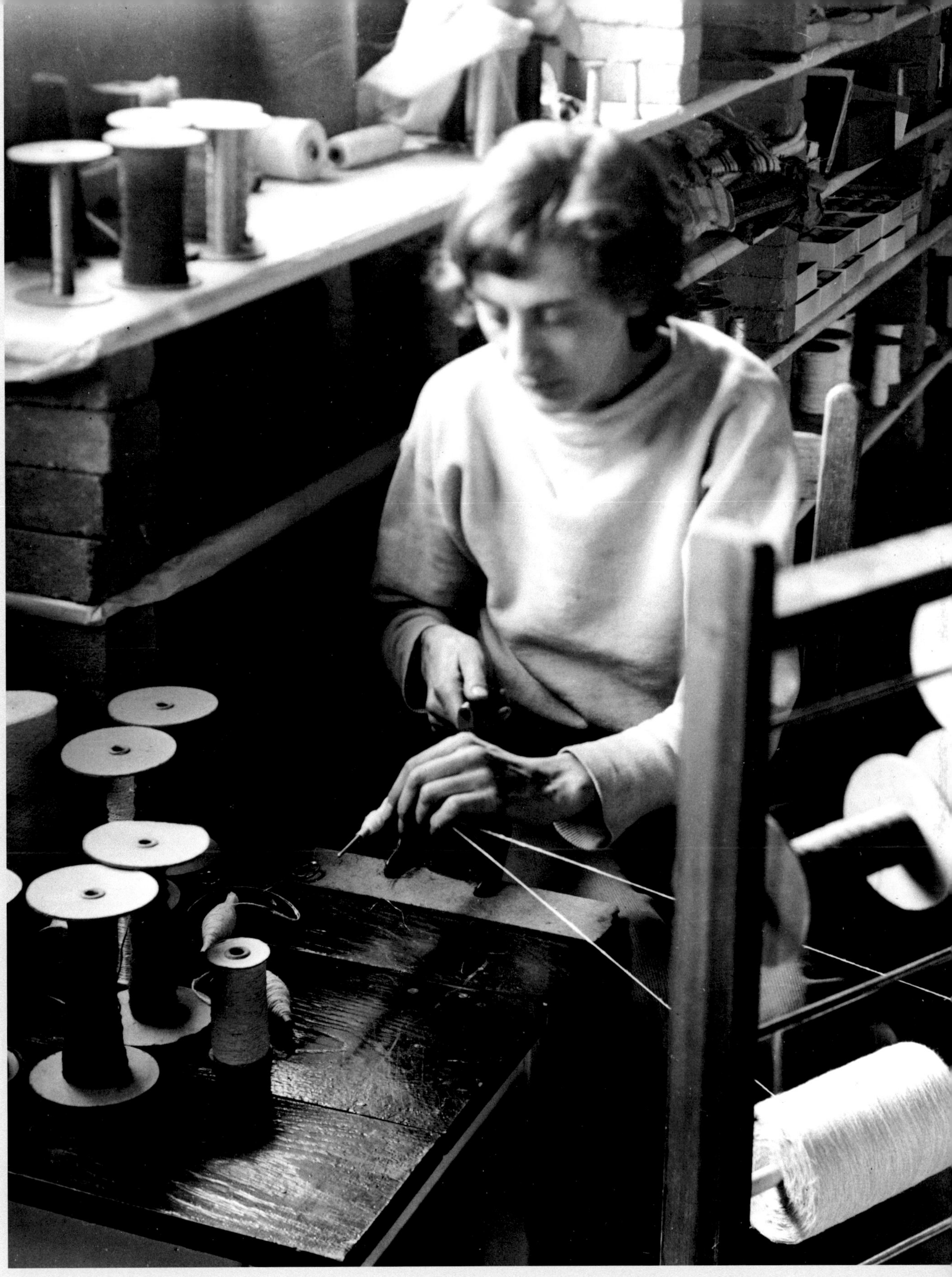

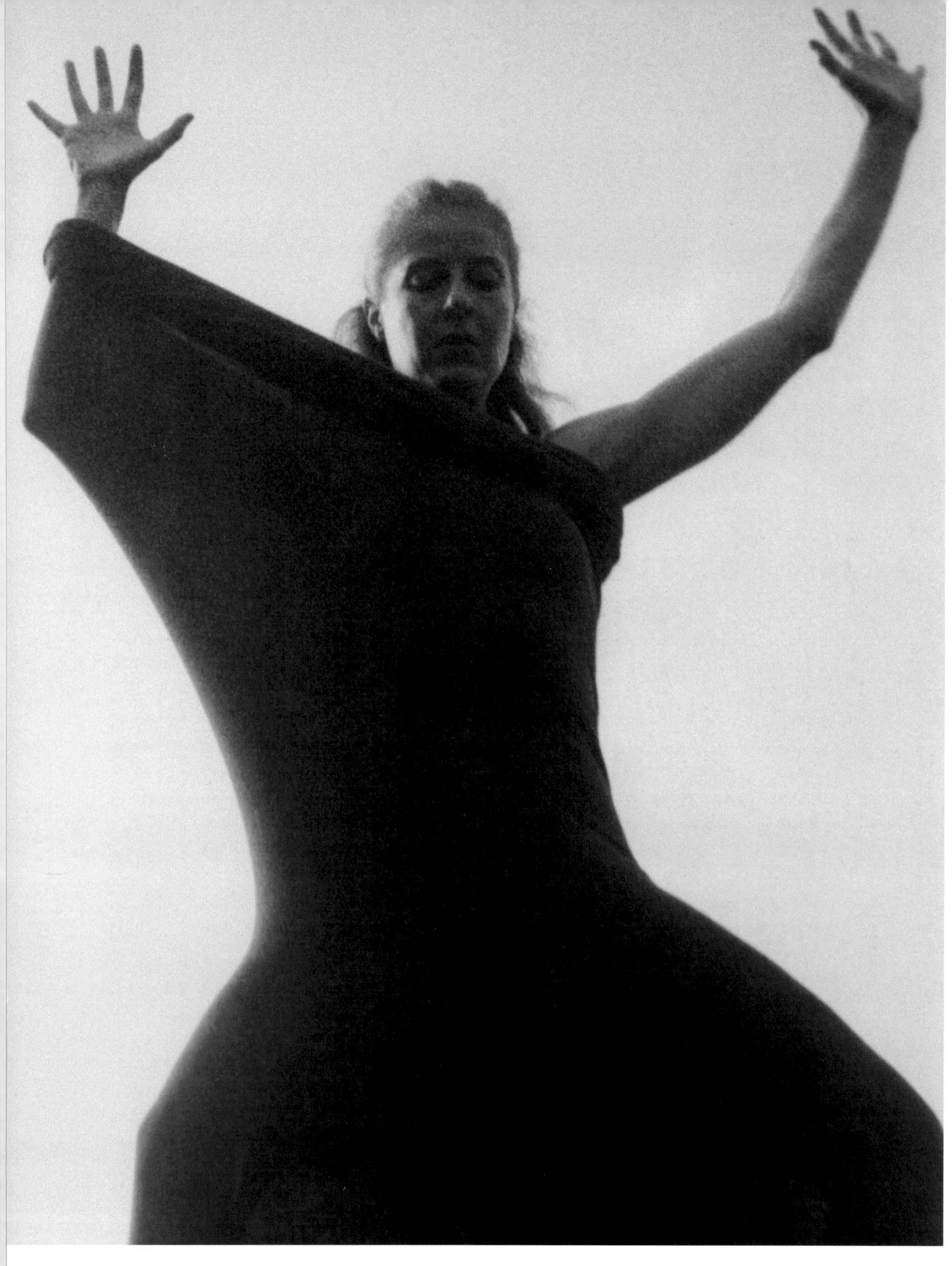

69. Katherine Litz dancing *The Glyph* at Black
Mountain College, 1951. Photographer unknown.

WEAVING LITERACY

WEAVING IN THE GENERAL EDUCATION CURRICULUM

MICHAEL BEGGS

The exhibitions and publications that featured work by Black Mountain weavers placed the College within a very small peer group alongside institutions like Rhode Island School of Design, Cranbrook Institute, and the Institute of Design. BMC was not only one of a very select group of schools to participate in these exhibitions, it was the only liberal arts college to do so. While weaving classes could be highly technical and specialized, they nevertheless were well integrated within Black Mountain's interdisciplinary academic culture, and nonspecialist students could interact with the medium in a variety of ways, including attending weaving classes, viewing exhibitions, purchasing and handling textiles, and receiving informal instruction in weaving from friends and classmates. These many ways of encountering textiles and textile thinking led to a high level of what we have termed *weaving literacy*—a familiarity with weaving and its processes, key concerns, and products—at Black Mountain College.

Students who took weaving at Black Mountain, including those who took weaving semester after semester, also seriously pursued studies in other subjects. Andy Oates and Willie Joseph, two creative and prolific weavers, wound up changing their majors at the College as their interests changed.[1] Joseph, who took ten weaving classes between 1945 and 1949, changed his major to math after becoming a dedicated student of the legendary mathematician Max Dehn. Joseph maintained an active creative practice after leaving Black Mountain College in which he continued to weave rugs and other textiles and also made rhizome-like sculptures in cast aluminum and bronze. Oates, who later had a successful career as a textile designer and master weaver in a cottage-industry model at Nantucket Looms, began to focus on photography in the late 1940s, studying with Hazel Larsen Archer and helping her to produce the photobook *5 Photographers* in 1950.[2]

Alternately, about half of all students who took weaving at BMC took only one weaving class. Some were art students, like Elaine Schmitt Urbain and Ray Johnson, who may have taken weaving as a way of broadening their art and design education. Others took weaving while pursuing other studies. Patsy Lynch Wood, who was a music major at Black Mountain College from 1942 to 1948, had been interested in taking weaving classes for most of her time at the College but did not take an official weaving class until the 1948 Summer Session, after she graduated.[3]

According to student records, more than 120 students officially enrolled in weaving classes, about ten percent of all students to ever attend Black Mountain College.

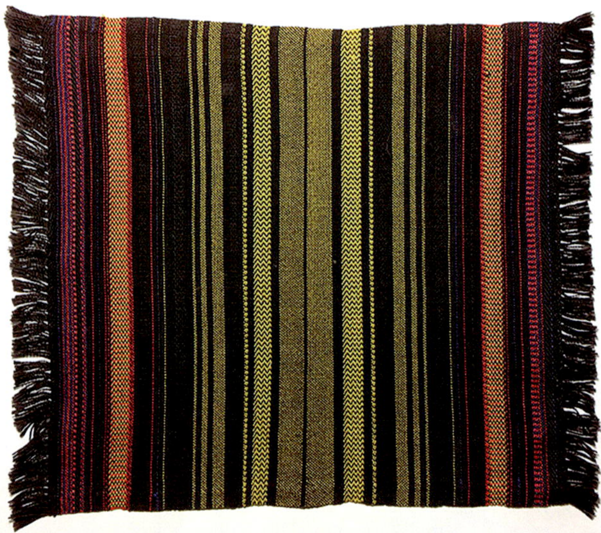

While this was certainly a smaller proportion of students than, for instance, those who took art classes with Josef Albers, at the humanities and arts focused BMC, enrollment in weaving classes was presumably comparable to or even greater than enrollment in mathematics, chemistry, physics, or biology despite the presence of excellent faculty in those disciplines.

One measure of weaving's prominence in the Black Mountain College curriculum is the prevalence of questions about weaving on the exams students took to be admitted to the Senior Division. In February 1942, students were given nine hours to answer questions of their choice from a total of nineteen options, three of which were about weaving. These included "Discuss the plain weave," a prompt answerable even by students who had taken only one term of Anni Albers's weaving class, and two design-oriented questions, "What is the sense of a back filling fabric?" and "In what way has the use of textiles in the interiors changed in the last decades?"[4] In 1946, the test asked students to "give some examples of the influence of the construction of a weave on the raw material of a yarn, such as wool, linen, etc.," and to "give examples of a) a balanced compound twill, b) a derivative twill, c) a warp satin."[5]

Nonspecialist students could also try their hand at weaving outside of formal instruction in classes. At both the Blue Ridge and Lake Eden campuses, the weaving room could be visited by anyone, and it is easy to imagine nonweaving students visiting their friends in the weaving room to chat or to see what they were working on during free weaving hours. Inevitably, some visitors were offered a seat at the bench and an opportunity to try weaving for themselves. Sometimes these informal encounters included Anni Albers herself, as in the case of Patsy Lynch Wood, who "did some informal work on the looms with Anni" in the years that preceded her eventual enrollment in Albers's class.[6] The opportunity to engage with weaving on an informal basis may explain why there are extant examples of weaving attributed to students who do not have official course card records for weaving classes, such as Joan Stack.[7]

The entire Black Mountain College community had many opportunities to touch, see, and purchase the products made by students in the weaving program. Occasional formal exhibitions of textiles were arranged at the College, including one organized by Trude Guermonprez in 1947 (figs. 93 and 94), recent acquisitions from the Harriett Engelhardt Memorial Collection (see page 108), and graduation exhibitions for Don Page, Marilyn Bauer Greenwald, and Lore Kadden Lindenfeld. In addition, textiles were informally displayed around the College, both in public spaces and in student and faculty studies. Photographs show Anni Albers's 1936 wall hanging *Ancient Writing* behind students playing a flute duet (fig. 76), Don Page in his study in front of one of his large wall hangings (fig. 20), and other textiles hanging in the hallway of one of the buildings at Lake Eden (probably the cottage known as "Mountain Stream").[8]

Textiles and the products of the weaving program also appeared in other classes at Black Mountain College. Textile rearrangements, first introduced at the Bauhaus, were a common exercise in Josef Albers's *Werklehre* classes. Working only in two dimensions, students manipulated woven screens of loosely woven fabrics like burlap or cheesecloth to create the illusion of three-dimensional volume (fig. 71). These materials, Josef noted, all shared a woven structure that "is emphatically flat and our study in its re-arrangement aims at spatial effects without changing its flatness . . . cutting and bending [the material] so that it is impossible to read anything but the illusion of volume."[9] His students also used products of the weaving program occasionally in other exercises, including skeins, tangles, and lengths of yarn in *matière* studies. In at least one instance, a student made a woven version of a drawing exercise in which spatial illusions are created using lines of varying width or spacing (fig. 75).

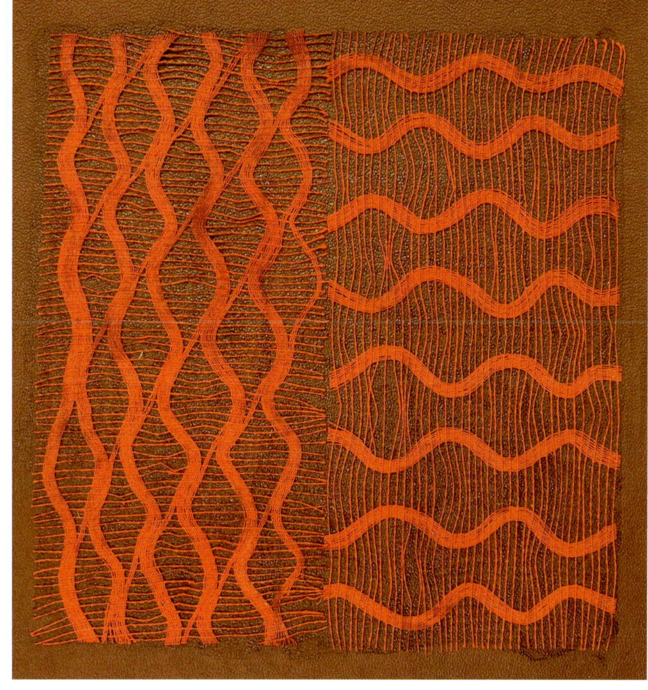

The disciplines of weaving and architecture were notably tied at Black Mountain College. With the exception of the classes given by A. Lawrence Kocher and Anatole

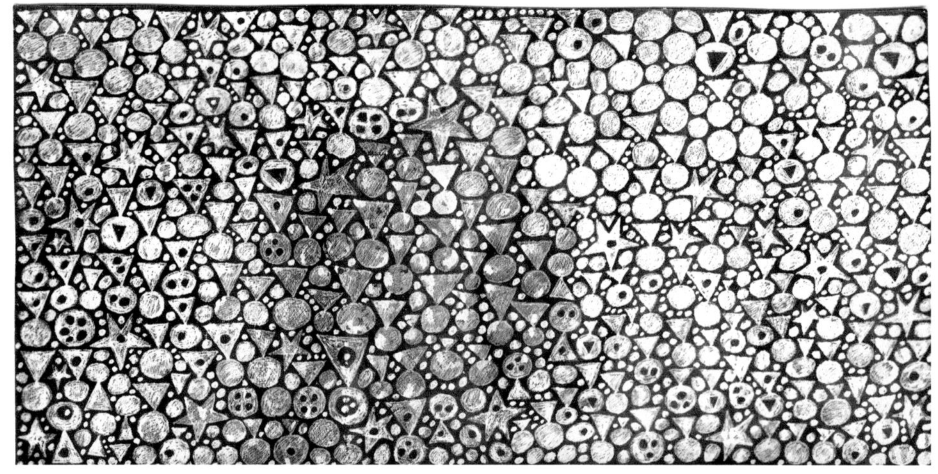

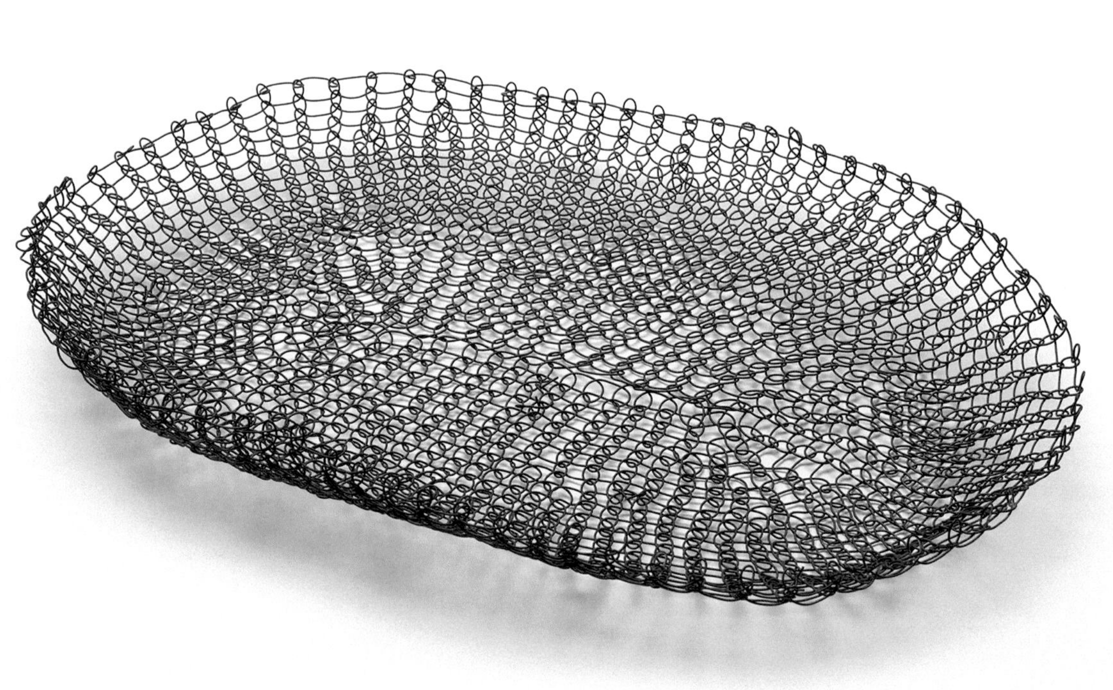

72. Ray Johnson, *Photogram Mailing to Josef and Anni Albers*, 1947. Photogram with typescript on verso. 3⅛ × 7⅛ in.

73. Ruth Asawa, *Untitled* (S.784, Free-standing basket), ca. 1948–49. Copper wire. 14 × 20 × 2½ in.

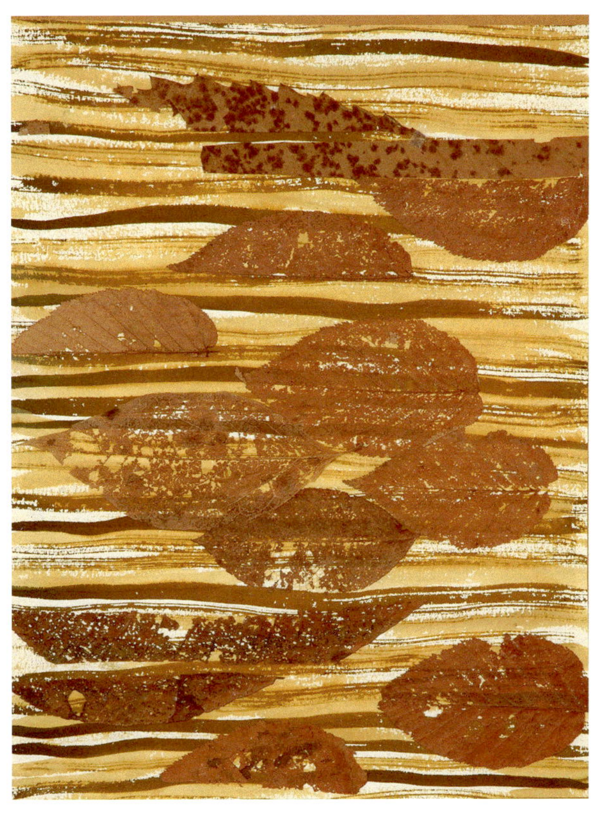

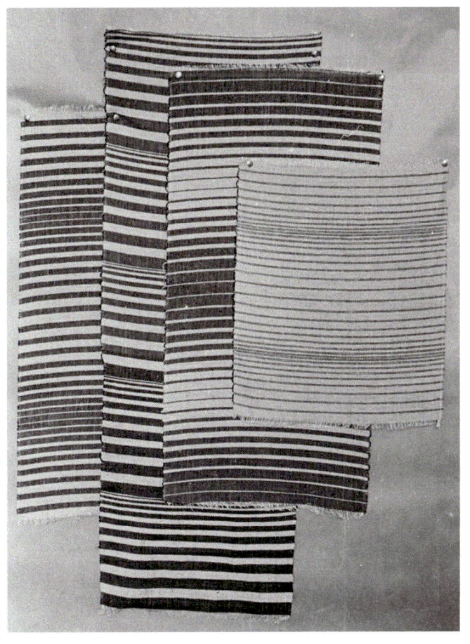

74. Lore Kadden Lindenfeld, *Leaf Study*,
ca. 1945–48. Mixed media, leaves, watercolor.
13 ¾ × 10 ½ in.

75. Four woven studies for a drawing or *Werklehre*
assignment, Black Mountain College, ca. 1939–41.
Photograph by Josef Albers.

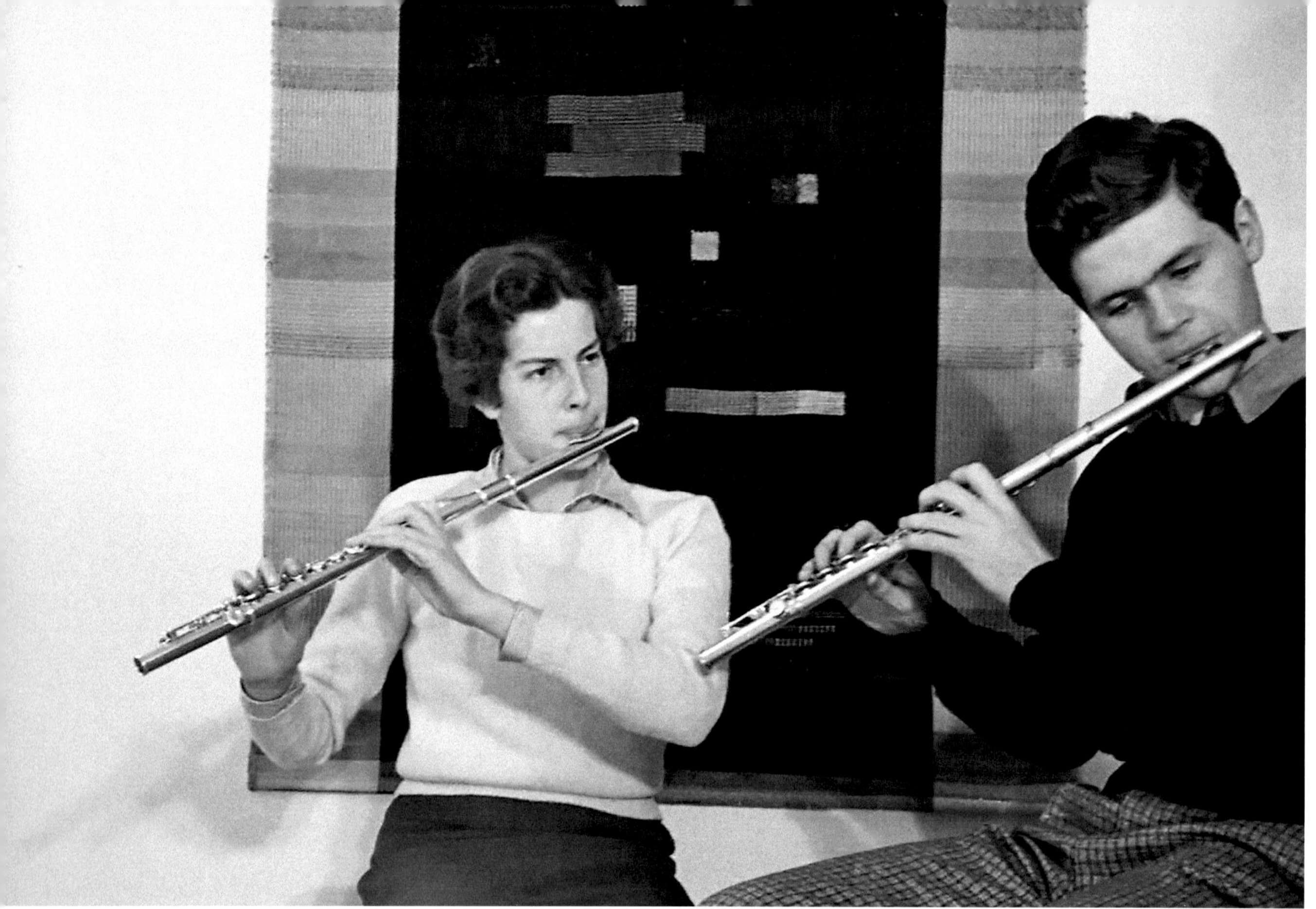

Kopp in the early 1940s, when the College's campus building program was at its height, instruction in architecture at Black Mountain College was largely intermittent and informal. As the College's primary design program, Anni Albers's weaving classes introduced students to rigorous design thinking, which they could later (or simultaneously) apply to work in architecture.

At a time when architecture was a heavily male-dominated discipline, the College's weaver-architects were primarily, but not exclusively, men. Nell Goldsmith, a female student who studied weaving and architecture, was a notable exception.[10] A notable trio of the College's strongest weaving and design students in the 1930s and early 1940s—Don Page, Alex Reed, and Claude Stoller—all took weaving classes with Anni Albers before later studying architecture at the Graduate School of Design at Harvard University after wartime service. In the postwar years, when architecture at Black Mountain consisted of student-led projects (such as the Minimum House and Science Building) that were supplemented by visits by notable architects and educators, like Walter Gropius and R. Buckminster Fuller, the College's architect-weavers included Paul Williams and Ragland Watkins.[11]

Aside from being a design discipline, Anni Albers's approach to weaving, with its emphasis on structure and material, made it highly comparable to architecture itself. Both practices dealt with mass-produced materials, the characteristics of which the designer did not control themselves. Like weaving, the overall design experience of a

76. Black Mountain College students Peggy Barton French and Duncan Dwight in front of Anni Albers's wall hanging *Ancient Writing*, 1937. Photograph by Helen M. Post Modley.

77. Alex Reed in the Quiet House, ca. 1943. Photograph by Will Hamlin.

completed piece of architecture was made up of many separate components brought into order, contact, and relationship with each other by the designer that combined to perform structural and aesthetic functions. For Albers, who had enjoyed particular success as a designer at the Bauhaus when designing textile commissions for use in buildings, integration with architecture was a natural and essential function of textile design. At the end of her time at Black Mountain, she designed a series of innovative free-hanging partitions or space dividers that were prominently featured in her 1949 MoMA exhibition. These dividers, sturdy and stiff while at the same time open and transparent, were meant to be ready-made architectural products, nonopaque walls to divide the open plans of modernist interiors.

The College's new buildings at Lake Eden created a need for more practical textiles for the College's furnishings. However, given the College's extremely limited ability to produce textiles in any quantity, most of the textiles for the College were purchased from other manufacturers. For the Studies Building, Anni Albers chose

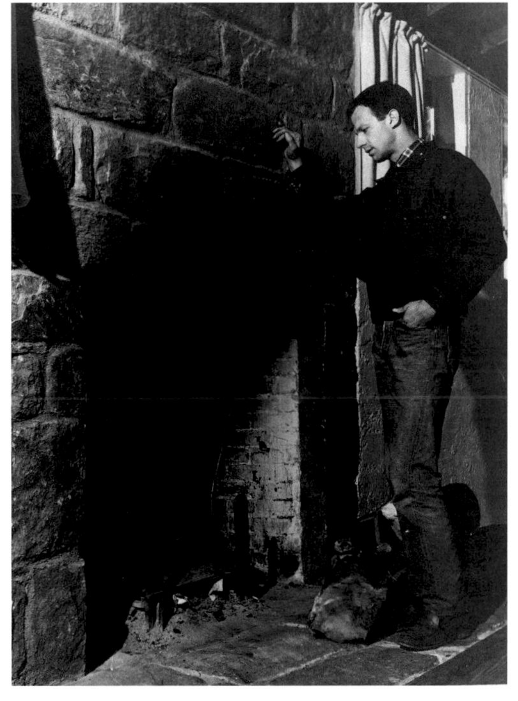

a suite of six white or off-white fabrics, produced by the Itasca Weavers Guild in Itasca, Texas, as suitable for "couch covers, pillows or [uses] other than for curtains" and two neutral-colored fabrics for curtains.[12] Students and faculty could order the fabrics of their choice in yard lengths at wholesale prices to furnish their studies. A large silvery drape was ordered to serve as a backdrop and curtain in the dining hall for performances. Though much of the interior of the Studies Building remained unfinished throughout the war due to a lack of availability of paneling, one notable aspect that was finished was the creation of ceilings made of woven wooden slats, of which seemingly no photographs or physical examples remain.[13] The Quiet House, a meditation space and de facto spiritual center for Black Mountain College, had handwoven white curtains made by Alex Reed, who had built the Quiet House himself with help from members of the community.

A general level of weaving literacy also supported interest in weaving-adjacent practices or disciplines. Ruth Asawa's work in looped wire has sometimes been misunderstood as being weaving or as stemming from Anni Albers's teaching, but in fact Asawa never took weaving at Black Mountain College. Indeed, the forms she created, from bowls to teardrop and vessel sculptures to Möbius-like involutions, are all impossible in weaving (which is a resolutely planar process) though eminently possible in structures like crocheting and knitting, where complex, double-curved

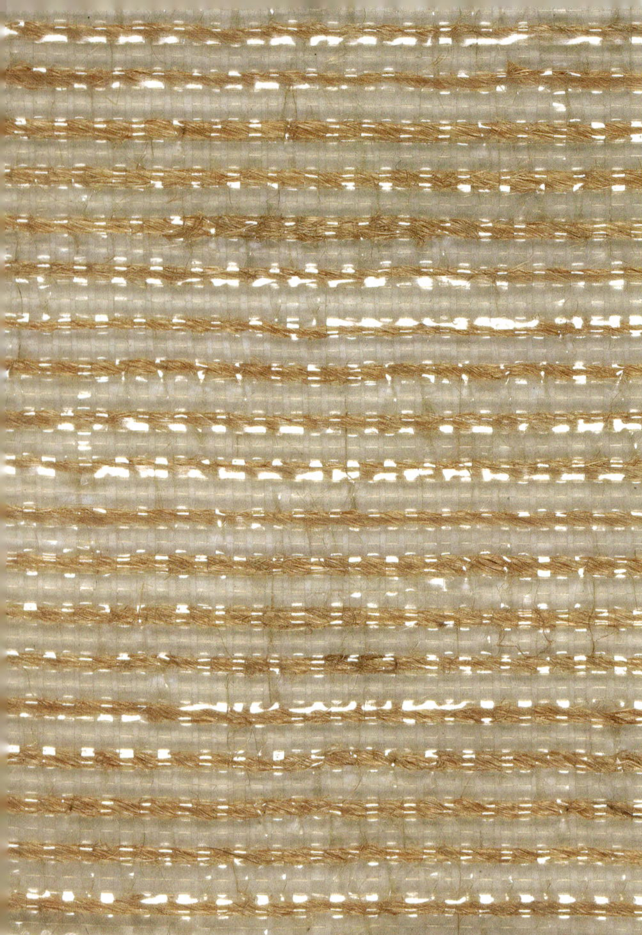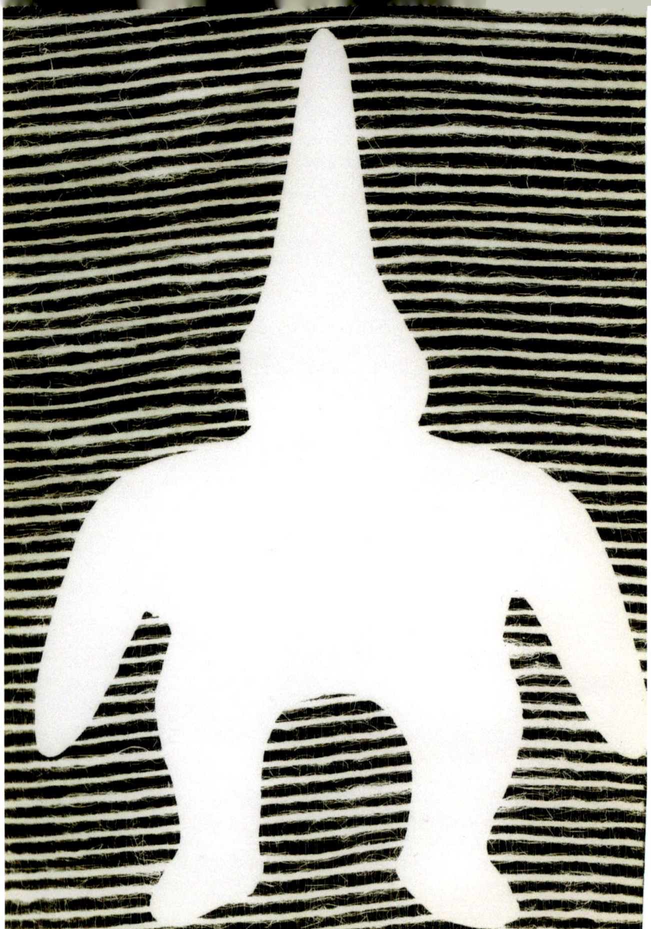

surfaces can be easily made through the addition of extra loops or stitches. Asawa's wire work is related in some senses to weaving at Black Mountain in that it makes use of a textile-like process, but it also stands apart and stems from many other sources, including Josef Albers's guidance as Asawa's advisor and teacher; craft traditions in Mexico where Asawa first learned to make wire baskets; and, most notably, Asawa's own prodigious talent, skill, and vision as an artist. Black Mountain's academic freedom also meant that when Asawa first turned her hand to making objects out of wire, her work was taken seriously and encouraged, and she was not shunted into weaving or basketmaking or discouraged from allowing her curiosity to guide her.

Anni Albers's interest in publicizing the products of the weaving program naturally created a need for photographs of textiles, and Black Mountain's photographers took their depictions of textiles beyond mere documentation. Claude Stoller's photographs of textiles designed and made by Albers, Stoller himself, and other student weavers often emphasize the textiles' transparency, highlighting Albers's interest in using open-weave structures and clear materials like cellophane. Albers herself used the inherent transparency of one of her fabrics, woven of cellophane and jute, in a series of collaborations with Nancy Newhall made in 1948, where the cut-out silhouette of a pre-Columbian Colima clay figurine from the Alberses' collection floats in a sea of fibers. Other photographic works, like a photogram by Ray Johnson (fig. 72) sent as a postcard to the Alberses when they were on sabbatical, do

78. Anni Albers, *Textile sample* (detail), n.d. Linen and cellophane.

79. Nancy Newhall and Anni Albers, *Untitled (photogram)* (detail), n.d. (ca. 1948). Gelatin silver print. 6½ × 3½ in.

not depict textiles but instead evoke Anni Albers's material studies and their use of nonweavable materials to create *textile orders*.

Interdisciplinary education at Black Mountain College happened largely on a personal level as students made connections between diverse topics for themselves, a process that the College's faculty recognized. Josef Albers wrote that "we at Black Mountain are content when our student, for instance, sees a connection between a modern picture and music by Bach, or a relationship between patterns of textiles and music."[14] Naturally, the very personal level of such connections makes it hard to find documentation of weavings' interdisciplinary connections. We do not, for instance, have many examples of how students connected studies in music and weaving, even if for Albers the connection was a natural one.[15] Perhaps the most literal example of weaving and music being linked is found in a copy of *Johannes Brahms: Fifty Selected Songs*, a collection of music manuscripts covered with a fabric woven at Black Mountain College, made by Janet Heling Roberts. Johanna Jalowetz taught bookbinding at Black Mountain for many years, and her students often covered books in heavy or handwoven cloth. Jalowetz's affinity for interesting textures and fabrics was one she shared both with Anni Albers and with her daughter, Trude Guermonprez.

Connections to other disciplines like writing, poetry, and dance are often even more elusive. Elizabeth Schmitt Jennerjahn, who was a prolific dancer and weaver at the College, seemingly never spoke specifically about any connections she found between the two disciplines. In the 1951 Summer Session, Katherine Litz created *The Glyph*, a dance in which she moved within a stretchy black jersey tube, which some have suggested was made by Johanna Jalowetz (fig. 69).[16] Illuminated in a way to enhance contrast, the costume becomes flat, an undulating moving black blot constantly reshaping itself, a word constantly shifting its meaning. Her performance, which is both humorous and poignant, is almost Albersian in the ways in which Litz pushes, stretches, and tests the properties of the tube, allowing it at times to swallow her whole, while at other times fighting with it. Like the best works by the Alberses and their students, dancers of *The Glyph* manipulate material in transcendent ways, allowing a simple fabric to become something more: shapeless and definite, flat and volumetric, a dancing partner, a monster, a collaborator.

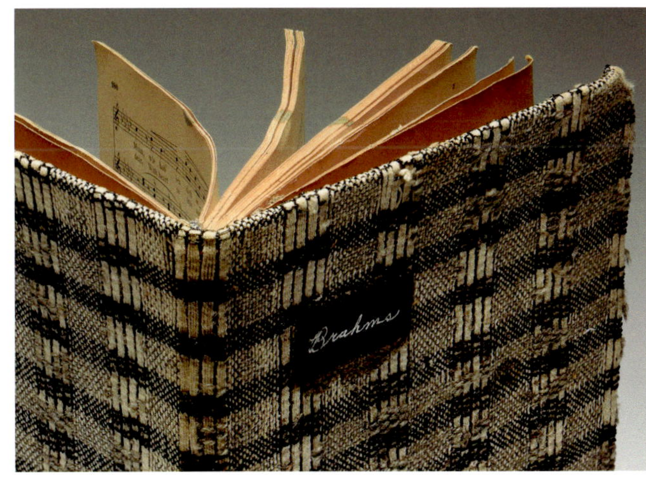

80. Janet Heling Roberts, *Bookbinding:
Johannes Brahms: Fifty Selected Songs*, ca. 1945.
Paper, thread, and handwoven bookcloth.
12 × 10 × 1⅛ in.

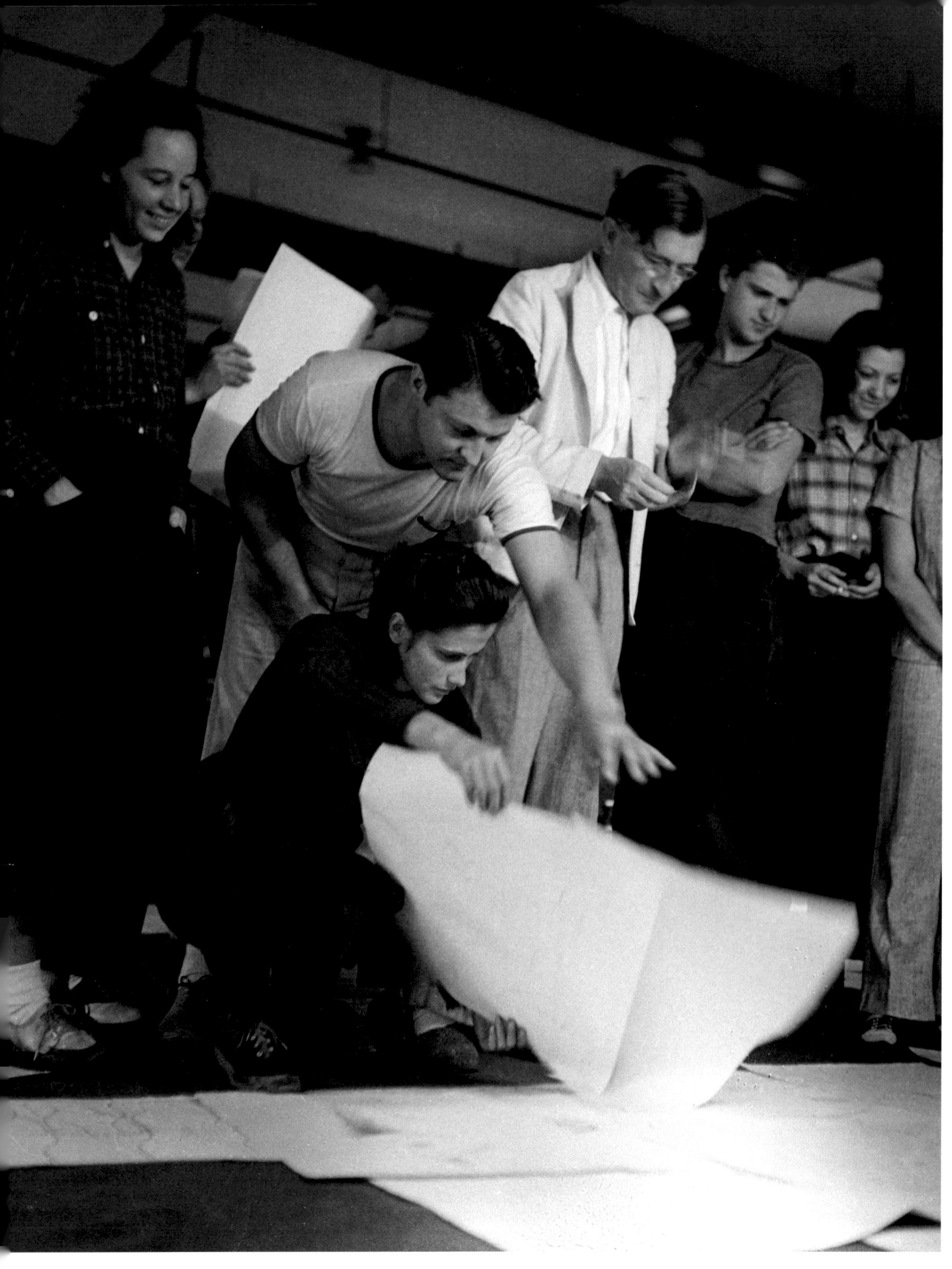

81. Harriett Engelhardt (left) in one of Josef
Albers's classes, 1940. Photograph by Robert
Haas.

THE HARRIETT ENGELHARDT MEMORIAL COLLECTION OF TEXTILES

JULIE J. THOMSON

The Harriett Engelhardt Memorial Collection of Textiles, formed between 1946 and 1949, honored a former Black Mountain College student. With the donations made in Harriett Engelhardt's name after her death in 1945, Anni Albers and Black Mountain College decided to assemble a textile study collection. The collection represented both the work in weaving and art history Engelhardt had "been particularly interested [in] and which she later hoped to pursue."[1]

WHO WAS HARRIETT ENGELHARDT?

Harriett Engelhardt was born in 1919, in Montgomery, Alabama. She enrolled at Hollins College in Virginia, where in her second year she learned of Josef Albers's art and Black Mountain College.[2] She applied for admission in the summer of 1939 and Winifred Leon, who knew Fred and Anne Mangold at Black Mountain, sent a colorful recommendation:

> The stage is set for Harriett to grow up a Southern lady, as Mr. [John] Rice would put it for me. And Harriett thinks it's all swell and dandy, but it sorta smothers her. . . . She's really very anxious to go, and I'd like to see such an honest youngster represent Alabama in Black Mountain College.[3]

Harriett was accepted for the fall of 1939, and she remained at the College until the spring of 1942, with some intervening leaves of absence. At Black Mountain she

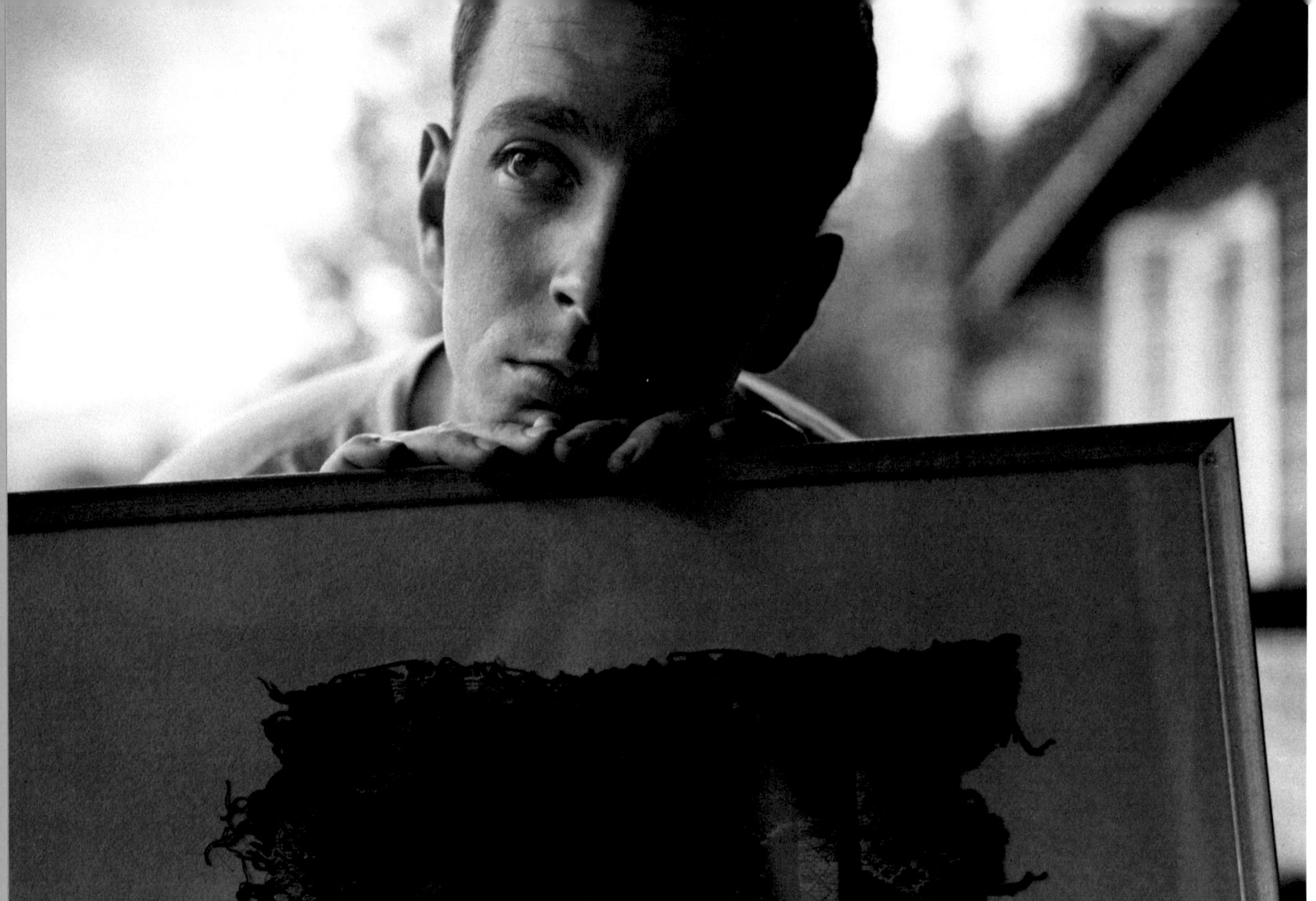

strangely it is one from Guatemala. It is quite beautiful, and I am quite excited about the idea of getting something really worthwhile together."[20]

A few months later, in July 1947, Anni wrote to Harriett's parents to report that she had acquired twenty-three pieces and that "the little collection is gradually turning into something very interesting and quite precious."[21] Josef also wrote to a friend that the Engelhardt Collection was "although still very small, already very valuable and exciting."[22] By the end of their trip Anni had acquired one hundred pieces; most were woven textiles but there were also embroideries and some braided pieces.[23]

Harriett's parents were very pleased with this memorial to their daughter.[24] Anni shared with them: "It is a really great experience for me to gather this material and I am indeed grateful to you for [e]ntrusting me with this task. To judge by the thrill these textiles give me, I feel hopeful that they will be stimulating to others too."[25]

Anni's hope to display the Engelhardt Collection upon her return to the College in 1947 was delayed by U.S. customs. Her plan was to show the textiles "in the Art Room or Weaving Room until the day when Black Mountain College builds its own museum."[26] Finally, with the help of a customs broker, Anni's acquisitions were released to the College in March 1948.[27] A few months later, in May 1948, the first exhibition of the Engelhardt Collection opened at the College.[28] While Anni could have organized this exhibition, she gave the opportunity to two of her weaving students, Willie Joseph and Nancy Dunn. The College's *Bulletin* praised their curatorial

83. Donald Droll with a textile from the *Harriett Engelhardt Collection*, ca. 1948–49. Photograph by Hazel Larsen Archer.

84. Embroidered cloth, 1000–1300, Central Andes, Peru, North Coast, Chimú, Wool, dyed and embroidered. 10 ¼ × 9 ⁷⁄₁₆ in.

work: "The quietness which has been achieved in the placement of these textiles brought out each piece, despite the great variety."[29] The *BMC Bulletin* concluded: "We admire these textiles for their craftsmanship and artistic values, but what is even more important is the stimulation they will give to some, opening new ways in the use of materials and tools."[30] The popularity of this exhibition led to its being extended through the end of the summer.[31]

The Engelhardt Collection consisted of ninety-two objects. The majority were textiles: sixty from Mexico, fourteen from Peru, and assorted other textiles from Italy, Bolivia, Guatemala, the Pacific Islands, Egypt, and Africa. A few were ancient.[32] Most were practical textiles made in the last one hundred years: belts, clothing, bags, hats, mats, blankets, tortilla cloths. Anni also purchased some weaving tools for the collection, including a backstrap loom and a spindle, both from Mexico.[33]

TEACHING WITH AND STUDYING THE HARRIETT ENGELHARDT COLLECTION

To understand how the Engelhardt Collection functioned as a teaching and study collection at Black Mountain College, we can look at interviews, notes, and writing from faculty and students. Textiles from Peru were particularly important to Anni, and she would later dedicate her 1965 book, *On Weaving*, "to my great teachers, the weavers of ancient Peru."[34] In one chapter Anni wrote: "It was the loom of ancient Peru, for instance, on which the great masterworks of the textile art were woven. . . . [T]he fabrics made on this loom stand as a testimonial to heights of inventiveness in weaving never reached again anywhere at any time."[35] In ancient Peruvian (Andean) textiles Albers found both inspiration and evidence for her theories about weaving and the role of the weaver in society as both an artist and textile designer.[36]

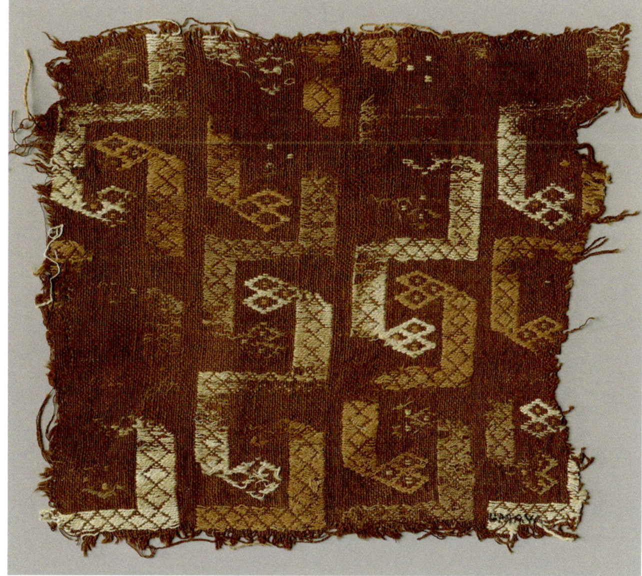

Once the Engelhardt Collection arrived Albers used it as a teaching tool. Trude Guermonprez recalled that the collection "came very much alive through her, and then through her trips to Mexico and the contemporary versions of South American weaving."[37]

In the spring of 1949 Guermonprez offered a Weaving Tutorial in the Study of Peruvian Techniques, which was attended by Andy Oates, Barbara Stone Rice, and Donald Droll.[38] A poignant photograph of Droll with an embroidered cloth from Peru suggests a feeling of personal connection to the collection (figs. 83 and 84). These feelings extended to Hazel Larsen Archer, who made this photograph, and who later became one of the caretakers of the collection.

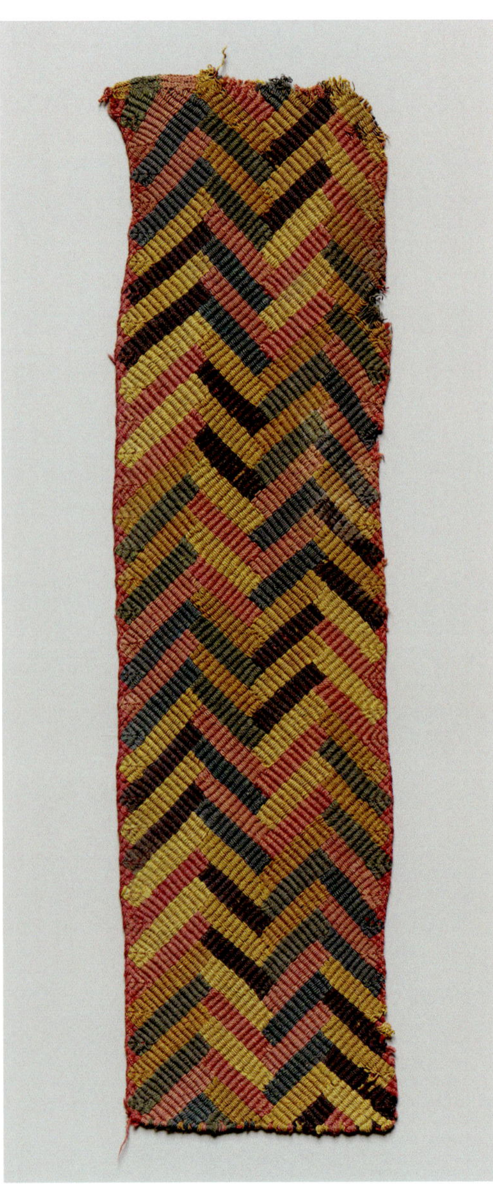

Later Guermonprez recalled how she was "indebted to Anni because she opened up the whole world of pre-Columbian textiles to me."[39] After her time at Black Mountain ancient Andean textiles became part of Guermonprez's teaching. At Pond Farm, an artists' colony, she offered a tutorial on Peruvian techniques by special arrangement.[40] When she returned to Black Mountain in 1952, she discussed Peruvian textiles as "superb in design" and envied their position within Andean society where their weaving was "part of their life."[41]

Lore Kadden Lindenfeld's weaving notebook thoroughly illustrates her interaction with the Engelhardt Collection. In careful, annotated drawings, Lindenfeld describes fourteen textiles, including clothing (serapes, scarves, and a Huipil) and accessories (a bag and blanket).[42] Looking closely at one page of her notes (fig. 87) Lindenfeld's drawings can be matched to specific textiles in the Engelhardt Collection, including this nineteenth-century serape made in Querétaro, Mexico (fig. 88). Her handwritten notes include analyses of patterns, colors, construction, and techniques, with particular attention to the finishing details for scarves and tassels. As part of her graduation exam Lindenfeld wrote about ancient Peruvian textiles: "We are enchanted by the choice of color, the techniques employed, they show an exceptional understanding for the pliability of yarns and a deep understanding for the material."[43] Lindenfeld's notes clearly convey that she shared Anni's interest in these textiles and that she was indeed stimulated by her close study of them.

85. Textile fragment, A.D. 500–650, Central Andes, Peru, possibly Nazca, Cotton. 13 × 3 9/16 in.

86. Elizabeth Jennerjahn, *Untitled (Woven Peruvian Tapestry)*, n.d. Wool, cotton, and linen. 21¼ × 7½ in.

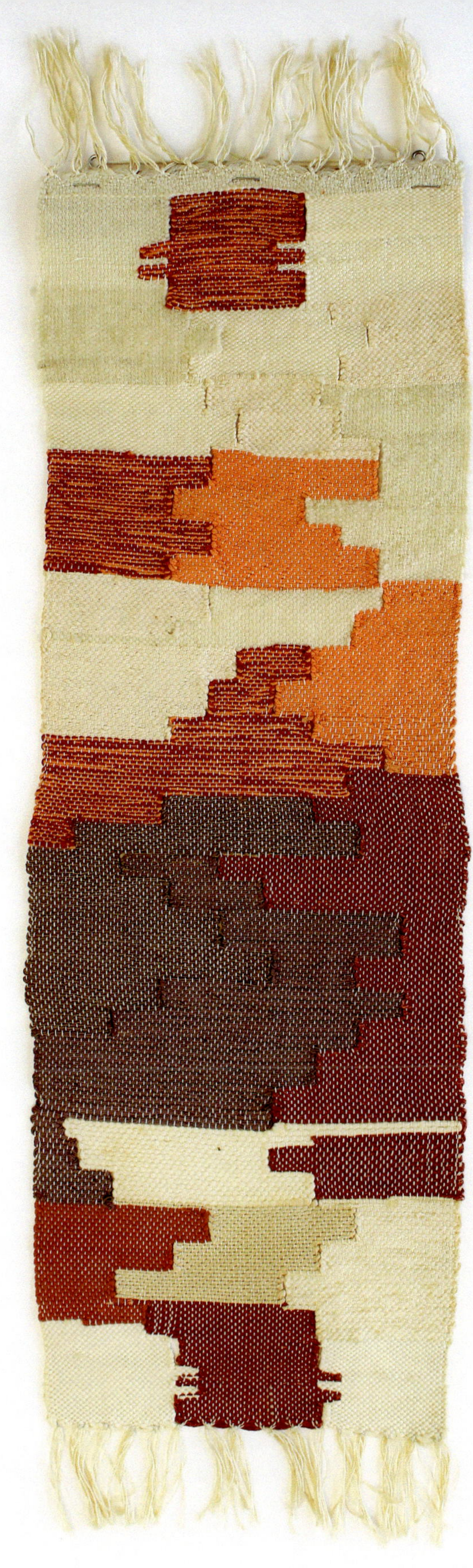

SPECIALIZATION AND GENERALIZATION, 1940–1947

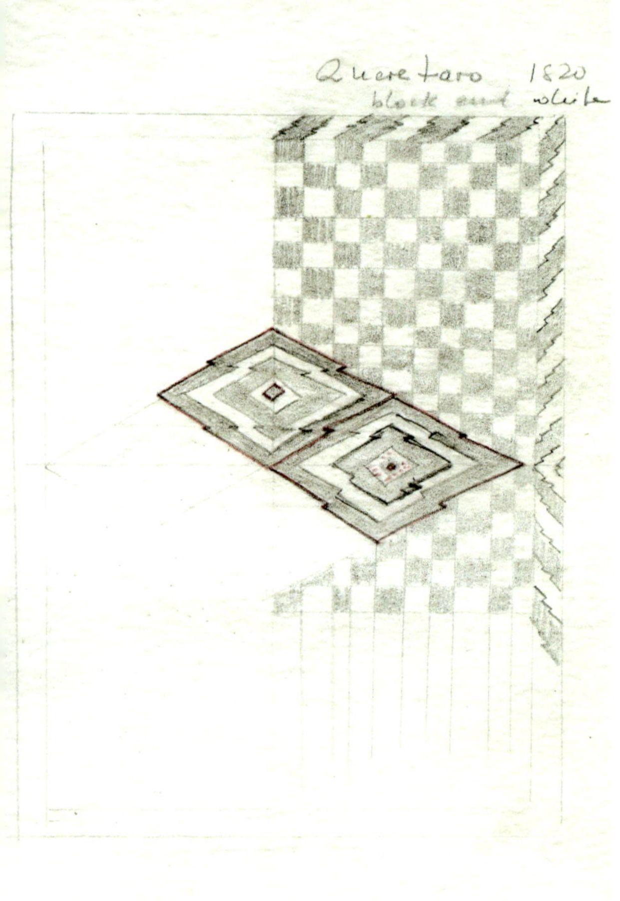

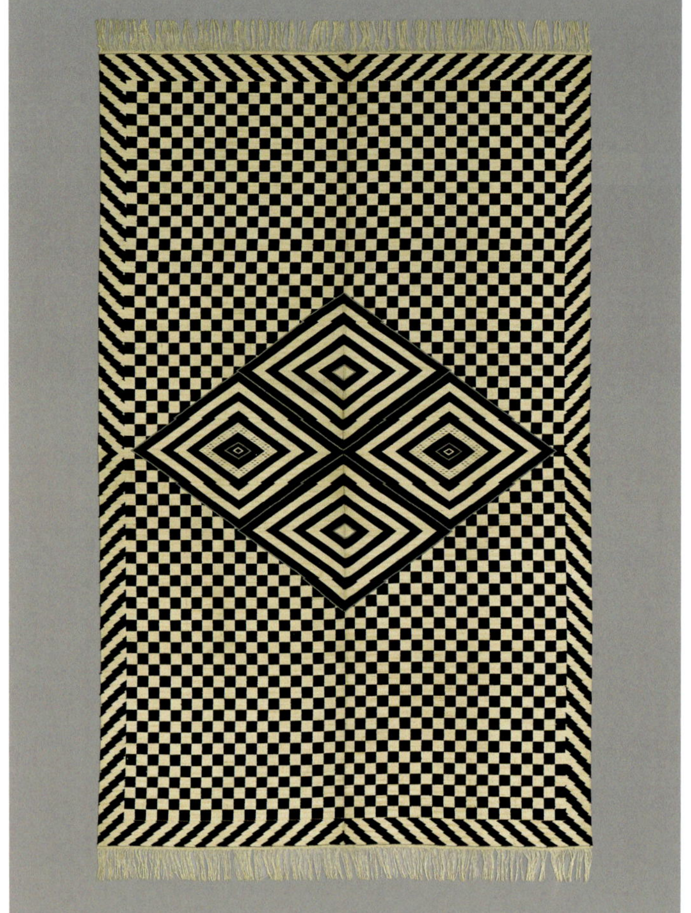

The Engelhardt Collection had a direct impact on student learning in the practice of weaving. The closest connection is Elizabeth Jennerjahn's *Untitled (Woven Peruvian Tapestry)* (fig. 86). Jennerjahn studied weaving and textile design with both Anni and Trude after the Engelhardt Collection arrived at the College. The slit-tapestry technique was used by ancient Andean weavers in the Later Intermediate period and revived by weavers at the Bauhaus.[44] Jennerjahn's repeated use of this technique results in clear, vertical lines between her changes in colors.

While Ruth Asawa did not study weaving at BMC she undoubtedly saw the Engelhardt Collection exhibition and talked about it with her friends.[45] The similarities between an ancient Nazca Peruvian textile (fig. 85) and her *Untitled* painting (fig. 89) are striking.[46] Asawa's repeating chevrons in the upper part of this painting, as well as the varied ways the colors join and separate in the lower part, resemble details in the fragment and suggest her close examination of it.

Anni's work on the Engelhardt Collection could have ceased when she resigned from Black Mountain College in February 1949. However, after leaving the College she felt obligated to continue building and caring for it and tried to establish it as a separate trust. Albers planned to serve as one of the collection's trustees along with former weaving student Alex Reed.[47] Since not all the donated funds had been spent, she continued acquiring textiles. However, in December 1949 the College asked her to stop, saying they needed to save funds for the collection's future care.[48]

87. Drawing of Querétaro Serape in Lore Kadden-Lindenfeld's notes from Anni Albers's weaving course at Black Mountain College (detail), ca. 1946–48.

88. Serape, 19th–20th century, Mexico, Querétaro. Woven cotton, silk, and wool. 81 × 50 in.

Albers didn't inquire again about the collection until 1954 when she wrote to Charles Olson to check on it. Olson replied that the collection was intact, and that it had been cared for by Hazel Larsen Archer, Willie Joseph, Andy Oates, and Herb Roco. Olson assured Anni that Black Mountain wanted to keep the Engelhardt Collection and added that if anything happened to the College, they would consult with her about its placement.[49]

A few months later Olson wrote to Albers to let her know of the appointment of Tony Landreau as Weaver at Black Mountain College.[50] In addition to teaching weaving, Landreau inventoried the Engelhardt Collection and identified the textiles' historical and material details: place of origin, date, materials, and sizes. His inventory lists ninety-seven objects and includes this assessment:

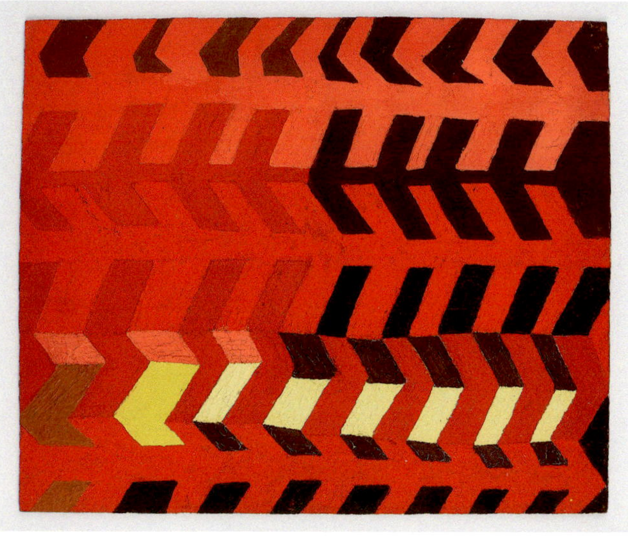

> This collection is primarily of study value, in so far as it is demonstrative of the techniques and designs of Peruvian and Mexican weavers. It is limited, in the ancient Peruvian section[,] to fragments which are good examples of their kinds, but not whole pieces. The antique and modern Mexican section[s] are the most complete. Some pieces from other peoples are included, but it should be noted that the textiles in this collection are closely allied in their approach to the art of weaving.[51]

Landreau's inventory statements assess the Engelhardt Collection with consideration for how it would be viewed outside the College and by nonweavers.

When Black Mountain College officially closed in 1957, Anni arranged the transfer of the Engelhardt Collection to Yale University, where Josef Albers was chair of the Department of Design. In October 1958 the Yale University Art Gallery announced the acquisition as a gift from Mrs. Paul Moore, a major benefactor of the museum.[52] Although objects from the Engelhardt Collection have rarely been exhibited, the art gallery continues to safeguard the collection and make it available to researchers, both through in-person visits and their online collections database. Through the Harriett Engelhardt Memorial Collection of Textiles Anni's efforts to "save the lasting" continue today, both in preserving the work of ancient Andean weavers and perpetuating the memory of Harriett Engelhardt.

89. Ruth Asawa, *Untitled* (BMC.95, In and Out), ca. 1948–49. Oil and water-based paint on Masonite. 11⅞ × 14¾ in.

SPECIALIZATION AND GENERALIZATION, 1940–1947

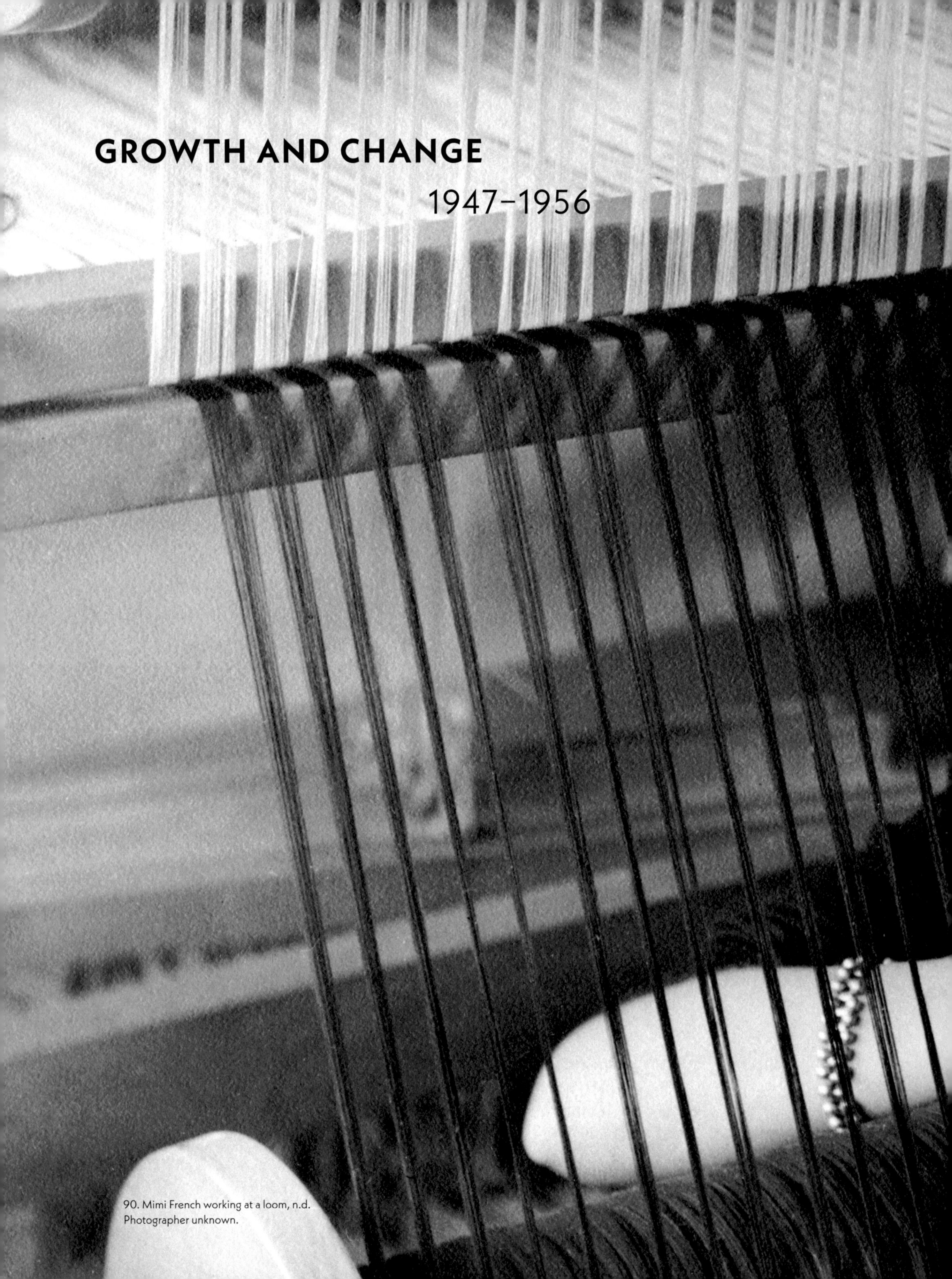

90. Mimi French working at a loom, n.d.
Photographer unknown.

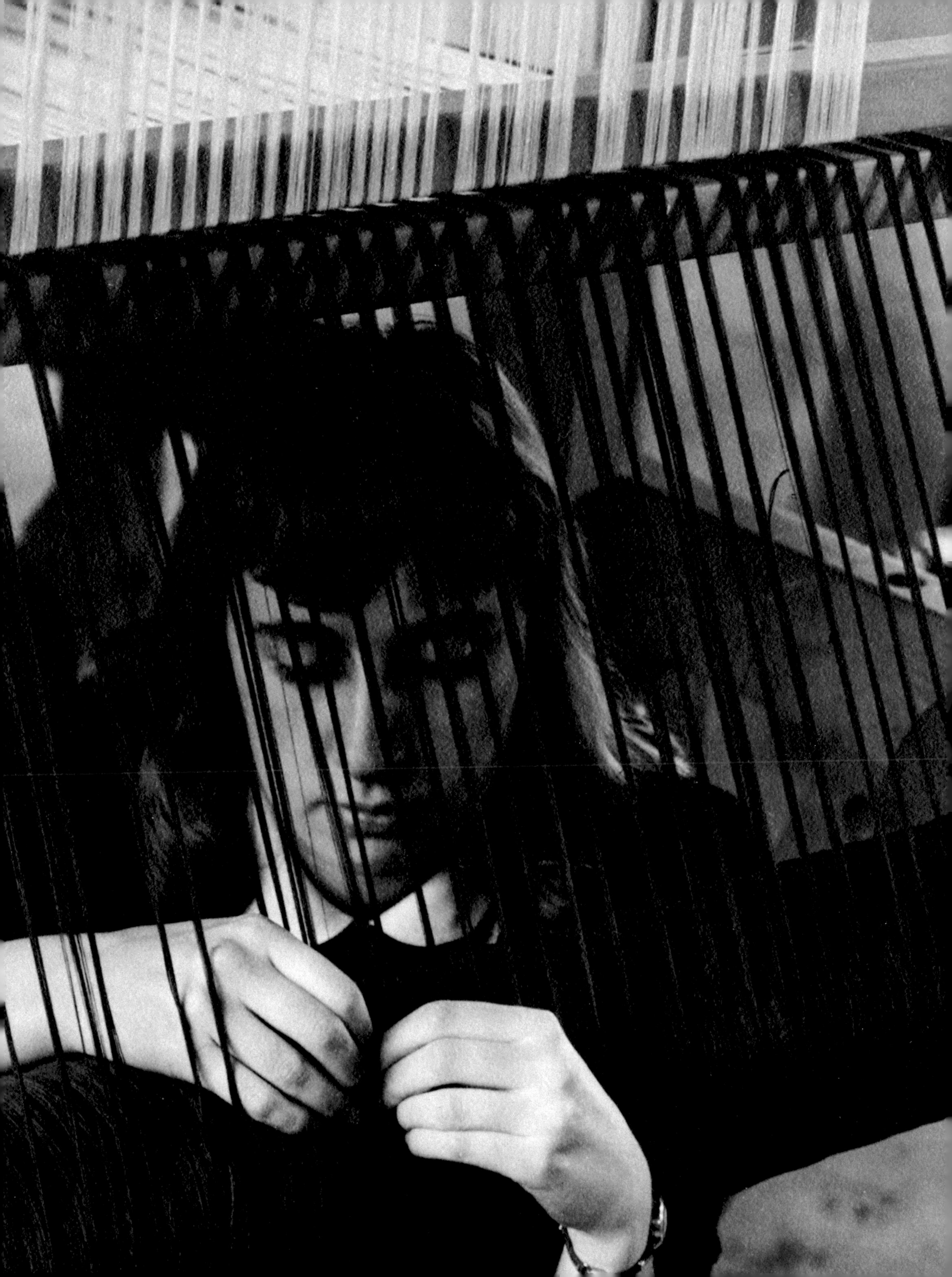

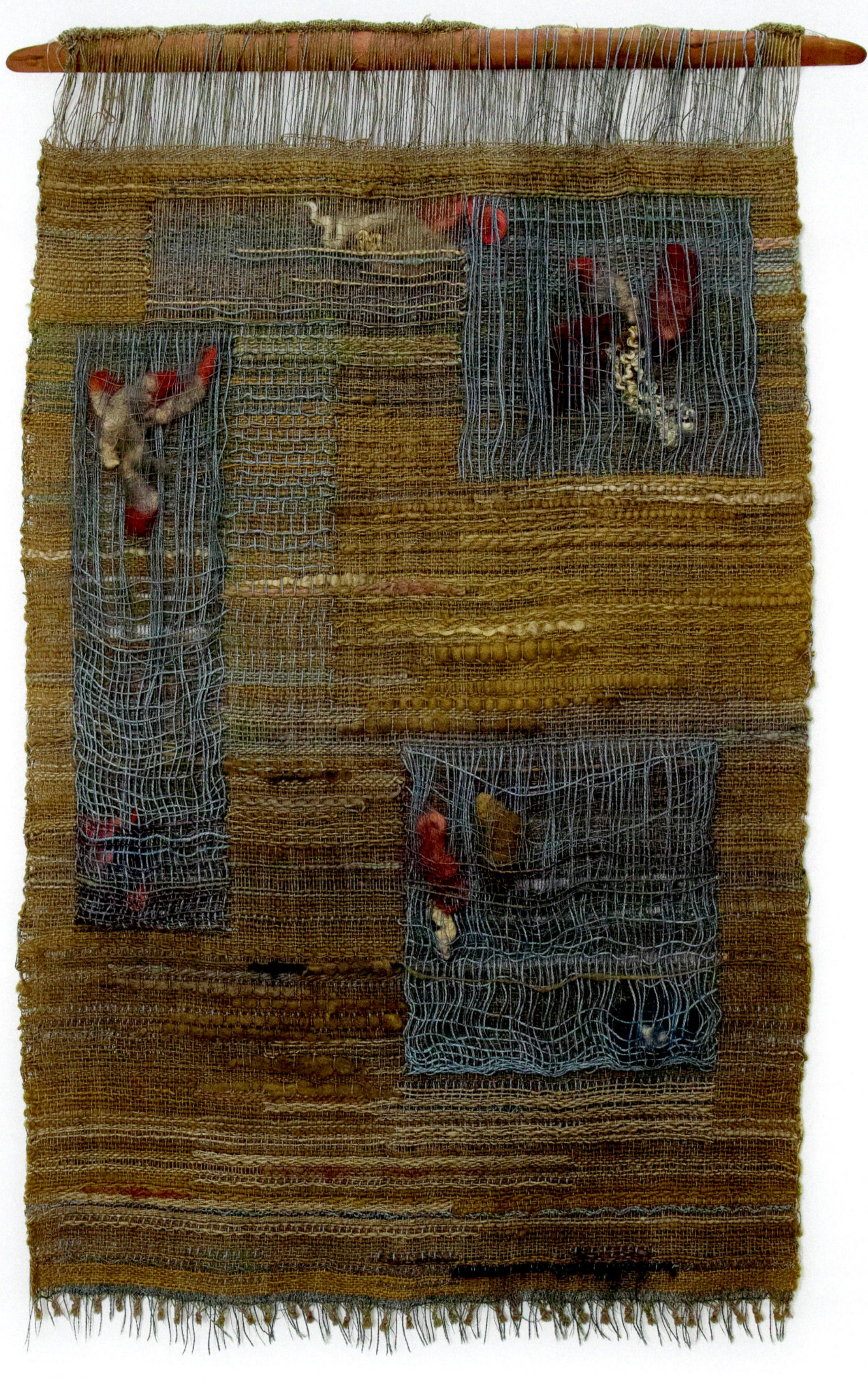

91. Trude Guermonprez, *Hummingbird Cages*,
ca. 1963. Linen and silk. 41 × 26 in.

TRUDE GUERMONPREZ
TEACHING AND
TEXTILE GRAPHICS

JULIE J. THOMSON

The Weaving and Textile Design program at Black Mountain College experienced its biggest change when Anni Albers went on sabbatical from the fall of 1946 to early 1948. Two experienced weavers—Franziska Mayer and Trude Guermonprez—both new to the College, taught weaving classes in Albers's absence. Both Franziska and Trude had previous teaching experience, but the pedagogical freedom of Black Mountain College gave them the opportunity to choose what and how they taught. Prior to Albers's departure, Franziska, who as a teacher felt "more competent in draft writing and technical procedures than in designing," assisted Albers teaching weaving during the 1946 Summer Session and took Theory of Weaving as well as Basic Design with Josef Albers.[1] After Trude's arrival, she and Franziska were able to coordinate their co-teaching to suit each of their strengths.

This period was also one of personal growth for Anni, Franziska, and Trude. Anni had the first solo exhibition for a textile artist at the Museum of Modern Art and resigned from BMC after sixteen years of teaching.Franziska reunited with family members in the United States and then with her two brothers in Peru. Trude rejoined her mother and sister after years of being apart, then moved to California, remarried, and founded two textile programs there. All three would continue to teach after leaving Black Mountain. Anni taught privately in Connecticut. Franziska established a weaving workshop in Peru. Trude would teach at Pond Farm, the California School of Fine Arts, and the California College of Arts and Crafts. Only Trude would return to Black Mountain College, when she delivered a lecture titled "Design" during the 1952 Pottery Seminar.

Trude Guermonprez arrived at Black Mountain College as an experienced textile designer and production weaver (fig. 92).[2] From 1931 to 1933 she studied weaving and textile design with *Bauhausler* Benita Koch-Otte at the School of Fine and Applied Arts in Halle, Germany.[3] Additional professional training came through the Textile

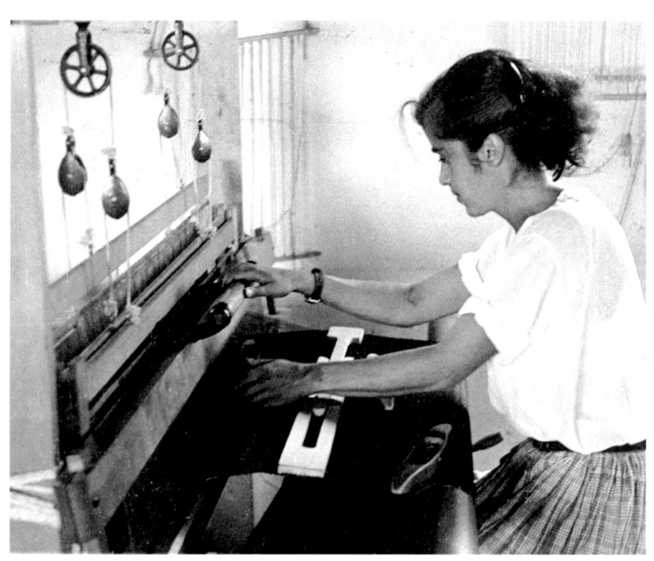

Engineering School in Berlin and an apprenticeship in a Czechoslovakian cotton mill.[4] Following these experiences she was hired as a textile designer at Het Paapje, a Dutch handweaving studio, where for six years she designed rugs, upholstery, and custom textiles, eventually becoming head of design.[5] She also did freelance design work for De Ploeg, a Dutch cooperative that produced household textiles, including curtains and upholstery.[6] Freelance design work was something Trude did throughout her career. Her studies in weaving were furthered with funding she received to travel to Finland to study Scandinavian weaving techniques (a scholarship in 1936) and to Sweden to study weaving institutions there (a fellowship in 1946).[7] Trude's weaving and teaching were informed by Bauhaus approaches to design, color, and materials; her experience designing for industry; and her own research. This essay examines the ways Black Mountain College allowed Guermonprez to develop a more personal textile expression and traces the development of her weaving and textile design pedagogy.

Trude's Bauhaus connections carried through to her personal life when she married Paul Guermonprez in 1939. Paul had studied briefly at the Bauhaus in Berlin—taking the Preliminary course and studying photography—before the Nazis forced the school to close. In the Netherlands Paul taught art at Bauhaus-inspired schools: photography at Amsterdam's Nieuwe Kunstschool and advertising design at the Hague's Koninklijke Academie van Beeldende Kunsten. From 1934 to 1942 Paul also owned and operated his own advertising agency, Co-op 2, in Amsterdam, where Trude assisted while she took a break from her textile design career.[8] Partners in design and in life, Trude and Paul shared a mutual commitment to modernism and living an artful life.

Two tragedies changed the direction of Trude's life and career. Her marriage to Paul, who had joined the Dutch Resistance during World War II, ended with his execution by the Nazis in 1944. While they both understood the risks he was taking, Trude was devasted by his death and wrote to her parents: "It shall be difficult to refind the happiness of life without Paul."[9] Then in 1946 her father, Heinrich Jalowetz—beloved professor of music at Black Mountain—died suddenly from a heart attack. With her mother, Johanna Jalowetz, still at BMC and her younger sister, Lisa Jalowetz Aronson, in New York, Trude traveled to the United States on a vistor's visa to see them, made possible through a one-year appointment at BMC.

TEACHING AT BLACK MOUNTAIN COLLEGE

In February 1947, at the age of thirty-six, Trude started as a visiting consultant in Weaving at Black Mountain College.[10] For the first semester she co-taught weaving and textile design with Franziska Mayer. This was not Trude's first experience teaching. In the Netherlands she taught for two years (1944–46) in an adult education program.[11]

Black Mountain, however, gave Trude the pedagogical freedom and the opportunity to discover which aspects of teaching weaving and textile design interested her most.

A 1947 exhibit in the dining hall shared Trude's vision for textiles with the BMC community.[12] Shown with a "Textiles" title card, this exhibition presented the many forms and functions of woven textiles illustrated by numerous examples. Entering the exhibit viewers saw a finished, banded textile on the left panel and a backstrap loom mounted on the panel to the right (fig. 93). The display of the loom emphasizes the warp, the basis for all weaving.

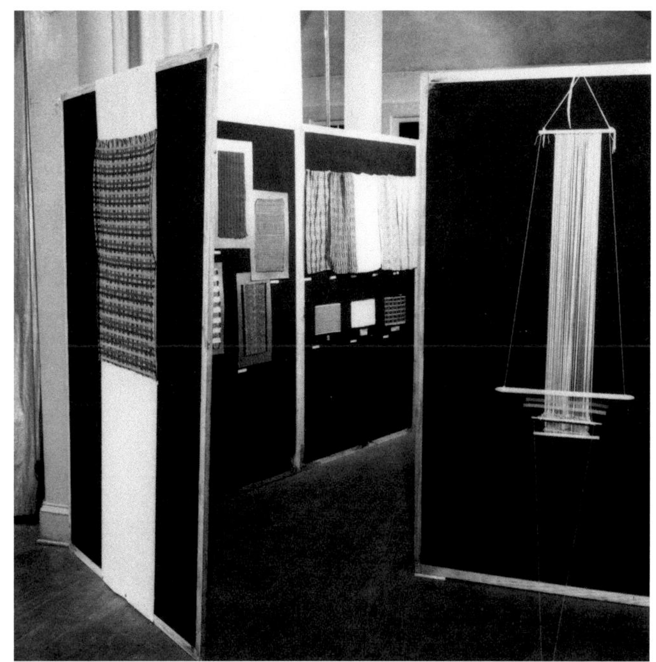

This pairing offers an invitation to contemplate how textiles are designed and made.

The interior exhibit panels show the fundamentals of textile design: how the weaver's choice of weaves and thread result in different effects, and how the appearance of a textile varies with function and length, seen in the sets of short and long curtains. Another photograph shows an installation of practical textiles: a pillow, a tunic, books covered with handwoven cloth, and behind the installation a larger handwoven sample covered the wall (fig. 94). Even in black and white, the pictured fabrics clearly have a variety of textures, colors, patterns, and functions and are compelling examples of weaving's versatility. Shown in the dining hall, a building every person at Black Mountain College visited multiple times a day, the exhibition is a great example of how Trude's presence at the College helped to increase *weaving literacy* among the community.

Like Anni, and following her own Bauhaus-influenced education, Trude did not believe weaving should be taught by following preexisting draft notation patterns from books.[13] Notes from the 1947 Summer Session, when Trude and Franziska split teaching responsibilities, indicate that for one hour each week Trude taught design, and for another hour Franziska taught theory. Trude's topics included "material in relation to design, what is a textile?, color and texture, stripes, draft reading, and planning for special purpose." Franziska covered the "four basic raw materials and their manufacture into thread, the drafts of the four basic weaves and some derivatives." Additional

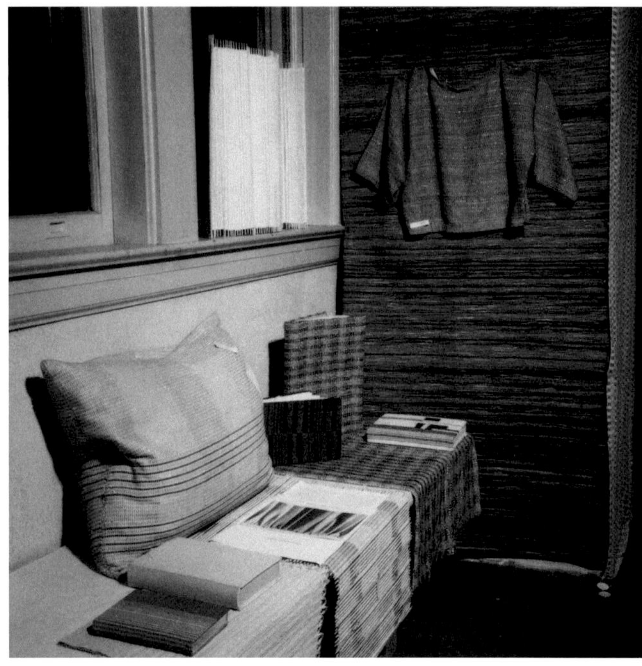

notes suggest that if time permitted, card weaving and vegetable dyeing would also be taught, and that Trude would offer tutorials on the types of looms as well as design for industrial textiles.[14] Franziska's BMC appointment ended following the 1947 Summer Session and soon after she moved to Huancayo, Peru, where her two brothers lived.[15]

When Anni Albers returned to BMC in February 1948 she taught Textile Design and Trude taught Textile Construction. Trude described Anni's teaching as Socratic, letting "the student make the deductions that she wanted them to know about," which she often did through the design problems that she gave out as assignments.[16] Trude believed that her teaching differed from Anni's in the way she "emphasized more freedom on the basis of the structural and technical knowledge into a more free-use of the loom, the thread, and so forth."[17]

Like Anni, by helping her students understand the construction of various weaves, showing them possibilities for designing the warp, and developing their understanding of how looms worked, Trude allowed her students to understand the choices open to them to create their own designs. Describing her teaching at BMC, she later explained:

"I was able to make the structural aspect of weaving very clear and out of that, draw the design aspects."[18]

BMC student Lore Kadden Lindenfeld recalled that Trude was "simply extraordinary as a teacher. She had a special gift of making the process of weaving logical. [She] would explain weave constructions in such a way that they became totally clear and could be taken into other directions. I learned from her how to think independently."[19] Trude and Lore became close friends, due in part to Lore's age and their shared European backgrounds (Lindenfeld was older than most of her peers and had been born in Wuppertal, Germany).

Trude's logic and clarity is evident in this poetic passage found in one of her notebooks:

> Fiber makes thread
> Thread are lines
> Weave with lines
> Up and down
> Back and forth
> Over and under
> In and out
> Weaving makes materials
> Materials are flat areas
> Flat areas make forms[20]

MAKING ART AT BLACK MOUNTAIN COLLEGE: TEXTILE GRAPHICS

Freed from the stipulations of her prior position as an industrial textile designer, at Black Mountain College Trude was able to experiment with her weaving in a more personal way. This space and time allowed her to create *Leaf Study* in 1948, a work she would later call her first "textile graphic" (fig. 96).[21] A close examination of this tapestry illuminates Trude's design process.

The basis for this pictorial tapestry came from a leaf study—a free study in Josef Albers's Color class—made by Nicholas Muzenic, a BMC student.[22] Trude made a sketch based on Muzenic's collaged leaf study (fig. 97). Her drawing emphasizes the graphic qualities of the tuliptree leaves he used, while also further abstracting them into bold shapes. Photographs show Trude at the loom working on *Leaf Study*, with a similar, but different, reference drawing hanging at eye level (fig. 95). These sketches suggest that Trude's process was iterative; she used different stages of drawing during her initial planning. This process of gradual transformation from drawing to weaving reflects her belief that "in weaving you *must* plan ahead and then take time in executing your work. The preparatory steps are an organic aspect of the weaving."[23]

Trude painted parts of the leaf study onto the jute warp before weaving this tapestry with linen threads, a combination of painting and tapestry weaving that she thought she had done for "probably the first time [at BMC]."[24] Calling *Leaf Study* a *textile graphic* allowed her to distinguish it from traditional tapestry weaving. Writing in 1974 she explained:

> At that time pictorial weaving had been done mostly in the Gobelin technique, where the weft thread carried the color and formed the image. Often painters were the designers of those tapestries, and trained weavers executed them. My thought then was this: Painters used woven canvas as the base for their brushwork; when then should not I, as a weaver, enter the process at an earlier phase. I would paint on the warp and see how subsequently the perpendicular interlacing of the weft would alter color and texture."[25]

Trude's use of black paint to transfer her drawing onto this warp gives the warp an active role in the textile's design, beyond its typical structural role. While edges of the leaves are still visible, the central section, outlined in black, has faded, making the central figure of the graphic less clear than it once was.[26] While Trude later attributed

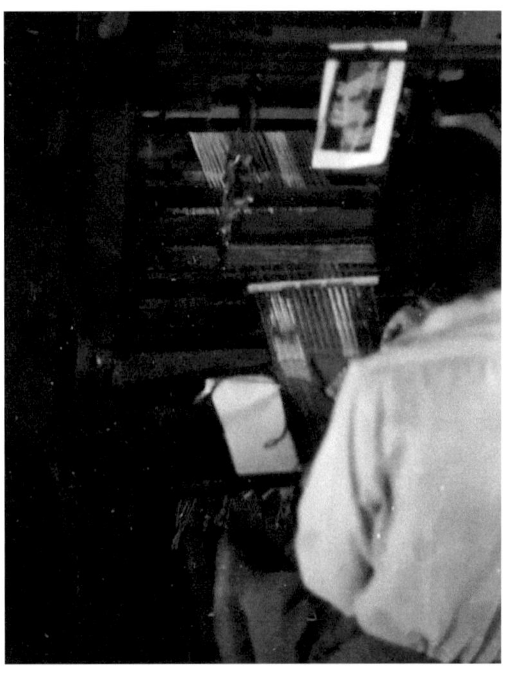

her use of Muzenic's collage for the figure for her textile graphic, as a result of being "still in the grip of tradition," eventually she would apply the same process to images of her own.[27] Many of her subsequent textile graphics would involve her parallel interest in photography in her process, using painted warps and other techniques to translate photographic pictures into woven ones.[28]

Both Trude and Anni were familiar with European tapestry traditions, but as modern weavers they each created new terms for describing the innovative woven pictorial work they were doing.[29] Anni—who used the phrase *pictorial weaving*—explored structural approaches based in part on her close study of ancient textiles. Trude's *textile graphics* use a structural approach to weaving to depict a range of subjects including nature (leaves, seasons, birds, mountains, and clouds), portraits and self-portraits, and text. While both Anni and Trude focused on the structural aspects of weaving in their own work, Trude saw her weaving as "concerned with concept and content more than Anni's."[30] In *Leaf Study* and *Hummingbird Cages* she paired a distinct weaving technique with different pictorial subjects from nature.

96. Trude Guermonprez, *Leaf Study* 1948.
Natural linen and jute. 20 × 8¼ in.   122

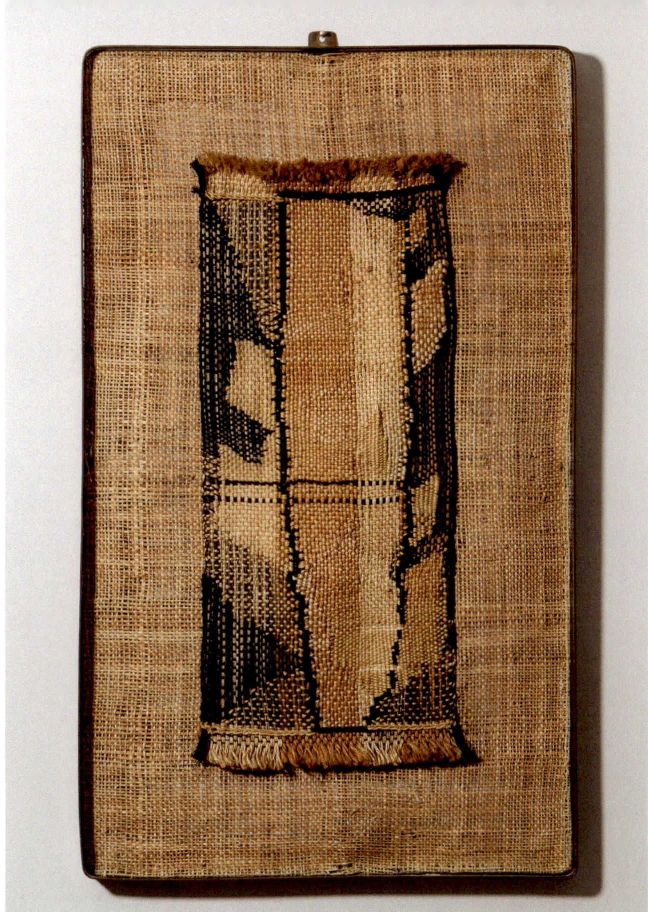

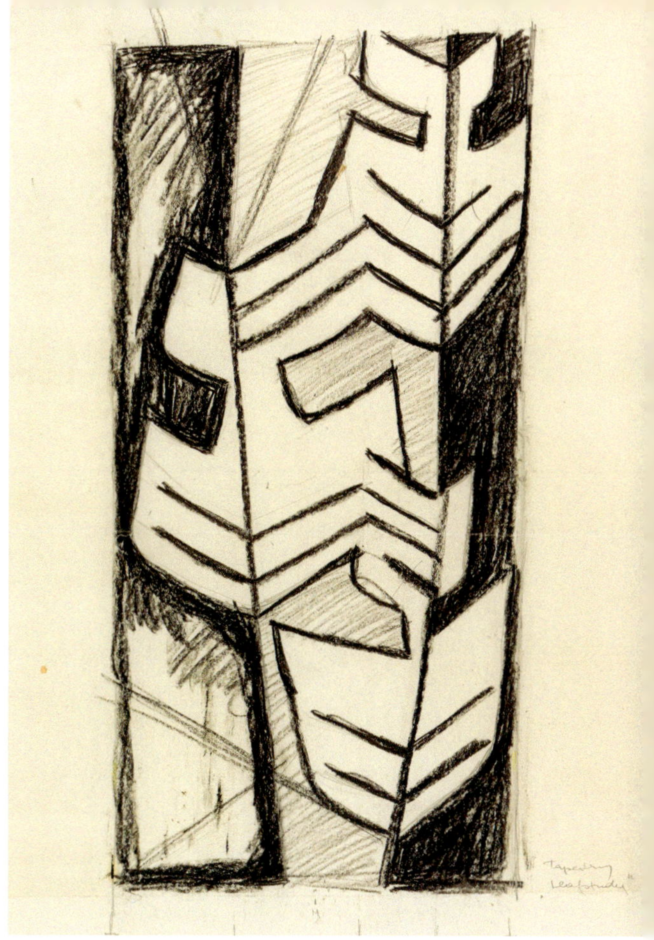

Trude's commitment to experimentation and the depiction of natural subjects is evident in her 1963 wall hanging *Hummingbird Cages* (fig. 91). Seemingly inspired by her own encounters with hummingbirds (in her yard and the San Diego Zoo), she formed these fast, small, wild birds with unspun wool. Making them blurry and indistinct suggests they are in motion, while her use of white and magenta resembles the coloring of California's Anna's hummingbird.[31] The cages that cover the hummingbirds are made from thin, floating warp and weft threads. The varying thicknesses of thread she used results in a riveting variety of textures throughout the rest of this wall hanging. Trude's concept and content of caged hummingbirds presents us with the perplexing question: How did these wild birds become caged?

A year after Trude made *Hummingbird Cages* she wove *Space Hanging* (fig. 102). Comparing these textiles shows the impressive range of her imaginative ability and her continual striving to expand weaving's possibilities. Woven on the loom *Space Hanging* can be thought of as an X, where the thread goes from the upper left to the bottom right to form one diagonal, and the thread goes from the bottom left to the upper right to form the other diagonal. On the loom each of these layers is flat, but because of the double-weave structure, they are joined at the center and can be opened up and turned ninety degrees. This warp effect parallels Kay Sekimachi's (a later student of Trude's) structural innovation in *Cross Warp* where she wove two

97. Trude Guermonprez, *Design for Leaf Study*, 1948. Black crayon and graphite on paper. 22 1/16 × 17 in.

GROWTH AND CHANGE, 1947–1956

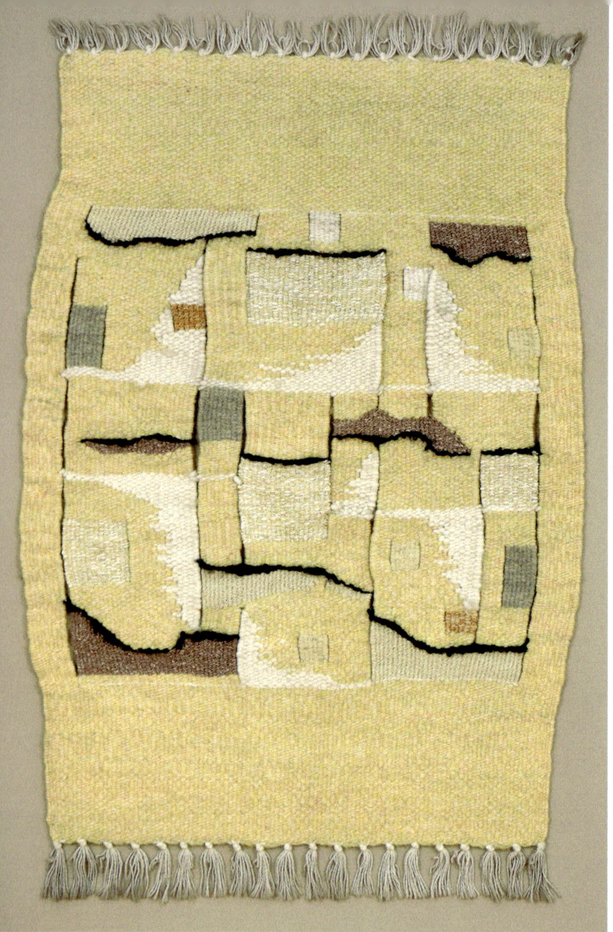

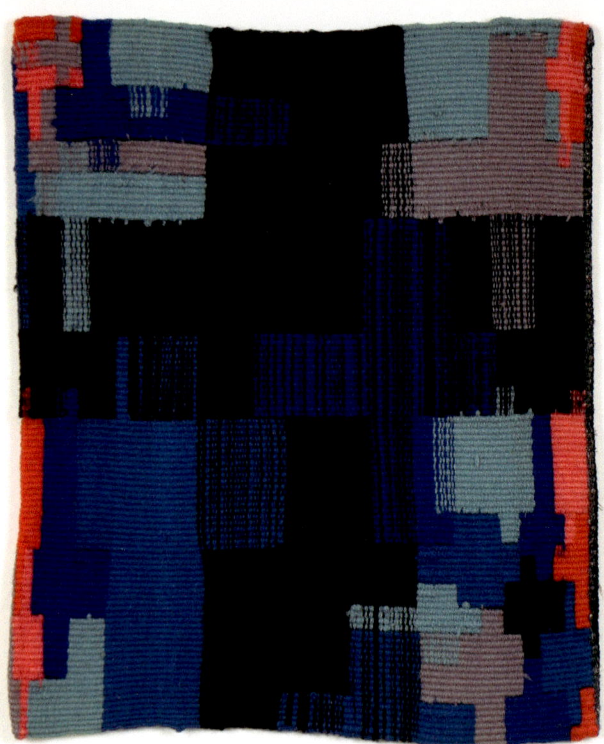

tubes on top of each other (fig. 134). In these works Trude and Sekimachi transform weaving from a two-dimensional medium into a three-dimensional one, with space and movement being integral parts of the work.

While some of Anni's students had explored tapestry before Trude's arrival, the known wall hangings by students who studied with both Anni and Trude tend to be smaller and more freely composed. Elizabeth Jennerjahn made *Cross* in 1949 with a dominant black cross filling the center of the composition (fig. 99). A closer look reveals a repetition of multiple, smaller cross forms in other colors, as well as shapes that don't quite coalesce into crosses. Following the European tapestry tradition, Jennerjahn's wool weft threads in orange, salmon, gray, three shades of blue, and black completely cover the warp threads. As the central large black cross becomes subsumed by overlapping crosses, Jennerjahn's close interleaving of different colors evokes an illusion of transparency, an exercise that she and other BMC students did in the Color Course using paper, which she achieved here with thread.[32] A sense of the energy of working across the warp both horizontally and building up vertically is palpable to viewers.

When we compare *Cross* to Jennerjahn's *Woven Tapestry* we see her use of a very different slit tapestry technique (fig. 86). A handwritten note by Jennerjahn suggests she was inspired by ancient Peruvian weavers. This slit tapestry technique was also used by Eini Sihvonen in her later tapestry titled *Pale Yellow* (fig. 98).[33]

98. Eine Sihvonen, *Pale Yellow*, n.d. Cotton, wool, and metallic thread. 28½ × 19 in.

99. Elizabeth Schmitt Jennerjahn, *Cross*, 1949. Wool. 12½ × 10 in.

CHANGES AT BLACK MOUNTAIN COLLEGE

In February 1949, at the beginning of the spring semester, Anni and Josef Albers, Trude Guermonprez, Ted Dreier, and Charlotte Schlesinger resigned from Black Mountain College.[34] This choice was especially precarious for Trude, since unlike the Alberses, she was not a U.S. citizen. Trude later recalled that one of the main reasons the Alberses felt the need to resign was a difference of opinion between faculty members about how to restructure the College.[35]

Trude's and Anni's teaching during their final semester seems more individualized to the students in their classes. The course cards show them teaching Textile Construction to advanced students Barbara Stone (Rice) and Jennerjahn and beginning students Donald Alter, Donald Droll, and Robert Rauschenberg. Trude remembered Rauschenberg coming up with an imaginative solution to a design challenge, possibly inspired by the work of Irene Schawinsky, "to design garments where you would not cut out the fabric, only retain it in its rectangular shape."[36] While Rauschenberg's project is not documented, she remembered that he used white muslin to make "all kinds of versions of rectangular pieces."[37]

Another garment made by Rauschenberg around this time is preserved in photographs made by Trude (fig. 100). Described as a Mardi Gras costume for his sister, in this picture BMC student Inga Lauterstein models the costume, while Rauschenberg drapes the materials around her. Trude recalled Rauschenberg made a "paper mache horse body" and a "wreath of flowers" for her chest, both visible in her photographs.[38] While Rauschenberg previously studied Fashion Design at the Kansas City Art Institute, taking Textile Construction with Trude and Anni directed his attention to the structure of textiles and expanded his knowledge of them as materials. Rauschenberg's attention to textiles, evident in his later Combines and costumes for dancers, was informed by his studies with Trude and Anni.

Ray Johnson also studied weaving with Trude. Knowing this and reviewing the work he made at Black Mountain College allows us to reassess his designs in relation to weaving. In a letter he sent to designer Alvin Lustig, Johnson filled the page with wavy, colorful lines and wrote in pencil in between them (fig. 101). At the top of this letter, Johnson wrote the unexpected sentence "Reptiles on the path

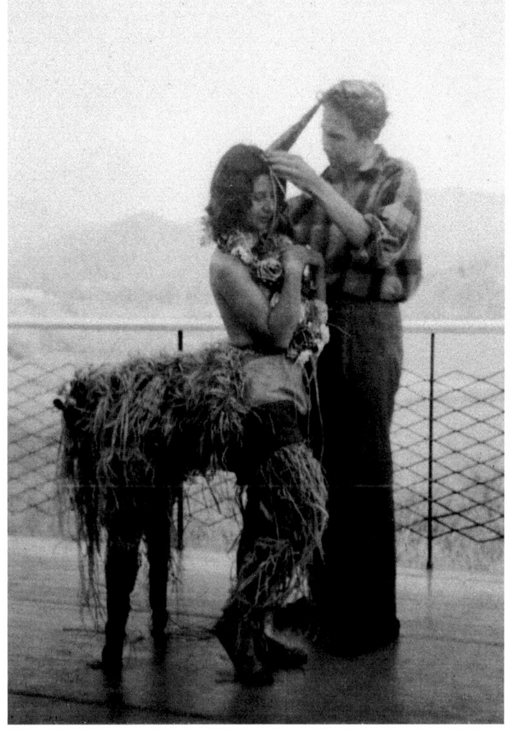

100. Robert Rauschenberg with Inga Lauterstein, who wears a costume designed by Rauschenberg, 1949. Photograph by Trude Guermonprez.

in the snow." This statement provides an idea for the multicolored lines printed on the paper that Johnson wrote between. Creating an idea for the design in this letter demonstrates how design can result in a psychological effect, the type of effect that Lustig had previously lectured about at BMC.[39] Halfway through the letter he says, "I am weaving too." When one views this letter through the weaving class Johnson took with Trude, these lines resemble what a loose warp of wool threads looks like on a loom when it's not under tension. While Josef Albers and Alvin Lustig have been linked to Ray's design education at BMC, Trude Guermonprez needs to be added to this list, even if she said there was "not enough consistent effort" from Johnson in her class.[40]

Trude's and Anni's last semester at BMC was also student Andy Oates's first semester at the College. He came to BMC to study weaving and took Weaving I and II with both Anni and Trude, trying to learn the most from them in the one semester that he would have with them.[41] Oates later said that he liked Trude "very much as a teacher and as a person."[42]

In addition to studying with Trude, he recalled weaving the fabric that she was commissioned to design for the Weizenblatt House, a private residence designed by Marcel Breuer in 1940–41 in Asheville. Before she left, Trude set up a countermarche loom and asked Oates to weave the fifteen yards of fabric. Oates found this loom very challenging to weave on and without Trude there, he stopped working on it. However, after hearing from Dr. Sprinza Weizenblatt, he resumed weaving and finished this commission.[43] The yardage was used to upholster a chair (fig. 106).[44]

The upholstery's pattern, made of shifting blocks of unbalanced twills woven with the same three colors in warp and weft, recalls Lore Kadden Lindenfeld's eight-harness group weaving sample (fig. 40), suggesting that this pattern might have been designed for BMC's textile production program, though this fabric's design is credited to Trude.[45] Trude continued to make practical textiles throughout her life, including draperies, rugs, and fabric for clothing.

Anni and Trude enjoyed teaching together at Black Mountain College. Anni referred to their time together as "fruitful joint work" and wrote: "It was a great pleasure for me to have the exchange of knowledge and ideas with someone as experienced in the work and as eager for new experience in the field as Mrs. Guermonprez."[46] Trude thought that Anni was kind and inspiring. Later Trude said that she was indebted to Anni in particular for introducing her to pre-Columbian textiles.[47]

TEACHING IN CALIFORNIA

After resigning from Black Mountain College, Trude needed to figure out what to do next. The solution came through Marguerite Wildenhain, the master potter and former *Bauhausler* whom Trude knew from her days as a student in Halle and when both were émigrés in the Netherlands. Wildenhain asked Trude to direct the weaving workshop at Pond Farm—an artist's colony located in Guerneville, California—founded by architect Gordon Herr and his writer wife Jane as "a sustainable sanctuary for artists away from a world gone amuck."[48] Wildenhain had moved to Pond Farm in 1942 and set up a pottery workshop there. The Herrs envisioned Pond Farm being able to support itself through fees collected from summer workshops. The summer of 1949, Trude's first at Pond Farm, was the artist colony's first session of workshops.

While she had shared teaching responsibilities at Black Mountain, Pond Farm offered Trude her first opportunity to develop her own weaving curriculum. Black Mountain allowed Trude to realize that teaching was a career path she could pursue.[49] The announcement for Pond Farm's weaving workshop stated the aim to "initiate the inventive capacity of thinking in a specific medium," the medium being weaving. Her teaching included experimental studies on color and texture and also "analytic studies on designing for special purpose." For beginners she taught basic raw materials, basic weaves, and drafting. For "those interested" Trude also offered to teach tapestry techniques.[50] Her notes mention the opportunity for students to schedule tutorials about more advanced weaves, including double weaves and coated weaves, as well as Peruvian techniques.[51] Another document about Trude's weaving workshop stated the aim to develop "Contemporary Craftsmen-Designers."[52]

Trude's connections to Black Mountain continued in California. In the summer of 1950 Lore Kadden (Lindenfeld) came to assist Trude with teaching weaving.[53] Then in the fall of 1950 Trude's teaching expanded to San Francisco, where she taught Elements of Textile Design at the California School of Fine Arts (later the San Francisco Art Institute), a position that Josef Albers had recommended her for.[54] Balancing teaching with making her own work was challenging for Trude during this time. She wrote her sister Lisa, "I don't like the fact that one thinks I am such a good teacher, leaves too little time for weaving."[55]

A RETURN TO BLACK MOUNTAIN COLLEGE

In the fall of 1952 Trude returned briefly to Black Mountain to deliver a lecture during the eight-week Crafts Institute, which included the famous two-week Pottery Seminar hosted by Marguerite Wildenhain.[56] Professionally this allowed Trude to return after a few years of teaching her own weaving curriculum and to share her perspectives about textile design. Personally, it allowed her to visit her mother, Johanna Jalowetz, who was still living at BMC, and to introduce Johanna to her new husband John Elsesser, whom she met at Pond Farm.[57]

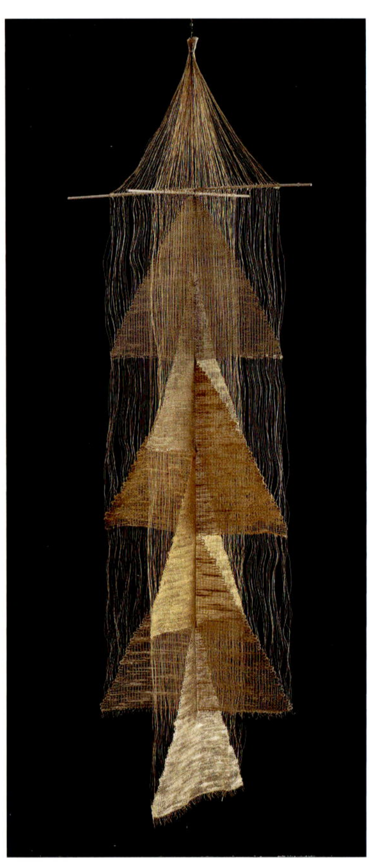

The lecture Trude gave about textile design is published for the first time in this book (see pages 132–137). In the lecture Trude reflected on her work and her field and grappled with how the overused words "design" and "designing" had lost their meaning. As a textile designer she tried to return meaning to the word and to explain how design is achieved.

She confronted these terms and referred to ancient Peruvian weaving as a tradition of weaving (not designing) as one that allowed them to make fabrics that were central to their lives and "timelessly beautiful." Trude offered the phrase *analytical designing* as a way to understand what weaving's reengagement with the handloom offered and emphasized the importance of deeply understanding weave structures and the loom itself as being as essential as imagination.

Most significantly in this talk Trude shared her perspective on the elements for textile design: "The elements for textile design are the weaver's yarns, his equipment, the purpose which the final fabric has to serve, the weaver's informative knowledge, his skills as a craftsman, and last [but] not least, his imaginative ability." She emphasized the importance of knowing the qualities of thread and how when one has "mastered this truthful integration of the nature of the yarn and the form of the weave, we are ready to design fabrics which serve certain functions."

RETURNING TO CALIFORNIA

Trude resigned from Pond Farm in 1951 and Pond Farm's workshops closed in 1953. In the summer of 1953, she was hired to teach weaving at the California College of Arts and Crafts (today California College of the Arts). The following year CCAC hired her

102. Trude Guermonprez, *Space Hanging*, 1964.
Cotton and metallic threads, metal rods. 42 in.

103. Kay Sekimachi, *Study for room dividers*, ca. 1960–70. Linen, group threading.
11¾ × 6¾ in.

to teach weaving and textile design full time, which allowed her the opportunity to create another weaving and textile design program in her field.[58]

Trude's teaching opened up a world of possibilities for her students. This is particularly evident in the career of Kay Sekimachi who first encountered Trude through a lecture that she gave at Pond Farm in the summer of 1951. She recalled, "Suddenly that summer, my eyes were opened, and I knew weaving was for me." Sekimachi began studying weaving with Trude at CCAC in the summer of 1954, and added:

> [Trude's] teaching was Bauhaus-oriented and included her own sensitive insights . . . She started the session by having us clarify in our minds what weaving was, and what function the parts of the loom played in the process of weaving. She stressed getting to know the loom.[59]

A teaching study titled "Approach to Fabric Design" that Kay made in the 1950s to show her students conveys the structural approach to weaving she learned from Trude. The draft notation in the lower right emphasizes that all four samples are made with the same structure. Viewing this as an experiment, with the structure as the control, the threads become variables, which Sekimachi tests: a thicker weft thread in the second sample, a red thread in the third, and how reversing the colors in the fourth obscure the weave's structure. This iterative and experiential way of learning recalls both Trude's Bauhaus-influenced training and the rigorous play and experimentation at the heart of the weaving program that she and Anni taught at Black Mountain College. For Kay, experimentation and sampling has remained a central practice throughout her career and led her to push structural weaving into new, three-dimensional realms. This is seen in her room dividers developed in open weaves, hanging monofilament sculptures, book-like accordions in double weave, and other experiments like the colorful *Cross Warp* (fig. 134).

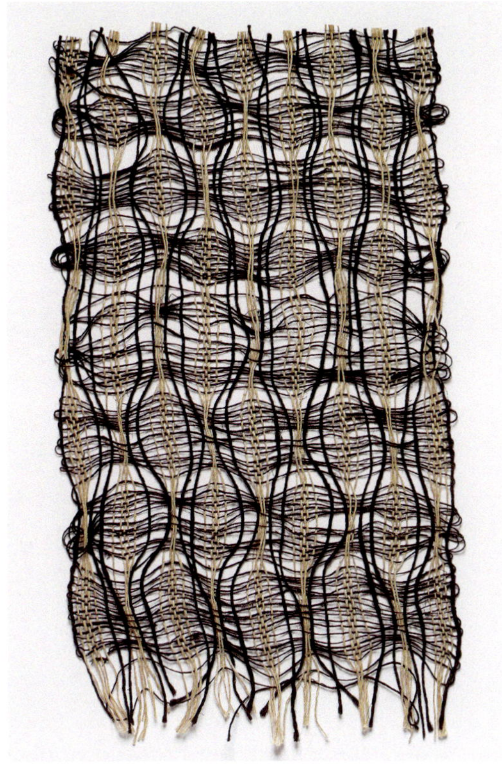

Kay and Trude became good friends, and this friendship led to Trude asking her to substitute for her during some of the CCAC summer sessions. Eventually Trude asked Kay to teach all of her summer classes. Without Trude's encouragement, Kay would not have pursued teaching,

DESIGN

1952

TRUDE GUERMONPREZ

The very fact that we speak nowadays about designing houses, designing furniture, designing textiles is a regrettable one. There was a time when people did not design anything but built houses, turned furniture, and wove textiles. With this introductory statement I am really giving you the essence of my ideas about textile designing. But since it has become such a common convenience of speech to use the word "design," I will stick to it after exploring the meaning of it from different angles.

Wherever a multiple process of productive activity turns out an object, we speak about the design of it. Why do we say: this chair is badly designed? Or we might also say: this chair is appropriate in material and workmanship, but poor in design. In the first statement we did not specify but expressed a general dissatisfaction of our receptive sensitivities. In the statement which followed we pass[ed] through a series of analytic thoughts and found that certain factors involved in the making of the chair did satisfy, but that nevertheless the total lacked something. It is very hard in such a case to put [a] finger on the sore spot. But one thing has become clear: that there is no such thing as "design" [as] an element in itself. The design of a chair then is the sum of a series of factors. It is the whole impact of impressions which the onlooker gathers from the object, mixed with his own expectations (preconceptions) of a chair. Poor designers.

But my own stationery shows the title, textile designer and I will now try to defend this expression for what it is worth. The Webster [dictionary] defines design as a plan or scheme formed in the mind for the making of anything, the adaptation of means to an end. Or more specifically related to our fields it says: the arrangement of elements or details which make up a work of art.

105. Trude Guermonprez, *Sample*, ca. 1950.
Linen, cotton, viscose rayon. 30⅛ × 24 in.

WOVEN FABRICS
TRUDE + GUERMONPREZ
810 CLIPPER STREET
SAN FRANCISCO 14
VALENCIA 6-7607

Thus again it becomes clear that for the maker as well as for the spectator, design is not one part of the whole, but design is the motoric intention which determines the choices of elements, forming a complete, new thing. Design can be truthful and adequate. Design can be fake and superficial. In exceptional cases it can be genial [show genius]. How do we the designers go about it (in my case: the weavers)?

Here I would like to substantiate my very first statement with a reminder. Some of the most beautiful pieces of weaving from the past, which we are able to see in our museums, are the fabrics of the Pre-Columbian weavers in Peru from the 11th until the 14th century. They are superb in their design; some are genial [ingenious], as near to art, as a piece of craft work can get. These Peruvian weavers wove what they had learned from their predecessors with what thread they had discovered to spin for the use of their clothes [or] for the worship of their gods. They wove as they lived. Their intention to make a certain fabric—what we call design—was one, determined by strict custom, by the mode of life. Their weaving was in no way a different part of their lives than is cooking in ours.

When the weaver was called upon to make the serape for the king, he wove it. He did not design it because there was no doubt as to the royal symbol to be woven into it. No doubt as to which colors expressed leadership. No doubt which were the most precious materials. And no doubt who was the most skill[ed] weaver. And it might have been not one, but several persons whose completely integrated knowledge and intuition of their world, their lives, and their mythology enabled them to weave fabrics which we call timelessly beautiful.

I feel that I don't have to say much about our time to justify our own stand as designers in comparison to the maker-designer. Here am I and the fabric which I wove by hand. There are the millions of yardage, which the machine turns out designed by one human mind. The discrepancy, the extension from the thinker-maker to the maker, is clear. [E]specially in the case of the machine.

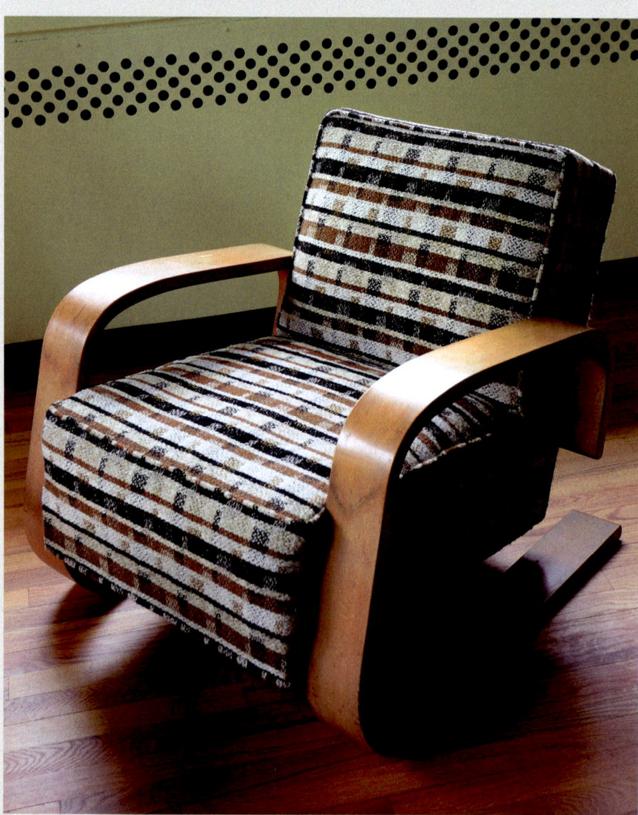

106. Trude Guermonprez and Andy Oates,
Upholstery fabric for Weizenblatt House, 1949.
Wool and synthetic fibers.

But look at the other part of the picture. Where is the universality of belief that carried ancient people? Where is the [inherited] tradition on which generations of artisans built their skill? We go to art schools, we also move with the speed of 100 horsepower through the streets, and yet [we] produce our crafts at the tempo of a medieval man. We have specialists in each field. We divide the production of one thing into several stages made by different highly specialized makers. We have hurried lives and most of our products don't answer a need, but [instead] seem an artificial luxury.

This to you must sound negative when I call our state as "designers" a regrettable one. Actually, I only [say] it to point out where and in which way we would be able to make as beautiful things as the past has shown us. As sad as our confused times may seem, [by] analyzing its limitations, recognizing its terrific advantages, determining our place as the mind-and-soul animal in it, we will be able to produce objects that have as fully an expression of our lives, as those from Peruvian times.

The very fact that in weaving the handloom has appeared on the scene again, after the machine had been developed to its utmost perfection, is of great importance. It does not mean that we want to turn the wheel back, but that we have recognized the limitations of the power-tool production. We, the same people who have focused our mind on technical perfection, find that we have to turn to the basic making of a thing in order to be imaginative, in order to animate the steel which is thundering in the mills. This development and insight [have] shown us the way to analytical designing.

The elements for textile design are: the weaver's yarns, his equipment (hand or power alike), the purpose which the final fabric has to serve, the weaver's informative knowledge, his skill as a craftsman, and last [but] not least: his imaginative ability.

You will readily admit that the range of various yarns provides the weaver with a palette, which the painter might envy. Not only that, the thread is [not only] a carrier of color, but it also has a texture and structural quality. How to interlace the threads provides the weaver with another possibility of design. He will either interweave the vertical threads of the warp with the horizontal threads of the weft in a loose fashion, thus producing a fine, flimsy fabric, or he will crowd the density of the warp and weft, thus achieving a canvas-like textile. And of course all the variations in between and beyond those two examples. How would he determine his choice of yarn and weave— his design—amongst the still staggering possibilities? Here enter laws of organic as well as of aesthetic nature. The thread, the weaver's main medium, demands to be treated according to its own organic structure. A brittle thread, although it might just have the right texture [and] color, can never be used as a warp thread, because it undergoes such strain during the process of weaving. Aesthetically speaking we want to enforce a form which does not reveal the natural quality of the threads we use.

We therefore would [look] to find the interlacing that makes wool feel wooly, warm, [and] protective, or linen, for instance, cool, strong, and flat. After we have mastered this truthful integration of the nature of the yarn and the form of the weave, we are ready to design fabrics which serve certain functions. Wanted is a drape, an upholstery, a dress fabric. With each item and its specific demands a series of suggestions spring to the mind, based on experience and information. We know that rayon drapes but linen does not. We have experienced that wool shapes easily into dresses, provided the right weave is applied, and so on. By elimination rather than by choosing at random, we approach the solutions that serve [our] defined purpose. By proceeding in this way, we can be more sure of truthful, adequate design (meaning planning); a craftsmanship which in turn comes nearest to what we would call timeless and beautiful.

There is no mind without a soul, and whatever logic has gone so far into the design process will be pulled out of the rationalist into the creative wherever the sensitive forces of man are involved. Nobody can abstain himself of likes and dislikes, of moods and impressions. A certain amount of this will penetrate the work at every step, and paired with the discipline of analytic design, it will make for the wholeness which we expect from good design.

There is still one point, to which I want to say a few words, without getting too technical. It had been felt that weaving might be a field where those that love to splurge in color can find an easy medium to express themselves. Here again, it is a false conclusion to think of a colorful fabric as a sum of colored threads. The way the threads are interlaced [means] that not only the thread has a texture, but also [that] the weave has ups and downs; has spots and linear elements. To place color so that this specific landscape of a fabric is not disturbed but rather emphasized, is what would be called an integrated use of color in weaving.[1] The effect is one of outstanding colorfulness, in a new and [characteristically] textile way.

From here on I would like to let the fabrics, which are exhibited, speak for themselves. And if you care to ask [questions] and discuss, please do.

Delivered to an art club in Sacramento in 1951/1952 and at Black Mountain College in October 1952 during the Pottery Seminar

Some light editing has been done on this typescript for clarity. Where there were X's in her typescript we have deleted those sentences.

[1] *While an x appears before this sentence, we have chosen to include it.*

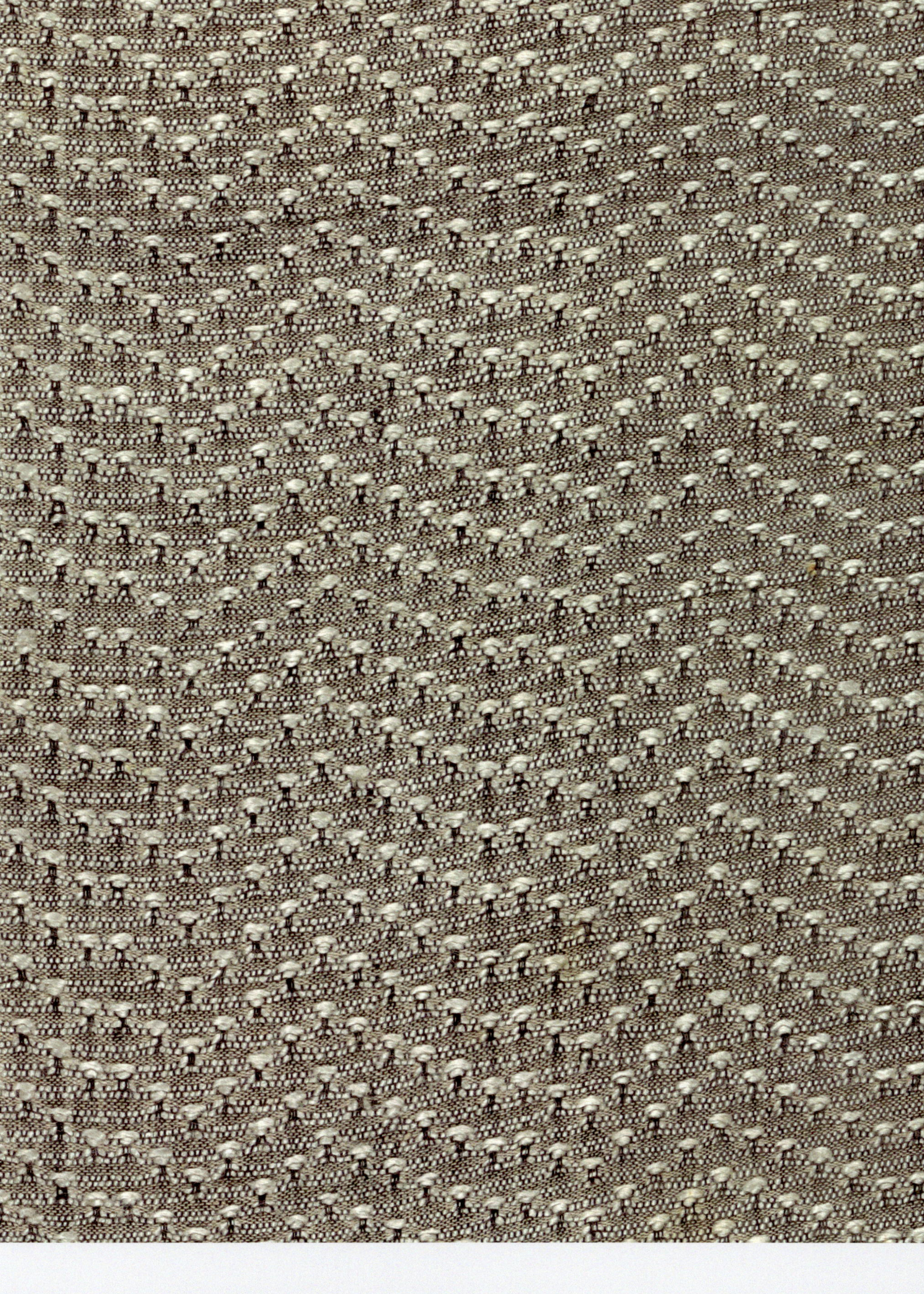

at Black Mountain College.[10] They would meet in New York later that month when Anni was en route to Cambridge where she was to give a talk at MIT.[11] On June 11, 1946, Molly Gregory wrote to Franziska confirming her appointment as "Instructor in Weaving" while Anni Albers was away on sabbatical. Gregory's letter ended with what may have been a reference to a question that had arisen during the New York meeting: "Mrs. Albers asked me to tell you that we have decided not to have sheep until we are in a better position to provide the right pastures, etc. I understand you were interested in the project."

Mayer arrived at Black Mountain College in early July, in time for the start of the 1946 Summer Art Institute. Eager to expand her education, she took Josef Albers's course in Design and Anni Albers's Theory of Weaving course while assisting with weaving instruction. In the fall, when the Alberses left on a year-long sabbatical, Mayer took up her one-year contract in the weaving workshop. Of her experience at the College, Franziska wrote:

> The weaver [Anni Albers] whom I was to replace stayed on for a few weeks before she went on leave, and from her I learned a new aspect of weaving. It was to try out, at the loom, experimental patterns not previously drawn on paper. The best results would then be sold to industry as "designs." She also told me of Peruvian weaving with four weaving borders, still made today by the Indios on pre-colombian [*sic*] looms. . . . Black Mountain College was a great experience for me not only professionally but also humanly . . . Knowledge of the problems of colleagues made for patient collaboration. . . . When we ran short of housekeeping money . . . faculty and students shared the dishwashing. At the end of the year, I went west by Greyhound bus to see my relatives in California and then to join my family in Peru.[12]

Trude Guermonprez, who joined Franziska Mayer in the weaving department in February 1947, also acknowledged her debt to Anni Albers who "opened up the whole world of pre-Columbian textiles to me."[13] To Franziska she wrote on November 7, 1947:

> Annie [*sic*] Albers is now here. I think it will be very fine for me to work with her. She is very kind and grateful and inspiring. She must have formed a real exciting collection. Some of the pieces which she had personally bought (the others are still on the way) . . . she showed us during class. You will have the time of your life in Peru.[14]

Mayer, largely cut off from events in Europe, had made the most of the war years in isolation in Newfoundland where she endured cultural dislocation, uncertainty, and bureaucratic obstacles to regaining her personal status after the war ended. Trude Jalowetz Guermonprez, on the other hand, experienced the war up close in the Netherlands. Trude had moved from Germany to Amsterdam in 1933. There, in a series of coincidences, she met and married Josef Albers's former Bauhaus student, the talented Belgian-born photographer and graphic designer, Paul Guermonprez, on April 1, 1939.

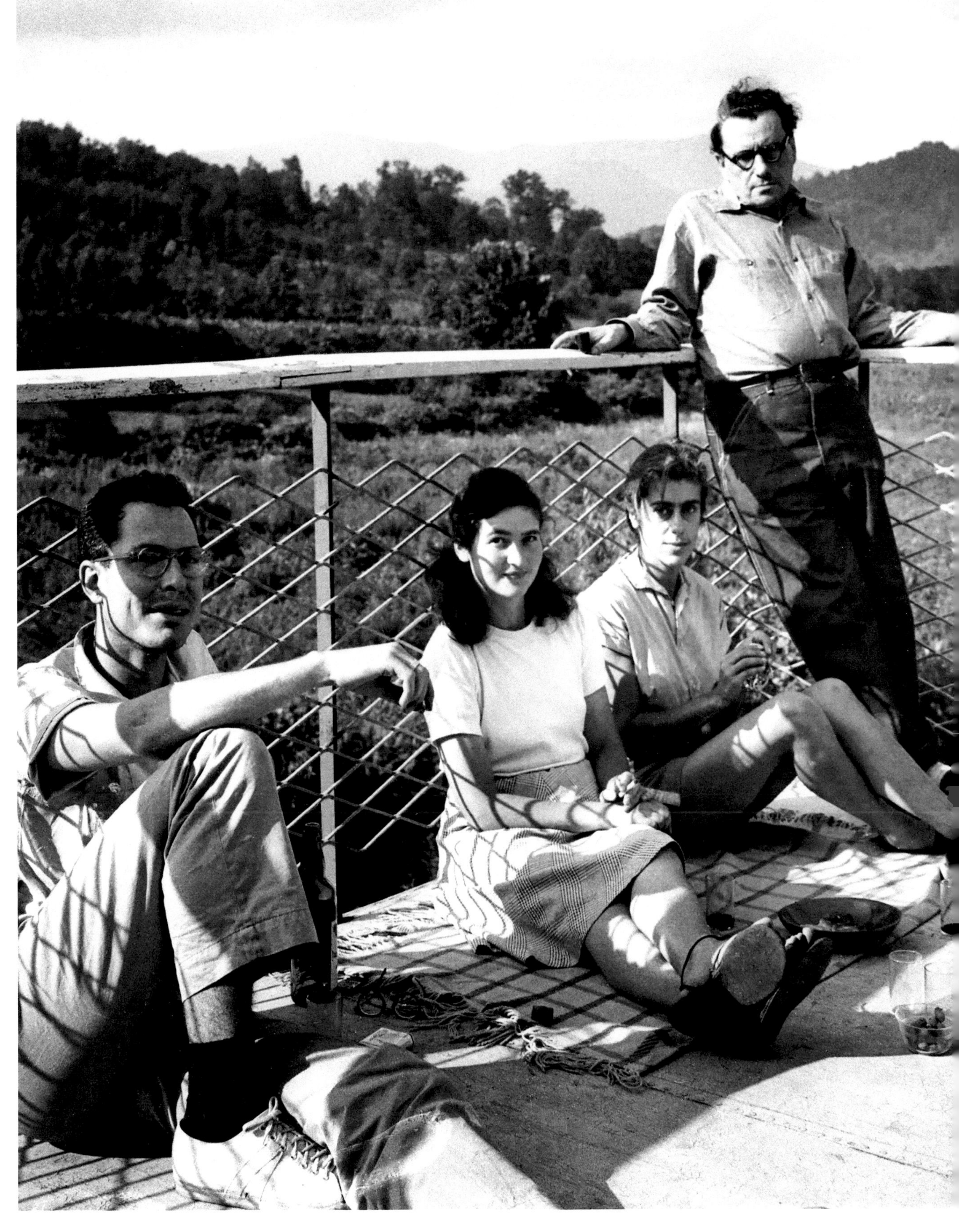

Trude's parents, Heinrich and Johanna Jalowetz, on the run from the Nazi threat, managed to get a passage to New York in 1938 and by late 1939 were happily settled at Black Mountain College where they were at the center of a classical music renaissance. Trude's younger sister, nineteen-year-old Lisa, who had been living with her sister in the Netherlands, after celebrating Trude and Paul's marriage in Amsterdam, joined her parents at Black Mountain where she completed her education.[15]

Barely a year later, on May 10, 1940, Trude's and Paul's lives were threatened, and then shattered, by the Nazi invasion and takeover of the Netherlands.[16] Communication with her family was cut short, and it was not until the war in Europe had ended that Trude was able to relate her personal history of the preceding six years in a letter to her parents. Writing in unfamiliar English, Trude explained:

> Paul escaped the first day [of his imprisonment in August 1943] with the firm idea to fight as a partisan against the system that oppressed the people of Europe. I knew this and I consented to do it because I knew his intens[e] spirit of liberty and right and I saw the misery and knew that it was necessary to do so. We both knew that it was dangerous work. [In] the time from Aug. 43 until 4 April 1944 [when Paul was arrested] and 10 June [1944 when he was killed] we saw each other frequently. We had no home. This was too dangerous. But sometimes we were a week together. . . . It was a thrilling time, but we were very, very, happy. . . . [Now] I have no home and no work. perhaps can I start weaving again in Holland. . . . We lost many of the best people. . . . I got very old this past year, but I did not loose [*sic*] courage. . . . [Paul's] life was a very adventurous one, but he lived 100%.[17]

In this and other communications with her parents Trude was torn between rebuilding her private and professional life in a Europe that she clearly loved, even though "everything has fallen apart" and the fates of friends and relatives remained unknown, or of following her family and emigrating.[18] The decision was made for her less than six months later, when her father, Heinrich Jalowetz, suffered a fatal heart attack as he made his way home after a recital of sonatas by Mozart, Brahms, and Bach at the College.[19] This was a signal for Trude to get to the United States to be with her widowed mother. It was several months before Trude, with help from the College, which applied for her visitor's visa as a "specialist in weaving," was able to enter the US. She arrived at Black Mountain in February 1947.

Trude was somewhat prepared for life at BMC, having heard from her father earlier how "he very much relished working with young people and felt that there was an abundance of talent . . . [and] from his letters I understood the philosophy of the college."[20] Despite this and a warm welcome from students, since she had little teaching experience and "hardly" spoke English, it was also "a shock" . . . "the new country, the new language, the new environment, everything." In Anni Albers's absence it was Franziska who would have initiated Trude into the curriculum of the weaving department.[21] What Trude did recall was that her own work questioned the medium specificity of Albers's approach:

where maybe my instruction differed slightly or branched out slightly from Anni Albers
was that I emphasized more freedom on the basis of the . . . structural and technical
knowledge, . . . into a more free use of the loom. . . . I made a tapestry [at Black Mountain College] where I used painting as well as tapestry weaving combined. And that
was probably the first time that was done here. . . . [T]he students must have picked up
some . . . feeling of more freedom away from the strictly geometrical . . . that's determined
by the structure.[22]

Elaborating on her teaching experience at Black Mountain College, Guermonprez observed that she learned about teaching *through* teaching, and contrasted her
own methods with those of Albers who would "bring the students in" by using "the
analytical . . . Socratic . . . way of educating." Albers would set a functional task for
a fabric and then allow the students to come up with a structure through a process
of deduction. About her own teaching Trude observed, "I was always able to explain

the drafting very clearly . . . which is sort of
like . . . writing the score for an orchestra, you
write things down for weaving, and you have
to read it like you do an architectural plan." She
might have added that being from a family so
closely connected to the process of composing
and performing music may have developed
her sophisticated understanding of weaving's
underlying codes of draft notation.

Early in March 1949 Anni Albers wrote
to her friend and former Bauhaus weaving
workshop colleague, Marli Ehrman, with
an invitation for Ehrman to teach at BMC
during the summer session that year. Albers
explained that she and Josef as well as Ted
Dreier, Trude Guermonprez, and Charlotte
Schlesinger would be leaving at the end of June,
adding, "you would not be completely without old friends because you still would find the

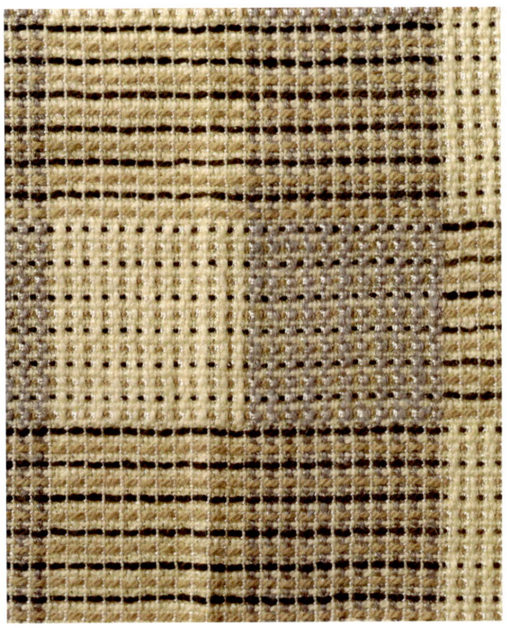

Dehns, . . . and Mrs Jalowetz [here]." Gently, Anni suggested that Ehrman might "look
at the possibility of continuing through the year" and went on to describe the equipment in the weaving workshop, reminding her friend that the workshop was "one of
the coolest places [on the BMC campus] during summer."[23]

The friendly tone of the letter indicates the close association of the two women
that stretched back at least twenty-five years. Indeed, Josef Albers's series of photographs of Ehrman, and a memorable collage he made of her parents at the Bauhaus
in 1930, is evidence of the friendship. Ehrman's previous visits to the College had
been to act as examiner for graduating weaving students Don Page, Marilyn Bauer

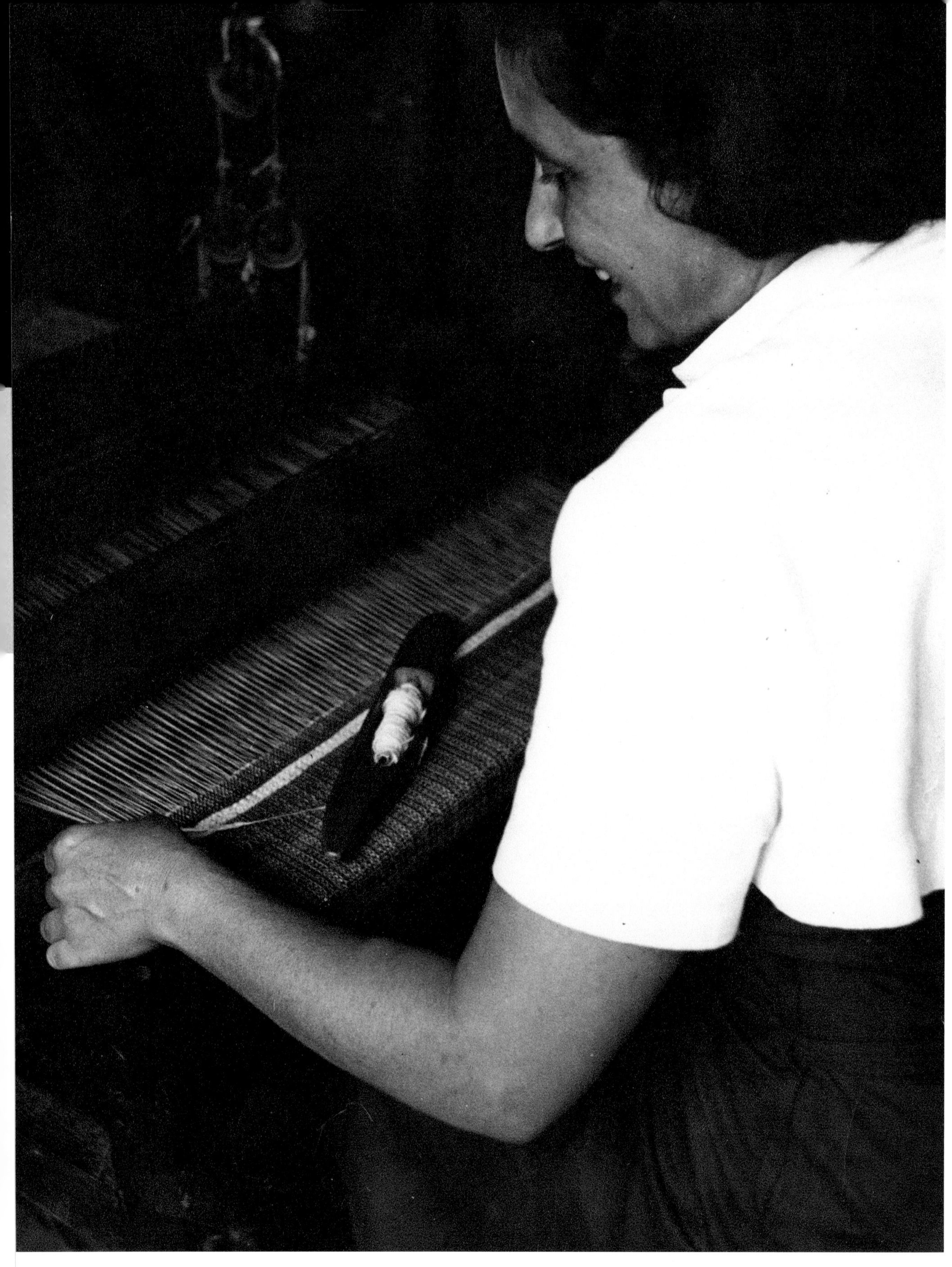

114. Marli Ehrman weaving at BMC, 1949.
Photograph by Diana Woelffer.

DEPARTURES, SHORT STAYS, AND CLOSURE

JULIE J. THOMSON

Both Anni Albers and Trude Guermonprez departed from Black Mountain College following the Spring 1949 semester. Their absence could have meant the end of weaving at the College. Despite their leaving, the program continued with a series of shorter stays by recognized weavers. For the 1949 Summer Art Institute, Marli Ehrman taught weaving (fig. 114). Ehrman studied at the Bauhaus alongside Anni and they continued to stay in touch while in the United States. Anni invited Ehrman to BMC three times to serve as the outside examiner for graduates in weaving and textile design. Ehrman, as a result, was familiar with both Black Mountain's weaving program and the skills and knowledge that students could learn through it.[1]

Ehrman came to BMC as an experienced teacher, having founded and directed the weaving workshop at the Institute of Design, Chicago from 1939 to 1947, but the workshop was closed when the school merged with the Illinois Institute of Technology.[2] As a result of this merger, Ehrman was experiencing a period of great personal change while at Black Mountain.

At BMC Ehrman offered both elementary and advanced levels of weaving and textile design. Her approach for teaching beginners resembled Anni's and Trude's and covered "basic weaving and fundamentals of textile designing including basic weaves, materials, color, design, as well as fabric texture and structure." Her advanced class included "construction of fabrics with backing, double cloth, and combination of various fabric structures for specific purposes in function and design."[3]

Returning to Chicago Ehrman continued to teach privately to a group known as the "Marli Weavers," and architects continued to commission her work, including

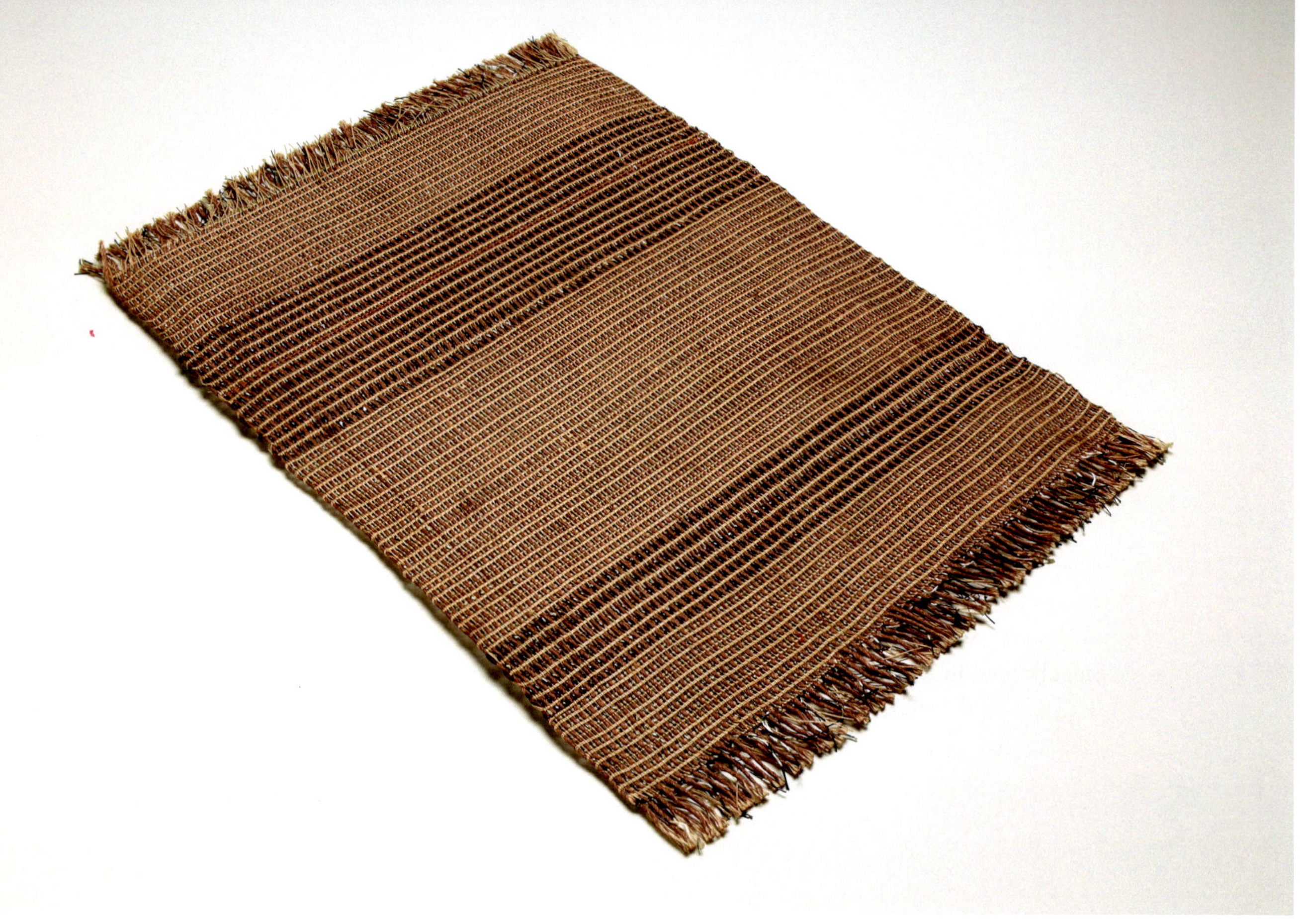

the draperies for Mies van der Rohe's Lake Shore Drive Apartments in 1951.[4] One of
her later students recalled:

> Marli's lessons developed sensitivity to the visual and tactile qualities of fabrics, as well
> as a rigorous technique with which to enlarge our vocabulary of structures. She opened
> our eyes to the colors and proportions of nature. She recommended study of Raoul
> d'Harcourt's *Textiles Ancien de Peru* before it was translated into English and gave us
> an appetite for all kinds of visual experiences and research.[5]

Like Albers, Ehrman learned about d'Harcourt's classic book on Peruvian weaving at the Bauhaus. At BMC she likely viewed and encouraged students' use of the
Harriett Engelhardt Memorial Collection, which featured Peruvian textiles.

At the end of the 1949 Summer Session, the BMC community was introduced to
Ellen Siegel through an exhibition of her work.[6] Soon after the exhibition opened Siegel arrived as the College's weaving instructor for the next academic year.[7] A recent
graduate of Cranbrook's weaving program, Siegel studied weaving and textile design
for two years with the Finnish-American textile designer Marianne Strengell.[8] Siegel
was twenty-five years old when she arrived at Black Mountain and this was her first
position teaching at the college level. Her weaving accolades included receiving an
honorable mention in the 1948 International Textile Exhibition in Greensboro, North

115. Errisinola Ginesi (Burnett), *Placemat*, 1950
Cotton, rayon, and synthetic fibers. 19 × 13 ¾ in.

116. Saran casement cloth designed by Ellen Siegel
in 1956. Photograph by Mary Emma Harris.

Carolina, and the exhibition of her work in New Orleans and Detroit. Records show that Siegel's class attracted three students: Errisinola "Erris" Ginesi (Burnett), Patricia Campbell, and John "Jack" Cannon. Andy Oates, signed up for her class but then shifted to focus on studying photography with Hazel Larsen Archer.[9]

A closer look at Erris Ginesi's four placemats made in Siegel's Spring 1950 class (fig. 115) reveals a very modern approach to textile design. The placemats prominently feature the use of synthetic threads, perhaps to make them more durable or easier to clean. For the warp Ginesi alternated thin tan synthetic threads with thick, brown-painted cotton and thin black plastic–coated rayon. Woven in plain weave, the varied textures of the mats come from modulating the weft threads, which include pairs of the same tan synthetic as the warp, brown synthetic bands, and occasional highlights of orange cotton.

Siegel's own interest in using modern materials, including rayon and saran (fig. 116) is apparent through the known examples of her work.[10] The drapery and casement fabric that she wove with saran was shown in *Textiles USA* at the Museum of Modern Art in 1956. After leaving BMC, Siegel taught weaving in 1954 at the Haystack Mountain School of Crafts.[11] In 1958 she founded Ellen Siegel Designs in Fort Lauderdale, Florida, and designed drapery, upholstery, and apparel fabrics.[12]

While Andy Oates chose not to study weaving with Ellen Siegel, after her departure he became the College's apprentice weaving instructor, teaching from the fall of 1950 through the summer of 1951.[13] Teaching weaving was part of his graduation plan, and in the spring of 1951 he graduated in photography. Oates believed that "weaving teaches a discipline and satisfaction that come with learning how to use the mind and hands together."[14] Once again, Black Mountain offered a young weaver their first opportunity to teach weaving at the college level. Oates's classes were popular, perhaps because he was an established member of the BMC community. A remarkable number of six new students took his summer 1951 weaving class, the most of any weaving class in the 1950s.[15]

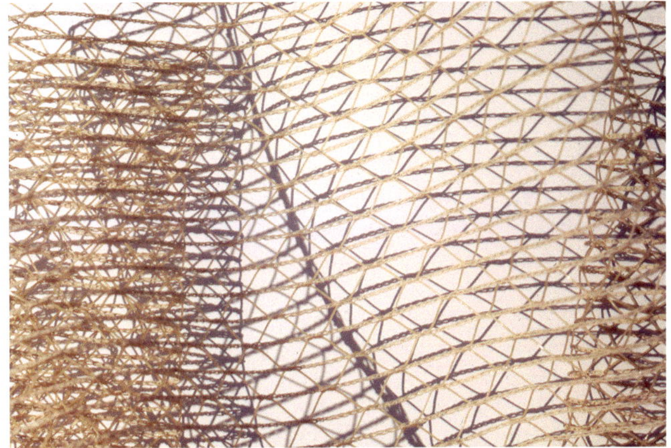

With Oates's departure for Boston, weaving classes ceased for the first time since 1934, and the absence of a weaving instructor lasted for five semesters.[16] Weaving was reintroduced for the 1953 Summer Session by San Francisco–based weaver and designer Marie Murelius. College records show that she only had one official student, Betsy Weinrib (Williams), sister of potter David Weinrib.[17] After BMC Murelius taught weaving at the California College of Arts and Crafts alongside

Trude Guermonprez, and it is likely that Guermonprez recommended her to Black Mountain.[18]

The following summer, after all of these teaching stints, a chance for a return to stability arrived with the appointment of Anthony "Tony" Landreau as the College's weaving instructor in July 1954.[19] Landreau was a painter who learned to weave while working for textile designer Dorothy Liebes.[20] Charles Olson wrote that they hired

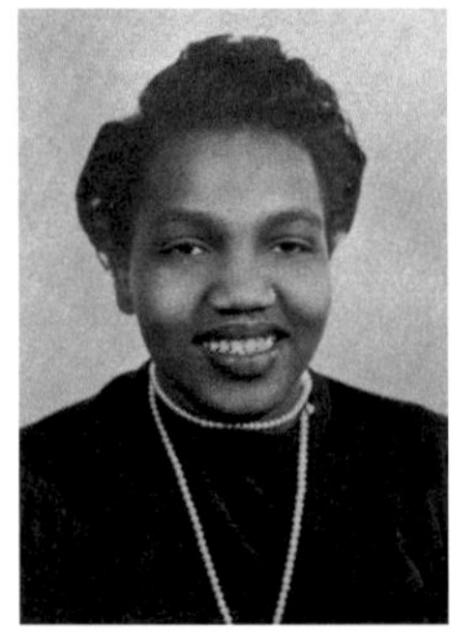
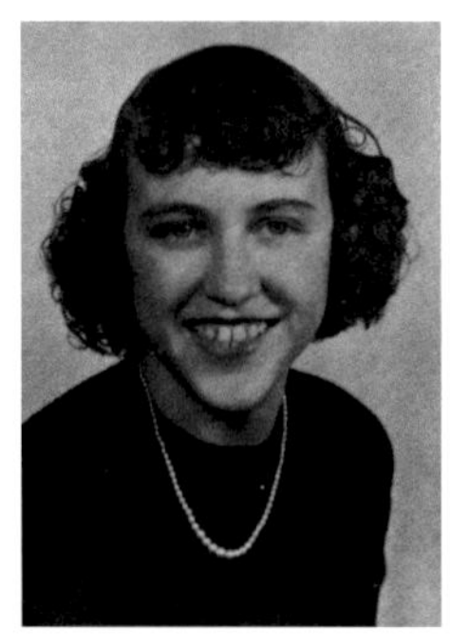

Landreau because he was young, his weaving showed "good workmanship" and "conservative" design, and they felt that he could "grow" at Black Mountain College.[21]

Landreau's students included Mona Stea (Burns), Lorraine Feuer, and Martha Davis (King), as well as two African American day students from Asheville, Jean Brewton and Lelia Murphy (fig. 117), both recent graduates from Stephens-Lee High School. BMC's student numbers were declining and allowing local students to attend classes during the day was an attempt to increase enrollment.[22] However such efforts by the College didn't always match the needs of the students. Black Mountain student Paul Alexander thought Brewton and Murphy "took weaving, because it was something they could conceivably get something out of." He added, they "could have benefitted more from a typical junior college environment than [from] Black Mountain."[23]

Mona Stea, who took four quarters of weaving with Landreau, was the most committed weaving student during this time. She remembered him as "a very good teacher."[24] Stea later recalled that the weaving program was still very much influenced by both Alberses. With Landreau she studied basic weaving techniques, tapestry, double weave, and dyeing with local plant materials.[25] Fellow student Martha Davis attended the 1955 Summer Session. She recalled trying to dye wool with found plant materials and learning Josef Albers's color theory from Landreau. She added, "the Weaving Lab still had a large stock of supplies and some extremely fine looms as well."[26] How Landreau learned and taught the Alberses' approaches is not known.

Three color slides of Stea's weaving exist, preserving two larger weavings and two belts (fig. 118), which were likely woven with cards or on an inkle loom.[27] She later recalled designing and hand-dyeing a belt for her lead role in the College's production of *Women of Tachis* by Ezra Pound.[28] Stea's most dynamic fabric, a double weave with a motif of multicolored rows of staggered blocks, shows her to be a very capable weaver with a subtly complex grasp of composition (the patterns of staggering are different between the rows) and a good sense of color.

In addition to teaching, Landreau also served as curator and caretaker of the Engelhardt Collection. Stea recalled that he showed and used the "wonderful" textiles

118. Belts made by Mona Stea Burns in 1954–55.
Photograph by Mary Emma Harris.

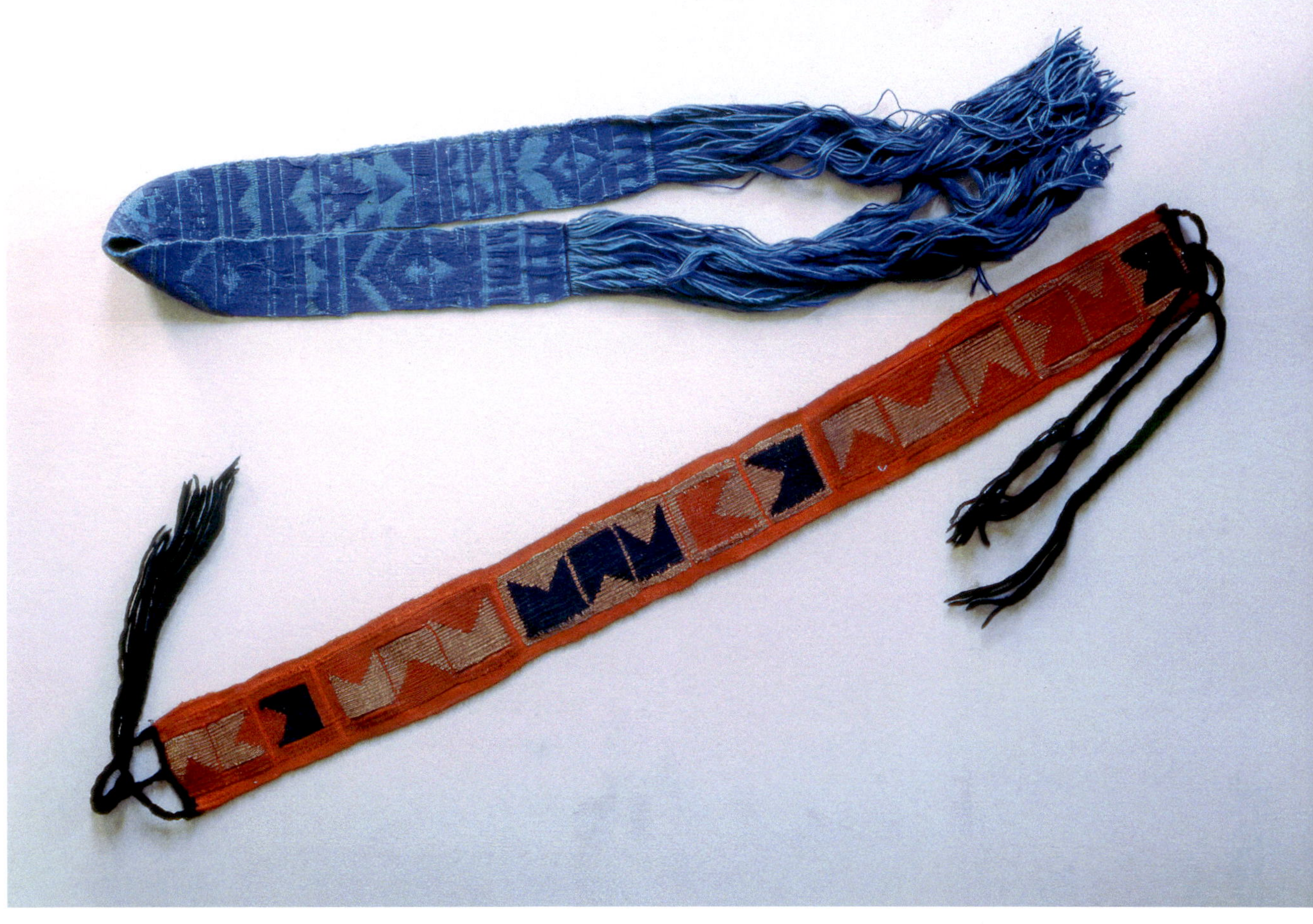

from it with his students; the belts she made may have been inspired by belts in the collection.[29] Cataloging and inventorying the Engelhardt Collection gave Landreau his first experience in textile history. Later he would serve as a curator (1967–71) at the Textile Museum in Washington D.C., and then as its executive director (1971–75).[30] There he gave seminars on textile analysis and textile conservation, wrote for the *Textile Museum Journal*, and curated exhibitions. Eventually he undertook field research and wrote about weaving in Turkey and the Middle East. In 1995 he earned his doctorate degree from Temple University with his dissertation "Anatolian Rug Weaving: Mirror of Change."[31]

Records indicate that by the winter quarter of 1956 Brewton and Murphy were the only weaving students at Black Mountain College.[32] Landreau remained at the College through at least late September, but it is not clear how much he taught in the final year.[33] Like everything else at BMC, the weaving program ended with the closure of the College in the fall quarter of 1956. Eventually the remaining materials and looms would be sold along with the rest of the College's property, but the experiences students and faculty had with weaving and textile design, and the weaving literacy that was fostered in the College's community would continue to reverberate through them to the world.[34]

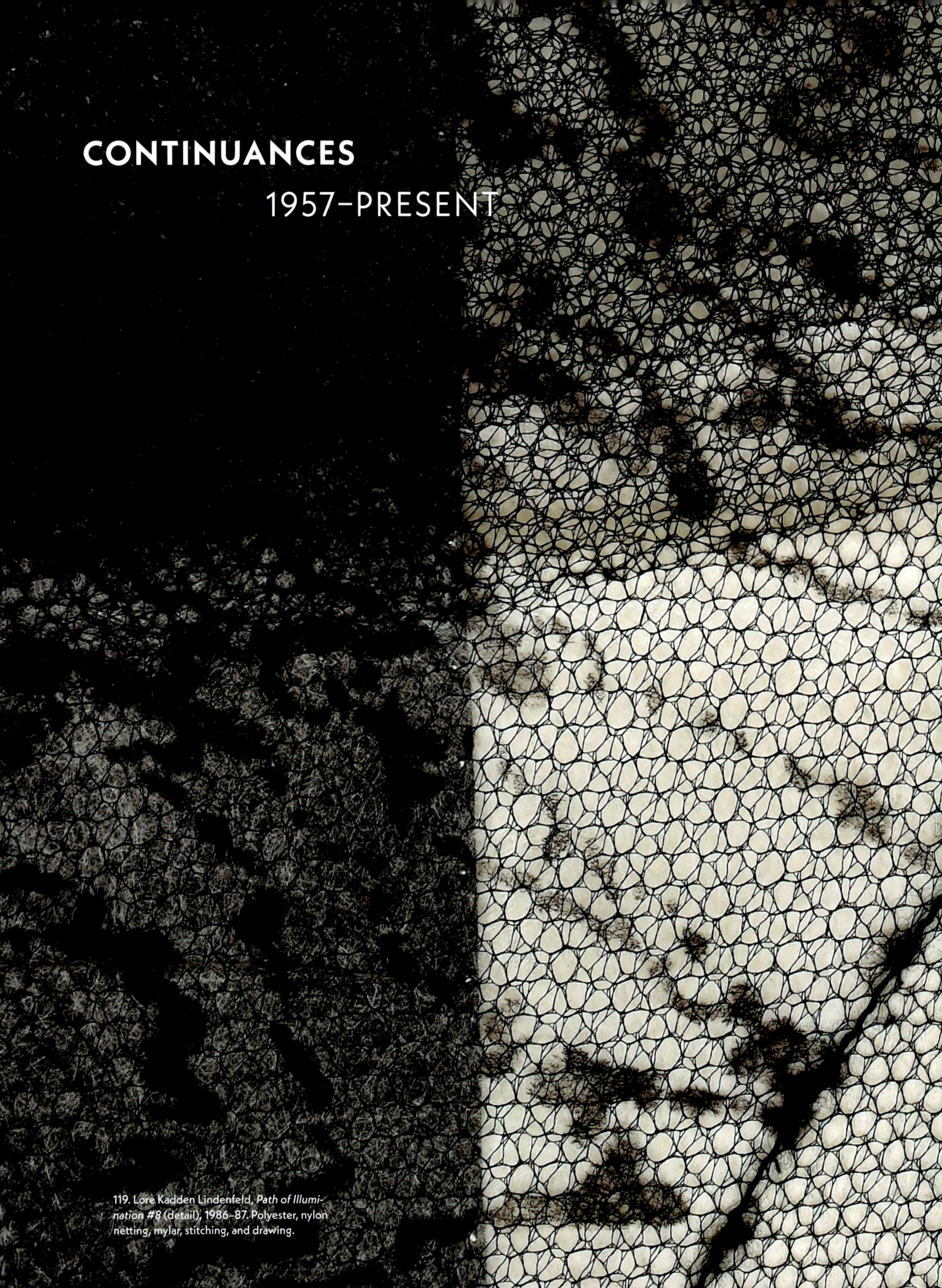

CONTINUANCES
1957–PRESENT

119. Lore Kadden Lindenfeld, *Path of Illumination #8* (detail), 1986–87. Polyester, nylon netting, mylar, stitching, and drawing.

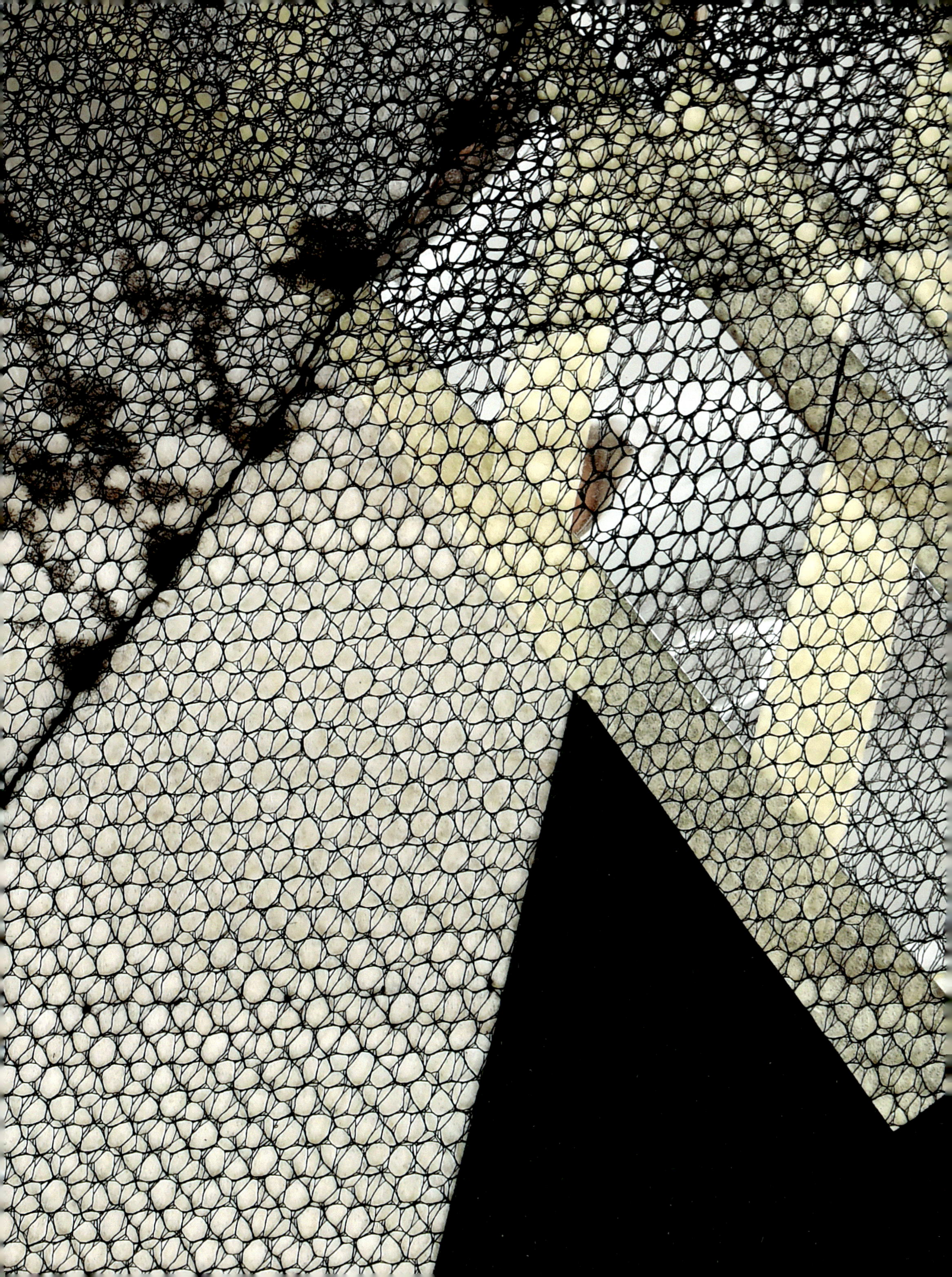

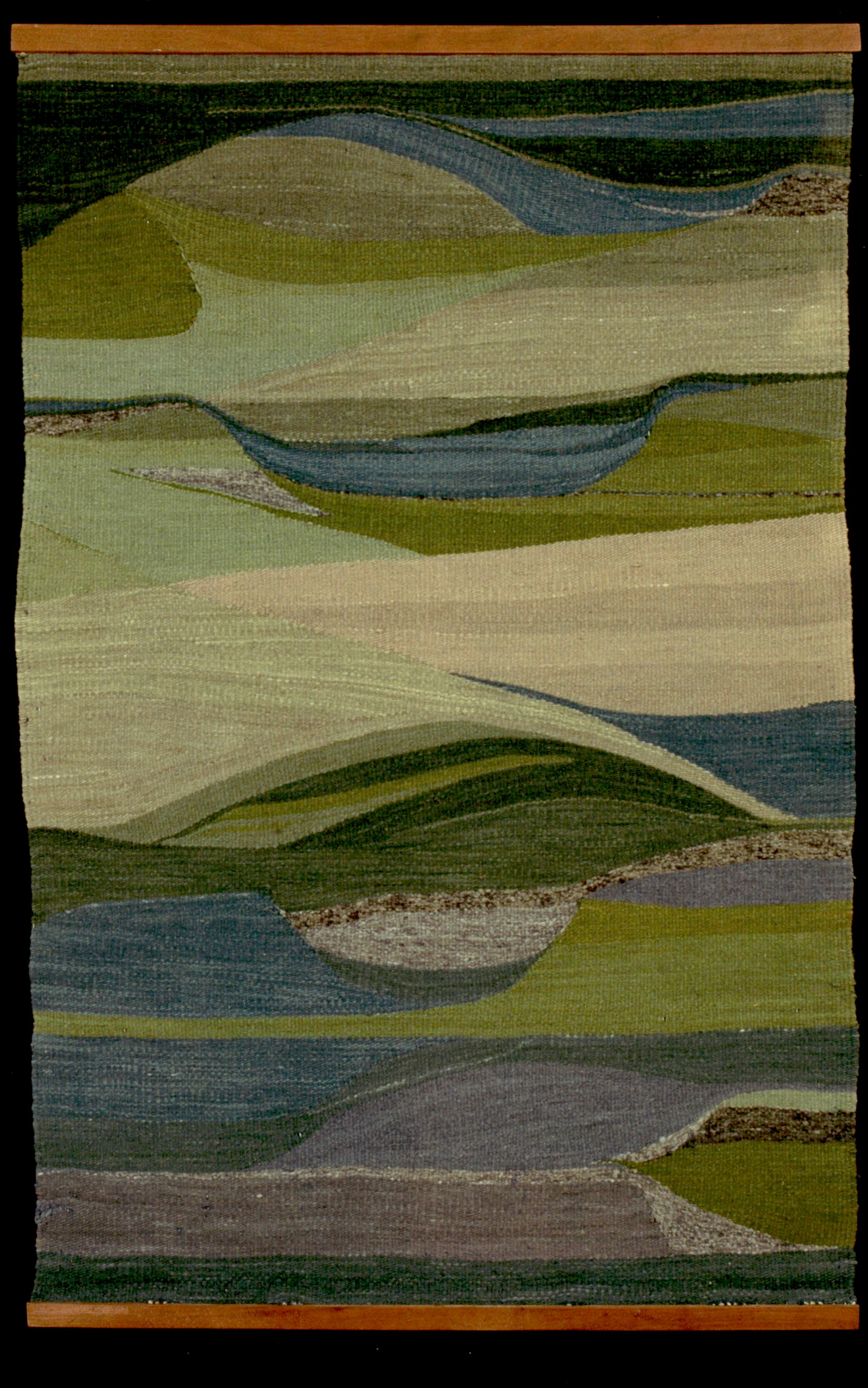

120. Joan Potter Loveless, *Bay Area*, ca. 1960–70.
Wool. 56 × 37 in.

WEAVING AFTER

BLACK MOUNTAIN

MICHAEL BEGGS

Even after the College closed in 1957 and weaving classes ceased, the influence of Black Mountain College textile thought and design lived on. The College's former faculty and students in the weaving program, through their later work, teaching, and writing, continued to participate in weaving discourses and to inspire subsequent generations of textile artists and designers.

After leaving Black Mountain College in 1949, Trude Guermonprez and Anni Albers took very different paths as they both entered into the greatest years of their respective careers. Albers became the first textile artist to have a solo exhibition at the Museum of Modern Art when the exhibition *Anni Albers: Textiles* opened in the fall of 1949. In the 1950s, she taught one-on-one tutorials to select weaving students from her home in New Haven, Connecticut. Her students included artists who studied with her husband Josef at Yale University, such as Sheila Hicks, as well as other people within the Alberses' greater Yale or New Haven orbits, including Dolores Dimbus Bittleman and Dorothy Cavalier Yanik. Freed from the community, teaching, and production responsibilities she had at Black Mountain, Albers's art practice flourished, and she created the pictorial weavings for which she has now become famous. In 1965, she published *On Weaving*, a book that has become a seminal text in weaving and design theory. Perhaps fittingly, *On Weaving* was published near the end of Albers's weaving career; Albers made her last weaving in 1969 before turning to a second artistic career as a printmaker and graphic artist. The first visual motifs she explored as a printmaker during a 1964 visit to Tamarind Lithography Workshop in Los Angeles were loose, complex knots, which she had first drawn in 1947, while on sabbatical from Black Mountain College.[1]

Guermonprez's post-BMC career saw her achieve maturity in her artistic practice, which both built on the early experiments in pictorial and painted-warp techniques she made in *Leaf Study* at Black Mountain College and included adventurous structural developments that took her weavings off the wall and into three dimensions. At the same time, her highly successful tenure as a teacher at California College of Arts and Crafts brought her methods and approach to hundreds of students, many of whom became teachers themselves. Today there are countless weavers who, like Susie Taylor, can identify teachers they studied with who themselves studied with Trude Guermonprez. While Albers's primary influence on contemporary textiles is through her writing, Guermonprez's influence can be measured in her large family tree of students.

Other entries in this book have described the post-BMC careers of student weavers like Lore Kadden Lindenfeld, Lili Blumenau, Else Regensteiner, Marilyn Bauer, Don Alter, Don Wight, Andy Oates, and Don Page, but many other Black Mountain weavers continued to work in weaving or in related media long after leaving Black Mountain College, or found their own voices in weaving and fiber arts that departed from the ways in which they were taught at the College.

Some of the College's weavers found ways to work in related media, even if they did not return to weaving on the loom. Mimi French (Batchelor) made a series of needlepoint embroideries that show a highly personal graphic style coupled with the careful and balanced approach to color that Josef Albers admired in her when

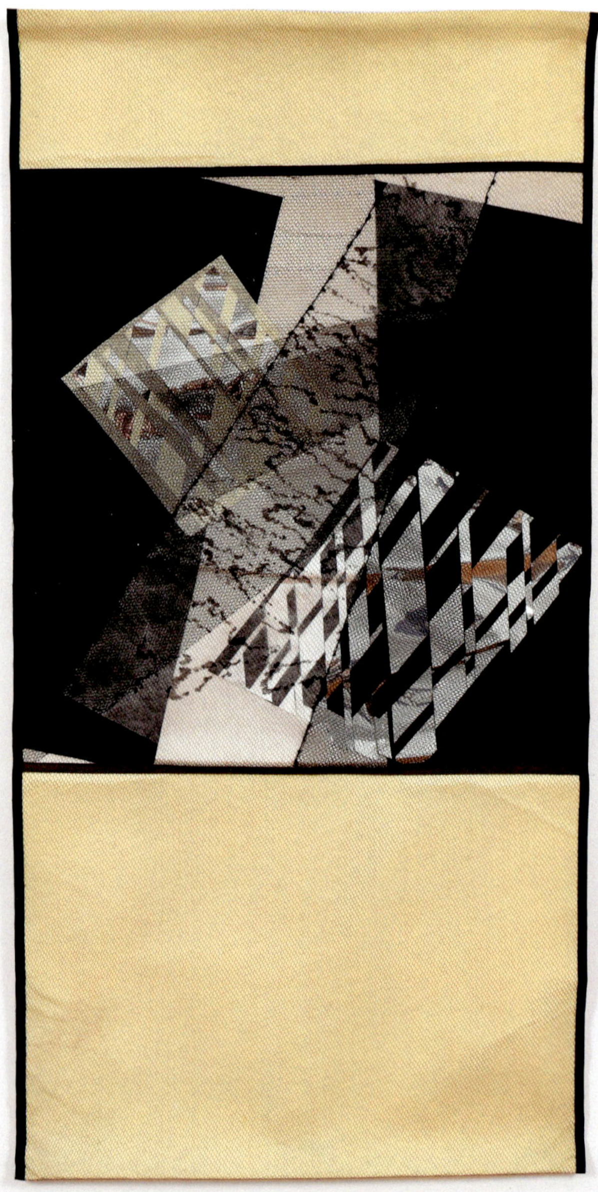

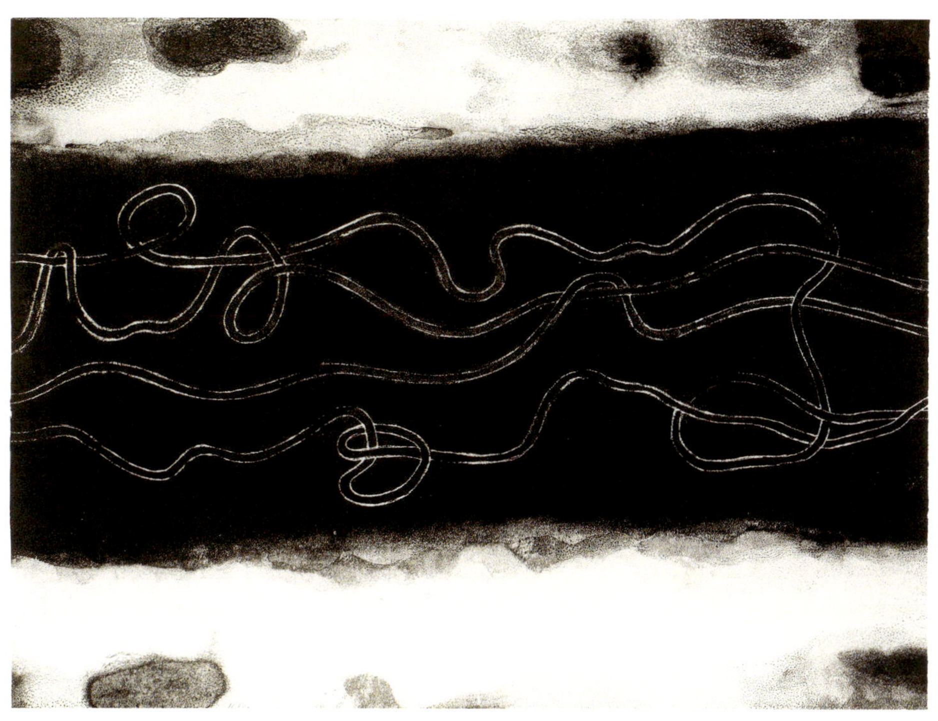

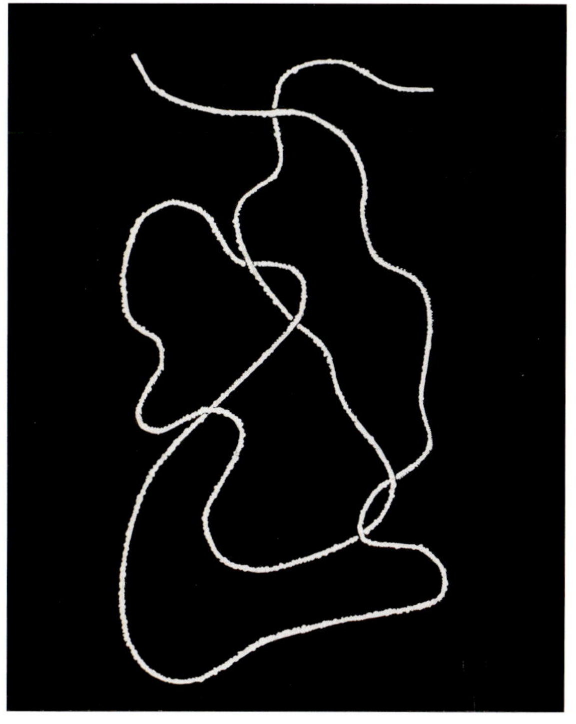

123. Anni Albers, *Drawing for a knot*, 1948.
Gouache on paper. 13 ¾ × 10 ¾ in.

she was his student. Her needlepoint of black-and-white striped and spotted leaves recalls the leaf studies she would have done at Black Mountain as Albers's student, a small nod to BMC's continuing impact on her life and creativity.

The use of found materials was a hallmark of art and design instruction at Black Mountain College. In addition to the non-loom studies done in Anni Albers's weaving classes, Josef Albers's students made *matières,* which explored material and textural interaction and deception and were so ubiquitous that students made jokes and sang songs about them.[2] Reflecting the joint lineage of their materials-oriented education, and their heightened textile literacy as former weavers, several former Black Mountain weavers made fabric collages after leaving the College. Elizabeth Schmitt Jennerjahn, who had taken weaving at Black Mountain, made several pieces using collage and hand and machine embroidery techniques, which often featured found textiles. Robert Rauschenberg, whom Anni Albers had described as an "erratic" weaver who was "sometimes brilliant, sometimes just average," also made prominent use of found fabrics in many of his works, including, in some cases, whole shirts.[3] In

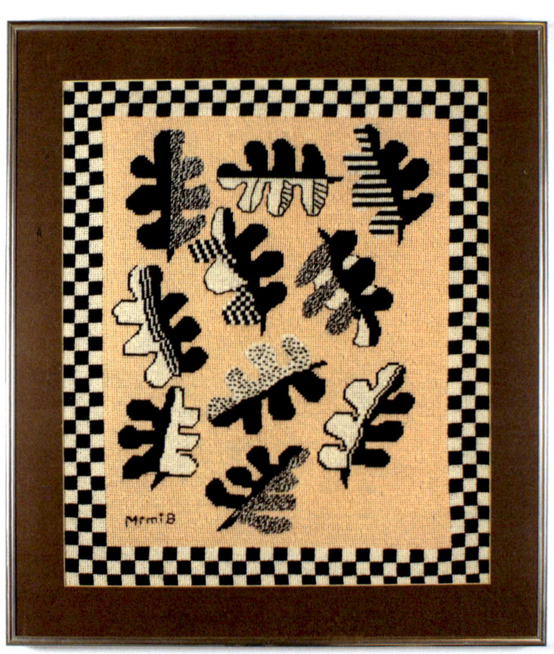

the 1980s, inspired by Robert Wilson and Philip Glass's opera *Einstein on the Beach,* Lore Kadden Lindenfeld began making a series of fabric collages titled *Paths of Illumination* (fig. 121). Merrill Gillespie, who had studied weaving with Andy Oates in 1950 and 1951, returned to textiles much later, contributing a panel to the 1992 AIDS Quilt in memory of James Robison.

Some of those who continued to weave forged their own paths by embracing more traditional approaches. Joan Potter Loveless, who attended Black Mountain College under the names of Joan Couch or Joan Sihvonen and had taken weaving with Anni Albers, Franziska Mayer, and Trude Guermonprez in 1946–47, became a prolific weaver of handspun and hand-dyed tapestries in Taos, New Mexico. Loveless continued to weave after leaving Black Mountain in 1948, weaving with cards, frame looms, and a small table loom made at Black Mountain by her sister-in-law, Miriam "Mim" Sihvonen. Throughout her "loomless" years she remained "sure that I would one day start weaving tapestries," and, after moving Taos in 1956 with her husband, painter and BMC alum Oli Sihvonen, she finally began weaving tapestries "primarily about the landscape."[4]

125. Joan Potter Loveless with two tapestries, 1963. Photographer unknown.

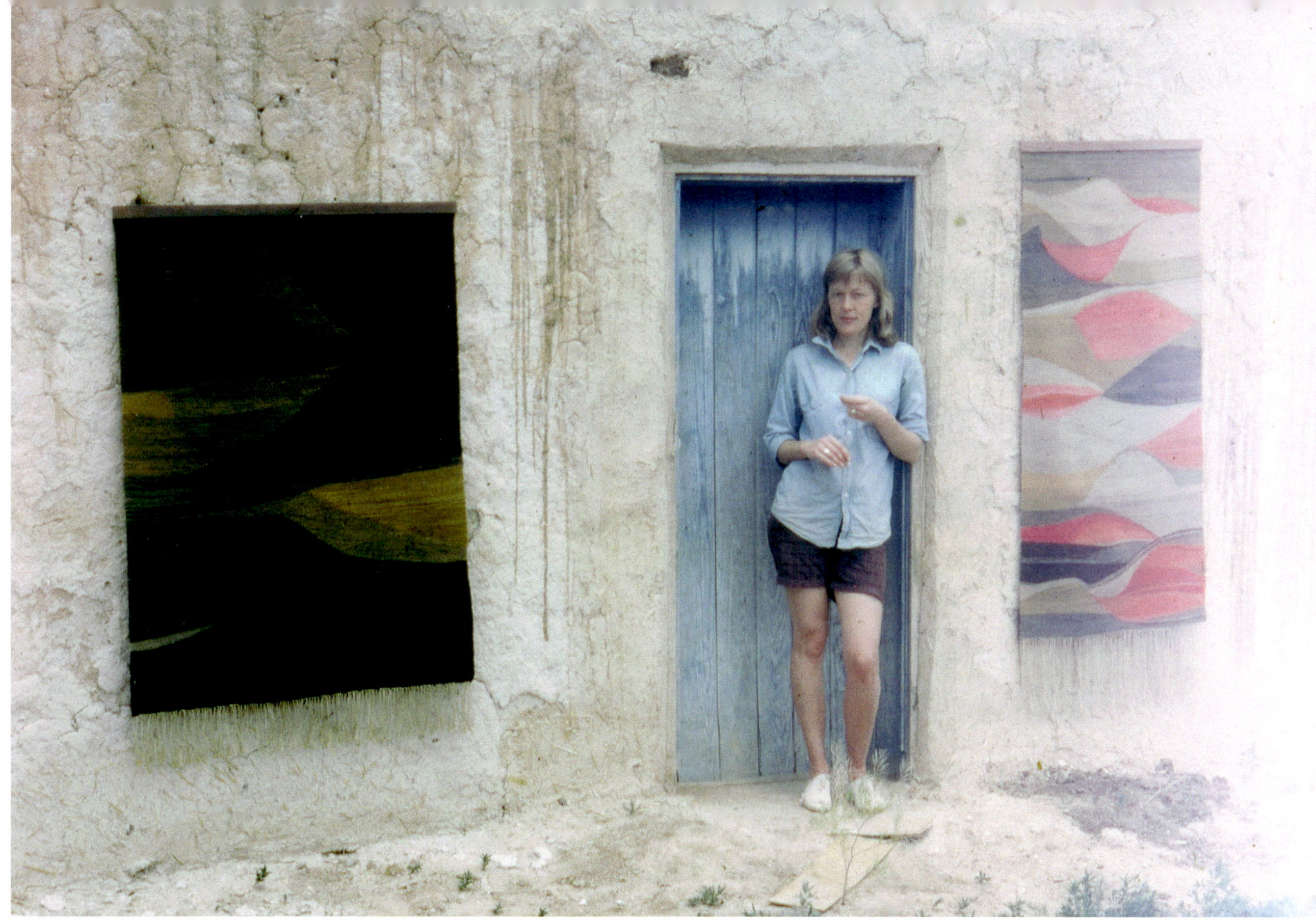

> In a way, I was weaving the activity of what I saw—the mysterious ways in which a bit of
> shadow would seem to become a form where it lay across a vast stretch of the desert
> floor, or how distant mountain peaks would appear to become blended when their
> inclines where thrown into similar shadow at the same time of day. I didn't try to weave
> these specific physical events; I simply watched them and they became part of my
> visual vocabulary, experiences from which to draw when I began to weave a tapestry.[5]

Loveless recounted her experiences as a weaver in her book, *Three Weavers,*
which became a classic text on handweaving and handcraft as a way of life, continuing
the legacy of Black Mountain weavers promoting their medium in the written word.

The impact of Black Mountain College continues to be felt, and the legacy of its
weavers continues. In the following essay, Jennifer Nieling charts the history of Nantucket Looms, a company co-founded by BMC alumnus Andy Oates, which operates
to this day. At the very end of this book, we feature the work of contemporary artists
whose work connects to the themes and techniques explored by weavers at Black
Mountain College. In keeping with Black Mountain's interdisciplinary environment,
these artists work in a variety of methods and media. Their words and work serve as
a bridge between Black Mountain and contemporary craft, art, and design.

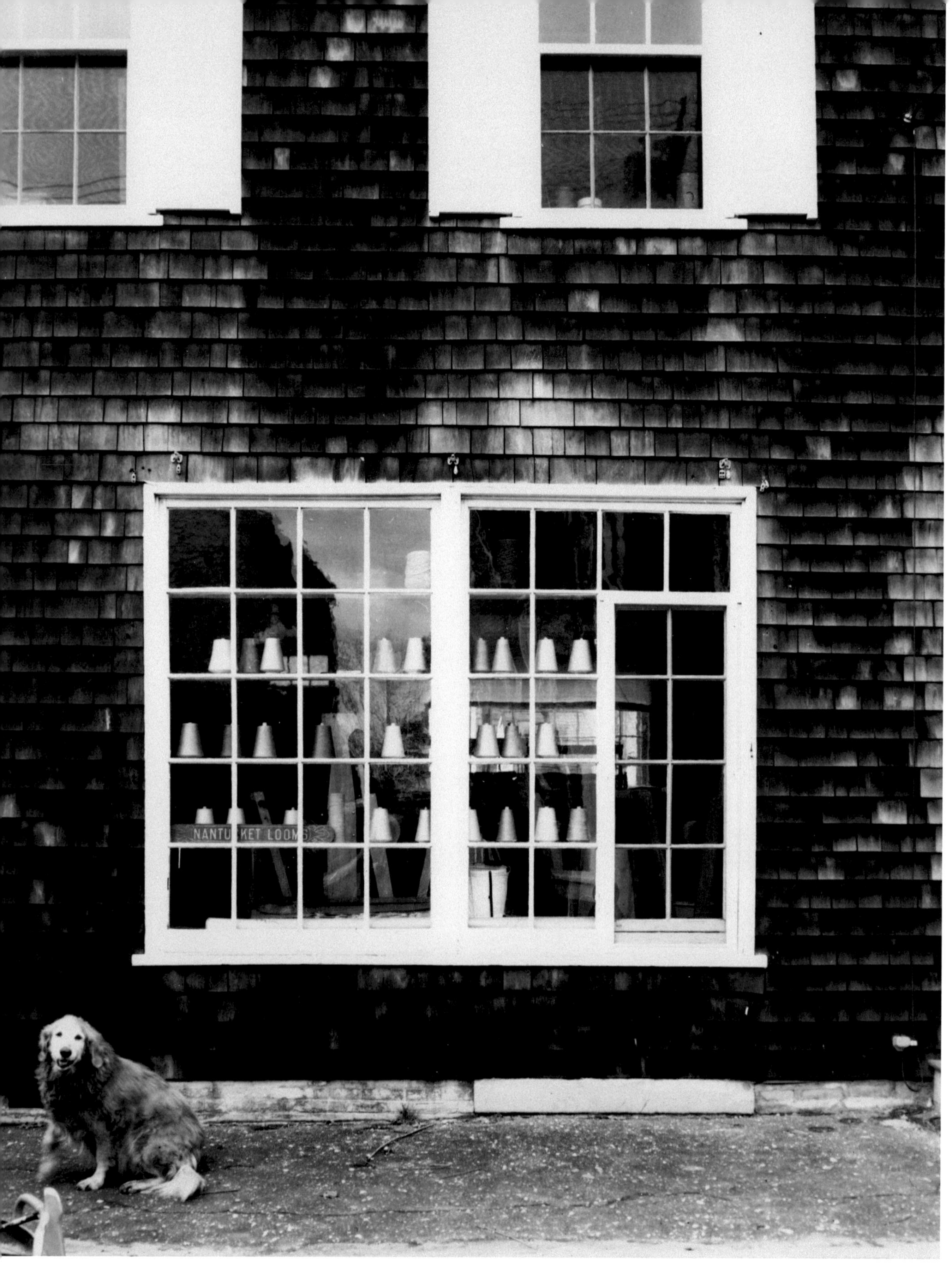

126. Nantucket Looms building at 16 Main Street,
Nantucket, 1968. Photograph by Jack E. Boucher.

A BLACK MOUNTAIN LEGACY ON NANTUCKET

ANDY OATES AND NANTUCKET LOOMS

JENNIFER NIELING

Nantucket may seem an unlikely place to find the influence of Black Mountain College, but it was on that island thirty miles off the coast of Cape Cod in Massachusetts that Black Mountain alumnus Andy Oates built his life and career. In the 1960s, the sleepy island of sandy beaches and cedar-shingled cottages was just beginning to transform into the luxury destination it is today. Longtime summer resident Walter Beinecke Jr. was buying up and rebuilding the town's waterfront in an effort to revitalize the town, promoting historical tourism and capitalizing on the island's early history as a whaling port.[1] It was out of this period of renewal that Nantucket Looms was born. Working as co-founder and head weaver of Nantucket Looms, and influenced by the teachings of Black Mountain College, Oates found his calling and left a legacy that endures more than fifty years later.

Oates was interested in the arts from a young age and fell in love with weaving while attending Rhode Island School of Design on the GI Bill. Upon specializing in weaving in his second year, Oates was disappointed with the "boring" way that it was taught at RISD by retired industry men. He wanted to approach weaving more creatively. Encouraged by a friend to contact Black Mountain College, he decided to transfer there based on the personal response he received from Anni Albers.[2] Oates attended BMC from the spring of 1949 through the summer of 1951, and while he studied weaving under Anni Albers and Trude Guermonprez and color under Josef Albers for only one term before they left the College, they made a profound impact on him.[3]

Oates's first assignment in Anni's class was to create a backstrap loom, like the looms ancient Peruvian weavers used. At Black Mountain, he developed an appreciation for historic textiles, even serving as curator of the Harriett Engelhardt Memorial

Collection for a short time after Albers left the College.[4] Oates got to know the Alberses on a personal level and later echoed his former roommate Robert Rauschenberg in calling Josef Albers the best teacher he ever had.[5] Shortly after the Alberses' departure, Oates switched his focus to photography, ultimately becoming Black Mountain College's first (and only) graduate in that specialty.[6] His graduation program included both photography projects and teaching a summer weaving class at the college.[7]

Andy Oates first came to Nantucket, as many have, for just a summer. It was the late 1950s, and Oates's Boylston Street Print Gallery in Harvard Square was quiet during the summer months, so he closed shop and headed to the island at the invitation of a friend who suggested he start an art supply store there for the season. One job led to another, and Oates soon found himself working year-round in the kitchen at the Woodbox Inn, where he met his partner in life and business, William "Bill" Euler, as well as Walter Beinecke Jr. and his wife Mary Ann.[8] Mr. Beinecke's nonprofit Nantucket Historical Trust was in the midst of renovating the Jared Coffin House, a brick mansion-turned-hotel, purchased by the Trust in 1961 and renamed for the wealthy

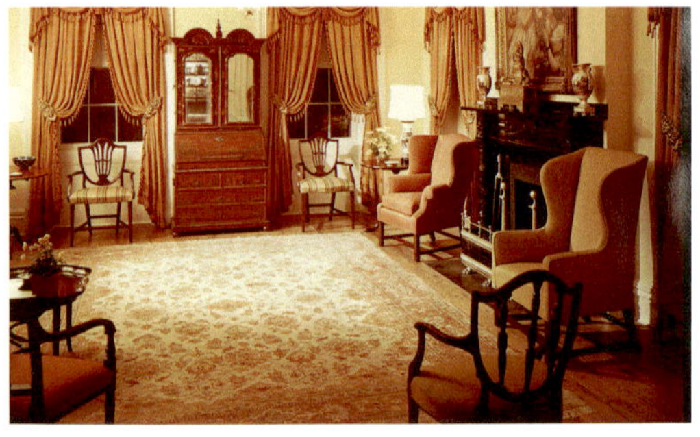

whaling merchant who built it in 1845.[9] Over coffee one night, the Beineckes asked Oates what he would do if he had a lot of money. He replied that he would start a craft movement. Serendipitously, Mary Ann, a passionate weaver, needleworker, and textile historian, had the same idea.[10] The hotel project was the perfect opportunity to make their dream a reality. The hotel would be redecorated in an historic style that recalled the whaling era and would include antiques from the seventeenth and eighteenth centuries. They decided that the textiles, too, should look historic. They would create them on-island, building a new local industry with year-round employment.

Mrs. Beinecke acted as manager and recruited Oates as master weaver to train locals in handweaving. Together, they set up a

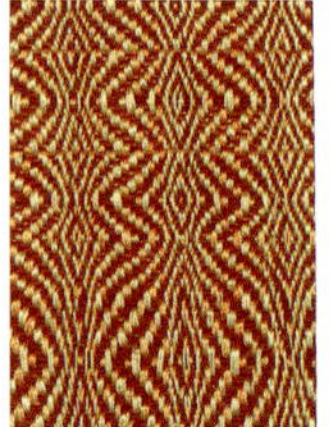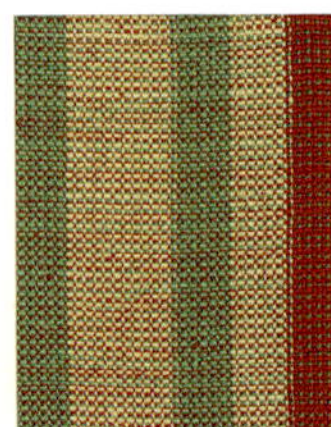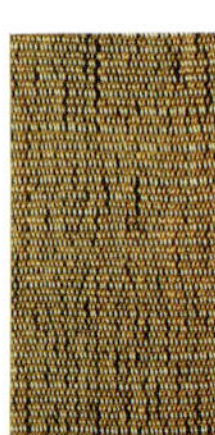

weaving workshop on Main Street and researched early nineteenth-century fabrics in libraries and in Mrs. Beinecke's own rare book collection.[11] Over the next two years they produced more than 6,000 yards of textiles for the hotel, including upholstery, draperies, coverlets and bed hangings, as well as carpets and rugs. The designs, which included herringbone weaves, traditional overshot patterns, and a special chenille weave for rugs, were woven with the highest quality natural fiber yarns sourced from suppliers around the world and custom-dyed to Mrs. Beinecke's specifications.[12]

By the time the Jared Coffin House opened in May 1963, Oates and Beinecke's weavers were already taking private commissions, and an extensive public relations campaign promoted not only the hotel and island but also the new weaving venture. They were officially called Nantucket Looms by that fall in an extensive feature in *Handweaver and Craftsman*. Over the next several years, the company went through a period of growth and transition as they worked toward commercial viability. Andy's team grew from four to eleven full-time weavers, the sub-

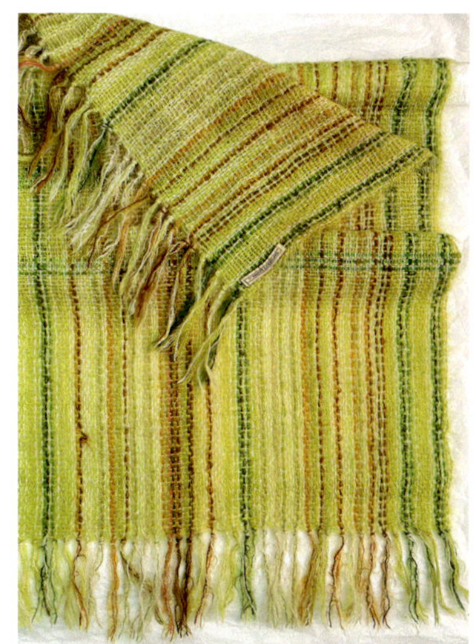

stantial workshop acquired new Macomber looms outfitted with custom production-friendly warp frames, and they added 125 designs of sportswear tweeds to their already extensive offerings, which included interior fabrics and custom options.[13]

In 1964, Nantucket Looms, still under the Nantucket Historical Trust, designed a new line of more than two dozen upholstery and drapery fabrics to be marketed by New York–based luxury textile distributor Thaibok Fabrics.[14] These new offerings signaled a shift from reproduction historic textiles to a conscious effort to appeal to the modern market, including architects and interior decorators. Nantucket Looms branded itself as "Modern Interpretations of Fine Traditional Handcrafts" and illustrated this shift in focus in a sample book that contained photographs and textile samples from the Jared Coffin House followed by eight new modern fabrics, each in several colorways, named after geographical features of Nantucket.[15] Promotional images from this time show textiles in both historic revival settings and more modern spaces, as with the casement fabrics *Hummock Pond, Coskata,* and *Sacacha Pond.*[16] These textiles, designed by Oates to gently filter light with more open weaves in a soft, neutral-colored worsted wool embody the modernist approach of textiles designed to interact with space—an approach promoted by Anni Albers and others at the time.[17]

The modern designs Oates created for Nantucket Looms show his distinctive approach and reflect the spirit of experimentation, focus on materials and texture, simplicity of design, and adept handling of color that he learned at Black Mountain. Anni Albers encouraged her students to experiment with different materials to hone their "tactile sensibility" and their understanding of the relationship between structure and material. Oates continued this experimentation by using a wide range of unique yarns in his early textiles, which included "intricate couture constructions made with leather strips and velvet ribbons, blended with silk, mohair, and wool yarns."[18] Mohair shawls, scarves, and throws with accents of velvet and satin ribbons or strips of fabric quickly became a trademark of Nantucket Looms that Oates would continue to weave throughout his career.[19]

Albers's influence can be seen in the understated fabrics in neutral colors that Oates designed in which simple weave structures allowed texture and material to be featured, such as the "particularly fine nubbed cotton with the texture of smooth linen and the appearance of unbleached muslin" and a "handsome box design in undyed

TRUDE REMEMBERED

1982

This was to be a very special day, that day in the summer of 1951. Two friends and I were driving up to Guerneville, [California] to [Pond Farm's] Octagon House to hear a talk by a weaver, newly arrived from Europe via Black Mountain College. The speaker was Trude Guermonprez, who became my teacher, friend, and mentor. She helped give a direction to my life, and her work and teaching would soon influence the course of weaving in the United States and abroad for the next three decades.

The large audience waited, silent with anticipation and excitement. Trude was sitting in the middle of the round room. She was slightly built and wiry; her skin was olive. Her dark bobbed hair, parted at the side, surrounded a long fascinating face dominated by large beautiful eyes (no wonder she had modeled for Gerhard Marcks, who did beautiful drawings and sculpture of her). The few things that stand out in my memory and from notes about her talk were her concerns about a handweaver's place in society; and the machine and its place and necessity in life; and the belief that understanding the machine allowed for creativity. She said that searching only for the new and different was rather noncreative, she cautioned us to be aware of the limitations of the loom and she urged us to take from nature—threads being nature.

Trude had a large cross-sectioned board on which she moved and pinned black squares representing warp thread to illustrate basic weaves. I had been weaving for two years and not one of my teachers had explained the loom or the weaves, and this made a deep impression on me. Here was a person with much greater knowledge about weaving than anyone I'd met before. Her thoughts and concerns were profound and went much deeper than anyone I knew. All the weavers around here seemed to be interested only in making pretty placemats and glittery fabrics. I was

133. Kay Sekimachi, *Sampler*, ca. 1950s.
Cotton and linen. 14½ × 9⅜ in.

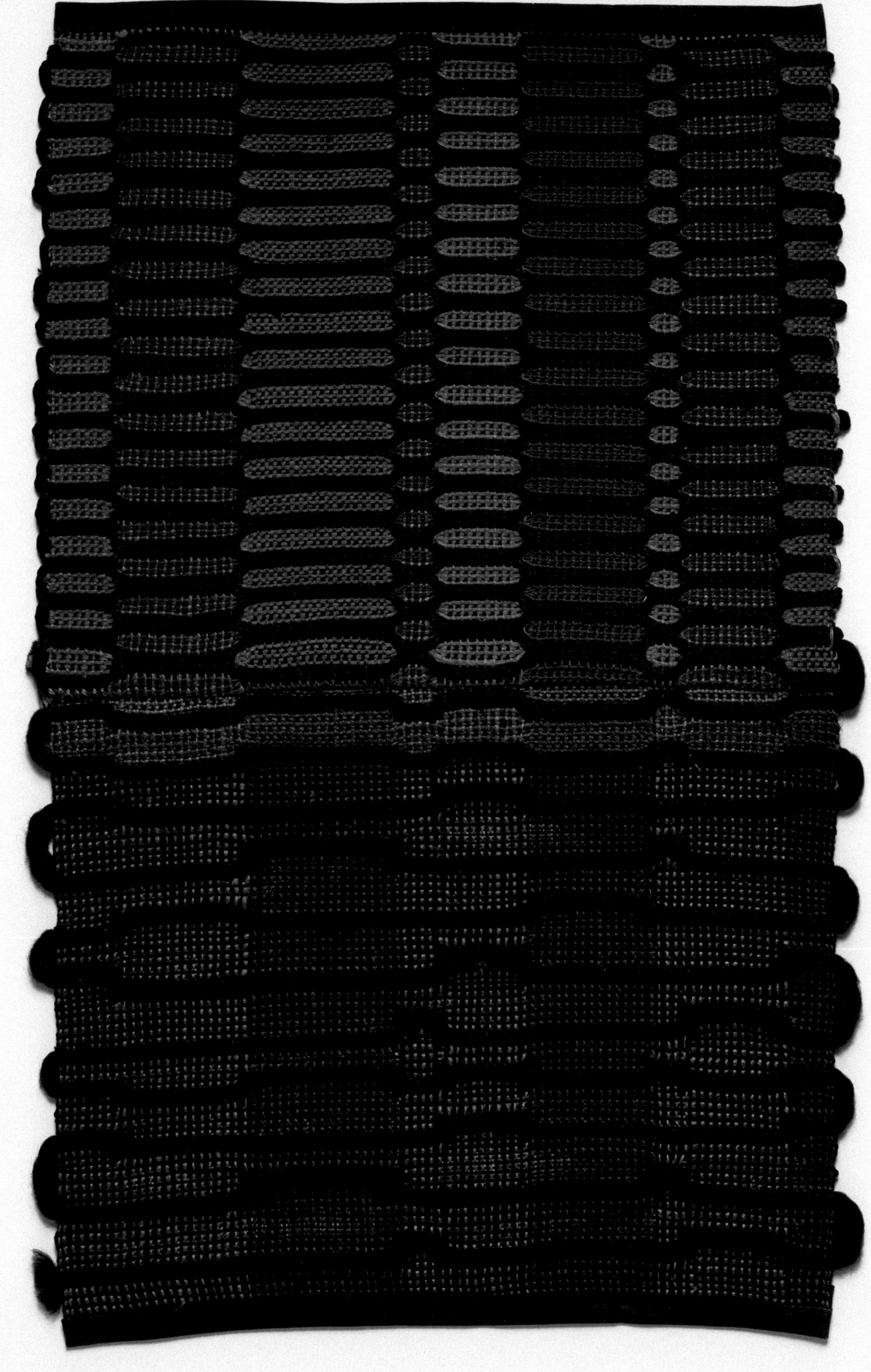

introduced to her but didn't have a word to say because I too was shy and already in awe of her.

My next encounter with Trude was at UC Berkeley. Lea Miller had asked her to speak to the faculty and students of the Decorative Arts Department, but it was open to the public. We found ourselves in a packed room in Dwinelle Hall. Trude seemed shy and spoke quietly. All I could remember is that afterward, when I could get close to her, I asked her if she wove samples (being so unsure of my own work, I guess I wanted to know how she worked), and she answered, surprised at such a question, "Oh, sure."

I wasn't able to take the first summer session she taught at the California College of Arts and Crafts in 1953, but the next summer was a turning point for me when I enrolled in her classes. It was the beginning of a life-long friendship with Trude.

Her teaching was Bauhaus-oriented and included her own sensitive insights. She studied in Germany with a Bauhaus-trained weaver, [Benita Koch-Otte]. She had also worked with, and substituted for, Anni Albers at Black Mountain College. It was just what I needed. I had been weaving for about four years then but had no understanding of what I was doing. She started the session by having us clarify in our minds what weaving was, and what function the parts of the loom played in the process of weaving. She stressed getting to know the loom and told how a backstrap weaver in a Oaxaca village becomes one with the loom. She was thorough in presenting and explaining technical material. She stressed the importance of understanding materials according to the origin of the fibers and urged us to get to know and love materials by touching, seeing, listening, tasting, and smelling them.

She spoke of texture as an important aspect of weaving: threads have texture and weaves make texture. We drafted, studied weaves, and wove samplers. We studied materials and made tactile charts. She spoke of color as an important design element, and we made color studies. We analyzed woven fabrics and learned to trace back a finished piece to list its point of departure. She impressed upon us the importance of being flexible, of having an open mind, and not starting with preconceived ideas. She made us think; we worked and questioned. Suddenly that summer my eyes were opened and I knew weaving was for me. By the end of the session I was in a state of euphoria. She broadened my vision and more importantly, I made a true friend.

In the classroom she was firm and critical and would let us know if something we did displeased her. She was not one to give praise lightly, but one day as she was leaving, she quietly said to me, "I like what you did today a lot." I was very pleased and at the same time felt a responsibility that I must continue to do much better. On another occasion, as I was struggling to solve a weaving problem, and trying too hard to come up with something fancy and different, she said, "Sometimes plain weave is the right solution." Of course, she was right. As I continue to weave today, I can almost hear her words: "Choose a weave that expresses the thread best. Listen to the warp. Imagination is wonderful, if toned down. Always think in terms of how can one do this more simply to achieve the same effect."

She was a great teacher; she gave just enough. We, on the other hand, were terrible students. We were so demanding and expected so much from her instead of trying to work out problems for ourselves and make our own discoveries.

I don't know if Trude had it planned that I should become a teacher but, before I knew it, she had me substituting for her during the summer sessions at CCAC, and she also gave me the courage to take on other teaching assignments.

Trude, like most people, had favorites and didn't get along with everyone—students and associates alike. But she loved life and people. She was stimulated by the sharing and the give-and-take that occurred in workshops and at American Craft Council meetings and conferences.

Dropping in on Trude was always fun. She invariably had something to show me and often it was her current work. She would insist that I stay for lunch regardless of who was with me, and we would feast on fresh salad with greens from John's organic garden and cheeses and homemade bread. John, if he were home, and Johanna Jalowetz, Trude's mother, would join us. We would talk, gossip, and laugh. As our friendship grew, we also shared a wider range of problems in our daily lives. As busy as Trude was, she entertained quite regularly. She had a need for company. Her dinners and Christmas parties, or slide shows upon returning from a trip, were always events to which I looked forward. If there was a weaver from out of state or abroad, she would have a few friends over for an evening of lively talk.

While I was teaching a summer session at UCLA in 1975, I had a call from Trude who was in the hospital. She had undergone surgery and asked me to substitute for her at CCAC that fall, while she recuperated. The report wasn't good, but she responded to chemotherapy and, amazingly, returned to teaching right after the new year. My last meeting with Trude was a few months later at the performance of a new folk opera, whose sets and costumes were designed by a mutual friend and colleague, Suzanne Schwartzman. When I returned from a trip a week later, there was a letter from Trude waiting, which had an ominous overtone. She asked me about monofilament nylon, and she was full of excitement about sending a photograph of her weaving to *Craft Horizons* for its cover. She was living her life to the end.

A fitting tribute to Trude's spirit comes from the work of one of her favorite poets:

> The conditions of a solitary bird are five:
> the first, that it flies to the highest point;
> the second, that it does not suffer
> for company, not even of its own kind;
> the third, that it aims its beak to the skies;
> the fourth, that it does not have a definite color;
> the fifth, that it sings very softly.
>
> —Carlos Castañeda,
> "San Juan de la Cruz, Dichos de Luz y Amor," *Tales of Power*

CONTEMPORARY CONNECTIONS

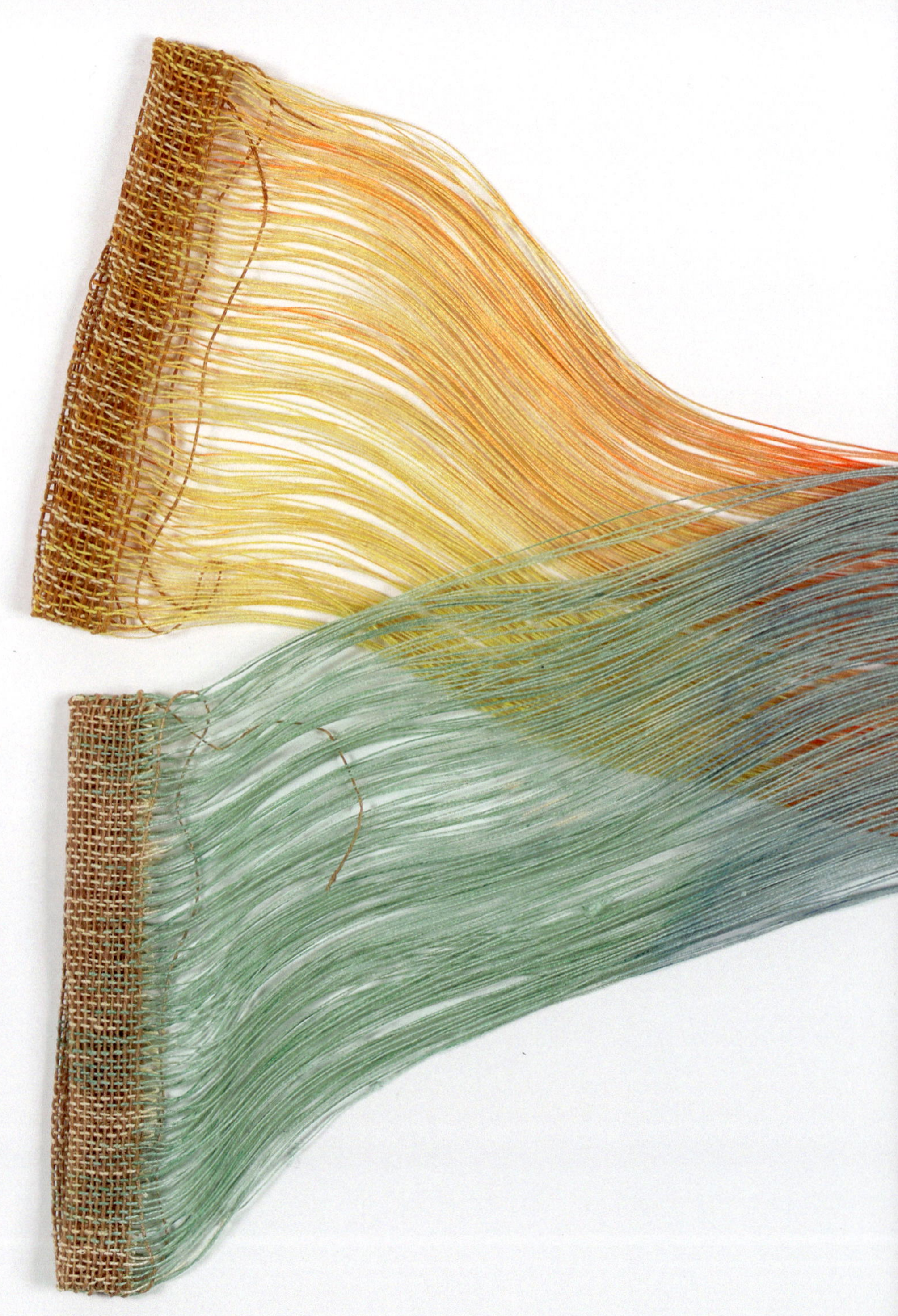

134. Kay Sekimachi, *Cross Warp*, ca. 1980s.
Linen. 8½ × 12½ in.

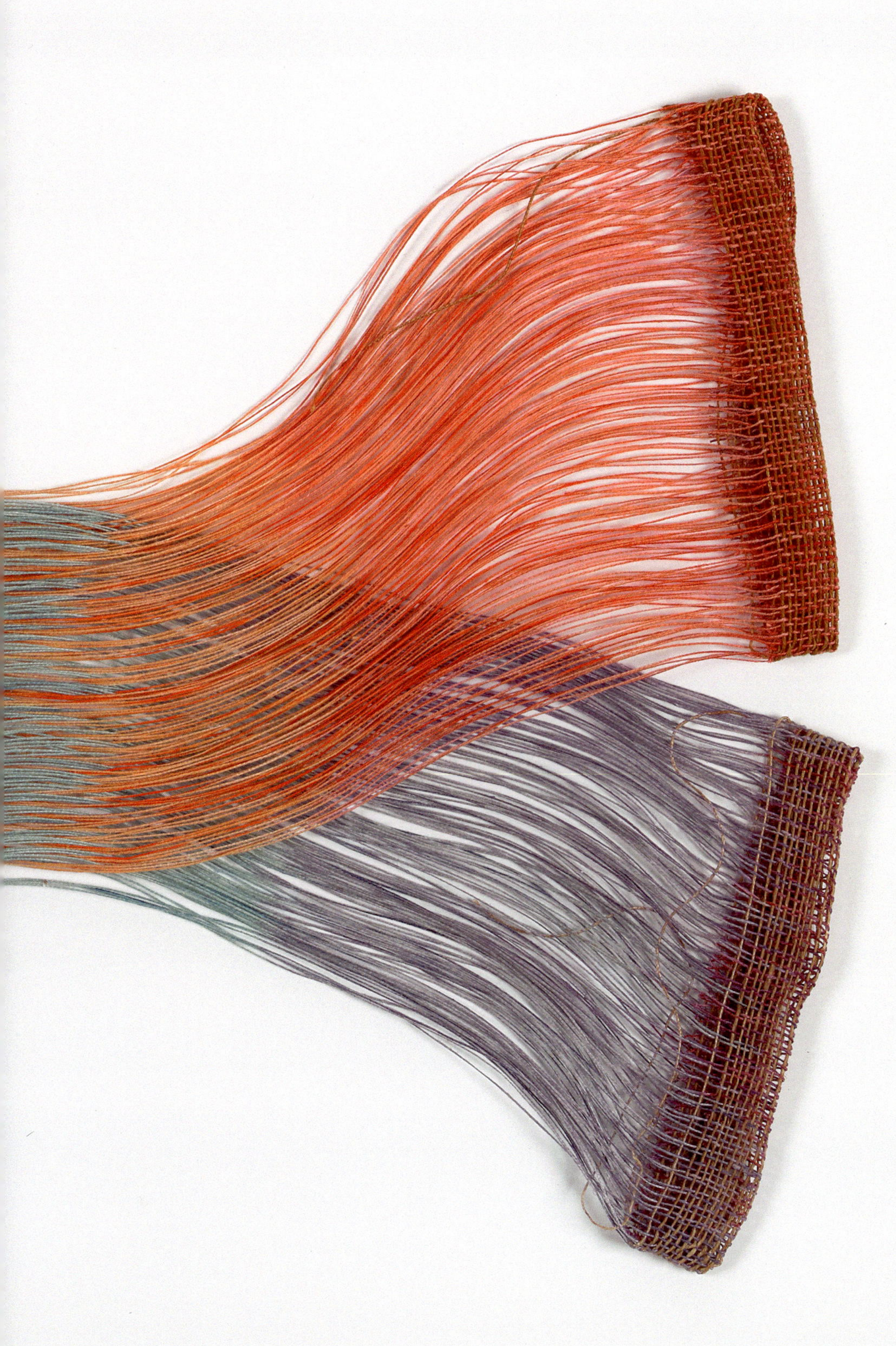

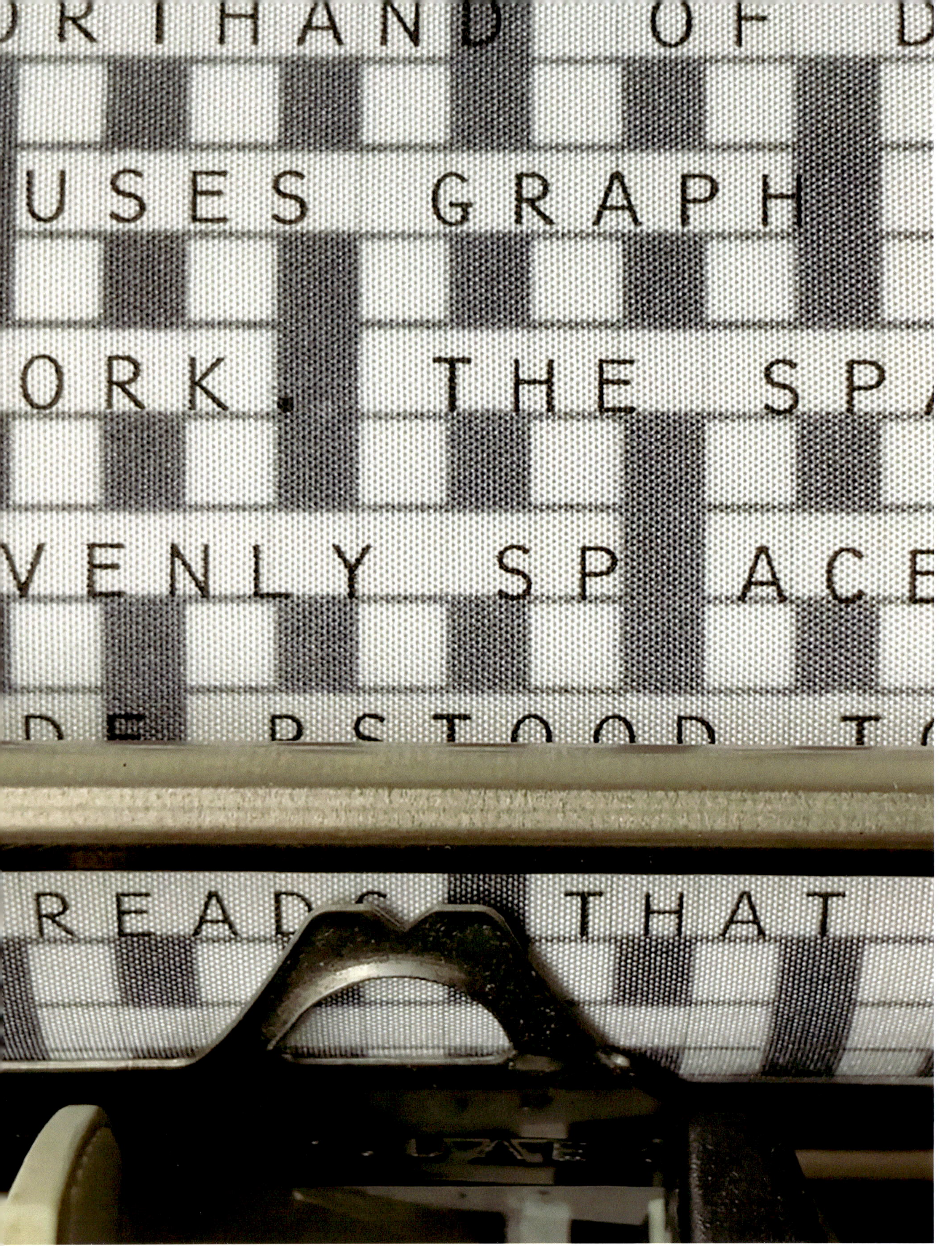

135. Jen Bervin, *On Weaving*, 2021.
Still from HD video.

JEN BERVIN

Jen Bervin is a poet and interdisciplinary artist based in Guilford, CT. Her work often explores the relationships between text and textiles and is based on long-term research. Her artist's book Draft Notation *(2014) expands upon the typewriter-based design studies done by Anni Albers and her students at Black Mountain, bringing those visual and haptic-textural studies into the realm of poetics.* On Weaving *(2021) converts Albers's written words into textile, interweaving and overlaying them on illustrations from Albers's book printed on silk. In these works Bervin does not repeat Albers's work, but instead uses her methods and words to get at something deeper (and perhaps tacit) behind and between the words and letters.*

HOW DID YOU BEGIN WEAVING? WHO WERE YOUR TEACHERS?

Anni Albers's landmark book *On Weaving* (Middletown, CT: Wesleyan University Press, 1965) was, is, and will always be my teacher. It was my stimulus to study weaving, one specifically motivated by her typed studies. "Studies"—the verb and noun—and the process-oriented thinking and doing held within—is a teacher too. Albers's work and this book are the basis of three works I've made over the last decade—a durational performance titled *Weaving at Gridspace* (2011), and artist book edition titled *Draft Notation* (Granary Books, 2014), and more recently *On Weaving* (2021), an edition and series of videos celebrating Anni Albers's book chapter by chapter, combining her three chosen mediums: writing, printmaking, and weaving.

I'm very grateful to The Josef and Anni Albers Foundation for multiple residencies and visits. In their archive, I studied Lore Kadden Lindenfeld's impeccable notes, meticulously detailing Anni Albers's BMC weaving course in drawings and typescript. Lore was one of the very few graduates of Black Mountain College. During one visit, I digitized her notes—I've been delighted to find many other artists have taken those up.

Reading is a form of weaving performed by the eyes and/or the finger. I don't remember learning to read, but I remember beloved hands holding index fingers in books, thumbs anchoring fore edges. Shu Bervin, my grandmother, read to us and taught my sister and I how to weave when we were very young. Fittingly, we made potholders, weaving together our shared love of the kitchen. I may have one from that time; though it easily could have been anyone in the family who made it. I'm guessing the second form of weaving that I learned—the lattice top crust of a pie—was from my mother.

My first formal weaving class was expertly taught by Ellie Hess at FIT in New York; she designed weave structures for heart valves. Madelyn van der Hoogt at The Weavers' School on Whidbey Island taught advanced weave structures—deflected double weave delighted me most. At some point, I learned how to weave the headbands of books at the Center for Book Arts in New York.

The best definition of teaching I have ever heard came from Lucy Ann Yakeleya (K'asho Got'ınę from Radilih Koe) at the Indigenous Haute Couture Fashion Residency at Banff Centre. She said she was there "in support." Present to pass on knowledge of hide tanning and porcupine quillwork that she had been taught to the next generation. Mutual, lived, interdisciplinary contexts that involve curiosity, questioning, and experimentation are my preferred. Francesca Capone, briefly my student, is still my weaving teacher and often supports my questions.

Spiders, silkworms, birds, hyphae—weavers and teachers are everywhere.

Every weaver, every weaving teaches.

TELL US ABOUT YOUR LOOMS AND HOW YOU USE THEM.

My primary loom—the one I use the most—is an IBM Wheelwriter II by Lexmark. Though technically a typewriter, it has a "memory" and can be programmed to replay texts or patterns as a weft thread weaves back and forth. I've used it to make so many projects at this point, but *Draft Notation* and *On Weaving* are the most obvious examples. I also have a Glimakra countermarche floor loom, most often dissembled like Imi Knoebel's sculpture *Room 19*, and a double hexagonal loom (modeled on Dieter Roth's *Book 4A*) assembled from numerous sets of Speed-O-Weave looms. It is literally tabled, as triangular weaving takes a very particular mindset.

HOW DO YOU EXPLORE THE MATERIALS THAT YOU USE?
HOW DO YOU DRAW INSPIRATION FROM OTHER DISCIPLINES?

I gravitate toward what is beyond me, my knowledge, my skills, to explore materials. The way material scientists like Fiorenzo Omenetto at Tufts University Silklab work from the unique properties of a particular material outward—without preconceived ideas about where new understandings will lead—is very humbling and instructive to me. It strikes me as rooted curiosity. I also admire conservators like Debora Mayer at Harvard Library's Weissman Preservation Center who both intricately and structurally understand materials that must be regarded as transforming and in motion over long periods of time. She's the expert currently imaging embossments on Dickinson's fascicle manuscripts—her studies to arrive at an approach are stunning. Our conversations around the plant fibers, textiles, and paper as a continuum rooted in science, technology, history, and culture continue to inspire collaboration.

Research is a significant part of my practice. You might say I layer research experiences of material as one way of approaching deeper understandings of them. I often don't know where things will lead and draw tremendously from the haptic, from my sense of touch and embodied knowledge. I also take pleasure in making and gathering samples and tests, living ambiently with materials—being in their midst. Like books, materials sometimes find you at the right time, when you're ready for them, even when they've been there all along.

DO YOU FEEL CONNECTED TO BLACK MOUNTAIN COLLEGE? IF YES, HOW?

I have long held the dream of collaboratively participating in a new and very different Black Mountain College when the time is right. Anni Albers and Ruth Asawa are North Stars to me. Their ceaseless curiosity, active commitment to practice, emphasis on process and listening to materials, their larger vision in support of art education—all such a tall order! Experimental, experiential art education in community has always appealed deeply to me—the focus on innovation in pedagogy, questions, fluidity in learning from everyone and everything around you—these make for such wild, messy, rigorous, surprising spaces to try things out. When it works best, this community makes inclusive space to experiment and fail, encourages divergent, differentiated work, and holds space and time enough to nourish transformative, lifelong friendships.

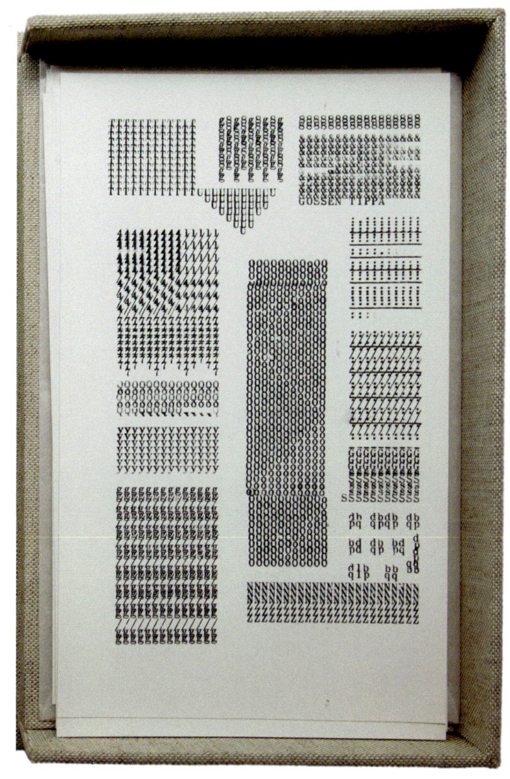

There are so many BMC artists I admire beyond Anni Albers and Ruth Asawa—Dorothea Rockburne, Gwendolyn Knight Lawrence, M.C. Richards, John Cage, Buckminster Fuller, Ray Johnson, Robert Rauschenberg, Jonathan Williams / Jargon Society, Trude Guermonprez, Leo Lionni and more. My wife, the artist Charlotte Lagarde, studied with Lucien Marquis. Lucien's wife Jane "Slats" Slater Marquis studied weaving with Anni Albers. One of the first things that lured Charlotte and me into conversation eleven years ago was the inordinate amount of BMC books in my library. Our library continues to grow.

On Weaving *courtesy of Catharine Clark Gallery.*
Draft Notation *is a Granary Books project.*

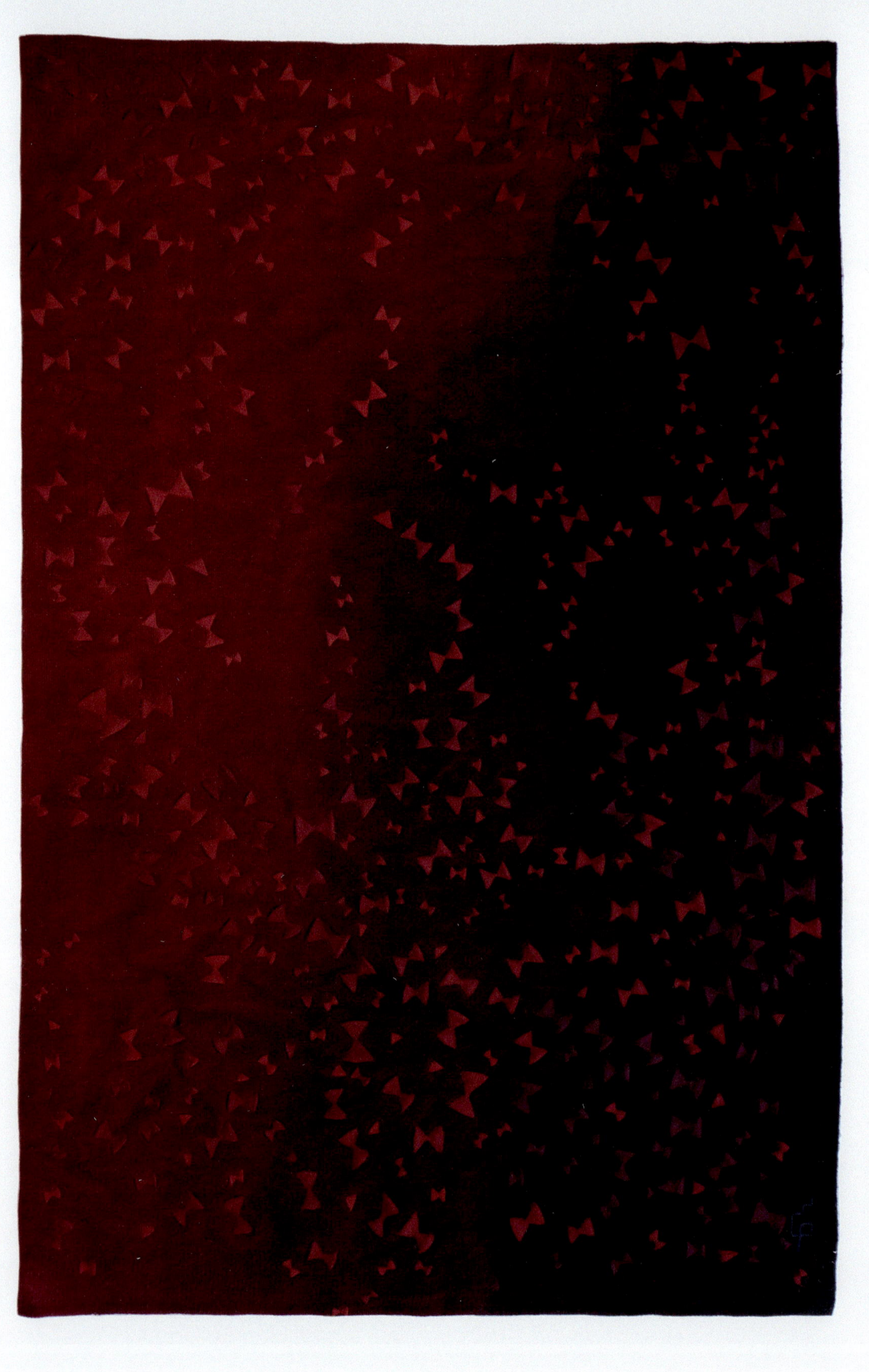

137. Porfirio Gutiérrez, *Untitled, from Transmigra-
tion*, 2022. Wool dyed with cochineal insects
72 × 47¼ in.

PORFIRIO GUTIÉRREZ

Porfirio Gutiérrez is a Zapotec American textile artist based in Ventura, California. He uses traditional Zapotec knowledge of dyes and materials and reinterprets Zapotec weaving language to create pieces that speak to his creative vision of the complexity of the Americas today. When the weavers of Black Mountain College viewed the textiles in the Harriett Engelhardt Collection, they saw them with Western eyes as ancient or foreign abstract art, devoid of symbolic meaning. Gutiérrez's work connects to the same legacy, but in a very different way: his work is part of and in communication with a continuing legacy that connects him to his ancestors.

HOW DID YOU BEGIN WEAVING?

I started to weave because weaving is in my DNA. My ancestors have been developing this art form for thousands of years and so I was born and raised within a tradition, within a family that also weaves. Weaving to me is my language. I started to learn the principles of making bobbins, cleaning a piece, making the yarn as I was also learning my first words in my language.

WHO WERE YOUR WEAVING TEACHERS?

My father, Amado Gutiérrez. I formally started to weave under his teachings when I was twelve. But weaving is not straightforward. You have all these preparations, making bobbins, cleaning the wool, the yarn. And in this case, too, then there would be my mother Andrea Contreras and my father, they're both my teachers.

WHAT IS YOUR RELATIONSHIP TO THE WORK OF ANNI ALBERS?

I think [Anni's] work has a relationship with mine. Aside from the commonality of loom, warp, and weft I can say her work is deeply inspired by my ancestors' work and forms. Some of the designs she is known for have such deep spiritual meaning to my culture.

HOW DO YOU EXPLORE THE MATERIALS THAT YOU USE?

For me, they are more than material just for art, they are living beings, medicine, and food, many of them grow in the wild and some are farmed. In our beliefs, a plant is alive just like us humans, water is sacred and divine, and before I can transform all of these elements into material for art, I need to have a deep understanding of the ecosystem of nature.

All of this communicates the colors that represent a memory of nature and a seasonal imprint. One piece of my work represents a time in history that will never be repeated again, they also carry the energy and the power of nature. Because the materials are nature themselves they behave differently every season depending on the rainy season, the soil they grew in, and the sun. You can have the same recipe but the colors might vary.

HOW DO YOU NAVIGATE TRADITION AND EXPERIMENTATION?

I come from an ancestral lineage and was raised by the last generation that continues to hold the deep worldview of our nation. This experience has been the core value of my work, but within our community much of this knowledge was disrupted by standardization of our traditions to the Western understanding of production. I was born and raised in this environment, an environment we call today tradition, this Western understanding of production of handcraft froze my creativity and stole my right of imagination. This inspired me and everyone I know to migrate to the United States.

Anyone who has experienced diaspora has experienced trauma but also enrichment; living and working in a more urban America enabled me rediscover my cultural identity. My weavings are expressions of the convergence of the two worlds that my soul dwells in. I find comfort and strength in the materials and techniques of my ancestors and now my life is based in modern America, my second world. This environment strikes a hard contrast to the simplicity of my early years. The effects of a high-tech, fast-paced, and complex world are at work in my need for expression. Urban life evokes a new interpretation of the ancient symbols that are at the base level of my psyche. I seek to impart a tactile sense of order and peace through the use of natural media and simplified imagery that are both unmistakably evolved from my Indigenous roots and urban life.

My art practice maintains my ancestors' spiritual belief in nature as a living being, sacred and divine. My grounding in Zapotec traditional knowledge manifests in my textiles, reinterpreting the traditional weaving language, subverting and re-imagining the symbols and forms, morphing my textile designs into the fractal forms and spaces of architecture and the movement I see in cities and urban environments. But [they] also create a dialogue around migration and perceptions of Indigenous people today. My designs draw deeply on my experiences of two cultures, moving between the traditional and the modern, but always reliant on the deep knowledge and spiritual dimensions of my work.

HOW DOES YOUR WORK ENGAGE THE SENSES?

[The senses] absolutely live every day in my work. I'm able to see when the plants are ready to be harvested. I can see that. Once I'm in the studio, dyeing in this case, so many things are obviously measured and there's a discipline to the chemistry of creating color. But with time so much of it is by feeling, smelling, and seeing. To understand the high alkalinity to be where I want it to be, I can just touch the water. I can tell by its smell. I can know by smell and touch when it is ready. I can tell you whether the yarn is handspun, or milled, or is machine spun. I can tell what material, if you close my eyes and give me different materials, I can tell exactly what they are. I can tell you all the plants I use by only smelling them. These senses are deeply embedded. I can tell obviously a piece when it's well woven by just touching it. I can even tell you by just looking at one piece and touch, I know exactly which of my team members wove a piece; who's doing what. Who are the families that are spinning in a certain style.

HOW DO YOU DRAW INSPIRATION FROM OTHER DISCIPLINES?

I absolutely love architecture. I love the movement of a building, the intentionality of a building, how the light comes into a building. What do you see, how do you feel, when you are inside a building. I used to play in ancient buildings, ancestral buildings, and for me that's one of the most minimal, abstract art within the buildings themselves. And then later on I learned that the only other art form that's relatable to weaving is architecture. The steps that [are found in] Mitla, in Monte Albán, [are] so relatable to weaving. Sure you could do curved lines, but that's not the structure of the warp.

My ancestors' work, these very intentional spaces that they built that connect to nature, to the movement of the sun, the moon, and studying the celestial roof and looking all around them in nature and the energy that's bringing to their space. I always say that if I wasn't a weaver I'd probably be an architect, or build homes.

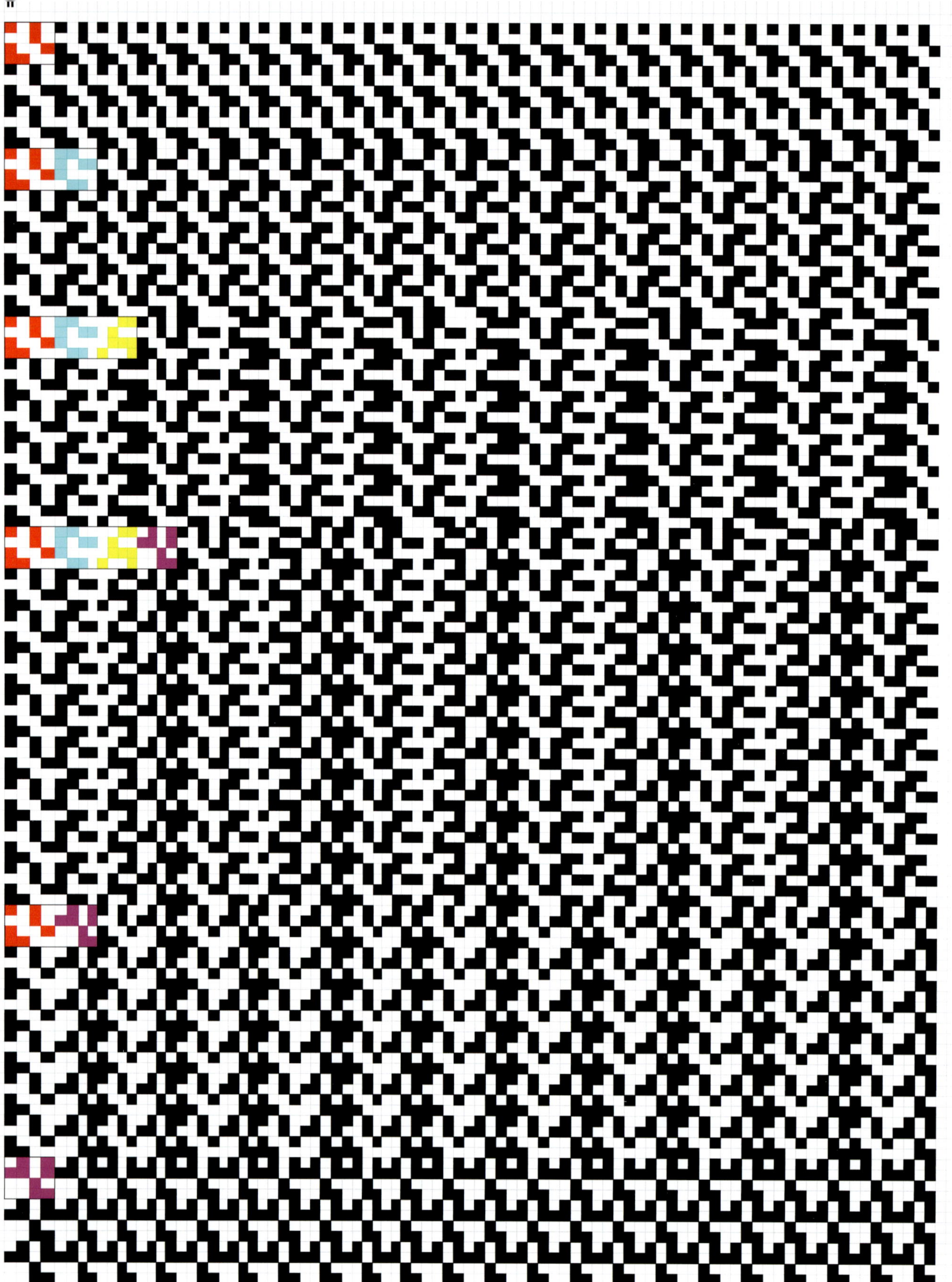

139. Bana Haffar, Graphic score from *Shed*, 2020
Digital illustration.

BANA HAFFAR

Bana Haffar is a synthesist currently based in Montreal, Canada. In 2019 she composed Shed, *commissioned by the Black Mountain College Museum + Arts Center and premiered at the Museum in a performance by Haffar and Third Coast Percussion on February 3, 2020. Haffar's piece translates weaving draft notation into musical notation but does so in a way that moves far beyond superficial similarities. Her process for composing* Shed *involved deep research into weaving, including private lessons and conversations and interviews with skilled weavers. As a result,* Shed *treats sound (synthesized, recorded, or live) as material and subjects it to structure according to draft notation. In doing so, her work echoes the kind of rigorous material experimentation characteristic of Anni Albers's weaving classes at Black Mountain College.*

HOW DID YOU BEGIN WEAVING?

Shed was my gateway into weaving. The Black Mountain College Museum + Arts Center commissioned me to compose a piece for the *Question Everything! The Women of Black Mountain College* exhibition in 2019. I happened to have a copy of *On Weaving* on my desk before they approached me. This is how the story began, this magical synchronicity. I hadn't opened the book yet and didn't really know how it was going to fit into my life. When I started reading it, and saw draft notation for the first time, I knew there was going to be some kind of connection between rhythm and draft notation. I had no idea what that was going to look like. In addition to starting to read about weaving, I decided I needed to learn how to weave to really understand the language of draft notation.

WHO WERE YOUR WEAVING TEACHERS?

I studied weaving with Ruth Gaynes. She learned how to weave in Huancayo, Peru, with Franziska Mayer. She later went to San Francisco State and graduated in 1968 and was in San Francisco in the 1970s in the height of the Fiber Arts movement. She ended up teaching at Penland, was a resident weaver at Penland, and was then hired to start the Professional Fiber Arts program at Haywood Community College with Catharine Ellis. I also interviewed many weavers while I was doing my research.

WHAT IS YOUR RELATIONSHIP TO THE WORK OF ANNI ALBERS?

Anni Albers was in essence my first teacher. I remember reading *On Weaving* early on and thinking how metaphorical her wording felt. I would read her texts and try to translate the concepts into sound or synthesis terms. She arrived at the perfect moment and encouraged me at the beginning of my journey to really sit with the materials, try to understand them, and to, above all, follow my intuition. Also the fact that she was into technology, which not all weavers are, gave me the sense that she would have approved of my efforts in applying her weaving knowledge to synthesis. There are so many connections, it's hard to distill and articulate. Her work and philosophies definitely manifested in many facets of *Shed* and remain with me as I move through subsequent projects.

HOW DO YOU EXPLORE THE MATERIALS THAT YOU USE?

In *Shed* I was working with the percussion quartet [Third Coast Percussion]. I traveled to Chicago and recorded sounds from their studio. They had a lot of hand-made instruments and I ended up sampling about 150 different sounds, which cre-

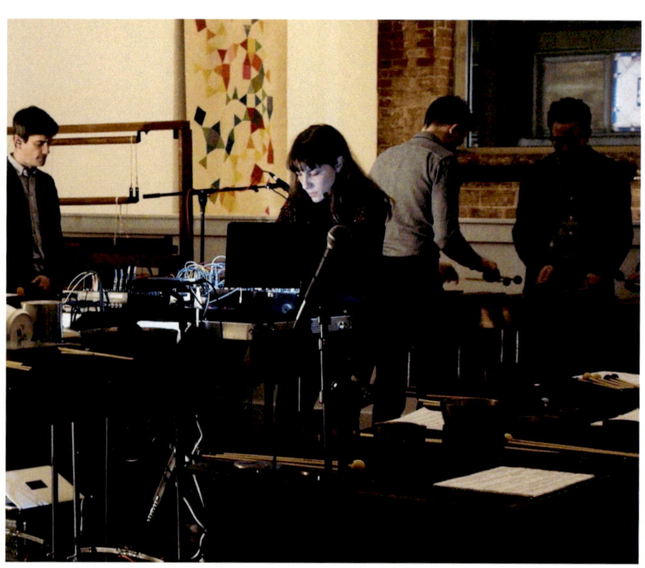

ated a rich sound bank to work from and program with. I was thinking a lot about what Anni Albers wrote about weaving drafts being an abstraction from the final product as I was transforming the sound banks through the weaving drafts.

My materials were percussion instruments and two sequencers. On one side were the drafts, and on the other, the samples, and in the middle was the sequencer that I used to weave the two worlds together. In terms of exploring materials, I like to start with a question:

What does this instrument want to do naturally? Kind of like a fiber. How does this sequencer, even though it's a machine, naturally want to be programmed? Which in terms of the Cartesian sequencer I was using in *Shed*, was an on-off process, not unlike a loom. It naturally wanted to be programmed using a similar thought process as a weaving draft. Now I approach materials and sound worlds starting with these questions: What does this sound want to be? How does it want to develop? Trying to understand the material itself by sitting with it, instead of trying to impose my own ideas onto it.

140. Premiere of *Shed* as performed by Bana Haffar and Third Coast Percussion at the Black Mountain College Museum + Arts Center, 2020.

WHAT DID WEAVING BRING TO YOU AS A MUSICIAN?

I think the process of repetition was a really big theme. And the emergence of patterns, from design cells, or rhythmic cells, through the process of repetition. When you're programming a synthesizer you don't hear what you're programming until much later. You're relying on meticulous planning, just like weaving. When you finally press play, you hear your sequence . . . you hear your pattern. Learning how to weave has profoundly changed the way I program sequencers. The connections are multidimensional. The idea of emergent patterns from smaller, repetitive fragments is one of many.

DO YOU FEEL CONNECTED TO BLACK MOUNTAIN COLLEGE? IF YES, HOW?

I'm very attached to the memory of Black Mountain College. I consider people like M.C. Richards and Anni Albers to be my creative ancestors. Black Mountain College in its memory is a vessel I feel comfortable in and a historical creative refuge I revisit often. I also think that the energy of BMC was just as attributable to the physical location as it was to the faculty and students, which is hard to understand if you haven't been there. How expansive the Lake Eden site is. That's the often overlooked character in the story, the land.

ARE YOU A DESIGNER? ARE YOU A CRAFTSPERSON? ARE YOU AN ARTIST?

I'm a synthesist and I engage in what I'm starting to call "expanded synthesis," which is work that extends beyond the idea of combining and ordering sound. Interpolation is a term used in synthesis that describes the idea of morphing between states, such as morphing between waveforms. Imagine designer, craftsperson, and artist as three different states that can be interpolated between. Instead of switching between designer to craftsperson to artist I embody different amounts of each archetype at different times—constantly interpolating between each of these archetypes. I am all of them in varying amounts, at different times.

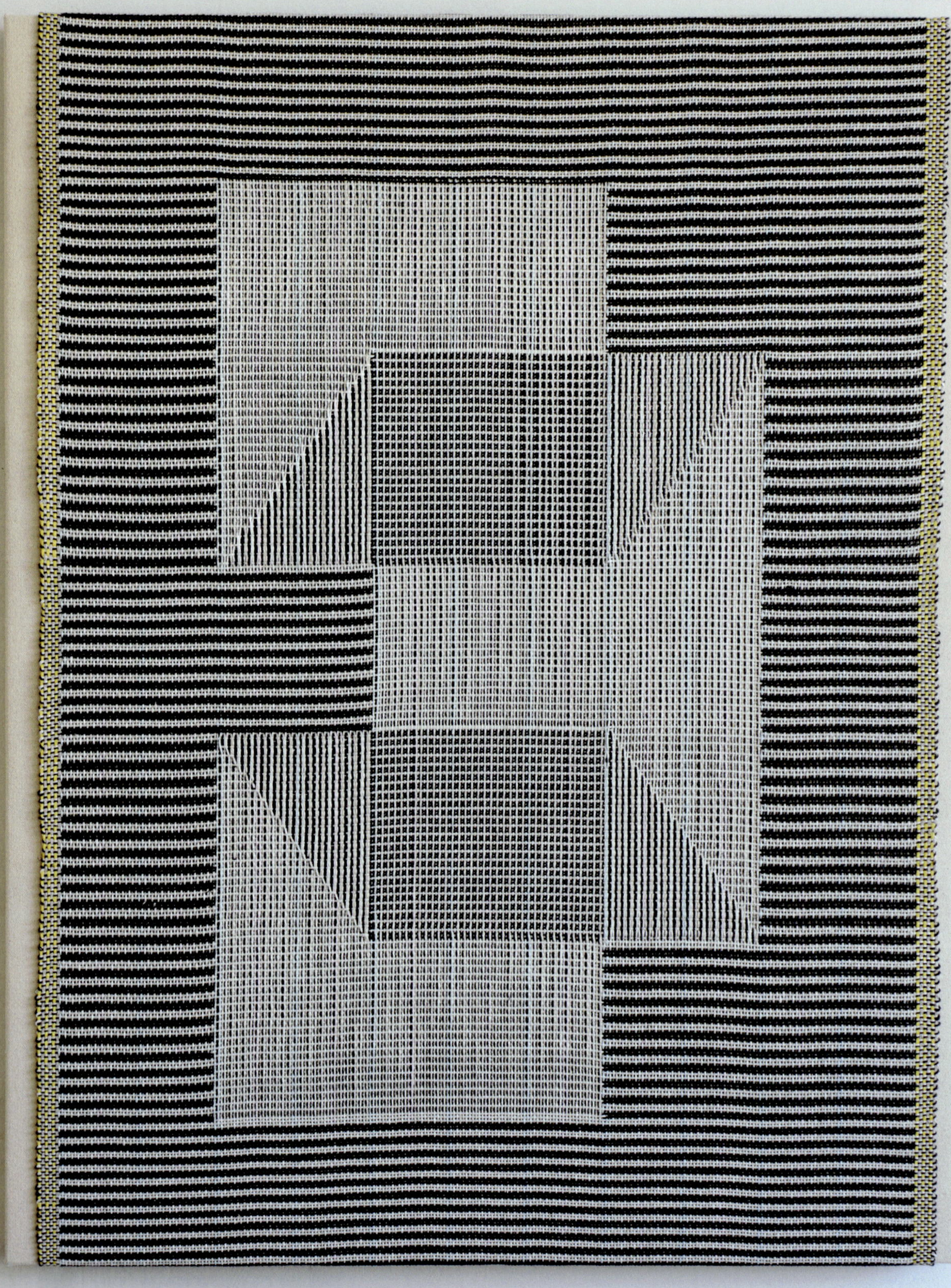

141. Susie Taylor, *X-Ray Folds*, 2023. Hand-dyed linen. 30 × 24 in.

SUSIE TAYLOR

Susie Taylor is a weaver and textile designer based in San Jose, California. A constant and prolific experimenter, Taylor takes an iterative approach to making her work, which she develops in series. By limiting her material palette, Taylor makes structure her primary tool for pictorial expression. Taylor's process recalls the work of the Black Mountain College weavers in her rigorous approach to experimentation, play, and iterative development. Her work in low relief and three dimensions, inspired in part by origami, also relates to the extended BMC legacy of weaving as practiced by Kay Sekimachi and Trude Guermonprez.

HOW DID YOU BEGIN WEAVING?

I am from a family of makers. The men in my family had tools and knew how to build and repair things while the women in my family knew how to sew and mend clothes. These skills made an impression on me. In addition to woodshop, drafting, home economics, and sports, I took as many art classes as possible while in high school.

My path through college was anything but straightforward, but after one semester at Colorado State University I had a general awareness of textile design as a possible career path. This led me to transfer to a more affordable school for the next two years (Fort Lewis College in Durango, Colorado) where I first experienced weaving while taking an Indian Arts and Craft class. I was immediately drawn to the loom. Working on a loom had a tool aspect, a physical aspect, and an art aspect. Weaving was an awakening for me, and it felt like I had found something that I was missing.

After another transfer, this time to Kansas City Art Institute, I was able to focus my studies on weaving within a well-rounded art/fiber curriculum. Also, during this time, I had a part-time job as a sample librarian at the Kansas City DesignTex showroom where I had access to a wide selection of Jacquard upholstery swatches that inspired me to elevate my weaving skills and to think about a career designing commercial textiles after completing my BFA at KCAI ('91 Fiber) and my MFA at UCLA ('94 Design).

WHO WERE YOUR WEAVING TEACHERS?

At KCAI, I studied with Jane Lackey, who coincidentally studied with Trude [Guermonprez] at CCAC [California College of Arts and Crafts], and then I studied with Jim Bassler at UCLA. They both offered basic instruction and critical feedback on my development as an artist. I am also a very independent learner and problem solver, which led me to mimic Jacquard structures and multilayered woven forms on shaft looms without formal instruction. Later, working as a Jacquard designer, my design director, Klaus Flock at Weave Corporation, was an important mentor. He taught me about Jacquard structures, introducing me to new constructions that elevated my problem-solving skills. I consider my twelve years working in industry as another part of my education that continues to shape my ideas.

WHAT IS YOUR RELATIONSHIP TO THE WORK OF ANNI ALBERS? TRUDE GUERMONPREZ?

Anni Albers's history, artworks, and writings are too overwhelming for me to address as a whole, but in general, I elevate her above all others. It is helpful to break down several qualities of her work that resonate with me. For the 100th anniversary of the Bauhaus, in 2019, I participated in the show *Material Meaning: A Living Legacy of Anni Albers* at the Craft in America Center in Los Angeles. During this time, I dove back into her work and was deeply moved by the *surface interest* that she explores through the multitude of elegant interlacements of warp and weft. Her work *Pasture* is my all-time favorite weaving. My desire to incorporate more surface interest in my own work led me to draft and sample many textured weaves. My goal was to identify a body of weaves that were compatible with the balanced double-weave construction that I was working on at the time. This process took a lot of extra work, but it gave me more tools to work with.

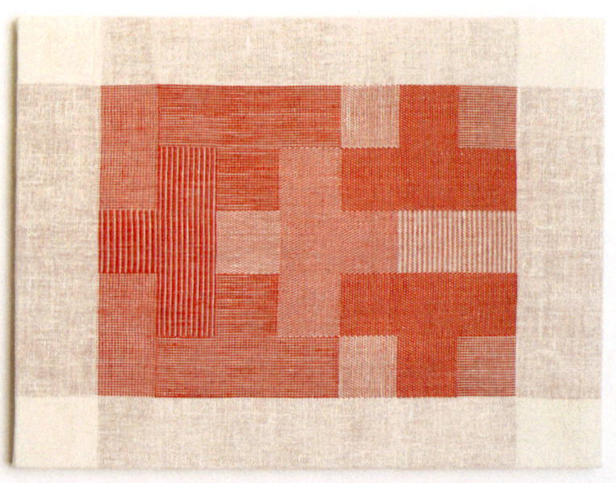

Also, like Anni, I have an interest in meandering lines, and it is fun for me to draw and weave compositions that move the viewer's eye around using linework. I often refer to weaving as a medium that allows me to solve visual and structural puzzles. In addition, I am drawn to her more graphic works that explore block and stripe compositions.

My awareness of Trude Guermonprez came after my interest in Kay Sekimachi's work. I am very impressed by her beautifully executed pickup techniques as well as her innovative dimensional pieces. Both methods of working really resonate with me as I explore similar processes. I think there is brilliance in the way she worked, and as an educator the seeds she planted continue to spread. Even though I am more familiar with and influenced by Kay's work, it goes without saying that I benefit from Trude's contributions to weaving and education. Also, I've heard Kay talk about the importance Trude placed on considering both warp and weft equally. The emergence of weaving as pictorial art only had tapestry (weft dominant) as a reference so this notion of considering both warp and weft equally opened up a new universe of possibility for weavers looking to innovate in new directions. In my own work, I strive to use balanced weaves that rely equally on warp and weft.

HOW DO YOU EXPLORE THE MATERIALS THAT YOU USE?

My practice is driven more by structure than material. I work with a basic stock of smooth linens and cottons and have never been very interested in weaving with wool or textured yarns. Over the last several years, I've been exploring textured weave structures because one of my goals was to add more surface interest to my work, and I would rather articulate texture through structure and color than by using textured yarns.

TELL US ABOUT YOUR LOOMS AND HOW YOU USE THEM.

I currently own two Macomber treadle floor looms: a forty-inch, sixteen-shaft and a forty-eight-inch, twenty-shaft. I enjoy the manual nature and the physicality of treadle looms because it feels like they are an extension of my mind and body. The neat thing about weaving is that you use your right and left brain, your right and left hand, your right and left foot; it's a full body experience.

I like being in full control of the manual functions of my weaving process. For me that combination of loom control structures and hand manipulation is playtime; it's when I get to apply all of my skills and tricks that I've developed. You can do anything on a manual loom, but some processes are very slow. When you really have strict limitations I think that's when I am most creative.

HOW DO YOU HANDLE TENSION AND SPACE IN YOUR WORK?

If one compares a loom to a human body, tension would be equivalent to blood flow. Tension is the fundamental element of weaving that I play with more than anything else. I often challenge myself to modify my processes and often that includes interrupting normal tension until it can be restored. Once you learn the rules of weaving then you can start to break them.

My relationship with space can be described as having an "origami mindset," which leads me to consider the transformation of 2D into 3D. Dimension is also an important element to my work that can be articulated through physical or visual means.

Susie Taylor is represented by Johansson Projects, Oakland, California.

LIST OF STUDENTS OFFICIALLY ENROLLED IN WEAVING CLASSES

ABBREVIATIONS

f w s Fall, Winter, Spring Quarters
(1933–35, 1942–46, 1953–56)

F S Fall, Spring Semesters
(1935–42, 1946–53)

SS Summer Session

[g] Graduate in Weaving
[d] Day Student
[a] Audited class

NOTE: The format for these abbreviations is consistent with those used by Mary Emma Harris in her list of "Faculty and Other Teaching Positions." Mary Emma Harris, *The Arts at Black Mountain College* (Cambridge, MA: MIT Press, 2002), 265–70. Where known, nicknames are given in quotes and married names are given in parentheses.

Donald Alter 49S
Vera Baker (Williams) 45f, 46s
Anne Furman Banks . . . 46w, 46F, 46S, 47S, 47SS, 48S, 48SS
Marilyn "Widget" Bauer (Greenwald)[g] 42f, 43w,
43s, 43f, 44w, 44s, 44SS, 44f, 45w, 45s
Nuvart Bedrossian 44SS
Henry Porter Bergman 46f
Joseph William Bex 47SS
Leonard Winter Billing 40F, 41F
Mary Alice Fielitz Bishop 51SS
Jane Cooper Bland 44SS
Lilli Blumenau 48SS
Arthur Thacher Boericke 49SS
Addison Sargent Bray 44w, 44s, 44SS
Jean Brewton[d] 55f, 56w
Alan McLean Brown 34f, 35w, 35s, 35f, 36w, 36s
Katherine Talbott Burnside 44SS
Patricia Genevieve Campbell 50S
John Granville Cannon 50S
Dorothy Tryon Carr 44f

Sheila Carr 45SS
Marcia Russell Chamberlain 51SS
Margaret Patterson Chandler 44s, 44f, 45SS, 46SS
Margaret Burns Cole 47SS
Carol Marie Comstock 51ss
Eleanor Marie Cosick 51ss
Joan Potter Couch (Sihvonen, Loveless)[1] 46F, 47S
Thomas Sparrow Dalton Jr. 40F, 41S
Martha Winston Davis 55SS
John Virgil "Jack" "Danny" Deaver . . . 41S, 41F, 41F, 42S, 42f
Mary Lou Derryberry 44SS
Mary Elaine Dodge 45SS
Marjorie Joan Dodge 45SS
Donald Edward Droll 48SS, 48F, 48F, 49S, 49S
Nancy Crawford Dunn 47F, 48F
Kendall Lathrop Durant (Ramsay) 48SS
Harriett Pinkston Engelhardt 38F, 39S, 40F
Lorraine Feuer 55s, 56SS
Laura Belle Fisher 34s
Francis Arthur Foster 41F, 46f
Phyllis Iris Franklin 51SS
Charles Wertenbaker Freeman 39F
Audrey Jane Freiheit 48F, 48F
Miriam "Mimi" Deware French (Batchelor) 40S, 40F,
41S, 41F, 42S, 42f, 42f, 43w, 43w, 43s, 43s, 44w
Wilma Gertrude Fuerstenberg (Joseph, Evans) . 48S, 48F, 48F
Merrill Edmund Gillespie 50F, 51S
Errisinola "Erris" Lombard Ginesi (Boyd, Burnett) 50S
Frederick Willius Goldsmith 44w
Cornelia "Nell" Goldsmith (Heyns) 42f, 43w
Beate "Ati" Eveliene Gropius (Forberg, Johansen) 44f, 45w, 45s
Donald Rae Grover 48S
Lynn Hatcher 45f, 46w, 46s
Eleanor Hawk 46SS
Margaret Willard (Helburn) 42SS
Janet Chloe Heling (Roberts) 44w, 44s, 46s, 46s, 47SS
Elizabeth Chalmers Hillard 35F
Elizabeth Marie "Betty" Schmitt Jennerjahn 44SS, 48F, 48F, 49S
Doris Martha Johnson 46SS
Raymond "Ray" Edward Johnson 47F
William "Willie" Wolff Joseph 45SS, 45f, 46w,
46s, 46SS, 46F, 47S, 47S, 47F, 48S

---

1. Loveless seems to have unofficially taken a weaving class with Anni Albers either during the 1946 spring term or 1946 Summer Session.

Victor Kalos 48F, 48F
Elizabeth Ferris Kelley 40F, 41S
Gloria Lolita Larsen 39S, 39F, 40S
Lore Kadden (Lindenfeld)[g] 46SS, 46F, 47S, 47SS, 47F, 48S, 48SS
Richard Lischer 48SS
Anna M. Schauffler Lockwood 44f
Jean Madeline Loop (O'Neill) 45f, 46w, 46s
Ann MacKinnon 44f
Moreen Maser 44SS
Jean Helen Maurice (Rochin) 45f, 46w, 46s, 47F
Robert Linne McAllester 50F
Alice Maria McCanna 44f, 45w
Nancy Hamblett Miller 47SS
Frances Moore 42SS
Esther Myra Moss 42SS
Lelia Murphy (Mallory)[d] 55f, 56w
Richard Negro . . . . .48F[a]
Wanda Beatrice Nelles 45SS
Andrew "Andy" Francis Oates Jr. . . . 49S, 49S, 49S, 49SS, 49F
Robert Orr 34s, 34f, 35w, 35s
Elizabeth Louisa Osbourne (Richards) 44f, 45w
Virginia Denman Osbourne 44w, 44s
Charles Donald "Don" Page[g] 36F, 36F, 37S,
     37F, 38S, 38F, 39S, 39F, 40S, 40F, 40F, 41S
May de Forest Payne 44SS
Ruth Mary Payne 38F, 39S
Mardi Mai Peterson (Pelkey) 40F, 41S
Milton Ernest "Robert" Rauschenberg 49S
Hubert Joseph "Bud" Ray 49SS
Rosemary Raymond (Stoller) 49SS
Alexander "Alex" Sylvester Reed[2] 38F, 39S, 39F, 40S
Else Regensteiner 45SS
Barbara Stone (Rice) 48F, 48F, 49S, 49S, 49SS
Emelyn N. Rogers 49SS
Nevalie Anne Ropp 38F, 39S
Elaine Louise Schmitt (Urbain) 44SS
Olga Maria Schubkegel 49SS
Agathe Maria Schurman (Elink-Schurmann) 36S
Laille Schutz 44SS
Renee Siegel 48F, 48F
Eini Irene Sihvonen 47F
Sewell "Si" Sillman 48S
Elizabeth Jane "Slats" Slater (Marquis) 42f, 43w,
     43s, 43f, 44w, 44s
Carolyn Constance Spencer 40F, 41S
Mona Stea (Burns) 54f, 55s, 55ss, 55f
Jean Hoffman (Stewart) 45SS, 45f, 46SS
Claude Stoller 40F, 41S
Adele Suska (Labrecque) 50F, 51S, 51S
Alice Lee Swan 34w
Sara "Sally" Natalie Sylvester 34f, 35w, 35s
Jacqueline K. Tankersley (Matthey) 42F
William Edmund "Bill" Treichler . . . . 47F, 48S[a]
William Ragland "Rags" Watkins III 47SS, 47F, 48S

Betsy Ann Weinrib (Williams) 53SS
Selma H. Weisberger 51SS
Nancy Clarke West 42S
Paul Francis Williams Jr. 47S, 47F, 48S
Mary Frances Wilson 39F
Don Emerson Wight 46SS, 46F
Helen Grace Wright (Marden) . . . 42f, 43w, 43s, 43f, 44w, 44s
Eva Carina Zhitlowsky (Milton) . . 39F, 40S, 40F, 41S, 41F, 42S

COMMUNITY MEMBERS AND FACULTY KNOWN TO HAVE STUDIED WEAVING

Ruth Bailey 37S
Barbara "Bobby" Loines Dreier . . . . 45w or 45s
Lolita Georgia . . . . ca. 1935, presumed 1937S

STUDENTS KNOWN TO HAVE STUDIED WEAVING NOT LISTED ON COURSE CARDS

Lorrie Goulet . . . . ca. 43f
Patsy Lynch (Wood) 48SS
Joan Shirley Stack . . . .
David Cleotis Stetzel . . . . ca. 49S, 49SS

WEAVING FACULTY

Anni Albers (b. 1899, d. 1994) . . . . .34w – 49S,
     (on leave 40F, 46F – 47F)
Don Page (b. 1917, d. 2007). . . . . 40F (student teacher)
Marilyn "Widget" Bauer Greenwald (b. 1924, d. 2009) . . . 44F
     (Introductory Weaving), 45SS (assistant)
Franziska Mayer (b. 1914, d. 1994) . . . . 46SS – 47S
Trude Guermonprez (b. 1910, d. 1976) . . . . 47S – 49S
Marli Heimann Ehrman (b. 1904, d. 1982) 49SS
Ellen Siegel (b. 1924, d. unknown) . . . . 49F – 50S
Andy Oates (b. 1926, d. 2012) . . . . 50F – 51SS
W. P. "Pete" Jennerjahn (b. 1922, d. 2020) 51S
     (Textile Design Tutorial)
Marie Murelius (b. 1907, d. 1991) 53SS
Anthony "Tony" Landreau (b. 1930, d. 2009) . . . . .54F – 56SS

2. Alex Reed also attended BMC under the name William Freeborn Reed and was commonly known as "Bill." He legally changed his name in the early 1940s and we have decided to use his chosen name in this book.

LIST OF KNOWN EXHIBITIONS OF BLACK MOUNTAIN COLLEGE TEXTILES

Note: This list is mostly compiled from casual mentions of exhibitions in Black Mountain College Community Bulletins, *where exhibitions are mentioned, but formal titles are not given. Where titles of exhibitions are known, they are presented within quotation marks.*

"Exhibition of Handweaving from Black Mountain College," *Sophie Newcombe College, New Orleans, Louisiana*, Spring 1942

Unnamed exhibition, *Mint Museum, Charlotte, North Carolina; Unnamed Location, Louisville Kentucky*, Spring 1943

Exhibition of modern textiles, *Skidmore College Gallery, Saratoga Springs, New York*, Spring 1945

"Exhibition of Modern Textiles," *Museum of Modern Art, New York, New York*, Fall 1945 (exhibition traveled for about two years to numerous other venues)

International textile exhibition, *Greensboro, North Carolina*, Fall 1945

Art association exhibition, *Fort Worth, Texas*, Fall 1945

Unnamed exhibition, *Cranbrook Academy of Art, Bloomfield, Michigan; Flint Institute of Art, Flint, Michigan*, Spring 1946

Textile exhibition organized by Anni Albers, *Massachusetts Institute of Technology, Cambridge, Massachusetts*, Summer 1946

Unnamed exhibition of textiles by Marilyn Bauer, *Ten-Thirty Gallery, Cleveland, Ohio*, Spring 1947

Unnamed exhibition, *University of North Carolina, Chapel Hill, North Carolina*, Fall 1947

"Textiles by Black Mountain College Students," *Busch-Reisinger Museum, Cambridge, Massachusetts*, January 3 – 24, 1950

NOTES

ABBREVIATIONS USED IN THE NOTES

ADAH — Alabama Department of Archives and History, Montgomery, AL

BMCM+AC — Black Mountain College Museum + Arts Center Collection, Asheville, NC

ERC — Else Regensteiner (1906–2003) Collection, Ryerson and Burnham Art and Architecture Archives, The Art Institute of Chicago

FMP — Franziska Mayer Papers, JAAF

JAAF — The Josef and Anni Albers Foundation, Bethany, CT

JAFC — The Jalowetz Aronson Family Collection, Maplewood, NJ

HPEP — Harriett Pinkston Engelhardt Papers, Montgomery, AL

NA — Nantucket Atheneum, Nantucket, MA

NHA — Nantucket Historical Association, Nantucket, MA

RRFA — Robert Rauschenberg Foundation Archives, New York, NY

TGP — Papers of Trude Guermonprez, 1947–1976, Oakland Museum of California, Oakland, CA

WRA — Western Regional Archives, State Archives of North Carolina, Asheville, NC

    BMCC — Black Mountain College Collection

    BMCFF — Black Mountain College Faculty Files

    BMCGF — Black Mountain College General Files

    BMCPC — Black Mountain College Project Collection

    BMCRP — Black Mountain College Research Project

    BMCSF — Black Mountain College Student Files

    COP — Charles Olson Papers, Photocopied from Archives & Special Collections, Thomas H. Dodd Research Center, UConn

    DBMCC — The Theodore and Barbara Loines Dreier Black Mountain College Collection (Dreier BMC Collection)

    MDC — Martin Duberman Collection

NOTES TO THE ESSAYS

INTRODUCTION

1. Kenneth Kurtz, "Black Mountain College: Its Aims and Means, *Black Mountain College Bulletin*, no. 8, 1944, BMCRP, WRA.

2. John Andrew Rice, quoted in Louis Adamic, "Education on a Mountain: The Story of Black Mountain College," *Harper's Monthly Magazine* 172 (April 1936): 519.

3. A brief history of BMC's weaving program can be found in Mary Emma Harris, *The Arts at Black Mountain College* (Cambridge, MA: MIT Press, 1987); and Jenni Sorkin, "Weaving," in *Leap Before You Look: Black Mountain College, 1933–1957*, edited by Helen Molesworth (New Haven, CT: Institute of Contemporary Art/ Boston in association with Yale University Press, 2016), 166–69.

4. Thank you to Heather South, lead archivist at the Western Regional Archives for searching through the College's student records in order to compile a list of the students who took weaving and textile design. Without her work, our understanding of the weaving program would be a fraction of what the program actually was.

5. Trude Guermonprez, interview by Mary Emma Harris, 1971, 30, BMCRP, WRA.

ART, CRAFT, DESIGN

1. Anni Albers, interview by Martin Duberman, 1967, 59, MDC, WRA.

2. Nell Rice, John Andrew Rice's wife, was the College's librarian. Bobby Dreier, Ted Dreier's wife, taught in the kindergarten, which was named "The Cottage School." (See Barbara Dreier, letter to Henry E. Dreier and Ethyl Dreier, October 10, 1934, DBMCC, WRA.

3. Josef Albers, letter to Ted Dreier, October 31, 1933. Alberses-Dreiers Correspondence, JAAF. Translation from German by Michael Beggs. An article in the *Asheville Citizen* from November 30, 1933 also states that Anni Albers was expected to teach weaving upon her arrival: "As yet, Professor [Josef] Albers speaks very

little English, but his wife, who is to teach weaving, speaks the language quite precisely." "Germans Join College Staff," *Asheville Citizen*, November 30, 1933.

4. Josef Albers, letter to Director of Customs, US Treasury Department, February 12, 1934, JAAF.

5. Josef Albers, letter to Wassily and Nina Kandinsky, April 27, 1934, published in Jessica Boissel and Nicholas Fox Weber, eds., *Josef Albers and Wassily Kandinsky: Friends in Exile* (Manchester, VT: Hudson Hills, 2010), 32. Translation by Oliver Pretzel.

6. Anni Albers, interview by Duberman, 15–16, MDC, WRA.

7. Stephen Forbes, interview by Martin Duberman, MDC, 32. Don Page recalled that Georgia built the College's largest loom, "a beautiful loom out of maple," to Anni Albers's specifications. (Don Page, interview by Mary Emma Harris, 1970, BMCRP, WRA.) Another loom built by Georgia, an unusually narrow eight-harness countermarche sample loom recorded in a photograph in the collection of the BMCM+AC, may have left the College when Georgia and his wife, Lolita Georgia, who was an active participant in the College's weaving program, left Black Mountain College. Most of the College's later looms were purchased secondhand from local crafts schools in the greater Asheville area. See Treasurer's files, BMCC, WRA.

8. Related disciplines such as architecture and dressmaking, both of which were taught with a design approach, were intermittently offered at the College and attended by a much smaller percentage of the College's overall student body than weaving. Woodworking, bookbinding, and ceramics were treated as more traditional craft disciplines concerned either with hand production or the creation of unique objects.

9. Anni Albers, "Designing," *Craft Horizons* 2, no. 2 (May 1943), 3, offprint, collection JAAF.

10. Anni Albers, "One Aspect of Art Work," published under the title "We Need the Crafts for Their Contact with Materials," *Design* 46, no. 4 (December 12, 1944), unpaginated offprint, JAAF. Reproduced in this book on pages 90–93.

11. Anni Albers, letter to Ted Dreier, July 17, 1938, JAAF.

12. Anni Albers first formulated this complex relationship between craft, industry, and the designer nearly a decade before arriving at Black Mountain College, in her first published writing on weaving (Annelise Fleischmann, "Bauhausweberei," *Junge Menschen* 5, no. 8 [November 1924]). T'ai Smith does an excellent job relating this essay to the development of weaving as a design discipline in her book *Bauhaus Weaving Theory: From Feminine Craft to Mode of Design* (Minneapolis: University of Minnesota Press, 2014).

13. Albers, "One Aspect of Art Work," unpaginated. Reproduced in this book on pages 90–93.

14. Albers, "Handweaving Today: Textile Work at Black Mountain College," *The Weaver* 6, no. 1 (January–February 1941), 5, offprint, JAAF. Reproduced in this book on pages 48–51.

15. On the renaming of *Werklehre*, see Fred Horowitz, "Design," in *Josef Albers: To Open Eyes*, by Fred Horowitz and Brenda Danilowitz (London: Phaidon Press, 2006), 126. Josef Albers could easily have taught design classes aimed at the creation of practical objects or industrial products. At the Bauhaus he had run the Cabinetmaking Workshop (1928–29) and starting in 1929 directed the highly successful wallpaper division of the Wall-Painting Workshop. The absence of practical design from Albers's classes at Black Mountain further supports the idea that Anni Albers was the College's primary design instructor.

16. The nearest senses in American or English usage were either instructional: "to produce a scheme or plan for the making of anything" (*Webster's New International Dictionary*, 1927) or decorative: "to plan and execute (a structure, work of art, etc.); to fashion with artistic skill or decorative device, to furnish or adorn with a design" (*Oxford English Dictionary*, 1933).

17. MoMA had used the verb "design" once before, in 1937, in *Rugs from the Crawford Shops Designed by American Artists*, but the meaning invoked is an earlier English sense of the word design: developing the drawing or scheme for a decorated object. MoMA Exhibition History List, https://www.moma.org/research-and-learning/archives/archives-exhibition-history-list, accessed October 23, 2022. Albers's article "One Aspect of Art Work," published in *Design* magazine in the mid-1940s, was subtitled "Art Appreciation and Practice," and used the same, older definition for "design."

18. MoMA Exhibition History List, https://www.moma.org/research-and-learning/archives/archives-exhibition-history-list, accessed October 23, 2022.

19. Anni Albers, *On Weaving* (Middletown, CT: Wesleyan University Press, 1965), 53.

20. Anni Albers, interview by Duberman, 15.

21. Anni Albers, interview by Duberman, 15.

22. Claude Stoller, "Claude Stoller," in *Black Mountain College: Student Experience in Experimental Education in the Early Years, 1933–43*, edited by Robert Sunley, unpublished, 103, JAAF.

23. Joan Potter Loveless, *Three Weavers* (Albuquerque: University of New Mexico Press, 1992), 14.

24. Marilyn Bauer Greenwald, interview by Emma Harris, 1971, 11, BMCRP, WRA.

25. Janet Heling Roberts, Notes from Anni Albers's Weaving Class, ca. 1944, WRA.

26 Loveless, *Three Weavers*, 15.

27. Greenwald, interview by Harris, 1971, 11.

28. Marilyn Bauer Greenwald recalled that "some people would take the weaving class and wouldn't do sufficient free weaving, and Anni would get very annoyed with them." Greenwald, interview by Harris, 1971, 11.

29. To give some examples: the structure of wood is fibrous; hammered metal has a distinctive facture as a result of how it is worked; combed hair has a distinctive texture that is the result of the combination of its structure (many strands of hair) and its facture (combing).

30. For more on *matière* studies, see Michael Beggs, "Photographs of Matières," in *Leap Before You Look: Black Mountain College, 1933–1957*, edited by Helen Molesworth (New Haven, CT: Institute of Contemporary Art/Boston in association with Yale University Press, 2015), 86.

31. Lore Kadden Lindenfeld, Notes from Anni Albers's Weaving Class, 1946, JAAF.

32. Albers writes incredibly compellingly of the slow loss of tactile engagement in the chapter, "Tactile Sensibility," in *On Weaving*, 62–65.

33. The typewriter studies also recall Albers's Bauhaus roots. Katja Rose, who was in the weaving workshop at the Bauhaus from 1931 through 1933, made multiple designs for print textiles using typewriter characters in 1932. Rose's husband, Hajo Rose, also designed print textiles that were put into production and that used typewriter characters. See *Katja Rose: Weberei am Bauhaus 1931 bis 1933, Bildwebereien 1964 bis 1983*, edited by Magdalena Droste (Berlin: Bauhaus-Archiv, 1983).

34. The accessibility of Anni Albers's non-loom material and design exercises mirrored the use of colored paper in Josef Albers's color class, which separated the study of color from the guesswork and skill required to mix paints. According to Joan Potter Loveless, when she took Albers's weaving class in the spring of 1946, these material and design exercises preceded work on the loom. Loveless, *Three Weavers*, 14.

35. Anni Albers, "March 1965 Interview: Teaching Weaving and Design," in *Black Mountain College: Sprouted Seeds; An Anthology of Personal Accounts*, edited by Mervin Lane (Knoxville: University of Tennessee Press, 1991), 43.

36. Loveless, *Three Weavers*, 14.

37. Anni Albers, letter to Ted Dreier, August 21, 1939, JAAF

38. It is not clear if the photograph depicts a weaving "class" or students weaving on their own time. If it is a class, the combination of identifiable students likely dates the photograph to the end of the winter term of 1944.

39. The known belts are by Mimi French, who took twelve weaving classes between 1940 and 1945, and Bobby Dreier, who took one weaving class in 1945.

40. Anni Albers, interview by Sevim Fesci, July 5, 1968, Archives of American Art, Smithsonian Institution, https://www.aaa.si.edu/download_pdf_transcript/ajax?record_id=edanmdm-AAADCD_oh_211924, accessed November 24, 2022.

41. Albers, interview by Fesci, 1968.

42. Dorothy Cavalier Yanik, interview by Brenda Danilowitz, February 2012, quoted on the former website for the Josef And Anni Albers Foundation, https://web.archive.org/web/20200511160622/https://albersfoundation.org/teaching/anni-albers/introduction/, accessed November 24, 2022.

43. Lindenfeld, Notes from Anni Albers's Weaving Class, 51–52, JAAF.

44. Note that the use of the word "design" in this case means a surface decoration on a fabric. Lindenfeld, Notes, 51–52.

45. The original curtains are lost, but a gouache study is in the collection of the Museum of Modern Art, New York.

46. Anni Albers, "Weaving at the Bauhaus," in *On Designing* (Middletown, CT: Wesleyan University Press, 1961), 39.

47. Anni Albers, "Design: Anonymous and Timeless," in *On Designing*, 6–7. Originally printed in the *Magazine of Art* 40, no. 2 (February 1947).

48. Lindenfeld, Notes, 51–52.

MAKING CLOTHES AT BLACK MOUNTAIN COLLEGE

1. Unfortunately, there is not space in this essay to discuss a parallel history of clothes making at BMC: that of costume making for parties and theater productions, which were often highly experimental and involved materials like paper (such as the "Paper Ballet" in Xanti Schawinky's *Spectodrama* or the wigs and costumes made for the 1942 production of Moliere's *The Affected Young Ladies*), metal (such as Bobby Dreier's and John Stix's costumes for the College's 1940 Valentine's Day Party), or plants (such as Robert Rauschenberg's costume for his sister from 1949, fig. 100).

2. Mary Emma Harris lists Schawinsky as a tutor from the fall of 1936 to the spring of 1938 (the entirety of the Schawinskys' tenure at Black Mountain College) in her list of College faculty (Harris, *The Arts at Black Mountain College* [Cambridge: MIT Press, 2002], 269). Bobby Dreier sets the date of Schawinsky's first class as 1937 in a letter to her in-laws: "I would love to have a subscription to *Harper's Bazaar* beginning with the Jan number because Anni, Irene Schawinsky and I are going to have a class in clothes cutting and construction next term" (Barbara Dreier, letter to Henry and Ethel Dreier, December 7, 1936, WRA). In a letter to Ted Dreier from July 10, 1938, Anni reports that the Schawinskys are about to leave BMC and mentions in passing their "last dressmaking classes."

3. Rice, who as Rector was the College's administrative head and its leading personality in the Blue Ridge years, can be seen in photographs taken by Helen M. Post Modley in the spring of 1937. Whether he attended all meetings of that term's dressmaking class or merely showed up for the photoshoot is unknown. In Modley's photographs, he appears to be an attentive observer, rather than a participant.

4. Bobby Dreier, Notes from Irene Schawinsky's dressmaking class, spring 1937, DBMCC, WRA.

5. Don Page, interview by Mary Emma Harris, 1970, 16–17, BMCRP, WRA.

6. Dreier, Notes from Irene Schawinsky's dressmaking class.

7. Dreier, Notes from Irene Schawinsky's dressmaking class.

8. Page, interview by Harris, 1970, 17.

9. Page, interview by Harris, 1970, 17.

10. Anni Albers records some of this sentiment in a letter to Ted Dreier, writing that music teacher John Evarts "feels that we simply cannot keep on having [the Schawinskys] here . . . that the students have no respect for him and dont want to go to his classes and so on . . . " Anni Albers, letter to Ted Dreier, "Wednesday" [March 23], 1938, JAAF.

11. Harris, *The Arts at Black Mountain College*, 45.

12. Indeed, Schawinsky never taught at the New Bauhaus, which closed before the Schawinskys could get to Chicago. Harris, *The Arts at Black Mountain College*, 45.

13. Story told to the author by Addie Lanier, Ruth Asawa's daughter, November 9, 2022.

14. Mimi French wrote in a letter to Anni Albers, "I haven't done anything with my two jacket materials yet, but there is no place around here to have them made." Mimi French, letter to Anni Albers, August 17, 1943, Mimi French Student File, BMCSF, WRA.

15. "Black Mountain College," *Junior Bazaar*, May 1946, 132, JAFC.

16. Harris, *Arts at Black Mountain College*, 99.

17. Harris, *Arts at Black Mountain College*, 99.

18. Student Claude Stoller was photographed wearing sandals while participating in the work program at Lake Eden around 1940, and Alex Reed is shown wearing sandals at a loom in his study at Blue Ridge in a photograph from 1938–40.

19. Mimi French also mentions espadrilles being popular in an essay in her student file. Whether she meant open-toed or closed-toed espadrilles is not clear, nor is it clear if the students were making espadrilles themselves. Mimi French, "Describe Black Mountain College in 10 Years," ca. 1943, Student File of Miriam Deware French, BMCSF, WRA.

20. "Tradition Challenged in Museum of Modern Exhibition, Are Clothes Modern?" press release from the Museum of Modern Art, https://www.moma.org/documents/moma_press-release_325448.pdf, accessed November 25, 2022.

21. Bernard Rudofsky, *Are Clothes Modern? An Essay on Contemporary Apparel* (Chicago: Paul Theobald, 1947), 203.

22. Rudofsky, *Are Clothes Modern?*, 203.

23. Albers specifically uses the term "dress design" in his letter. Josef Albers, letter to Irene Schawinsky, March 11, 1945, WRA.

24. Irene Schawinsky, letter to Josef Albers, March 10, 1945, WRA. Translated from German by Michael Beggs.

25. See pencil note by Josef Albers on Josef Albers, telegram to Irene Schawinsky, April 22, 1945, WRA.

26. See Anni Albers, letters to Ted Dreier, December 4 and December 28, 1947, JAAF.

27. Rudofsky, "Tradition Challenged in Museum of Modern Exhibition, Are Clothes Modern?"

SPECIALIZATION, PRODUCTION, AND PUBLICATION

1. Sigrid Wortmann Weltge, *Women's Work: Textile Art from the Bauhaus* (New York: Chronicle Books, 1993), 112.

2. "Sears," Anni Albers, letter to Hans Farman, June 6, 1938, JAAF. "Kaufmann," Ted Dreier, letter to Anni Albers, November 25, 1940, JAAF.

3. It should also be noted that when the Bauhaus turned away from craft production and toward industry in 1923, Walter Gropius hired Emil Lange to "help broker deals between the workshops and buyers," a resource Albers never had at Black Mountain. T'ai Smith, *Bauhaus Weaving Theory: From Feminine Craft to Mode of Design* (Minneapolis: University of Minnesota Press, 2014), 41. "Print fabrics," see Don Page, interview by Mary Emma Harris, 1970, 1, BMCRP, WRA.

4. Records of some of these production commissions can be found in the Anni Albers Papers, JAAF.

5. "Weaving Report 1940," Treasurer's files, BMCC, WRA.

6. Marilyn Bauer Greenwald, interview by Mary Emma Harris, 1971, 11, BMCRP, WRA.

7. Robert S. Kumabe, letter to Mrs. Dwight Morrow Jr., May 3 1944, BMCC, WRA. Margot Loines was also the owner of one of Albers's early pictorial textiles, *Untitled*, 1941 (fig. 50).

8. Page, interview by Harris, 1970, 2–3.

9. Page, interview by Harris, 1970, 7–9.

10. Letter from J. H. Daughdrill to Anne Mangold (Mrs. F. R. Mangold), September 27, 1939, BMCC, WRA.

11. Page, interview by Harris, 1970, 9.

12. Page, interview by Harris, 1970, 9. Anni Albers also tried to set up industry jobs for other weaving students, including Marilyn Bauer Greenwald and Willie Joseph. See Greenwald, interview by Mary Emma Harris, 1971; Arthur C. Brill, letter to Anni Albers, June 18, 1946, JAAF.

13. Lawrence Rogin, letter to Morton Steinau, August 10, 1942, WRA.

14. Textile Workers Union of America, CIO, "Southern Training Institute," WRA.

15. It is possible that the Textile Workers Union did not return to Lake Eden in the intervening years between 1943 and 1950 due to conflicts with BMC's summer sessions. Lawrence Rogin, letter to Robert C. Orr, September 2, 1943; Pat Knight, letter to Donald Worthington, July 26, 1950. Both letters found in BMCC, WRA.

16. Anni Albers, letter to Mr. and Mrs. Lindol French, June 11, 1943, Student file of Miriam Deware French, BMCSF, WRA.

17. Anni Albers, letter to R. D. Sailors, April 23, 1946, Cranbrook Academy of Art, Registrar's Office. Quoted in Robert Judson Clark, *Design in America: The Cranbrook Vision, 1925–1950* (New York: Harry N. Abrams, 1983), 320.

18. Franziska Mayer, Statement on her role at BMC, January 19, 1947, WRA.

19. Mayer, Statement on her role at BMC.

20. In a letter to Josef Albers, Ted Dreier explained: "We are still discussing Trude; except for the production weaving angle that she and Anni are going to work out together, most people would feel doubtful about having two teachers of weaving. But nearly everyone likes her and feels that she is good." Ted Dreier, letter to Josef Albers, December 2, 1947, JAAF.

21. Mary "Molly" Gregory, letter to Trude Guermonprez, September 9, 1947. Trude Guermonprez, letter to Black Mountain College Board of Fellows, August 22, 1947, BMCC, WRA.

22. Sigrid Wortmann Weltge, *Lore Kadden Lindenfeld: A Life in Textiles, 1945–1997* (Asheville: BMCM+AC, 1997), 16.

23. Weltge, *Lore Kadden Lindenfeld*, 7, 17.

24. Polly Weaver, "Jobs Looming: Jobs and Futures for the Artist-Weaver," *Mademoiselle* (July 1950): 117, quoted in Weltge, *Women's Work*, 173.

25. Weltge, *Lore Kadden Lindenfeld*, 17. Lindenfeld was also the subject of an article in *Craft Horizons* in 1953.

26. Anni Albers and Trude Guermonprez, letter to the Black Mountain College Board of Fellows outlining a proposal for production weaving at Black Mountain College, November 11, 1947, BMCC, WRA.

27. Albers described the non-loom exercises as based in arranging parts "in specific orders, which are textile orders." Albers in Mervin Lane, ed., *Black Mountain College: Sprouted Seeds: An Anthology of Personal Accounts* (Knoxville: University of Tennessee Press, 1991), 43.

28. The similarity to rearrangement works has also been noted by Sigrun Åsebø and Vibece Salthe, "Art as an Approach to Living," in *Ruth Asawa: Citizen of the Universe*, edited by Emma Ridgway,

Vibece Salthe, Sigrun Åsebø, John R. Blakinger, and Emily Pringle (Oxford: Modern Art Oxford, Stavanger: Stavanger Art Museum, 2022), 102.

29. Indeed, Åsebø and Salthe posit that Asawa developed the design for this purpose, although this cannot be confirmed. Åsebø and Vibece Salthe, "Art as an Approach to Living." The viewbook seems to have been printed in late 1947. In a letter to Josef Albers, Ted Dreier wrote: "Hazel Larsen, who is leaving, has just proposed staying on for an extra month if we want her to design a new picture folder for the college. She did some awfully good work under [Beaumont] Newhall last summer and he thought she would be good for the job." (Ted Dreier, Letter to Josef Albers, September 29, 1947, JAAF.)

30. My thanks to Isabel Bird, whose conference paper, "Ruth Asawa's Stamp and the Imprint of Black Mountain College," given on October 8, 2022, at *ReVIEWING Black Mountain College 13*, introduced me to the use of Asawa's stamp designs for print fabrics and helped to frame much of my discussion of these works.

31. Åsebø and Vibece Salthe, "Art as an Approach to Living," 104.

32. Mary Emma Harris, "Donald Alter" biography on the Black Mountain College Research Project website, n.d., https://www .blackmountaincollegeproject.org/Biographies/ALTERdonald/ ALTERdonaldBIOGRAPHY.htm, accessed December 14, 2022.

33. Alison Rooney, "A Lifetime of Art," *The Highlands Current*, January 10, 2020, http://highlandscurrent.org/2020/01/10/a -lifetime-of-art/, accessed December 14, 2022.

34. Student file of Don Emerson Wight, BMCSF, WRA.

35. Ray Johnson, "Art News," *Black Mountain College Community Bulletin*, no. 2 (November 1, 1946), WRA, https://digital.ncdcr .gov/digital/collection/p249901coll44/id/1096/rec/7, accessed December 14, 2022.

36. Larsen quote found in Kelsey Keith, ed., "Jack Lenor Larsen's Greatest Hits," online collection to accompany profile of Jack Lenor Larsen in *Dwell*, October 2013, https:// www.dwell.com/collection/jack-lenor-larsens-greatest-hits -9bf0e08a/6133564659413528576, accessed December 7, 2022.

37. "Leaves of Grass, 1971–1987," object text on the Minneapolis Institute of Art website, n.d., https://collections.artsmia. org/art/86990/leaves-of-grass-larsen-design-studio-new-york, accessed December 14, 2022.

38. Maleyne Syracuse, "The Effulgence of Country Gardens," article on the Cooper Hewitt, Smithsonian Design Museum website, posted March 9, 2016, https://www.cooperhewitt .org/2016/05/09/the-effulgence-of-country-gardens-2/, accessed December 7, 2022. The embedded quote is from "Annual Design Review," *Industrial Design* 8, no. 12 (December 1961): 72.

39. "Benin Brocade," Victoria and Albert Museum website, posted June 24, 2009, https://collections.vam.ac.uk/item/O267664/

benin-brocade-furnishing-fabric-don-wight/, accessed December 7, 2022.

40. Josef Albers, quoted in *Black Mountain College Community Bulletin* (July 1945), WRA.

41. "Black Mountain College Art Institute Summer 1944, July 17–Sept. 16," card or flyer published by Black Mountain College, 1944, DBMCC, WRA.

42. "Black Mountain College Art Institute Summer 1944."

43. See List of Students Officially Enrolled in Weaving Classes, pages 192–193, in this book.

44. Smith, *Bauhaus Weaving Theory*, 45.

45. Anni Albers, letter to Ted Dreier, July 3, 1938, JAAF.

46. Eve [Eva Zhitlowsky] Milton, statement for Black Mountain College Reunion, M. H. De Young Museum of Art, San Francisco, California, March 6–8 1992, 39.

47. Hudnut, who was dean of the Graduate School of Design at Harvard University, and Barzun, a prominent cultural historian and professor at Columbia University, had divergent views on the article. Hudnut agreed with Albers that manual and experiential work in the arts should precede historic analysis and critique, whereas Barzun, who favored a historical approach, disagreed. Joseph Hudnut, letter to Anni Albers, March 9, 1945, JAAF; Jacques Barzun, letter to Anni Albers, May 8, 1945, JAAF.

48. Arthur A. Brill, letter to Anni Albers, June 18, 1946, JAAF. This special issue of *Design* also played a major role in the recruitment of art and design students in the late 1940s. Writing in the "Art News" section of the *Black Mountain College Community Bulletin* in April 1946, the second issue of the *Community Bulletin* published after the special issue of *Design*, weaving student Jean Maurice reported, "The Black Mountain College Art Institute is gaining wide recognition and appears to be making an important contribution to American Art. The fame of previous summer sessions is shown by the fact that over 100 inquiries for this summer were received before even a preliminary announcement had been sent out." Jean Maurice, "Art News," *Black Mountain College Community Bulletin*, Spring Quarter (April 1946): 2.

49. Alexander H. Girard, letter to Anni Albers, undated (ca. 1947), JAAF.

50. Weltge, *Women's Work*, 167. To Atwater's credit, her book *Byways in Handweaving: An Illustrated Guide to Rare Weaving Techniques* (New York: Macmillan, 1954), while still full of the "recipes" for traditional forms that characterize her method books, offers an interesting exploration of alternative and non-Western weaving techniques, including card and inkle weaving, twining, braiding, plaiting, and other techniques.

51. Mary Meigs Atwater, "It's Pretty—But Is It Art," *The Weaver* 6, no. 3 (July–August 1941): 13–14, quoted in Weltge, *Women's Work*, 167.

52. Atwater, "It's Pretty—But Is It Art," quoted in Weltge, *Women's Work*, 168.

53. In this way, Albers's *On Weaving* is fairly closely aligned with Josef Albers's *Interaction of Color*, which Albers called "a record of an experimental way of studying color and teaching color." Josef Albers, *Interaction of Color* (New Haven, CT: Yale University Press, 2009), 3. Josef Albers does not give guidance on how to use color, what color means, or rules to follow. *On Weaving* and *Interaction of Color* are books best viewed as invitations to begin experimenting and guides for how to interpret the success of the results of experimentation, rather than as instructional manuals.

54. In a letter to the BMC Board of Fellows requesting an extension to her 1946–47 sabbatical, Anni wrote: "A further consideration is that I want to continue writing on a book uninterrupted by class-work. I lost these past months so much working time that I am unable to meet the date set by the publisher for it." (Anni Albers, letter to Black Mountain College Board of Fellows, May 14, 1947, JAAF.) Albers expert Karis Medina believes that such a book would have been largely similar in content to *On Weaving* [Karis Medina in conversation with the author, May 4, 2022].)

55. Museum of Modern Art, New York (MoMA), "Modern Textile Design: Check and Installation List," master checklist for exhibition organized by the Museum of Modern Art, New York, August 29–September 23, 1945, https://www.moma.org/documents/moma_master-checklist_325485.pdf, accessed December 7, 2022.

56. *Black Mountain College Bulletin*, April 1943.

57. See p. 194 for a full list of known exhibitions featuring textiles designed by Black Mountain College students and faculty.

58. MoMA, "Modern Textile Design: Check and Installation List."

59. Anonymous, possibly Jean Maurice, "Art News," *Black Mountain College Community Bulletin* (June 1946).

WEAVING AS ART

1. In 1941–42 the necklaces were shown at the Katharine Kuh Gallery in Chicago, Illinois; the Willard Gallery in New York City; the Addison Gallery in Andover, Massachusetts; and Outlines Gallery in Pittsburgh, Pennsylvania.

2. Bobby Dreier to Ethel Eyre Valentine Dreier, December 22, 1941, DBMCC, WRA.

3. Since the weaving is only recorded in a black-and-white photograph, I am assuming that it is woven in black and white, though it is possible that its colors were in fact different.

4. It is not clear if Reed wove the entire textile in two blocks controlling the white and black warps separately, or using pick up at the piece's midline.

5. Eva Zhitlowsky Milton, interview by Mary Emma Harris, 1971, BMCRP, WRA.

6. Milton, interview by Harris, 1971.

7. Albers, "Handweaving Today: Textile Work at Black Mountain College," *The Weaver* 6, no. 1 (January–February 1941): 3.

8. Milton, interview by Harris, 1971.

9. Milton, interview by Harris, 1971. This quote has been lightly edited for clarity.

10. Marilyn Bauer Greenwald, "('Widget') Marilyn Bauer Greenwald," in *Black Mountain College: Student Experience in Experimental Education in the Early Years, 1933–43*, edited by Robert Sunley, unpublished, 37.

11. *Black Mountain College Community Bulletin* 12, no. 33 (June 4, 1945), BMCC, WRA.

12. *Black Mountain College Community Bulletin* 5, no. 4 (May 1947): 4, BMCC, WRA.

13. Albers first seems to have used pick-up leno in her pictorial weavings in the work *Untitled* (1950), formerly owned by Merce Cunningham and now in the collection of the Crystal Bridges Museum of American Art.

FOLLOWING THE THREAD

1. Sayde Tune Wilson, *Else Regensteiner: Biography of a Weaver* (Nashville, TN: Tunstede Press), 70–71; and Jenni Sorkin, "Weaving," in *Leap Before You Look: Black Mountain College, 1933–1957*, edited by Helen Molesworth (New Haven, CT: Institute of Contemporary Art/Boston in association with Yale University Press, 2015), 169.

2. Wilson, *Else Regensteiner*, 71.

3. Wilson, *Else Regensteiner*, 73.

4. Jane Addams, "Chapter V: First Days at Hull-House," in *Twenty Years at Hull-House with Autobiographical Notes*, edited by Mary Mark Ockerbloom (New York: Macmillan, 1912), 89–112.

5. Wilson, *Else Regensteiner*, 113.

6. Wilson, *Else Regensteiner*, 76. The year 1945 is noted by Regensteiner in a summary of her time at SAIC (submitted March 30, 1975), see Series III: Instructional Papers, box 4, folder 4.6, ERC.

7. Letters to Else Regensteiner from the School of the Art Institute of Chicago, Office of the Dean [Hubert Ropp] dated June 1, 1946, and September 13, 1946, Series III: Instructional Papers, box 4, folder 4.2, ERC.

8. Letters to Else Regensteiner from the School of the Art Institute of Chicago, Office of the Dean dated June 10, 1948, June 27, 1951, July 6, 1953, July 1, 1954, April 27, 1955, June 20, 1956, May 20, 1957, April 1, 1958, and May 5, 1959, Series III: Instructional Papers, box 4, folder 4.2, ERC.

9. Wilson, *Else Regensteiner*, 83.

10. Letter to Else Regensteiner from the Art Institute of Chicago, Chairman of the School Committee, Andrew McNally, III dated July 1, 1957, Series III: Instructional Papers, box 4, folder 4.2, ERC. Regensteiner received tenure in 1968. Letter to Else Regensteiner from the School of the Art Institute of Chicago, Acting Dean, Roger Gilmore dated April 15, 1968, Series III: Instructional Papers, box 4, folder 4.2, ERC.

11. This assignment, "Problems V and VI," is undated but is closely related to another titled "Study of leaves" in the same folder, dated October 1, 1953, Series III: Instructional Papers, box 13, folder 13.9, ERC.

12. Briony Fer, "Black Mountain College Exercises," in *Anni Albers*, edited by Ann Coxon, Briony Fer, and Maria Müller-Schareck (New Haven, CT: Yale University Press, 2018), 65. See also Anni Albers, "March 1965 Interview: Teaching Weaving and Design," in *Black Mountain College: Sprouted Seeds: An Anthology of Personal Accounts*, edited by Mervin Lane (Knoxville: University of Tennessee Press, 1991), 43.

13. Syllabus, undated, p. 23, Series III: Instructional Papers, box 4, folder 4.10, ERC.

14. María Minera, "Discovering Monte Albán," in *Anni Albers*, 75.

15. Lecture for the Ontario Handweavers and Spinners Conference, October 1961, Series III: Instructional Papers, box 7, folder 7.26, ERC.

16. Mary Catherine Howell, "Hand Weaving Is Both a Hobby and the Subject of Serious Study in New York," *Women's Wear Daily* 80, no. 89 (May 8, 1950): 20, and "To Open Weaving Workshop Oct. 1," *Women's Wear Daily* 83, no. 55 (September 18, 1951): 30.

17. Howell, "Hand Weaving," and "To Open Weaving Workshop."

18. Although these studies are undated, their format precisely matches with the description of Albers's 1941 BMC exercise. Anni Albers, *On Weaving*, new expanded ed. (Princeton, NJ: Princeton University Press in association with the Josef and Anni Albers Foundation, [1965] 2017), plates 37–40.

19. Lili Blumenau, "On Textures—Notes of a Contemporary Weaver," *Handweaver and Craftsman* 1, no. 2 (Summer 1950): 9.

20. Alice Adams, "Lili Blumenau: 'Each Limitation a Challenge, Each Job a New One,'" *Craft Horizons* 22, no. 2 (March/April 1962): 19.

21. Mary Alice Smith, "Editorially Speaking . . . ," *Handweaver and Craftsman* 1, no. 1 (April 1950): 2.

22. Gail M. Redfield, "Experiences with a Weaving Workshop," *Handweaver and Craftsman* 6, no. 1 (Winter 1954–55): 59.

23. Notably, Dorothy Liebes, Jack Lenor Larsen, and Trude Guermonprez also were profiled in this issue. "Marli Ehrman," *Handweaver and Craftsman* 2, no. 2 (Spring 1960): 26.

24. Haystack Mountain School of Crafts advertisement, *Craft Horizons* 16, no. 4 (August 1956): 50. In addition to her work as an artist

and educator, Ehrman also was a foundational member of the Midwest Designer-Craftsmen, see Sigrid Weltge-Wormann, *Women's Work: Textile Art from the Bauhaus* (New York: Chronicle Books, 1993), 179. Trude Guermonprez also studied and taught at Black Mountain, see Sorkin, "Weaving," in *Leap Before You Look*, 169.

25. Series III: Instructional Papers, boxes 7–12, ERC. See also Wilson, *Else Regensteiner*, 104–7. In addition to her practice and in-person teaching, Regensteiner also went on to write three books on weaving: *The Art of Weaving* (1970), *Weaver's Study Course: Ideas and Techniques* (1975), and *Geometric Design in Weaving* (1986).

26. Jack Lenor Larsen, "The Weaver as Artist," *Craft Horizons* 15, no. 6 (November/December 1955): 31–34; and M. Rachael Arauz, "The Best Ideals of Socially Useful Living: Haystack, 1950–1960," in *In the Vanguard*, edited by M. Rachael Arauz and Diana Jocelyn Greenwold (Portland, ME: Portland Museum of Art, 2019), 48–52.

27. M. Rachael Arauz and Diana Jocelyn Greenwold with Shea Spiller, "Chronology," in *In the Vanguard*, 144.

28. Larsen, "The Weaver as Artist," 31.

29. Albers, "Handweaving Today," 3.

30. Anni Albers, "Design: Anonymous and Timeless," in *On Designing* (Middletown, CT: Wesleyan University Press [1947] 1961), 6.

31. Regensteiner, quoted in Wilson, *Else Regensteiner*, 71.

32. "Do You Know Our Name?" *Craft Horizons* 1, no. 1 (November 1941): 4.

33. Smith, "Editorially Speaking . . . ," 2.

34. "Weavers' Workshops and Summer Classes," *Handweaver and Craftsman* 1, no. 1 (April 1950): 21–25, 41; and "Summer Courses in Weaving," *Handweaver and Craftsman* 6, no. 2 (Spring 1955): 18–20.

35. Blumenau's first issue as Textile editor was for *Craft Horizons* 16, no. 4 (July/August 1956). See also Nell Znamierowski, "Craft World: Lili Blumenau, 1912–1976," *Craft Horizons* 37, no. 1 (February 1977): 10.

36. Sorkin, "Weaving," in *Leap Before You Look*, 169.

WEAVING LITERACY

1. Both Joseph and Oates changed their focuses away from weaving after Anni Albers and Trude Guermonprez left Black Mountain College in 1949, but both had also begun to nurture their other interests prior to that time.

2. Julie J. Thomson, *Begin to See: The Photographers of Black Mountain College* (Asheville, NC: BMCM+AC, 2017), 86.

3. Mark Davenport (son of Patsy Lynch Wood) in email to the author, January 10, 2022.

4. "Examination for Admission to the Senior Division, Part II," February 23, 1942, JAAF. It is interesting to consider whether Albers's prompt about the use of fabrics in interiors recalled Otti Berger's 1930 essay "Stoffe im Raum" ["Fabrics in Space"], which, according to T'ai Smith, "theorize[d] an aspect of cloth that had largely gone uninvestigated" prior to its publication (Smith, *Bauhaus Weaving Theory: From Feminine Craft to Mode of Design* [Minneapolis: University of Minnesota Press, 2014], 81). Anni also wrote examination questions that were not related to weaving. Her prompt in Part I of the fall of 1943 Senior Division examination, in which the students had to answer all questions posed, was: "Formulate a night-letter of fifty words in which you give a prospective student the main points of the BMC program." (According to annotations by Josef Albers on "Senior Division Examination, Part I," October 29, 1943, JAAF.)

5. "Senior Division Examination—Fourth Day—Spring, 1946," WRA. Note that in the original "satin" is mistyped as "satis."

6. Mark Davenport, email to the author, January 10, 2022. Another possible example can be seen in a 1944 photograph of the weaving room by Joseph Breitenbach, showing weavers Mimi French and Ati Gropius (fig. 7). Although Breitenbach visited the College in the summer of 1944, Gropius was not officially enrolled in weaving until the fall of 1945, which suggests that Ati was either placed and posed for Breitenbach's photo deliberately, or more likely, a loom became available and Ati was able to begin her education in weaving early on a more informal basis.

7. A throw or shawl attributed to Joan Stack is in the collection of the Black Mountain College Museum + Arts Center, Asheville, North Carolina.

8. The photographs of weavings in "Mountain Stream" can be found in an album of photographs by Philip Hug, BMCC, WRA.

9. Josef Albers, *Search Vs. Research* (Hartford, CT: Trinity College Press, 1969), 73.

10. Goldsmith planned to major in architecture but left BMC in 1944 to join the WACs. Mary Emma Harris, "Nell Goldsmith Heyns," biography on the Black Mountain College Research Project website, n.d., https://blackmountaincollegeproject.org/Biographies/GoldsmithHeynsNell/GoldsmithHeynsNellBIO.htm, accessed December 14, 2022.

11. Williams was seemingly a particularly active and creative weaver, whose practical textiles included a blouse that he wove in Trude Guermonprez's class that was worn by Vera Baker when she married Williams at Lake Eden in the Quiet House. Mark Davenport, email to the author, January 10, 2022.

12. Anni Albers, Note about samples of material for curtains and furnishings at Lake Eden, ca. 1942, WRA.

13. "Unfinished," see Marilyn Bauer Greenwald, interview by Mary Emma Harris, 1971, 5, BMCRP, WRA. "Wood slats," see Don Page, interview by Mary Emma Harris, 1970, 23, BMCRP, WRA.

14. Josef Albers, "Art as Experience," *Black Mountain College Bulletin*, no. 2, 1935, WRA.

15. Eva Zhitlowsky explained that she was thinking about musical counterpoint when weaving her pictorial weavings with warp and weft floats. See "Eva Zhitlowsky," in "Weaving as Art," pages 75–78, this book.

16. Jason Andrew and Julia Gleich, "And No Birds Sang: The Life of Choreographer and Dancer Katherine Litz," *Journal of Black Mountain College Studies* 10, February 2020, https://www .blackmountaincollege.org/katherine-litz, accessed December 29, 2022.

THE HARRIETT ENGELHARDT MEMORIAL COLLECTION OF TEXTILES

1. Ted Dreier, letter to Bernard Lobman, October 14, 1946, BMCGF, WRA.

2. Harriett Engelhardt Application, BMCSF, WRA.

3. Winnifred Leon, letter to Fred and Anne Mangold, September 8, 1939, BMCSF, WRA.

4. Harriett Engelhardt, Course Cards, BMCSF, WRA.

5. Anni Albers, recommendation letter to Dan Wells, January 5, 1942, BMCSF, WRA. To our knowledge Harriett's own work in weaving and art have not been preserved.

6. Harriett Engelhardt, letter to Fred Mangold, June 22, 1942, BMCSF, WRA.

7. A short biography of Engelhardt can be found at https://digital .archives.alabama.gov/digital/collection/voices/id/7223/rec/2; and American Red Cross, letter to Engelhardt, April 8, 1944, HPEP, ADAH, https://digital.archives.alabama.gov/digital/ collection/voices/id/11433/rec/1, both accessed September 30, 2022.

8. For more about the Clubmobile women and their role as female combat troops, see Julia A. Ramsey, "'Girls' in Name Only: A Study of American Red Cross Volunteers on the Frontlines of World War II," master's thesis, Auburn University, 2011, https://etd.auburn .edu/bitstream/handle/10415/2616/ramsey_julia_ma_thesis_ history_post_defense_and_AUETD_check_5.9.11.pdf;sequence=3, accessed January 1, 2023.

9. These details come from Harriett Engelhardt's letters, HPEP, ADAH, https://digital.archives.alabama.gov/digital/collection/ voices/search/searchterm/Engelhardt%2C%20Harriett%20 Pinkston%2C%201919–1945/field/subjec/mode/exact/conn/ and, accessed September 30, 2022. Thank you to Michael Beggs for locating these letters.

10. Zygmunt Bilwin, letter to Mr. and Mrs. Engelhardt, September 3, 1946, HPEP, ADAH.

11. *BMC Newsletter* 4, no. 1, November 1945, BMCGF, WRA.

12. *BMC Newsletter* 5, no. 1, November 1946, BMCGF, WRA. Harriett earned $150 a month working for the American Red Cross; Ida May Born, letter to Harriett Engelhardt, April 8, 1944, HPEP, ADAH, https://digital.archives.alabama.gov/digital/collection/ voices/id/11433/rec/1, accessed September 30, 2022.

13. Anni Albers, "One Aspect of Art Work," 1944, in Anni Albers, *Anni Albers Selected Writings on Design* (Middletown, CT: Wesleyan University Press, 2000) 25.

14. Virginia Gardner Troy, *Anni Albers and Ancient American Textiles: From Bauhaus to Black Mountain* (Aldershot, England: Ashgate, 2002), 132.

15. Don Page, letter to Virginia Gardner Troy, February 19, 1996, courtesy of Virginia Gardner Troy. Also Troy, *Anni Albers and Ancient American Textiles*, 132.

16. Page, letter to Troy, September 4, 1996.

17. Anni also assembled her own personal collection of Andean textiles. See Troy, *Anni Albers and Ancient American Textiles*, 14 and 176n47.

18. *BMC Bulletin* 6, no. 4 (May 1948): 3, BMCGF, WRA.

19. In the fall of 1942 Harriett studied Spanish with Fred Mangold, Engelhardt Course Cards, BMCSF, WRA. She asked Anni for a recommendation letter and mentioned possibly traveling to Mexico to look for employment. Harriett Engelhardt to Anni Albers, August 16, 1943, Engelhardt Student File, BMCSF, WRA.

20. Anni Albers to Ted Dreier, May 18, 1947, JAAF. Anni's first acquisition was one of the two textiles from Guatemala in the Engelhardt Collection (Yale University Art Gallery object number 1958.13.28 or 1958.13.39).

21. Anni Albers, letter to Mr. and Mrs. Engelhardt, July 4, 1947, BMCSF, WRA.

22. Josef Albers, letter to Ludwig Grote, July 7, 1947, quoted in Jenny Anger and Kiki Gilderhus, *Anni and Josef Albers: Latin American Journeys* (Ostfildern: Hatje Cantz, 2007), 215.

23. *BMC Bulletin* 5, no. 7 (November 1947), BMCGF, WRA. This count of ninety-two objects is from August F. Stauff Co., customs list in letter to BMC, March 15, 1948, BMCGF, WRA.

24. Annie Floyd Engelhardt, letter to Anni Albers, July 18, 1947, BMCSF, WRA. BMC Minutes and Attendant Papers, box 9, BMCC, WRA.

25. Anni Albers, letter to Mr. and Mrs. Engelhardt, July 4, 1947, BMCSF, WRA.

26. *BMC Newsletter* 5, no. 1 (November 1946), BMCGF, WRA.

27. Stauff Co., letter, 1948.

28. *BMC Bulletin* 6, no. 4 (May 1948): 2–4, BMCGF, WRA.

29. *BMC Bulletin* 6, no. 4 (May 1948): 3, BMCGF, WRA.

30. *BMC Bulletin* 6, no. 4 (May 1948): 4, BMCGF, WRA.

31. Troy, *Anni Albers and Ancient American Textiles*, 143.

32. Stauff Co., letter, 1948.

33. Yale University Art Gallery collection numbers 1958.13.79 and 1958.13.20.

34. Anni Albers, dedication in *On Weaving* (Princeton, NJ: Princeton University Press, 2017).

35. Albers, *On Weaving*, 11.

36. For a detailed discussion of Anni's role to revive and redefine ancient Andean weaving and also act as an intermediary, see Troy, *Anni Albers and Ancient American Textiles*.

37. Trude Guermonprez, interview by Mary Emma Harris, 1971, 28, BMCRP, WRA.

38. Thanks to lead archivist Heather South for locating these details. Student Course Cards, BMCSF, WRA.

39. Trude Guermonprez, interview by Mary Emma Hariss, 1971, 28, BMCRP, WRA.

40. Trude Guermonprez, document that starts with "Schedule and the dates July 6–August 31," TGP.

41. Trude Guermonprez, "Lecture: Design," see pages 132–137, this book.

42. Thanks to Michael Beggs for matching Lindenfeld's notes to textiles in the Engelhardt Collection.

43. Lore Kadden, "Aspects of Modern Textiles," February 25, 1948, Lore Kadden, BMCSF, WRA.

44. See Troy, *Anni Albers and Ancient American Textiles*, 50.

45. Anni held this fragment in high regard since she reproduced it in *On Weaving*.

46. Thanks to Michael Beggs for sharing this observation.

47. Anni Albers, letter to Donald Warrington, December 7, 1949, COP, WRA. A December 19, 1949, letter from Natasha Goldowski to Anni Albers indicates the trust Anni requested had not been set up due to the departure of Bill Treichler from BMC, BMCRP, WRA.

48. Donald Warrington, letter to Albers, December 2, 1949, COP, WRA.

49. Charles Olson, letter to Anni Albers, May 28, 1954, COP, WRA.

50. Charles Olson, letter to Anni Albers, August 9, 1954, COP, WRA.

51. Harriett Engelhardt Research File, BMCRP, WRA.

52. Yale University, *News Bulletin*, no. 111, October 26, 1958, COP, WRA.

TRUDE GUERMONPREZ

1. Franziska Mayer, Typewritten statement about her work at BMC, January 13, 1947, BMCFF, WRA.

2. For a biography of Guermonprez (in German), see Albrecht Pohlman, *Modell, Künstlerin und 'wahre Eva' das Abenteuerliche Leben der Trude Guermonprez* (Halle an der Saale: Verlag Janos Stekovics, 2003).

3. For a discussion of Benita Koch-Otte, see Sigrid Wortman Weltge, *Women's Work: Textile Art from the Bauhaus* (San Francisco: Chronicle Books, 1993), 60–61.

4. "Meet the Author," in Trude Guermonprez, "Tapestry Through the Ages: The Weaving of Tapestries Part II," *Shuttle Craft Bulletin* 34, no. 6 (June–July 1957): 16.

5. Hazel V. Bray, "The Tapestries of Trude Guermonprez," in *The Tapestries of Trude Guermonprez* (Oakland, CA: Oakland Museum, 1982), 5.

6. Bray, "Chronology," in *Tapestries of Trude Guermonprez*, 26.

7. Bray, "Chronology," in *Tapestries of Trude Guermonprez*, 26.

8. Rik Suermondt, "Paul Guermonprez," in *PhotoLexicon* 9, no. 19 (September 1992), https://depthoffield.universiteitleiden .nl/0919f01en/, accessed December 4, 2022. According to Pohlman, Trude worked as an office clerk at Co-op 2. Albrecht Pohlman, email to author, September 16, 2016.

9. Trude Guermonprez, letter to Heinrich and Johanna Jalowetz, May 13, 1945, JAFA.

10. Guermonprez's visitor's visa did not allow her to be appointed to the faculty. See Albert William Levi, letter to Guermonprez, February 24, 1947, Guermonprez BMCFF, WRA.

11. Bray, "Chronology," in *Tapestries of Trude Guermonprez*, 26.

12. Guermonprez included the following credit line with these photographs: "Trude Guermonprez, Textile Exhibit, BMC, 1947." Guermonprez, Photo Release Form, BMCRP, 1973. From this credit, it appears that Trude Guermonprez organized this exhibition of textiles. The title card "Textiles" for it suggests, however, that it included more than just her own work.

13. Trude Guermonprez, interview by Mary Emma Harris, 1971, 23, BMCRP, WRA.

14. Mayer and Guermonprez, Handwritten notes "Weaving for Beginners," Summer Session 1947, BMCGF, WRA.

15. Maike Bruchmann, "Heinrich Mayer" research, translated by Erwin Fink, 2017, https://www.stolpersteine-hamburg.de/ en.php?MAIN_ID=7&BIO_ID=1934, accessed January 15, 2023.

16. Guermonprez, interview by Harris, 1971, 8.

17. Guermonprez, interview by Harris, 1971, 5.

18. Guermonprez, interview by Harris, 1971, 4.

19. Weltge, *Women's Work*, 172.

20. Guermonprez, [A poem from her notebook, translated by Bianca Landworth], https://ccatextilehistory.weebly.com/trude-guermonprez.html, accessed October 25, 2022.

21. *Leaf Study* was purchased by Jeanette MacMillan Pruiss, a weaver who studied eight-harness double weave with Trude. Gregg and Linda MacMillan, email to the author, March 14, 2022.

22. For more on Albers's Leaf Studies, see Josef Albers, *Interaction of Color* (New Haven, CT: Yale University Press, 2006), 144. About Muzenic's leaf study, see Mary Emma Harris, *The Arts at Black Mountain College* (Cambridge, MA: MIT Press, 1987), 256n47.

23. Guermonprez, quoted in Yoshiko Uchida, "Trude Guermonprez," *Craft Horizons* 19, no. 2 (March/April 1959): 29.

24. Guermonprez, interview by Harris, 1971, 5.

25. Trude Guermonprez, *Notes*, June 27, 1974, quoted in Bray, *The Tapestries of Trude Guermonprez*, 6.

26. See image in Harris, *The Arts at Black Mountain College*, 134.

27. Guermonprez, in Bray, *Tapestries of Trude Guermonprez*, 6.

28. These include *Alter Ego*, 1970; *Family Portrait*, 1970; and *We Are But Two Shadows*, 1971. See Bray, *Tapestries of Trude Guermonprez*, 20.

29. See Anni Albers, "Tapestry," in *On Weaving* (Princeton, NJ: Princeton University Press, 2017), chap. 9. Trude Guermonprez, "Tapestry Through the Ages: The Weaving of Tapestries Part I," *Shuttle Craft Bulletin* 34, no. 4 (April 1957): 5–10; and Trude Guermonprez, "Tapestry Through The Ages . . . Part II," *Shuttle Craft Bulletin* 34, no. 6 (June–July 1957): 8–16. Mildred Constantine and Jack Lenor Larsen coined the term "Art Fabric" for the textiles they discussed, since they found the varied approaches to "defy classification." Both Albers and Guermonprez are discussed in Constantine and Larsen, *Beyond Craft: The Art Fabric* (New York: Van Nostrand, 1974), 7.

30. Guermonprez, interview by Harris, 1971, 8.

31. Accounts of Trude's hummingbird observations are found in two of her letters to Lisa Aronson, postcard December 1964 and letter dated December 18 [no year], JAFC.

32. Josef Albers taught Color through the spring of 1949 after which his student, Warren "Pete" Jennerjahn (Elizabeth Jennerjahn's husband) taught it until the spring of 1951.

33. In *On Weaving* Anni shows diagrams of slit tapestry from Peru and also the former Persian Empire where it is called Kelim technique, see Plates 64 and 68.

34. Anni Albers, Josef Albers, Theodore Dreier, Trude Guermonprez, and Charlotte Schlesinger, Resignation letter, February 18, 1949, BMCGF, WRA.

35. For further discussion of their resignation, see Harris, *The Arts at Black Mountain College*, 164–65; and Lisa Jalowetz Aronson and Trude Jalowetz Guermonprez Elsesser, interview by Martin Duberman, 1967, 18, MDC, WRA.

36. Trude met Irene Schawinsky in the winter of 1947 to discuss production weaving at BMC. See Beggs, "Making Clothes at Black Mountain College," pages 40–47, this book.

37. Aronson and Guermonprez Elsesser, interview by Duberman, 1967, 27.

38. Aronson and Guermonprez Elsesser, interview by Duberman, 1967, 27.

39. See Julie J. Thomson, "The Art of Graphic Design: Lustig, Albers, Johnson, and the 1945 Summer Session," *Journal of Black Mountain College Studies* 6, https://www.blackmountaincollege.org/art-of-graphic-design-1945-thomson/, accessed January 13, 2023.

40. Ray Johnson, Course Cards, Fall 1947, BMCSF, WRA.

41. Andy Oates Course Cards, BMCSF, WRA

42. Andy Oates, Oral History by Connie Bostic, 2010, BMCM+AC.

43. Oates, Oral History by Bostic.

44. Hertha O. Horwitz, conversation with author, November 30, 2022.

45. Pohlman, *Modell, Künstlerin und 'wahre Eva' das Abenteuerliche Leben der Trude Guermonprez*, 387.

46. Anni Albers, Recommendation letter for Guermonprez, June 6, 1949, BMCFF, WRA.

47. Guermonprez, letter to Franziska Mayer, November 7, 1947, FMP, JAAF; Guermonprez, interview by Harris, 1971, 28.

48. Jonathan Guthrie Herr, "love because nothing else matters," in Dean and Geraldine Schwarz, eds., *Marguerite Wildenhain and the Bauhaus: An Eyewitness Anthology* (Decorah, IA: South Bear Press, 2007), 315.

49. Aronson and Guermonprez Elsesser, interview by Duberman, 1967, 44–45.

50. Pond Farm Workshops, Announcement, TGP.

51. Guermonprez, Schedule for the weaving workshop at Pond Farm, TGP.

52. Guermonprez, "Weaving" typewritten document, TGP.

53. "Apprenticeship Under Working Artists Offered at Pond Farm," *The Press Democrat* (Santa Rosa, California), August 20, 1950, 17.

54. Hazel Bray, "Trude Guermonprez," *American Craft* 43, no. 3 (June/July 1983): 42.

55. Guermonprez, letter to Lisa Aronson, undated circa 1951, JAFC.

56. *BMC Bulletin* 10, no. 4 (November 1952): 18, BMC.

57. Guermonprez and John Elsesser were married in 1951.

58. For a discussion of Guermonprez's teaching at CCAC, see Jacqueline Grace Sullivan, "'All That Concerns Us' The Art and Life of Trude Guermonprez," master's thesis, Parsons School of Design, New York, 2016.

59. Sekimachi, "Trude Remembered," see pages 170–173, this book.

60. [Kay Sekimachi,] "The Weaver's Weaver": Oral History Transcript, BANC MSS 97/128, 26. © The Regents of the University of California, The Bancroft Library, University of California, Berkeley.

61. "California College of the Arts Textiles History," California College of the Arts, https://ccatextilehistory.weebly.com/timeline.html, accessed October 25, 2022.

62. Marilyn Hagberg, "CCAC's Trude Guermonprez Is the U.S.'s Craftswoman of the Year," *CCAC Review* (Autumn 1970): 13, https://vault.cca.edu/file/5dfa7c69-a2d1–44c8-be77–92ef5fa1cbb6/1/20201020003.pdf, accessed January 20, 2023.

63. Guermonprez's *Notes to John I and John II* are in the Museum of Arts and Design Collection, 1977.2.33a,b.

64. Mary Emma Harris, "Marquis & Stoller, Rodef Sholom Synagogue," n.d. https://blackmountaincollegeproject.org/Biographies/StOLLERclaude/, accessed August 4, 2022.

65. Tyrel Holston, "Weaving the Old with the New," 2013, https://www.cooperhewitt.org/2013/09/05/weaving-the-old-with-the-new/, accessed January 24, 2023.

66. Trude's preparatory drawing is in the Cooper Hewitt, Smithsonian Design Museum Collection, 1993–121–68, https://collection.cooperhewitt.org/objects/18643409/, accessed January 22, 2023.

67. Lauren Eichler Berkun, "The Symbolism of Light," The Jewish Theological Seminary, https://www.jtsa.edu/torah/the-symbolism-of-light/, accessed January 24, 2023.

CONNECTING THE THREADS

1. See Anne Whidden, "Learning Weaving: Johanna Brunsson's Weaving School," https://theswedishrugblog.wordpress.com/2016/11/01/learning-weaving/, accessed January 29, 2023.

2. In 1937 Bauhaus weaver Otti Berger, after a similarly demoralizing experience in the UK, returned to her native Croatia. From there she was deported to Auschwitz and murdered in April 1944.

3. Franziska Mayer recounted her life in Newfoundland in "Reminiscences from Franziska Mayer's (7.4.14–11.13.94) Life: 50 Years in North and South America," an animated and detailed talk about her life that she presented after she returned to Hamburg in 1989. Located in FMP, JAAF. Mayer's family donated her papers to the archives of the Josef and Anni Albers Foundation in 2015 and 2022.

4. In the United States Mayer anglicized the spelling of her name to Francisca. Mayer initially had a three-year contract as weaving teacher; however, the Grenfell Association kept her on in various other capacities until the war ended.

5. Mayer, "Reminiscences," 5.

6. Maike Bruchman, "Heinrich Mayer, 1866," *Stolpersteine in Hamburg*, October 2017, https://www.stolpersteine-hamburg.de/en.php?MAIN_ID=7&BIO_ID=1934&VIEW=PRINT, accessed February 28, 2023.

7. Mayer gives an address on Riverside Drive on all her New York City correspondence but does not identify the relatives.

8. Max Dehn to Franziska Mayer, October 19, 1945, FMP, JAAF.

9. Letter from Dorothy Liebes to Franziska Mayer, March 12, 1941; letter from Toni Dehn to Helmut Dehn, May 20, 1943, FMP, JAAF.

10. Franziska Mayer, letter to Anni Albers, April 8, 1946, BMCFF, WRA.

11. Anni Albers, letter to Ted Dreier, April 26, 1946, JAAF; *Black Mountain College Community Bulletin*, June 1946, 3, WRA. The minutes to the June 4 BMC Board of Fellows meeting noted that "A. Albers joined the meeting and reported on her interviews with Franziska Mayer candidate to the Faculty in weaving," BMCC, WRA.

12. Mayer, "Reminiscences," 7. The bus trip took her "via the Grand Canyon, Los Angeles, San Francisco . . . Miami . . . and through the Panama Canal Zone to Lima."

13. Trude Guermonprez, interview by Mary Emma Harris, 1971, BMCRP, WRA.

14. Guermonprez was referring to the Engelhardt Collection, which Anni Albers had assembled during her sabbatical, FMP, JAAF.

15. Lisa Jalowetz Aronson described her experiences as a BMC student in a 2010 interview by Sigrid Pawelke, https://black-mountain-research.com/2015/06/10/interview-with-lisa-jalowetz-aronson/, accessed February 9, 2023.

16. Arrested by the Nazis and imprisoned in 1942, Paul Guermonprez escaped, became a leader in the Dutch Resistance, RVV, and was recaptured and murdered in 1944. Trude had gone into hiding in 1942, but they kept up a correspondence. For more on the RVV, see https://www.cryptomuseum.com/intel/rvv/index.htm, accessed February 9, 2023.

17. Trude Guermonprez, letter to her parents, May 13, 1945, JAFC.

18. Trude Guermonprez, letter to her parents, August 30, 1945, JAFC.

19. Article in the *Asheville Citizen*, February 4, 1946. Heinrich and Johanna Jalowetz Dreier Correspondence, DBMCC, WRA.

20. Guermonprez, interview by Harris.

21. In this interview Harris appears to show Trude some notes about the weaving program, but it is unclear whether these were Franziska's or Trude's notes. Guermonprez, interview by Harris, 4–5.

22. Guermonprez, interview by Harris.

23. Anni Albers, letter to Marli Ehrman, March 4, 1949, BMCFF, WRA.

24. The dates of the 1949 Summer Session were July 6 to August 31. *Black Mountain College Bulletin* 7, no. 1, March 1949, BMCGF, WRA.

25. Anni Albers to Marli Ehrman, March 29, 1949, BMCFF, WRA.

26. Anni Albers to Marli Ehrman, May 31, 1949, BMCFF, WRA.

27. Toni Ullstein Fleischmann, "Thrown off the Track," was written in the summer of 1939 after her arrival in Mexico with Anni's father, Siegfried Fleischmann, as refugees from Germany. Copy of original typescript "Aus de Bahn geworfen" found in JAAF. English translation by Theodore Benfey.

28. Anni Albers, letter to Ted Dreier, March 18, 1937, JAAF.

29. Theodor Adorno, *Minima Moralis: Reflections from Damaged Life*, translated from the German by E. F. N. Jephcott (London: Verso Editions 1978), 104.

DEPARTURES, SHORT STAYS, AND CLOSURE

1. Marli Heimann (later Ehrman) studied weaving at the Bauhaus from 1923 to 1927 and graduated as a journeywoman.

2. See Michael Reid, *Convergence/Divergence* (Asheville, NC: BMCM+AC, 2015), 12.

3. Marli Ehrman, "Textile Design Course," Summer Session 1949, BMCGF, WRA.

4. Ehrman taught and served as a mentor to her former students, who were known as the "Marli Weavers," from 1951 to 1956, though the group continued through 1991. See Joan Cotter and Barry Cotter, "Traditions: Marli Ehrman," *Handwoven*, January 6, 2020, https://handwovenmagazine.com/traditions-marli-ehrman/, accessed December 1, 2022.

5. Nancy Spiegel, "Marli Ehrman, 1904–1982," *American Craft* 43, no. 3 (June/July 1983): 87. D'Harcourt's *Textiles Ancien de Peru* was published in 1934 and was not translated into English until 1960. See Mary Elizabeth King, "Book Review: *Textiles of Ancient Peru and Their Techniques*," *American Journal of Archaeology* 67, no. 3 (1963): 324–26, https://doi.org/10.2307/501404, accessed December 1, 2022.

6. Andy Oates, letter to Ellen Siegel, August 21, 1949; Siegel, letter to Natasha Goldowski, August 22, 1949; Goldowski, letter to Siegel, August 31, 1949. All correspondence from BMCGF, WRA.

7. In the spring of 1949 Siegel wrote to Josef Albers asking if there were any teaching positions. Siegel, letter to Josef Albers, April 11, 1949, BMCGF, WRA. In July 1949 Natasha Goldowski invited Siegel to teach weaving at BMC for the next academic year. Goldowski, letter to Siegel, July 20, 1949, BCMGF, WRA.

8. Laura MacNewman, email to author, Cranbrook Archives, July 8, 2022.

9. Andy Oates, Student Course Cards, BMCSF, WRA.

10. Ellen Siegel, Casement Cloth 1956, MoMA object 505.1975, https://www.moma.org/collection/works/2036, accessed July 15, 2022. Color slides of Siegel's work, photographed by Mary Emma Harris, BMCRP, WRA.

11. M. Rachael Arauz, "Gathered Momentum: Black Mountain College and Haystack Mountain School of Crafts in the 1950s," *Journal of Black Mountain College Studies* 12 (May 2021), https://www.blackmountaincollege.org/arauz-haystack/, accessed July 15, 2022.

12. Ellen Siegel biography in *Designed for Production: The Craftsman's Approach* (New York: Museum of Contemporary Crafts, 1964), https://digital.craftcouncil.org/digital/api/collection/p15785coll6/id/2647/download, accessed July 15, 2022.

13. Student Course Cards, BMCSF, WRA.

14. Weaving Course description, *Black Mountain Bulletin*, Summer 1951, BMCGF, WRA.

15. Weaving student course records compiled by Heather South, BMCC, WRA.

16. A BMC 1952 Summer Institute announcement lists Willie Joseph as teaching weaving. No records for students taking weaving with him have been found. This announcement also lists a photography trip to the Yucatán with Hazel Larsen Archer, which did not happen. BMC Second Announcement, Summer Institute, 1952, JAFC.

17. Betsy Weinrib's work from this class does not seem to have been saved. Email to the author from Mark Davenport, January 10, 2022.

18. Mary Emma Harris, notes from an untaped telephone conversation with Marie Murelius, December 12, 1971, BMCRP, WRA.

19. Faculty Board Meeting minutes, July 20, 1954, BMCC, WRA.

20. Joe Holley, "Painter, Weaver Headed Textile Museum," *Washington Post*, June 8, 2009.

21. Charles Olson, letter to Anni Albers, August 9, 1954, COP, WRA.

22. Brewton and Murphy each paid $125 a quarter to attend BMC. Treasurer's files, BMCC, WRA.

23. Paul Alexander, interview by Mary Emma Harris, 1971, 28, BMCRP, WRA.

24. Terence Burns and Mona Stea Burns, interview by Mary Emma Harris, 1971, 19–20, BMCRP, WRA.

25. Terence Burns and Mona Stea Burns, interview by Harris, 1971, 22.

26. Martha King, *Outside/Inside . . . just outside the art world's inside* (Kenmore, NY: BlazeVOX), 36.

27. Color slide collection, photographed by Mary Emma Harris, BMCRP, WRA.

28. Terence Burns and Mona Stea Burns, interview by Harris, 1971, 18.

29. Terence Burns and Mona Stea Burns, interview by Harris, 1971, 21.

30. Anthony (Tony) Landreau, Curriculum Vitae, 2003, BMCPC, WRA.

31. "Tony Landreau Collection on Turkish Carpet Weaving and Village Life," University of Washington Libraries, https://content.lib.washington.edu/landreauweb/, accessed August 1, 2022.

32. Copies of Course Cards, Jean Broughton [*sic*] and Lelia Murphy, COP, WRA.

33. Faculty Board Meeting minutes, September 27, 1956, COP, WRA.

34. One of BMC's looms was donated to the Black Mountain College Museum + Arts Center in 2000 by Elma Johnson.

WEAVING AFTER BLACK MOUNTAIN

1. For more on these forms, see Brenda Danilowitz, "Tangles, Knots, Braids, Loops and Links," in *Anni Albers*, by Ann Coxon, Briony Fer, and Maria Müller-Schareck (New Haven, CT: Yale University Press, 2018), 86.

2. Michael Beggs, "Photographs of Matières," in *Leap Before You Look: Black Mountain College, 1933–1957*, edited by Helen Molesworth (New Haven, CT: Institute of Contemporary Art/ Boston in association with Yale University Press, 2015).

3. Student file of Milton Ernest Rauschenberg, BMCSF, WRA.

4. Joan Potter Loveless, *Three Weavers* (Albuquerque: University of New Mexico Press, 1992), 17, 30, 36.

5. Loveless, *Three Weavers*, 45.

A BLACK MOUNTAIN LEGACY ON NANTUCKET

1. "Walter Beinecke's Fight for Nantucket: Buying up an Island for Its Own Good," *Life*, September 6, 1968.

2. Andy Oates, Oral History by Connie Bostic, BMCM+AC, 2010, video https://vimeo.com/498658988, accessed December 4, 2022.

3. Andy Oates Student File, BMCSF, WRA.

4. Oates, Oral History by Bostic.

5. Andy Oates, interview by Karen Thomas, *Interviews with Rauschenberg Friends and Associates*, Robert Rauschenberg Foundation Archives, 2001, https://www.rauschenbergfoundation.org/sites/default/files/2022–06/OatesAndy_part_I_and_II_RRFA08_redacted.pdf, 10–11, accessed November 11, 2022.

6. Oates, Oral History by Bostic; Julie J. Thomson, "Biography, Andy Oates," in *Begin to See: The Photographers of Black Mountain College* (Asheville, NC: BMCM+AC, 2017), 83.

7. Oates Student File.

8. Andy Oates, Oral History, 1999, Nancy Newhouse Oral Histories Collection, NHA; Andy Oates, *Interviews*.

9. H. Errol Coffin, "The Jared Coffin House, Formerly the Ocean House," *Historic Nantucket*, April 1962.

10. Andy Oates, Oral History, NHA; Marilyn Hoffman, "Where Weavers Weave," *Christian Science Monitor*, October 28, 1964, 5.

11. Marianne Hertlitz, "Interview Portraits," *Inquirer & Mirror*, March 7, 1968, NA. For more on Mary Ann Beinecke's life, career, and historic textile book collection, see Julie Beinecke Stackpole, *Mary Ann Beinecke's Nantucket Textile Renaissance: A History and a Memoir, by Her Daughter* (self-published, 2018).

12. For more on the early history of Nantucket Looms, see my essay "The Nantucket Looms: Historicism and Modernism in an Island Cottage Industry," in *Hidden Stories/Human Lives: Proceedings of the Textile Society of America 17th Biennial Symposium 2020*, digitalcommons.unl.edu/tsaconf/, accessed March 12, 2023.

13. Melva A. Chesrown, "Nantucket Looms, Fabrics by Island Weavers in Restored Inn," *Handweaver & Craftsman* (Fall 1963): 6–9; "Nantucket Weavers Read to Try Their Skills in Many New Areas," *Inquirer & Mirror*, January 2, 1964, NA; NHA, Ms.549 contains many articles from the PR campaign. The warp frames or "dressing frames," developed by Macomber with Mrs. Beinecke, allowed warps to be prewound then set into the loom.

14. "Nantucket Historical Trust Announces New Agreement for World-Wide Sale of Island Manufactured Fabrics," *Inquirer & Mirror*, May 28, 1964, NA; photographs with press releases, NHA, Ms.549.

15. Promotion book with samples, undated, NHA, Ms.550.

16. NHA, Ms.549 contains PR photos of *Coskata* and *Hummock Pond*, and NHA collections contain a sample of *Hummock Pond*. *Sacacha Pond* is in the collection of the Cooper Hewitt Smithsonian Design Museum, 1967–9-7, http://cprhw.tt/o/2CBvB/, accessed March 12, 2023.

17. Anni Albers, "Fabric," reprinted from *Arts & Architecture*, March 1948, accessed in the Anni Albers Papers, JAAF; Susan Ward, "The Design, Promotion, and Production of Modern Textiles in the USA, 1940–60," in *Knoll Textiles*, edited by Earl Martin (New Haven, CT: Published for Bard Graduate Center by Yale University Press, 2011), 36–72.

18. "Handlooms on Nantucket," *American Fabrics* (Fall 1965): 21–22. A wide variety of materials can also be seen in the early Nantucket Looms textiles in the NHA collections.

19. The NHA and the BMCM+AC hold examples of mohair shawls made by Nantucket Looms.

20. "Handlooms on Nantucket."

21. The article by Steve Sheppard, "Timeless Traditions," *Home & Garden Nantucket*, 2011, says that, "A few years ago a British trade magazine commissioned a group of designers to name the most important fabrics designed in the twentieth century" and included the linen & ramie. Several later sources also write that it was one of the top 10 textiles of the twentieth century. Despite searching widely for the original source, it has not yet been identified.

22. Liz Winship, conversation with the author, November 3, 2022; Karin Sheppard, conversation with the author, November 8, 2022.

23. Oates Student File.

24. Hertlitz, "Interview Portraits."

25. Rebecca Peraner, conversations with the author, November 8 and 14, 2022.

26. "New York Outfit Takes Over Looms," *Inquirer & Mirror*, October 28, 1965, NA. For more on the Tilletts' work on Nantucket, see Nieling, "The Nantucket Looms."

27. "Cloth Company Inventories Sold," *Inquirer & Mirror*, April 4, 1968, NA.

28. Oates, Oral History, NHA.

29. Oates, Oral History, NHA.

30. Winship, conversation; Oral History with Andy Oates, NHA.

31. Winship, conversation; Sheppard, conversation; Robert Frazier, "Right Place, Right Time: The Advent of Cottage Style Living," *Historic Nantucket* (Spring/Summer 2016); "Photographs of Andy Oates at Main Street Gallery," *Inquirer & Mirror*, September 10, 1987, NA.

32. Bess Clarke, conversation with the author, October 28, 2022.

33. Winship, conversation; Sheppard, conversation; Lia Marks and Karin Sheppard, conversation with the author, January 29, 2018.

34. Winship, conversation; Clarke, conversation.

35. Clarke, conversation; Peraner, conversation; Stephanie Hall, conversation with the author, November 14, 2022; "Who We Are," Nantucket Looms, https://www.nantucketlooms.com/pages/who-we-are, accessed December 2, 2022.

36. "Our Story," Sam Kasten Handweaver, https://www.samkasten.com/our-story, accessed November 17, 2022.

37. Sheppard, conversation.

38. Sheppard, conversation; Winship, conversation; Rogers and Goffigon, https://www.rogersandgoffigon.com/.

39. Neil Welliver, "A Conversation with Anni Albers," *Craft Horizons* (July/August 1965), Anni Albers Papers, JAAF.

40. "Handlooms on Nantucket."

41. Nostalgia is most notable in John Peter and Marilyn Kaytor, "Christmas on Nantucket," *LOOK*, December 15, 1964.

42. Clarke, conversation; Sheppard, conversation; Hall, conversation.

43. Oates Student File. In his 1948–49 course descriptions, Josef Albers wrote, "Art here means more a process and a way of living than a product or its production." Josef Albers Papers, JAAF.

44. Oates, Oral History by Bostic.

ACKNOWLEDGMENTS

We extend our gratitude to Alice Sebrell and Jeff Arnal at the Black Mountain College Museum + Arts Center who responded with enthusiasm and support to our vision for a *Weaving at Black Mountain College* exhibition and this accompanying book from the very beginning. Thank you to their staff, especially Carissa Pfeiffer for her help with grant writing, and to Maya Rosenbaum and Kira Houston for promoting this exhibition. We also thank the BMC Museum + Arts Center's Board for their help to make this exhibition possible.

The diligence, expertise, and encouragement of Heather South (lead archivist at the Western Regional Archives) helped make our research more detailed, our knowledge deeper, and our forays into the many BMC collections and papers at the archives successful and enlightening. Endless thanks to her for her assistance, expertise, and cultivation of archives magic.

We thank Brenda Danilowitz, Erica Warren, and Jennifer Nieling for writing essays for this book and the many conversations we've had with each of them. We extend our gratitude to artists Kay Sekimachi, Jen Bervin, Porfirio Gutiérrez, Susie Taylor, and Bana Haffar for their generous participation. We are grateful to Tom Eykemans and Taylor Miles Hopkins for the thoughtful approach they brought to designing this beautiful book. Many thanks to Jessica Ryan for copyediting it. Our thanks to Yale University Press for distributing this book, especially those with a direct hand in our collaboration: Nicholas Geller, Katherine Boller, Carlin Cassell, and Stephen Cebik.

A project that centers so much on the work of Anni Albers would not be possible without the generous assistance of the Josef and Anni Albers Foundation. Many thanks to Nicholas Fox Weber, Brenda Danilowitz, Jeanette Redensek, Sam McCune, Karis Medina, Amy Jean Porter, Fritz Horstman, and Anne Sisco for their help at all stages of this book and exhibition.

We thank the families who are lending works to our exhibition: Marc Aronson and Marina Budhos; Linda Batchelor and Peggy Perkins; Heidi and Guy Burgess; and Mark Davenport and Patsy Lynch Wood. Thanks also to Addie Lanier, Henry Weverka, and Vivian Tong at Ruth Asawa Lanier, Inc.

Thank you also to Farrol Mertes, Forrest Merrill, Gregg and Linda MacMillan, Ruth Erickson, and to the artists, estates, museums, and families who granted us permission to reproduce the images they hold permissions for in this book.

We have many people to thank at various institutions for discussions about loans to our exhibition: Susan Brown, Antonia Moser, and Matilda McQuaid at the Cooper Hewitt Smithsonian Design Museum; Susan Matheson, L. Lynne Addison, Megan Doyon, Ashley Kane, and Stephanie Wiles at Yale University Art Gallery; Paul Galloway, Marissa Klein, and Glenn Lowry at the Museum of Modern Art, New York; and Rachel Hansen and Willow Holdorf at the Museum of Art and Design, New York.

Thank you to the other archivists who assisted our research: Jane Kjaer and Rachael Rieck at the Swarthmore College Library; Anna Bunting and Violetta Wolf at the Oakland Museum of California; and Meredith McDonough and Amelia H. Chase at Alabama Department of Archives and History. Additional thanks to the Josef and Anni Albers

Foundation for funding the digitization of BMC-era letters in the Harriett Pinkston Engelhardt Papers at ADAH. Thank you to Mary Emma Harris for the invaluable interviews she did with Black Mountain College students and faculty, the works she preserved, the photographs she took of weavings by students, and her foundational writing about Black Mountain College's artists.

Additional thanks to the families of BMC faculty and students who gave us valuable information in the course of our research. Thank you also to the community of Black Mountain College scholars who we have met and learned with and from over the years through the annual ReVIEWING Black Mountain College Conference hosted by the BMC Museum + Arts Center and University of North Carolina, Asheville.

MICHAEL BEGGS THANKS

Julie J. Thomson for inviting me on this journey, for being an excellent collaborator, for providing many hours of enriching and exciting conversation, and most of all for her boundless (and contagious) enthusiasm for all things Black Mountain (both College and place).

My weaving teachers: Katherine Hutman, Ismini Samanidou, and Anni Albers.

Everyone at the Josef and Anni Albers Foundation for continuing to support my projects related to both Alberses, and for their generous gifts of time, accommodations, and conversation. George Loisos and Susan Ubbelohde for generously encouraging me to work on this project even when I had to reduce my work hours, and all my colleagues at Loisos + Ubbelohde.

My friends Ely Maris, Spencer Collom, Ryan Conroy, Emily Gallivan, Brooke Hair, Kate Lenahan, Colm McNally, and Jonah Merris, for their questions, patience, encouragement, edits, and advice.

My parents, George Beggs and Katherine Hutman, for too many things—large and small—to mention.

FROM JULIE J. THOMSON

I am grateful to Michael Beggs for collaborating with me on this exhibition and book and writing the essays that I've always wanted to read about Anni Albers, weaving, and design at Black Mountain College. As part of my research I learned to weave. Thank you to my weaving teachers: Maggy Inman at the NCSU Crafts Center and Ruth Howe at Heritage Weavers and Fiber Artists. I also appreciate the John C. Campbell Folk School for awarding me a Margaret C. Toth Scholarship so that I could take a tapestry class with Nancy Crampton.

I want to especially thank Marc Aronson and Marina Buhos for sharing their family's archives with me and helping expand my understanding of Trude Guermonprez and the Jalowetz family. Thank you also to these archivists for their assistance: Laura MacNewman at Cranbrook, Annemarie Haar at California College of the Arts, and Sarah Downing at the Western Regional Archives. I appreciate the conversations and exchanges that I had with Huston Paschal, Tom Frank, Mary Emma Harris, Hertha O. Horwitz, and Kate Anderson about this exhibition and my essays.

I am grateful to have grown up in a family of makers. Special thanks to my Mom and Dad for their continual support, and also to Brian Bockhahn.

FROM JENNIFER NIELING

My sincerest thanks to Bess Clarke, Stephanie Hall, Rebecca Peraner, Liz Winship, Karin Sheppard, Lia Marks, Seth Tillett, and Julie Beinecke Stackpole for sharing with me their memories and insights about Nantucket Looms; to Michael Harrison and Amelia Holmes at the Nantucket Historical Association for their continued support and assistance; to Brenda Danilowitz at the Josef and Anni Albers Foundation; and Heather South at the Western Regional Archives for generously making research materials available.

CONTRIBUTORS

AUTHORS

Michael Beggs is a designer and independent scholar who has been studying Black Mountain College since 2010. He previously worked at the Josef and Anni Albers Foundation and has written about the Alberses and Black Mountain College in *Leap Before You Look: Black Mountain College, 1933–57* (Yale University Press, 2015), *Josef Albers: Interaction* (Yale University Press, 2018), and *The Quiet House: Stillness in Lake Eden* (Black Mountain College Museum + Arts Center, 2022).

Julie J. Thomson is an educator, independent scholar, and curator who has been researching and writing about artists at Black Mountain College since 2006 and served as co-editor of the *Journal of Black Mountain College Studies* from 2018–20. She is the author of *Begin to See: The Photographers of Black Mountain College* (Black Mountain College Museum + Arts Center, 2017) and the editor of *That Was the Answer: Interviews with Ray Johnson* (Soberscove Press, 2018).

CONTRIBUTORS

Brenda Danilowitz is an art historian and chief curator at the Josef and Anni Albers Foundation. She has organized exhibitions of their work around the world and is the author of numerous books and essays including *Anni Albers: Selected Writings on Design*, ed. and introduction (Wesleyan University Press, 2001), *Anni and Josef Albers: Latin American Journeys* (Hatje-Cantz, 2007), *The Prints of Anni Albers: A Catalogue Raisonné, 1963–1984* (Editorial RM, 2009), as well as contributions to *Black Mountain: An Interdisciplinary Experiment, 1933–1957* (Spector Books, 2015), *Anni Albers: Camino Real* (David Zwirner Books, 2020), *Anni and Josef Albers, L'art et la vie* (Paris-Musees, 2021), and *Josef Albers: Discovery and Invention, the Early Graphic Work* (Art/Books London, 2022).

Erica Warren is a decorative arts and design curator and scholar, and is currently the editor of *Craft Quarterly*, the James Renwick Alliance for Craft's magazine. From 2016–22, Dr. Warren was a curator of textiles at the Art Institute of Chicago, where she organized numerous installations, including the critically acclaimed exhibition *Bisa Butler: Portraits* and *Weaving beyond the Bauhaus*. Her recent publications include "Fission: Design and Mentorship in the Dorothy Liebes Studio" in *A Dark, A Light, A Bright: The Designs of Dorothy Liebes* (2023) and "Beyond Weaving: Transdisciplinarity and the Bauhaus Weaving Workshop," in *Textile: The Journal of Cloth and Culture* (2021).

Jennifer Nieling is an independent costume and textile specialist and owner of JLN Costume Mounting LLC. She previously worked for the Fine Arts Museums of San Francisco, the Philadelphia Museum of Art, the Nantucket Historical Association, and the Fox Historic Costume Collection at Drexel University. Nieling holds a Master of Arts in Fashion and Textile Studies: History, Theory, and Museum Practice from the Fashion Institute of Technology, and a Bachelor of Arts from Boston University.

CREDITS

of the Western Regional Archives, State Archives of North Carolina.

82, 84, 85, 88 The Harriett Engelhardt Memorial Collection of Textiles, from the estate of Black Mountain College through a gift of Mrs. Paul Moore (1958.13.4, 1958.13.98 1958.13.8, 1958.13.22) Photograph by Yale University Art Gallery.

86 The Johnson Collection, Spartanburg, SC.

91, 95 Courtesy of the Jalowetz Aronson Family Collection. **91** Photograph by Jim Ludlow.

96 Collection Linda and Gregg MacMillan, Courtesy of Institute of Contemporary Art, Boston.

102 Collection Forrest L. Merrill, Photograph by M. Lee Fatherree.

103, 133, 134 Collection Kay Sekimachi, Photograph by M. Lee Fatherree.

106 Private collection. Photograph by Alice Sebrell.

117 Photograph from *The Bear*, 1955 Yearbook from Stephens-Lee High School, Asheville, North Carolina, Courtesy of Buncombe County Special Collections, Pack Memorial Public Library, Asheville, North Carolina.

135, 136 Courtesy of Jen Bervin.

137, 138 Courtesy of Porfirio Gutiérrez.

139 Courtesy of Bana Haffar.

141, 142 Courtesy of Susie Taylor. Photographs by James Dewrance.

TITLE PAGE IMAGES
(from left to right)

Anni Albers and Mimi French at a loom, 1944. Photograph by Josef Breitenbach. © Josef and Yaye Breitenbach Charitable Foundation, courtesy of Gitterman Gallery.

Trude Guermonprez weaving at Black Mountain College, 1947. Photograph by Beaumont Newhall. ©1947, Beaumont Newhall, ©2023, the Estate of Beaumont and Nancy Newhall. Permission to reproduce courtesy of Scheinbaum and Russek Ltd, Santa Fe, New Mexico. Image courtesy of Black Mountain College Research Project, Western Regional Archives, State Archives of North Carolina.

Anni Albers weaving at Black Mountain College, 1937. Photograph by Helen M. Post Modley. Courtesy of the Western Regional Archives, State Archives of North Carolina.

Donald Droll with textile from the Harriett Engelhardt Collection, ca. 1948–49. Photograph by Hazel Larsen Archer. © Estate of Hazel Larsen Archer.

TEXTS
(listed by page number)

36–39 Anni Albers, "Work with Material" originally published in *Black Mountain College Bulletin*, 5, (1938). Reproduced with permission of the Josef and Anni Albers Foundation.

48–51 Anni Albers, "Handweaving Today: Textile Work at Black Mountain College" originally published in *The Weaver* 6 no.1 (January–February 1941). Reproduced with permission of the Josef and Anni Albers Foundation.

90–93 Anni Albers, "One Aspect of Art Work" originally published in *Design*, 46, no. 4 (December 12, 1944) under the title "We Need the Crafts for their Contact with Materials." Reproduced with permission of the Josef and Anni Albers Foundation.

130 Jack Lenor Larsen, "Trude Guermonprez", 1982. Reproduced with permission of LongHouse Reserve.

132–137 Trude Guermonprez, "Design" unpublished lecture, 1952. Courtesy of the Oakland Museum of California, Trude Guermonprez Papers. Reproduced with permission from the Jalowetz Aronson Family Archive.

170–173 Kay Sekimachi, "Trude Remembered," from the *The Tapestries of Trude Guermonprez* exhibition catalog published by the Oakland Museum of California, 1982. Courtesy of the Oakland Museum of California. Reproduced with permission of Kay Sekimachi.

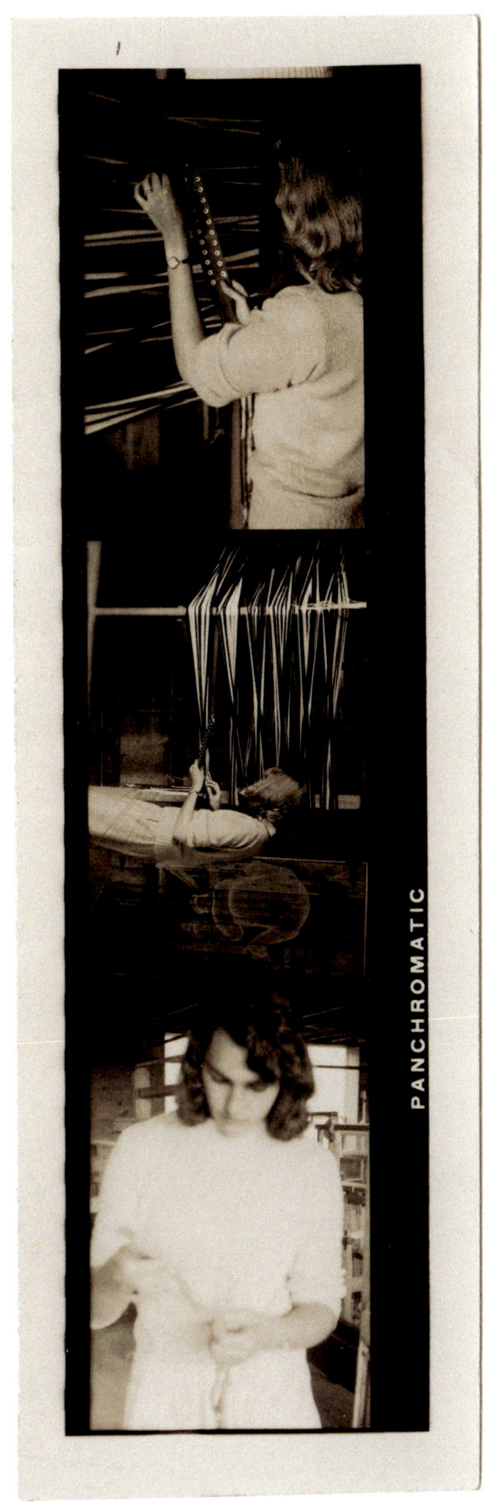
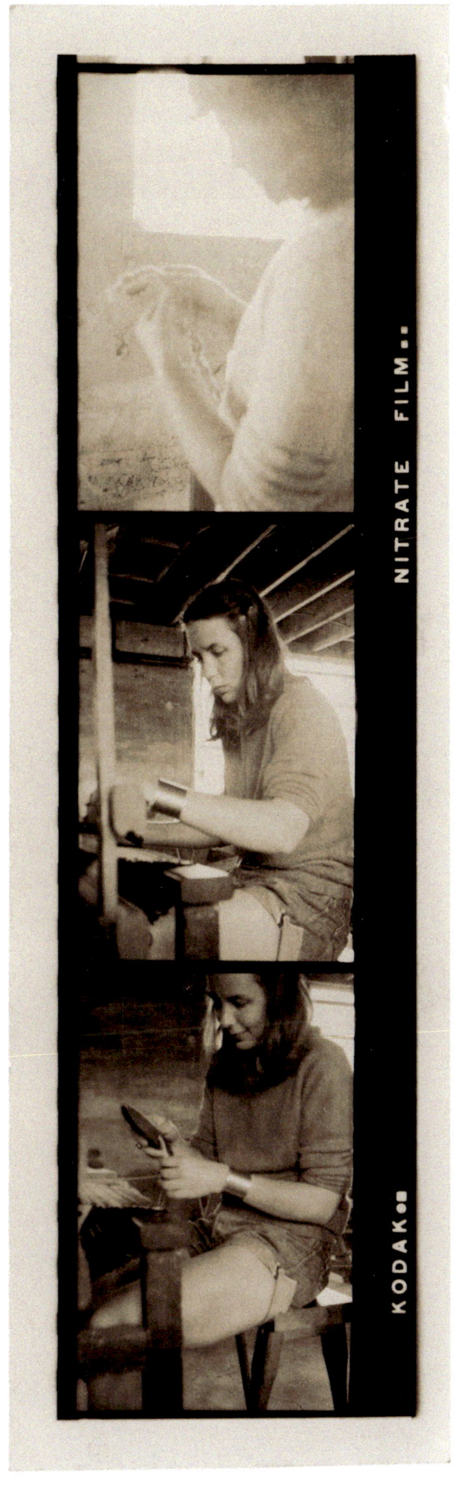

142. Mimi French, Jane "Slats" Slater, and Nell Goldsmith in the weaving room at Lake Eden, ca. 1942–44. Photographer unknown.

Published in conjunction with the exhibition
Weaving at Black Mountain College:
Anni Albers, Trude Guermonprez, and Their Students
September 29, 2023–January 6, 2024
Black Mountain College Museum + Arts Center
120 College Street, Asheville, NC 28801
blackmountaincollege.org

Support for this project has been generously provided by the
National Endowment for the Arts, Robert Lehman Foundation,
and Furthermore: a program of the J. M. Kaplan Fund.

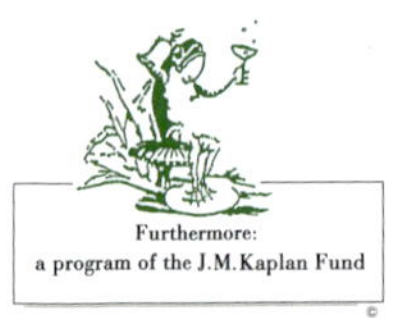 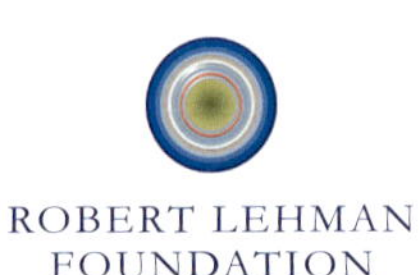 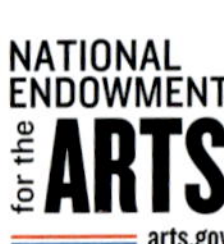

Distributed by Yale University Press
302 Temple Street
P.O. Box 209040
New Haven, CT 06520-9040
yalebooks.com/art

Front Cover: Handwoven fabric made at Black Mountain College,
n.d. Photograph by Claude Stoller, Courtesy of the Western
Regional Archives, State Archives of North Carolina

Back Cover: Alex Reed's hands and loom, n.d., Photograph by
Claude Stoller. Courtesy of the Western Regional Archives,
State Archives of North Carolina.

Cover Spine: Anni Albers, Drapery material, ca. 1937, Cotton
and silk, 27¾ × 21½ in. © 2023 The Josef and Anni Albers Foun-
dation/Artists Rights Society (ARS), New York. Photograph by
Tim Nighswander/Imaging4Art.

Book design by Taylor Miles Hopkins
Art direction by Thomas Eykemans
Print and color management by I/O Color, Seattle, WA
Printed and bound by Artron Art Group Co. Ltd.
in Shenzhen, China
Typeset in Neue Kabel by Marc Schütz
and Dapifer by Joshua Darden